SYNTHS, SAX & SITUATIONISTS

SYNTHS, SAX & SITUATIONISTS

THE FRENCH MUSICAL UNDERGROUND 1968-1978

IAN THOMPSON

To my three muses: Amanda, Georgina, Mia.

First published 2025
by Roundtable Books
www.thee-roundtable.com

All rights reserved
© 2025 Ian Thompson

The right of Ian Thompson to be identified as the author of this work has been asserted in accordance with Section 77 of the Copyright, Designs and Patents Act 1988.

ISBN 978-0-6454928-0-4

Cover
Original design by Tim Steward.
Remixed, relettered, and revibed by Andy Votel.
Photograph by Claude Palmer.

v 1.1

CONTENTS

Preface   ix

Introduction   xv

Foreword: Jean-Jacques Birgé   xxv

Foreword: Steven Stapleton   xxxi

PART ONE: A SHORT HISTORY OF THE FRENCH MUSICAL UNDERGROUND

1. Chanson, *yé-yé* & Teen Idols   3
2. May '68: The Explosion   11
3. A Brief History Pt 1: 1968-69   21
4. October '69: The Amougies Festival   25
5. A Brief History Pt 2: 1970   29
6. Summer '70: *L'été Pop*   35
7. A Brief History Pt 3: 1971-73   43
8. The MJC Touring Circuit   47
9. A Brief History Pt 4: 1974-78   51
10. Independent Labels   55

A Note on the Categories Used in this Book

PART TWO: THE EXCEPTION THAT PROVES THE RULE

11. Lard Free   63

PART THREE: THE POLITICAL UNDERGROUND

12. Introduction   89
13. Red Noise   97
14. Barricade   105
15. Maajun   127

16.	Komintern	139
17.	Fille Qui Mousse	153
18.	Dagon	165

PART FOUR: THE LYSERGIC UNDERGROUND

19.	Introduction	179
20.	Bananamoon	185
21.	Ame Son	195
22.	Gong	207
23.	Cheval Fou & Nyl	245
24.	Crium Delirium	253
25.	Clearlight (& Delired Cameleon Family)	263

PART FIVE: THE JAZZ UNDERGROUND

26.	Introduction	279
27.	Moving Gelatine Plates	283
28.	Magma	295
29.	Contrepoint	323

PART SIX: THE AVANT UNDERGROUND

30.	Introduction	331
31.	Camizole	335
32.	Jac Berrocal	347
33.	Etron Fou Leloublan	355
34.	Birgé Gorgé Shiroc	369

PART SEVEN: THE ELECTRONIC UNDERGROUND

35.	Introduction	381
36.	Philippe Besombes	387
37.	Heldon	395
38.	Ilitch	415

Discography	423
Bibliography	445
Illustrations	451
Sources	453
Index	480

PREFACE

In the ten years before Covid hit I was lucky enough to visit Paris a number of times. However, for some reason, I hadn't stepped into a French record shop before my last stay in 2017. I crossed the threshold of CrocoDisc, near the Sorbonne, on a quest to locate a copy of the French picture-sleeve release of Pink Floyd's "See Emily Play". The single wasn't to be found, but I *did* manage to stumble across a whole rack of albums labeled 'Prog Français'. That was a new one on me.

I'd vaguely heard of Magma and Heldon, but here was a huge selection of French progressive and underground rock. Intrigued, I dug through the records, leaving the shop with a copy of Moving Gelatine Plates' first LP and photos of some promising-looking sleeves. That evening I quizzed the internet about this unfamiliar scene. There was precious little information in French and next to nothing in English.* What I did find, thank the good Lord, were album uploads on YouTube. These allowed me to check out the likes of Red Noise and Heldon.

A few days later I was in Parallèles bookstore† and picked up a copy of Deshayes & Grimaud's book *L'underground musical en France*. By slowly working my way through this invaluable survey I was introduced to a world of fascinating-sounding bands: Lard Free, Barricade, Fille Qui Mousse, etc... I also began to understand the context in which this music was created, discovering that even 'successful' bands like Magma and Heldon had barely operated at a subsistence level. This was a truly subterranean, rather than simply underground, scene. It became clear why this music remained so unknown, as most bands left only vague traces of their existence.

Of course, this would be of no significance if the music itself didn't warrant investigation. It didn't take long to realise what outstanding

---

* The intervening years have seen a very welcome explosion in the amount of information available on-line.
† It was only much later that I would discover that this shop was actually a survivor from the very underground scene that I had begun to explore.

bands this scene had produced across such a broad range of genres. In the late '80s my mind had been blown when I'd been introduced to 'Krautrock' and now, decades later, I'd found yet *another* motherlode of fascinating and idiosyncratic music.

I returned to Australia with Deshayes & Grimaud's book and a healthy stash of vinyl. Over the next twelve months my interest turned into obsession, and the search for these records became a mission. It slowly dawned on me that if other anglophones were to discover this essential music they would need a reference - in English. And so, over the last five years I've digested everything I could find on the topic (obvious mainly written in French) and interviewed almost fifty musicians from the scene. Now, at long last, the result of my efforts rests in your hands.

Synths, Sax, and Situationists

The title suggested itself during the writing of the book and is intended to give a glimpse into what makes this music, and the scene that produced it, so distinctive. Last things first: the Situationist International (SI) was an avant-garde group active in Paris from the late '50s. Their potent mix of Marxist politics and artistic praxis gave vitality to political and social thought in '60s France. The SI's writings and provocations[*] were a huge influence on the social eruption of May '68, which in turn was a formative event for the musicians of the musical underground. The invocation of synths and sax is intended to highlight two major drivers in the evolution of French underground music: the introduction of electronic instruments and the influence of free jazz.

The time-frame covered (1968-1978) is somewhat arbitrary, given that the underground music scene continued into the '80s and beyond.[†] However this period, book-ended by the revolt of 1968 and the eruption of the punk movement, encompasses the first era of the

---

[*] The key provocation occurred in late '66 after a student union election at Strasbourg University. The new leadership collaborated with the SI to create *On the Poverty of Student Life*, a political polemic distributed at the university's commencement service. A nationwide scandal erupted, resulting in widely broadcasting the SI's incendiary ideas. The sparks from this event helped fuel the student uprising in May '68.

[†] I was encouraged to extend this time-frame by several interviewees, who believed the scene didn't fully mature until the early to mid-'80s.

French underground. By '78 two distinct waves of bands had risen and crested, and a third was building.

Defining the "underground"

On the question of what constitutes "underground music" I have been guided by the original members of the scene. I was particularly interested to ask them whether well-known (if not mainstream) bands like Magma or Gong should be included. On Gong the response was a resounding 'yes', but there was split opinion over Magma's role in the scene. What was very clear was that other major acts (Les Variations, Martin Circus, Triangle, and Zoo, etc.) and bands that identified as "progressive" (e.g. Ange, Atoll, and Pulsar) were never accepted by the underground,

Obviously, I must take full responsibility for the final choice of acts included in this book. I understand that there will be a range of opinion on my selection, and some valid criticism. One potential concern that I must immediately address is the absence of chapters on Brigitte Fontaine and Catherine Ribeiro. I fully recognise this could be viewed as creating a hole at the heart of the book.* The decision was made on the basis of my own shortcomings: my background is in alternative rock and electronic music, so I felt ill-equipped to do justice to Fontaine's and Ribeiro's *nouveau chanson*. Both artists can be appreciated without a knowledge of French poetry (as evidenced by the number of their albums in my own collection); however, they deserve an author with a better understanding of French literature than my own. Hopefully others will pick up the gauntlet and produce the book(s) that beg to be written about these very important artists.

Mode d'emploi

I have organised this book into a logical sequence: with introductory chapters and a historical overview followed by band histories, and a complete discography. However there's no need to approach it in a linear fashion. My own exploration of this scene initially focused on

---

* I also recognise that this has the potential to misrepresent the gender makeup of the underground. Not only were Fontaine and Ribeiro two of its most significant (and successful) artists, there was also a significant number of other women involved. The most visible of these were Gilli Smyth (Gong) and Stella Vander (Magma), but female musicians also featured in Barricade, Camizole, and Etron Fou Leloublan.

individual bands. Then, as I began to see common threads in their stories, I became interested in the historical and social context in which they operated.

I would suggest that a sensible way to approach the content is to read the book in sequence up to a point. The Introduction provides context for the underground scene as a whole, and the two Forewords recount personal stories from France and the UK: Jean-Jacques Birgé was involved in the underground from the very beginning and Steven Stapleton introduced many in the English-speaking world to these bands with the infamous 'Nurse With Wound List'. When a reader has finished Part 1 of 'A Brief History of French Underground Music' they'll have more than enough understanding of the scene to begin reading individual band stories. After this it's hoped that, like myself, they'll want to delve further into the historical context (the Amougies Festival, *L'été Pop*, the MJC Circuit, etc.).

Reissues and Streaming

My research for this book took place while a number of archival record labels were actively reissuing records from the underground on vinyl. The most significant of these were French (Souffle Continu, Replica Records, Monster Melodies), but they were joined by Finders Keepers in the UK and Superior Viaduct in the US. Over the last ten years albums that were out of print for decades have been made available again (although usually in limited releases). Perhaps more importantly, many of these albums have recently appeared on streaming services - making this previously inaccessible music instantly available. To help readers access this music there's a (hyperlinked) streaming discography (a 'streamography'?) at *french-underground.com/discog*

Acknowledgments

At times writing a book can appear to be a solitary activity, but it rarely is. They say that it takes a village to raise a child, and over the last few years I discovered that it takes at least a small hamlet to bring a book to life.

All of these people deserve my heartfelt thanks. The first among them are those who generously agreed to be interviewed for this book. The level of enthusiasm these people had for my project and their willingness to be available for follow-up questions was surprising, and humbling, to me. It was a genuine pleasure to hear your stories, and I sincerely hope that what I have written does justice to them.

There are several people who have been especially supportive and helpful. Gilles Yeprémian went above and beyond any call of duty by tirelessly tracking down contacts and giving invaluable feedback. Dominique Grimaud, responsible for so much ground-breaking work documenting this scene, has also shown tremendous support and enthusiasm, as has Michel Muzac. I thank you all. You may never know just how much you helped to keep this (sometimes overwhelming) project moving forward.

Thanks to Jean-Jacques Birgé and Steven Stapleton for writing such apt Forewords, for expressing so much interest in my project, and for being such interesting interlocutors over the last few years.

Andy Votel contacted me after reading an early draft, and in addition to providing enthusiastic support he has crafted a book cover better than I could have ever imagined. Andy was also responsible for bringing James Pianta into my orbit. James rivalled Andy in his enthusiasm, and I'm very grateful that this led to the opportunity to work with him in creating a series of vinyl compilations to accompany this book.

Tom Beaumont, Michael Helmstedt, Noel Mengel, Amanda Watson-Will, and Joe Woolley were a very willing and able team of proofreaders. Thanks to all of you there are many fewer errors in this text than there would have been otherwise...

Finally, I have to thank Aymeric Leroy for sharing some rare interviews with me, Klemen Breznikar for his ongoing work on the incredible *It's Psychedelic Baby* online magazine, and Philippe Robert for producing the three volumes of *Agitation Frite*, an essential resource for my research.

Brisbane, July '25.
frenchunderground1968@gmail.com

INTRODUCTION: What was French underground rock?

> We were sick of Anglo-American rock'n'roll with a three-chord structure and lyrics that were *oh so boring! so superficial!* People like Zappa and Beefheart came along and suddenly there was substance. They were talking about things that were interesting to our ears, to our hearts, to our concerns. Then the Velvet Underground showed the first sign of using drone and repetition - things that were sympathetic to our ears.
>
> There was something in *our* heads saying we don't want to be brainwashed, influenced, manipulated. This was the feeling in '68 and it led to political, social, cultural revolution. May '68 in France was the symbol, the peak of it. Our generation was born after the war and twenty years later we were confronted with all the shit that was left behind. We badly wanted something new, something of our own. We didn't need the Marshall Plan and three-chord rock'n'roll. And that's why in France (and even more so in Germany) there was a need for something new.
>
> Jean-Hervé Peron, Faust

Jean-Hervé Peron was born in France four years after the end of World War II. He was shaped by the shared musical, social, and political environment that primed his generation for the explosion of '68. In 1970 he moved to Hamburg, and immersed himself in the city's underground scene. He would go on to became a member of Faust, one of the most iconoclastic bands in Germany.

Peron is thus uniquely placed to compare the underground music scenes in France and Germany. He emphasises the common experience and motivations of the young musicians, noting only that he sensed a heightened impulse in Germany to create something new "because the vacuum left behind there was greater than the vacuum left anywhere else."

The near-revolution of May '68 was the zenith of the struggle of Peron's generation for a new kind of life. While its repercussions rapidly spread throughout Europe, in France itself the effect was seismic. A small, but vibrant, cultural underground had existed beforehand, but now it was kicked into overdrive, and the on-going aftershocks would birth the first wave of underground bands.

Patrick Fontaine was one of the small group of French musicians already on that path, as a member of Bananamoon (and later Ame Son). He recalls: "May '68 was the real turning point with the emergence of Patrick Vian's band Red Noise. After May the protest movement took hold of minds, especially among the young. Other bands followed the same path - but not immediately. These included Maajun, Crium Delirium, Crouille Marteau, Cheval Fou, Catherine Ribeiro, Musica Elettronica Viva. Then later, in the early '70s, Komintern, Barricade, and Fille Qui Mousse appeared."

Rock & Folk's Philippe Paringaux was one of the first to champion this new flowering of French rock. In '72 he reflected on the development of the underground:

"Two very clear and distinct, almost antagonistic, currents can be distinguished in French pop.* The first, the oldest, has tried in vain to measure up to British and American rock music though straightforward imitation. They've attempted to incorporate the spirit of blues and country music (which together give us rock'n'roll): two styles of music equally foreign to the French.

"The other, newer, current tries to take a step beyond these boundaries... turning its eyes and ears towards the more intellectual, precise music of the avant-garde... French musicians may never play like B.B. King, but they can grasp, reproduce, or even surpass the playfulness, surrealism, and musicality of Zappa, Beefheart, John Cage, and the free jazz players."

The first current that Paringaux identifies was the only game

---

* The use of the term 'pop' in French music journalism can be very confusing. In the '70's 'Pop' was used to differentiate rock music from *yé-yé* or *chanson*. One of the appeals of the term was its onomatopoeic representation of the explosive energy rock released into the French music scene. Of course the Pop Art movement was also in the mind of music writers.

in town before '68. Bands like Les Variations and Zoo continued *yé-yé*'s legacy of repackaging British and American music. While they featured highly talented musicians, each was firmly rooted in a specific Anglo-American genre and, significantly, both sang their songs in English.[1]

The second current was the path chosen by the French musical underground, leading it to produce music with much less rock purity than that coming from the UK and US undergrounds. French bands incorporated a profusion of different musical and cultural influences, foregrounding improvisation, disjunction, and genre-blending.

An article in *Pop 2000* underlined the paradigm-shift the underground groups brought to the French music scene: "Their musical tastes inclined them towards Soft Machine, Pink Floyd, Frank Zappa, Captain Beefheart and the big Californian groups. Their overriding ambition was to write completely new music, eliminating all imitation and every conventional influence. It was the beginning of a revolution..." The article goes on to draw a parallel with what was happening in France with the musical developments across the border in Germany and in Scandinavia.

The distinctive nature of the French underground is underlined by the reactions of British musicians who visited the country (and in some cases installed themselves there).

Soft Machine were embraced by the French, and returned the affection.[2] Robert Wyatt has stated that he felt more musically and artistically at home in France than in the UK:

"There is just a great tradition in France of listening to music and dealing with the arts that is completely conducive to the creation of, and the appreciation of, the sort of avant-garde set ups that we dealt in. Plus a whole avant-garde theatre tradition; Jarry[3] was French after all. It's quite different from [the UK], there's no sense of having to deal with the hit parade or anything like that... You could really stretch out in front of a French audience, you almost had to apologise for it in England.

"There was also the whole American expatriate thing that centred on the Shakespeare bookshop on the Left Bank and bars like the Chat Qui Peche, where they had racks of jazz albums behind the bar that you could request if you bought a drink. Fucking paradise as far as I was concerned."

The reaction of musicians raised in the working-class tradition of British rock was profoundly different. They found the more cerebral nature of the French scene hard to come to terms with.

Bachdenkel, an underground band from Birmingham, relocated to France in '69. On their arrival they were distinctly underwhelmed by the bands they played alongside. Karel Beer remains blunt in his assessment of the French's ability to play rock: "They couldn't do it! They were good at playing their instruments and writing music. They *weren't* very good at being rock bands. It wasn't in their DNA."

This initial impression was formed in the very early days of French rock, however Bachdenkel remained in France for years, allowing Beer to observe its development at close quarters. He points out that a major difference between French and British rock music culture can be seen in the influence of Frank Zappa: "Zappa was important in France, which gave credibility to being a good musician. A lot of the musicians had come out of jazz and could be credible in rock because they were playing music that could be kind of taken seriously. I have to admit that got on my nerves tremendously. We couldn't stand it. We considered it pretentious. If they'd wanted to they could've gone to university and gotten a degree. And that's got *nothing* to do with rock and roll!"

British and American rock was certainly appreciated within the French underground, with bands like The Pretty Things, The Pink Fairies, Edgar Broughton Band, and Third World War all being well-received. It was simply that French musicians looked further afield for inspiration, recognising what Paringaux had expressed: the direct influence of unalloyed Anglo-American rock could all too easily lead them down the *cul de sac* of imitation.

Beer overlooks an important factor in his assessment of Zappa's influence on these new French bands. A large part of his appeal was that many of *his own* influences were from French sources: the composer Edgard Varèse, musique concrète, Surrealism, and Dada. In many ways he gave French musicians permission to be themselves, to look to their *own* cultural history as a resource.

The strongly subversive side of the early Mothers of Invention was also crucial to the impact they made on the French underground. The most politicised members of the underground were suspicious of rock music as just the latest shiny consumer product served up by capitalism.[4] The sense of derision, and surrealist irreverence that the Mothers of Invention brought to their recordings and live performances echoed the sentiments that had exploded during May '68. This gave the band credibility even among the most radical elements of the underground.

Nevertheless, the major differentiating factor between the French and almost any other underground rock scene of the '70s was in the huge influence of free jazz as represented by figures like Pharoah Sanders, Archie Shepp, and Ornette Coleman. This was arguably more essential to its character than the influence of any kind of rock music.

Barricade's François Billard has written extensively on jazz, and points out that free jazz had a strong foothold in France long before the underground existed: "The two main jazz magazines, *Jazz Hot* and *Jazz Magazine*, gave great importance to free jazz and its political aspect from the mid-'60s. That's why many black jazzmen, often supporters of Black Power, came to France and sometimes settled here."

Free jazz was viewed by French youth as inextricably bound to the politics of the US civil rights movement. It was music that resonated in the ears, minds, and hearts of the generation of May '68.

A vibrant local free jazz scene had developed in the early '60s with Jef Gilson as a major catalyst. Gilson's groups gave a start to many of the most significant players of the era: François Tusques, Bernard Vitet, Barney Wilen, Jacques Thollot, and Jean-Luc Ponty amongst them. Adding to the ferment were the touring Americans who frequently played in Paris (often encouraging local players to sit in with them) and those who relocated to the city in the late '60s: Sunny Murray, Alan Silva, and The Art Ensemble of Chicago.

According to Patrick Fontaine there was a defining event that consummated the marriage of free jazz to rock in France: "The Amougies Festival in October '69 established the fusion of progressive rock and free jazz. For five days the biggest names from both styles followed one another onto the stage. Pink Floyd rubbed shoulders with Archie Shepp, Ten Years After and The Pretty Things with Pharoah Sanders and Don Cherry.

"The mix of rock and free jazz seems to be a very French phenomenon. England was quite separate from this movement - as

I understand it free jazz wasn't very successful there. At the end of the '60s a number of young people aspired to discover new musical domains that produced experimentation and creation. In my opinion that's what allowed these two musical styles to be brought together. We found it easy to listen to free jazz in a very natural way. The music spoke to us and we understood it intuitively."

The term "free-rock" is often used in French music journalism in reference to bands (like Red Noise, Ame Son, Lard Free, and early Gong) who set themselves apart by their ability to improvise in a style informed by free jazz.

One of the touchstones for this mix of rock and free jazz was Captain Beefheart and His Magic Band. Gilbert Artman of Lard Free credits seeing the Magic Band play at the Bataclan with inspiring him to bring his jazz drumming into a rock context: "For me Captain Beefheart was the synthesis of a kind of free-rock with a more offbeat and joyful attitude... the people on stage weren't earnest... It was more fun than free jazz, it was a new attitude that opened up new horizons... It was freedom! I'd heard a lot about Zappa who wrote very serious music, but to me Beefheart was much more free... It was seriously un-serious *(laughs)*."

A perhaps unexpected influence on the development of French "free-rock" came from the UK's Pink Floyd. Between '68 and '72, Pink Floyd was a major player on the European scene. As Nick Mason recalled in a 2016 interview: "Pink Floyd may never have survived without the French audiences. We toured a lot in France and appeared in many TV shows. It was our home from home in a way. France responded to our music quite rapidly, as opposed to England where our fan base was not always very reliable."

Part of Pink Floyd's appeal came from the European influences they brought to their music. Although named after the American bluesmen Pink Andersen and Floyd Council the band had never seemed particularly comfortable playing blues-based music. Early in their career Syd Barrett had introduced musical concepts from free improvisation into Pink Floyd's sound.[5] The most obvious manifestation of this influence was 'Interstellar Overdrive', a lengthy improvisation that would remain a centrepiece of the band's live set for years after Barrett's departure.

Pink Floyd continued to mine this vein of sonic exploration before eventually settling on a more conventional sound with *Dark Side of the Moon*. The French were particularly responsive to their musical experimentation, and commissioned the band to compose music for film soundtracks and ballet.[6]

In the decade between '68 and '78, French rock musicians found their own voice. As in Germany, the motivation was to leave the past behind, to cease imitating Anglo-American models. It wasn't purely artistic and aesthetic motivations that drove this desire, it was also a response to the social and political upheaval of the time.

Paradoxically the influences that opened the way for the French came from the very countries whose musical hegemony they were struggling against. From across the Atlantic came Frank Zappa and free jazz, and from across the Channel came Soft Machine and Pink Floyd. These musicians had all in their own ways rejected prevailing Anglo-American models of pop and rock, and were aiming for a musical freedom that resonated in France.

When Daevid Allen formed Gong in France, he responded to the musical freedom he experienced there. He has expressed a belief that Gong could only have developed as it did because of that environment:

"At the time, England was much narrower in its stylistic preferences; France was wide open... In England [Gong] would have been confined to a certain style of playing and would have stayed much less interesting, much less of a smorgasbord than it could be in France...

"I think in some ways France has always been an original country in the history of music. Their classical music, in the '20s, was some of the most original around - Erik Satie is a good example. There is something whimsical about France, which is delightful at the same time as really... fantastical. They love fantasy and whimsy. That's what I love too, and Gong was that...

"There wasn't really strong political aggro going on in England, either. There was a great deal of political passion in France and, of course, when I was thrown out of England and had to go to France, I ended up in the student riots. That was an initiation by fire and that influenced, enormously, the nature of Gong."

In his examination of the rise of the French underground, Philippe Paringaux concluded: "It's clear that there's more potential to find originality in playing a style of music that's completely understood rather than one that can't be grasped... The groups who try to go forward starting from bases other than blues and rock may one day find real spontaneity, a truth of their own..."

The story of the French underground is the story of that search for a new and authentic music. One that would allow French musicians to express their own truths.

Notes

1   This was actually a backwards step from the progress made by *yé-yé* in normalising French lyrics. See pp. 3-9 for more on *yé-yé* and the development of French pop music before '68.
In the early '70s a lively debate in the music press saw one side arguing that the French language might *never* find a home in rock music.

2   See pp. 179-180 for more on Soft Machine's influence on the French underground.

3   Alfred Jarry was an early influence on Surrealism and Dada. The 1896 debut of his play *Ubu Roi* created a scandal when the main character Père Ubu uttered the scatological first line: 'Merdre!'.

4   This often led to confrontations between radical groups and concert organisers over the "commodification" of popular music. These stand-offs could even become physical at times.

5   Barrett had been particular inspired by guitarist Keith Rowe from London-based group AMM.

6   The albums *More* and *Obscured By Clouds* were recorded as soundtracks for films by the French-based director Barbet Schroeder. In the early '70s Pink Floyd also created several ballet scores for French choreographer Roland Petit.

THE GOLDEN AGE
by Jean-Jacques Birgé

The story began for me with the events of May 1968, but it had really begun much earlier. History always begins earlier.

I was 15 when I realised that real life was elsewhere, to quote Rimbaud. As summer arrived, a three-month tour of the USA, alone with my little sister who was 13, was the revelation of all that was to come, especially listening to the Mothers of Invention's *We're Only In It For The Money*. I wrote a novel about this initiatory journey, *USA 1968 deux enfants*. No one at school had crossed the Atlantic ocean. I brought back some seeds that I grew on my balcony, that's how much of a hero I was in my college!

When I got back to Paris, I started the light-show group H Lights. We projected our psychedelic images on Red Noise and Crouille-Marteau (actors Pierre Clémenti on musical saw and Jean-Pierre Kalfon on guitar) for Melmoth's birthday (writer Dashiell Hedayat, author of *Chrysler Rose*).

We also organised the first rock concert at the Lycée Claude Bernard with Red Noise, Dagon and our band, Epimanondas. I met Dagon because the Lentin brothers were dealing hashish, fantastic black stuff from Afghanistan (Jean-Pierre Lentin went on to become a famous rock journalist). We also projected our images on huge screens behind Daevid Allen's Gong and other bands at concerts which were usually held in universities like Dauphine, Assas or the Maison de la Chimie...

In October 1969 I went by bus to the Amougies Festival in Belgium with my sister's little tape recorder. I recorded the concerts that can be found everywhere on the internet, in particular Zappa jamming with Pink Floyd, Caravan, Blossom Toes, Sam Apple Pie, Aynsley Dunbar

Retaliation, Captain Beefheart, etc. I discovered free jazz there; it was huge.

There were French bands like Ame Son, We Free, Cruciferius, Martin Circus, Pierre Mariétan's GERM (who played Terry Riley's 'Keyboard Study no.2'), and Gong of course, with Daniel Laloux on the Napoleonic drum. None of these groups exist any more. To my taste, however, the French groups were not as exciting as Soft Machine, Colosseum, The Nice, Archie Shepp, or The Art Ensemble of Chicago. There was something stiff and too clean about them, whereas the Anglo-Saxons swung and went for it.

The craziest French groups, like Lard Free and Red Noise, were inspired by free jazz, improvising rather than sticking to their repertoire. For six months I was a member of Lard Free as a trio with Gilbert Artman (Urban Sax) and Richard Pinhas (Heldon), playing at the Gibus Club and Bus Palladium, two historical rock'n'roll venues.

There were no borders between rock and jazz. Drummer Jacques Thollot was composing a very personal pop music, a true poet... Singers Colette Magny, Brigitte Fontaine, and Catherine Ribeiro were our Three Graces. They were often accompanied by jazz musicians. François Tusques, Bernard Vitet, Beb Guérin played on Colette's *Black Panther Suite*, and The Art Ensemble of Chicago made Brigitte's *Comme à la radio* famous. Patrice Moullet built a strange acoustic rhythmic instrument, the percuphone, for Catherine Ribeiro. You could listen to Zoo with Léo Ferré... It was a kind of melting pot!

However very few of us were interested in what we used to call pop music over here. Hippies wearing colourful clothes, stinky goat skin jackets and smoking joints. One important thing I remember is that during festivals I could leave the backpack with all my stuff in it under the big tent without fear of it being stolen. I felt like all the hairy people were part of the same community. It really was Peace & Love, believing that the Vietnam War would be the last if we didn't give up. Capitalism easily got the better of our naivety.

In Paris the rallying point was essentially the American Center on Boulevard Raspail, which offered rock and free jazz concerts. Their audiences were mixed. We also met the Krishna devotees who had taken up residence there. That's how I found myself accompanying them with George Harrison at Maxim's!

On my crappy tape recorder I regularly recorded French bands whose compositions were close to Zappa and Beefheart, like Moving Gelatine Plates, but also Mahjun, Komintern, Barricade, Fille Qui Mousse, Crium Delirium, Triangle, etc. Unfortunately I lost most of these tapes.

The following summer I hitch-hiked to the south of France to attend the Biot-Valbonne festival, which would become a disaster for the organisers, as young people stormed the gates to get in without paying. Free-riding is a favourite sport of the French. As in Amougies, we slept on site in sleeping bags. The festival didn't go ahead as planned, but I did borrow Patrick Vian's Marshall amp for Zappa and introduced him to Jean-Luc Ponty, Alby Cullaz and Aldo Romano. I recently sent the recording I made that night to Ponty who had never heard it before.

I was a very helpful kid, so I was appreciated by the musicians and the organisers. That's how, after the debacle, I found myself jamming with Eric Clapton in Giorgio Gomelsky's villa. Gomelsky had managed The Rolling Stones, The Yardbirds and Magma, among others. In a fit of anger he fired all the groupies, but not the kid who did the sweeping and washed the dishes! So then he took me to Pink Floyd's villa... In those days you could climb over the fences and go and talk to Zappa like I did in Amougies, without being beaten and violently thrown out...

If we wanted to know what was going on in Paris or London, we had to go to the Librairie Parallèles where we could find magazines like *IT*, *Le Parapluie* by Henri-Jean Enu or *Actuel* which Jean-François Bizot had relaunched. The guy in charge, Philippe Thyere, advised us on all the underground literature, from comics to Burroughs and Pélieu in the same bag. Further on, at the intersection of the boulevards Raspail and Saint-Germain, you could find imported records at Givaudan's, but it was obviously very expensive. That's how I discovered Sun Ra and Harry Partch. To tell the truth, the French scene seemed timid to me.

In 1973 I bought my ARP 2600 synthesiser, but most people were scared of it. Before that I played on a Farfisa Professional organ transformed by a few pedals. The synthesiser scared both rockers and jazzmen. It was automatically associated with krautrock. The rockers were into electric guitar, the jazzmen into saxophones.

Francis Gorgé and I recorded in my bedroom on headphones until

Sébastien Bernard offered to produce a record for Sun Records. He gave me the eight-track tape back six months later advising me to do something other than music. He had talked to Frank Wright, Alan Silva, and Noah Howard about our recording, but it was obviously not their cup of tea. So I founded GRRR Records and produced what became *Défense de* with Gorgé and Shiroc! At the time, it was only rare musicians who were aware of the importance of leaving a trace or distributing their work in this way. There were a lot of shows, but few recordings of French bands.

Three years later, as we were playing support concerts at the antipsychiatric clinic La Borde, I found myself once again jamming, this time with Opération Rhino. Jac Berrocal had gathered about fifteen musicians including Philippe Pochan and Pierre Bastien. Most of them preferred me to play the alto sax rather than the synth. Saxophonist Daunik Lazro had been kind enough to explain some tricks to me before the gig. At the other end of the stage Bernard Vitet was banging empty beer bottles until they exploded. The floor around him was littered with broken glass and he looked really scary. As I knew who he was, I went to meet him after the concert. We talked about Monk, Varèse, and Webern for three days and we remained together until his death in 2013. He became my best friend and I miss him a lot. I also remember taking part in a search for Brigitte Fontaine who had fled into the woods, and that Pierre Clémenti looked like the Antichrist from Buñuel's *The Milky Way* in his immaculate white suit, playing the saxophone!

From then on I devoted my life to Un Drame Musical Instantané, which was started by bringing together Francis Gorgé and Bernard Vitet. At the time, collective writing was not common and we really had the impression of living in the underground, on the fringe of the schools of thought that were beginning to flourish in France. Our independence, even within the movement, made us totally free, but also isolated us. It is paradoxical, but the schisms pushed us there.

Among the French musicians quoted on the Nurse With Wound List, who is still going on today? Jazz soloists such as Michel Portal, Bernard Lubat (who founded the Uzeste Festival), and Raymond Boni, outsiders like Albert Marcœur and Pierre Bastien (Nu Creative Methods), rock groups like Art Zoyd (mainly Gérard Hourbette and Thierry Zaboitzeff) and Magma… Guigou Chenevier (who founded the Gare aux Oreilles festival) is still playing. Gilbert Artman, Jean-François Pauvros and Jac Berrocal made it together with Catalogue... Many died or disappeared in the meanwhile. But they all remained very inventive artists.

At the beginning of the underground movement, musicians, whether they played rock or jazz, were very politically involved with the extreme left. They were clearly the fruit of May '68, which was essentially a revolution of morals. We had also inherited the Black Panthers, protest songs, jazz improvisations and the rage of rock... Rock, which is mostly a collective project, brought electricity but jazz, which promotes individuals, made us improvise. The economic conditions were favourable to these bohemian youth who enjoyed life and fulfilled themselves in their passion. Compared to today, their work was much less marginalised, it was broadcast on national radio (the *Pop Club* with José Artur) and television (*Bouton Rouge* with Pierre Lattès, then *Pop 2* with Patrice Blanc-Francard), reviewed in specialised magazines (*Rock & Folk*, *Best*) and even in the daily press. There were not many of us and our records sold quite well, both in small record shops and the large cultural stores (like Fnac) that were being set up at the time. There were also many more venues to play in!

At the beginning of the 1970s I remember taking part in the opening of the Andy Warhol exhibition at the Musée d'Art Moderne de la Ville de Paris with Dagon and Jérôme Savary's Grand Magic Circus, who had just returned to France from the USA. With my synthesiser I earned a living by recording film music. All this gradually changed after the oil crisis of 1974, but we didn't feel the disastrous effects until the 1980s.

You could say that despite the underground aspect of everything we were making, we lived a sort of golden age.

Jean-Jacques Birgé, Paris, March '23.

AN IMPORTANT AND OFTEN NEGLECTED MUSICAL UNIVERSE
by Steven Stapleton

I am sitting cross legged on a dusty scuzzy floor wedged between hippies, freaks and weekend hippies, someone just offered me a joint. It's the early seventies, it's a Sunday afternoon in London's Chalk Farm Roundhouse. I've been here before, Hawkwind, Man, Nektar and the Pink Fairies have all freaked out on this famous stage but today is something very special, today we have Ash Ra Tempel, Franco Battiato and Magma. An amazing lineup, but at the time Magma were unknown to me.

As I watched the roadies set up Christian Vander's drum set, loading huge metal weights around the cymbal stands and what looked like fixing the kit to the stage floor, I wondered what was in store for those drums and for us, the audience!

After incredible sets by Ash Ra Tempel and Battiato, Magma exploded with such fierceness it left me breathless, Christian Vander is truly a force of nature, to this day I have never experienced anything like the passion and mighty power of Magma on that occasion. The dynamism and intensity of their performance even led to bassman Jannick Top breaking several strings.

Since that pivotal moment I became a fan and soon learned of their all prevailing importance within the blossoming French music scene. The commanding mix of avant jazz, progressive rock and Carl Orff style operatics sung in Vander's own original idiosyncratic language, Kobaïan. Magma have dominated the French underground since the late sixties. Up until today their influence and legacy is inestimable, alongside Zappa, Soft Machine and Free Jazz, they have laid the foundations of this important and often neglected musical universe.

Since my Magma epiphany I became obsessed with this mysterious scene, I came across a little hand printed publication *Un certain rock(?) français* by Dominique Grimaud, xeroxed black and white pages stapled together containing all the dope on this secretive clandestine movement. Mystical and mystifying bands, artists with strange names like Mahogany Brain, Semool, Crium Delirium, Fille Qui Mousse, Horde Catalytique Pour la Fin. So intrigued was I that I had to get to Paris to check these out. Armed with *Un certain rock(?)*, I met and became friends with Gilles Yeprémian, Lard Free's manager and organiser, he kindly let me stay at his house and from this base I started my search into this most cryptic realm.

Following up clues found in my little xeroxed booklet, I met many artists and musicians, all friendly and happy to talk to a naive teenager. Records were elusive and difficult to find, many of what seemed the most interesting were on the Futura jazz label and some on their Futura Red imprint. Having no luck with record shops I decided to find the Futura headquarters as listed on the sleeves, I found the little dingy basement office and was warmly greeted by a lovely older lady who gave me copies of all the records I had read about, I would be forever grateful.

At the time the only other place to find these obscure gems would be the Parisian flea markets, where one could fill one's arms with as many abandoned and disregarded French records as you could carry! And oh so cheap - I remember finding the *Horrific Child* LP for 2 francs!

Some of the most interesting and incomparable music was produced in the golden years '70-'75, mainly issued on private or small self-financed labels with little or no distribution. Occasionally a major would take a chance, i.e. Komintern on Harvest or Zao on Vertigo, but for the most part they were almost entirely ignored. Some of my favourites from that early fertile period included: Maajun - *Vivre la mort du vieux monde,* Jean Guérin - *Tacet,* Chene Noir - *Aurora,* François Jeanneau - *Une bien curieuse planète,* Zao - *Osiris,* Jean Cohen-Solal - *Captain Tarthopom* amongst others.

Wonderful memories of meeting John Livengood who had played organ with Red Noise on the seminal *Sarcelles-Lochères* album, he had just formed the band Spacecraft with Ivan Coaquette of Musica Elettronica Viva, he invited my friend and I to their home studio to hear the album they had just completed. Instead of playing a tape he proceeded to perform the entire thing live, there and then.

Meeting Jac Berrocal was so important, I loved his music. I remember arriving at his flat unannounced, he was very kind and we became friends despite the language barrier. In '79 I invited him to London to play on our second Nurse With Wound album *Quiet Men*, he was so enthusiastic and vital to the project. Jac also created the astounding original 'Rock and Roll Station' with Vince Taylor, one of the most sublime 'songs' ever recorded.

Steven Stapleton, Cooloorta, June '24.

part one:
a short history of the musical underground

CHANSON, YÉ-YÉ & TEEN IDOLS: French pop before 1968

> In France, the radio and TV played only *variétés* singers, performing cover versions of Anglo-Saxon songs translated into French. The record companies swore by that, and had no desire to do anything else, it took up all of the space. Like many other bands, we wanted to take the opposite position, to express a rejection of French show-business as it was.
>
> *Michel Peteau (Cheval Fou/Nyl)*

Before the advent of rock'n'roll, French popular music was dominated by *chanson*, a distinctly French musical form with a long and rich tradition. In *chanson* the lyric was king, with aspirations to literature in some cases. The melodies and arrangements followed the rhythms of the French language, making *chanson* irrefutably French music.

When performed by Édith Piaf or Belgium's Jacques Brel *chanson* could be gritty or bawdy, but it was the smooth, middle-of-the-road *variété* style (epitomised by Charles Aznavour and Dalida) that totally dominated French radio and television until the late '60s. Despite the ubiquity of this commercialised music, singers of artful *chanson* like Georges Brassens and Léo Ferré would still be major figures on the musical landscape through the '60s and into the '70s.

Jazz was the other mainstay of French popular music before rock'n'roll. It had been introduced in the aftermath of World War One by American jazz musicians attracted to Paris by its relative lack of racial discrimination. There was some initial resistance to the importation of an American musical form, but by the '30s jazz was well-entrenched in France. That it was mainly instrumental undoubtedly assisted its acceptance, making the issue of non-French lyrics largely irrelevant. An important landmark came in 1934 when Django Reinhardt and Stéphane Grappelli joined forces to create the Quintette du Hot Club de France. Their gypsy-jazz fusion proved that jazz could be a truly French music.

When rock'n'roll finally arrived in France it was treated as nothing more than a passing musical fad. With neither the lyrical interest of *chanson* nor the musical complexity of jazz, it was considered an impoverished foreign form. Unlike jazz before it, rock'n'roll was inextricably bound to its English lyrics, leading to additional resistance.

The unexpected popularity of American rock'n'roll amongst the French youth led to a grudging acceptance from the music business, and the first recorded examples of French rock'n'roll began to appear in '56. These were firmly in the realm of pastiche, with already established artists like Boris Vian, Michel Legrand, and Henri Salvador releasing their approximations of the style (often under fanciful anglicised pseudonyms like Henry Cording).

The early history of rock'n'roll in France paralleled its development in the UK, with solo artists releasing cover versions (or French re-writes) of American songs. France's Richard Anthony and Danyel Gérard were the Gallic equivalents of the UK's Marty Wilde and Tommy Steele.

There would be little to distinguish either country's home-grown music until a breakout artist managed to locally eclipse the original American music. In the UK this came in '58 when Cliff Richard & The Drifters released 'Move It'. Two years later, on 14 March '60, Johnny Hallyday released 'T'aimer follement' (a French rewrite of Floyd Robinson's 'Makin' Love'). That date is widely accepted as the birth of French rock.

Richard and Hallyday would remain huge stars in their respective homelands, but neither could be said to have driven the evolution of rock or pop music. Their somewhat contrived images and derivative music underlined the innate foreignness of rock'n'roll. Teens in both France and the UK were aware that the teen rebellion celebrated by American rock'n'roll was inspired by an experience of adolescence totally different to their own.

In hindsight it's stunning that the British took only a few years to develop the confidence to innovate new musical and cultural styles inspired by American rock'n'roll. Starting with the Beat Boom of the early '60s, these new hybrid musical forms were distinctively British in their expression, and gave rise to idiosyncratically British subcultures. Indeed so novel were they that they caused a sensation in the home of rock'n'roll, leading to the so-called British Invasion.

Such innovation was sorely lacking elsewhere in Europe. It wouldn't be until the very end of the '60s that musicians in first Germany, then France would gain the confidence needed to develop their own new forms. They would leave imitation and pastiche behind, to search out a local expression of rock music.

In the meantime one factor differentiated France: it maintained a large market for songs in its native language. In 1960 only twenty percent of the songs that charted in France were by non-French acts, while the corresponding figure in Germany was around seventy percent. The language barrier was very real in France, creating resistance to simply importing British and American music (as occurred in most European countries). Thus, the French music business had good reason to continue to develop local artists. While musical innovation may have been thin on the ground, a slew of new French artists emerged in the course of the '60s.

Hallyday's success opened the breach for other French rock'n' rollers, the most significant being Les Chats Sauvages and Les Chaussettes Noires. However, while the music business rushed to embrace rock'n'roll, it was faced with growing opposition from a conservative adult population. Many viewed rock'n'roll as unwanted, foreign, and decadent music. For others it was symptomatic of an undesired Americanisation of French culture.

A *cause célèbre* at the time was the belief that gangs of youth were running amok under the influence of American movies and music. These *blousons noirs* (literally "black jackets") were the French equivalent of the British Teddy Boys and the American Rockers. They styled themselves on depictions of rebellious American youth seen in movies like *The Wild One* and *Rebel Without a Cause*. The French media attributed an increase in juvenile delinquency to these gangs, aided and abetted by the insidious effect of imported American rock'n'roll music.

Vince Taylor et ses Play-Boys, signed by Barclay Records in '61, became a lightning rod for these concerns. Their charismatic English-born singer (who'd been raised in the US) brought real rock'n'roll swagger to France, and along with it a reaction close to moral panic. Clad in head-to-toe black leather, Taylor was the living embodiment of rock'n'roll to French youth and their parents. Along with the strong image came a matching notoriety, and his concerts gained a reputation as the arena for gangs of *blousons noirs* to face off against each other. In reaction to the negative publicity, Barclay pulled back from their initial strong support of the singer.

The music business reacted to the backlash by flocking to the safe harbour of a new, more palatable home-grown style: *yé-yé*. While this new music was certainly related to rock'n'roll, lyrically it had much more in common with *variétés*. The sometimes louche suggestiveness of early rock'n'roll was replaced by a valourisation of innocence and wholesome fun. Its name was derived from The Beatles (*yé-yé* was a Gallicisation of their "yeah, yeah" exclamation), but the influence ended there. These new artists were marketed and styled in a distinctly French way, in an effort to make pop music more acceptable to French society.

Central to the development of *yé-yé* was the radio programme *Salut les copains* (roughly translated as "Hi pals") which began broadcasting on Europe 1 in '59. This nightly two hours of pop music quickly became a huge success, helping to foster *yé-yé* through its *chouchou de la semaine* (sweetheart of the week) segment. A featured song was guaranteed to shoot straight into the charts, and was a launchpad for singers like Françoise Hardy, Sheila, and Sylvie Vartan.

Salut les copains consolidated its position in '62 with the launch of an eponymous magazine. This pushed the idea that pop represented a community of *copains* (pals), made up of both fans and the stars themselves. The teen rebellion represented by youth subcultures (like the *blousons noirs*) was replaced by a much safer notion, with "teen idols" singing about (and portrayed as living) an idealised adolescence, something to be aspired to by all. In effect the *copains* formed a huge, inclusive youth club that advocated consumerism and an apolitical outlook. Even erstwhile rockers like Eddy Mitchell and Johnny Hallyday reinvented themselves to become leading members of this new community of *copains*.

The incredible popularity of *yé-yé* and of *Salut les copains* was brought home by the massive audience that celebrated the first anniversary of the launch of the magazine on 22 June '63. The La Nuit de la Nation concert, featuring Johnny Hallyday, Sylvie Vartan, Eddy Mitchell, Richard Anthony, and Danyel Gérard had been expected to attract 30,000. The actual attendance was well over 100,000.

Yé-yé reigned supreme into the mid-'60s. At the same time British bands like The Beatles and The Rolling Stones had made inroads into the French market, leading to the number of home-grown rock'n'roll bands plummeting between '62 and '64. A local group, like Les Chats Sauvages, was only rarely able to break the stranglehold of the *copains*.

While the *yé-yé* stars remained unchallenged by Anglo-American pop, the resistance to English-language rock music was evaporating. French youth began to prefer the original output of the new wave of British and American bands to locally-produced, Gallicised cover versions. As a result the proportion of non-French acts in the charts steadily grew to reach thirty percent in '65, and forty percent by '70. The ubiquity of *yé-yé* combined with the growing preference for original English-language rock combined to hasten the demise of French rock'n'roll bands. Even stalwarts like Les Chaussettes Noires and Les Chats Sauvages were forced into obscurity by the mid-'60s.

A new social phenomenon hit France in '64, a diffuse political and cultural fringe movement inspired by the American beat writers and the nascent hippy movement. These so-called "beatniks", long-haired, bearded poets and activists, caught the public's attention. The movement provided a welcome alternative to the consumerist conformism preached by *yé-yé*'s prophets. It soon became common for French youth to emulate the nomadic "beatnik" lifestyle, hitting the road to hitch-hike through foreign countries on their vacations.

In '65 a new generation of French musicians arrived representing these "beatnik" ideals. While their songs tended to emulate those of the US folk-singers, significantly they were written by the artists themselves. Foregrounding their own lyrics brought artists like Antoine and Michel Polnareff some of the cachet of *chanson*, and helped elevate the standing of French pop music.

It was the success of Antoine's 'Les Élucubrations d'Antoine', released in January '66, that signalled the beginning of a new era. The song represented the total antithesis of *yé-yé*, with a delivery soaked in Dylanesque insouciance, and a lyric presenting a sardonic youth manifesto (including an explicit dismissal of king of the *copains*, Johnny Hallyday). When the song hit #1 and remained in the charts for five months, it became obvious that the times were indeed finally changing in France.

Just a few months later a subversion at the heart of the world of *yé-yé* seemed to confirm the change in the air, even in this stultifying milieu. Serge Gainsbourg had developed a reputation for humourous wordplay, but he outdid himself in the lyrics for 'Les Sucettes' (Lollipops), written for France Gall. Unbeknownst to Gall, he had loaded the song with sexual double entendres, which she delivered with absolute innocence, serving to amplify the effect. The purported wholesomeness of the community of *copains* was sullied forever.

This year of change was capped in November by the launch of *Rock & Folk* magazine. It treated music as a serious cultural phenomenon (rather than the teen fantasy of *Salut les copains*), and would eventually grow into an important voice promoting the development of home-grown, truly French rock music.

By the end of '66 it finally seemed that French popular music had emerged from five years of arrested development caused by *yé-yé*'s domination.

An interesting twist in the tale of French pop music comes as a potentially apocryphal anecdote. A government memorandum had supposedly been circulated to radio stations directing them not to give airtime to French rock groups. The rationale: in the UK young people were being encouraged to experiment with drugs by rock musicians, and this must be avoided in France. The memo reportedly went on to state that *yé-yé* presented no such danger. True or not, the fact that this story had currency speaks volumes about the authorities' attitude to both popular music and French youth.

The following year may have been less dramatic, but the foundations for the changes to come after the social explosion of '68 continued to be put in place.

Firstly, inspired by the UK blues-rock boom, French bands began to re-emerge. The emphasis was still very much on emulation, with bands like Blues Convention, Les Variations, and Les Primitiv's playing cover versions of songs by their English contemporaries. These bands reflected the new French taste for rock sung in English by abandoning their native language on stage. Very few would find any lasting success (the most significant being Les Variations), but they were a training ground for many of the musicians who would form the core of the French underground.

Next, rock music was finally given a home on French television. The ORTF (the French equivalent of Britain's BBC) broadcast the first episode of *Bouton Rouge* on 16 April '67. The host Pierre Lattès followed *Rock & Folk*'s lead by presenting rock as serious music. The majority of the programme was given over to an extended live studio performance by a featured (almost always Anglo-American) band. These included The Jimi Hendrix Experience, The Yardbirds, Pink Floyd, Ten Years After, Cream, and Captain Beefheart. The coverage of *yé-yé* and pop was absolutely minimal. Unfortunately, along with all other regular programming, *Bouton Rouge* was taken off the air in May '68 when the general strike spread to the ORTF. However unlike other programming it never returned.

In the summer of '67 psychedelic rock was introduced onto French soil when Soft Machine played at a series of events around St Tropez. This put them directly in front of a Parisian artistic elite on its annual summer pilgrimage to the Côte d'Azur. While the band was barely known outside of the London underground at the time, they would quickly become a huge influence on the French music scene. When Soft Machine returned to the UK, their Australian guitarist Daevid Allen was turned back at the border. As a result he took up residency in Paris, where he would help transplant psychedelic culture directly into fertile French soil.

A reflection by Marc Blanc (who would be playing with Allen in Bananamoon by the beginning of '68) gives an insight into the early Parisian underground: "At the end of '67, there was a very small nucleus. When we met Daevid Allen he was playing in the cellar of La Vieille Grille where Brigitte Fontaine was headlining. Jacques Thollot and Barney Wilen also played there. Jean-Pierre Kalfon, the actor, was there... It was a very small underground group... rock was still small, especially underground rock! After '68, France changed... a whole scene came to light."

Much had changed in the French music scene since the introduction of rock'n'roll in the '50s. However as '67 drew to a close the underground remained a loose association of artists, film-makers, and rock and jazz musicians. The events of '68 would send shockwaves throughout the whole of French society, profoundly shaping the developing counter-culture.

MAY '68:
The Explosion

> France, compared to the rest of Europe and particularly the United Kingdom and Germany, was too French, too middle-of-the-road. There was no evolution, it was a controlled, very patriarchal society, not moving quickly to modernise... a very militarised, police state.
>
> The movement started at the university with the students, and the intelligentsia, plus the fringe of people like us (the artists). Then the working class came in, and 1968 became a snowballing process where all French were saying: "Enough is enough!" And it changed everything.
>
> *Roger Scaglia (Maajun)*

"The Year That Rocked the World" is the subtitle of Mark Kurlansky's history of '68. It's hard to find a better description for a year that saw such a succession of seismic events: the Tet Offensive in Vietnam, Russian tanks rolling into Czechoslovakia to crush the Prague Spring, the assassinations of Martin Luther King Jr and Robert Kennedy in the US, and a rash of student protests the world over.

In May of '68 all eyes turned to France when a series of student protests spilled over into the general public, fanning the embers of discontent into a wildfire of near revolution.

It all started with sex. Well, at least in part... For months students at the campus of Nanterre in the west of Paris had been campaigning against its antiquated rules, including a ban on male and female students visiting each other's dormitories. The authorities' attempts to suppress the protests only served to escalate them. This led to a series of overreactions that laid bare the authoritarian nature of not only the university system, but the whole of French society.

On 2 May Nanterre's dean, exasperated that his campus continued to be mired in protest, made the fateful decision to close it down. The next day, with the campus shut and expulsions threatened, the protest simply relocated to the Sorbonne in the heart of the Latin Quarter. The rector of the Sorbonne continued the spiral into chaos by calling in the police to clear the protesters away.

Scores of riot police entered the university, violently arresting around half of the 500 students who'd been staging a peaceful sit-in. Bystanders, shocked by the heavy-handed response, attempted to intervene and were given the same treatment. Running street battles ensued. Thrown paving stones were countered with tear-gas and baton charges.

The residents of the Latin Quarter were stunned by the authorities' overreaction. As demonstrations around the Sorbonne grew in size and the police clamped down with ever-increasing force, support for the students grew in proportion.

A week of protests culminated in a major demonstration on Friday, 10 May. Tens of thousands gathered at Place Denfert-Rochereau demanding the release of all those arrested so far, the removal of police from the Sorbonne, and the reopening of the university. The demonstrators decided to march across the city to bring their protest to the television studios of the ORTF, on the Right Bank. On reaching the Seine they were greeted by a phalanx of CRS riot police blocking every bridge. Incensed and cornered, the order went out for the protesters to occupy the Latin Quarter. As night fell police reinforcements arrived, further hemming them in, and by 9pm barricades began to spring up in anticipation of a police charge. The Night of the Barricades had begun.

Within hours more than 60 barricades had been constructed using anything to hand, including paving stones (*pavés*) dug from the street, cars, and uprooted trees. Sickened by the violence of the week-long police clampdown, the residents of the quarter offered the students help, bringing them food and drink (and later when the police attacked, providing them with shelter). At 2am the inevitable happened; the police stormed the barricades with tear-gas and truncheons. Members of the public who came to the assistance of injured protesters were beaten indiscriminately. By daybreak the authorities were back in control of the Latin Quarter, leaving what resembled a war zone in their wake. The final tally of the evening: 350 hospitalised, more than 1000 injured, and 468 arrested.

Public outrage exploded. The Night of the Barricades was the spark that ignited the tinderbox of French society. The savagery of the police response had exposed the darkness at the heart of Charles de Gaulle's France. In response the major trade unions called for a general strike and demonstration on Monday, 13 May. More than a million people took part in the march.

Then something totally unexpected happened: contrary to the unions' order a huge number of workers simply didn't return to work on Tuesday! Within days a spontaneous movement of wildcat strikes spread across France, and in a week the country was paralysed. At its peak ten million workers (about sixty percent of the workforce) had joined the protest. Their demands were much broader than student freedom or pay increases. The minimum they would accept was the resignation of de Gaulle and his government, but there was talk of even more radical change: demands for a new *kind* of France, a democratic, socialist, *workers'* Republic. This was something that the powers-that-be, even the unions and the Communist Party (a major political force at the time, with around twenty percent of the vote), would fight tooth-and-nail.

With the Metro ground to a halt, shops shuttered, fuel supplies dwindling, and uncollected rubbish piling up, the streets had begun to buzz. Everyone had an opinion, and communication and debate were welcomed.

Representatives of the major revolutionary groups took the floor in public forums and printed thousands of tracts arguing their case. Nevertheless the movement remained resolutely non-partisan. It was the ideas of a fairly marginal group, the Situationist International, that resonated loudest in May '68.

According to the Situationists the capitalist system had become so all-encompassing that *everything* had become a tradable commodity. We were living in The Society of the Spectacle: our entire lives, even our most intimate dreams and experiences, had been subsumed into the system to be sold back to us as pre-packaged product. The only solution was nothing less than the revolution of everyday life.

Tracts, flyers, and pamphlets flooded the streets, but in the end it was the walls that spoke loudest, and the graffiti, slogans, and posters

that plastered them spoke in unmistakeably Situationist language:
"Be realistic, demand the impossible"
"Never work"
"It is forbidden to forbid"
"Beauty is in the Street"
"The more you consume the less you live"
"Take your desires for reality"

For several weeks everyday life actually *was* transformed. The heightened atmosphere on the streets is captured in a contemporary account by an English academic caught up in the events:

"The great courtyard of the Sorbonne is crowded with people: students and workers, and some bourgeois, arguing, forming groups where people stand and discuss, dispute, bellow, disagree, create an atmosphere where one feels that they are awake! This goes on twenty-four hours a day...

"Walking out across the Place de la Sorbonne, you can see the same thing - groups, discussions, everywhere, perfect strangers joining arguments, exchanging views, in an atmosphere of charged excitement... The level of discussion is remarkably high, on the whole, and if you can imagine the sort of energy the French put into an argument between two drivers whose cars have collided, transferred to an argument about the organisation of the University, the class struggle, the whole organisation of our society, the possibility of revolution: all this conducted by a free-floating crowd of literally thousands of people, in the Sorbonne, in the street, in the cafés - this all going on day and night - then you may get some idea of the Quartier Latin at the moment."

The government, the unions, and the Communist opposition struggled to get things back under their control. A series of crisis talks were held in an attempt to defuse the strike with the promise of better working conditions. On 27 May the Grenelle Agreement was presented to the union membership - offering a ten percent hike in wages, a reduction in working hours, and a thirty-five percent increase to the minimum wage. It was comprehensively rejected by the rank-and-file.

As the workers refused their unions' pleas to return to work, it truly seemed that France was on the brink. The spirit of the 1789

Revolution and the 1871 Paris Commune had been rekindled.

In fact, on the morning of 29 May revolution looked so imminent that President de Gaulle fled the country. For six hours no-one in the government knew his location. More than a decade later it was revealed that he had flown to Germany to meet with one of his most loyal generals. Assured of the army's support, de Gaulle returned to Paris that evening. With his troops rallied (both figuratively and literally), he called a snap election the next day.

His gambit worked. During the election campaign people fell back into their prescribed roles, and by the end of June the revolutionary moment had passed. However French youth had experienced an exhilarating freedom they would never forget. In May it had seemed that not only was anything possible, it was sitting there for the taking. A whole generation was transformed.

Across the Channel, British musicians had been watching, and in August '68 both The Beatles and The Rolling Stones released songs inspired by the events of May. In 'Revolution' John Lennon proved to be ambivalent, while Mick Jagger openly celebrated the French students in 'Street Fighting Man'. Komintern's Michel Muzac notes that Jagger's support didn't go unnoticed: " 'Street Fighting Man' became symbolic in France, a kind of anthem for young rebels and protesters."

In a reflection written 50 years later, J.D. Beauvalet opined that French music had lagged behind the May events, rather than contributing to them: "No-one really amplified the hubbub like The Stones and The Beatles in England. Of course, there were exceptions, mainly from French *chanson*, such as Renaud, Evariste, and Dominique Grange. It's as if May '68 was too serious a thing to involve pop culture, as if the insurgents saw rock as an imperialist invention to be kept at bay. It's a shame, because the same slogans, set to the psychedelic or free-rock music that some tried to adopt (such as Patrick Vian's group Red Noise), would have resonated to the flight of paving stones. While the youth were screaming 'no! no!' to the old world, the music was mostly *'yé-yé'*."

While the musicians who would go on to populate the underground were forever marked by May '68, the established pop and *yé-yé* artists generally viewed it negatively. A number of them spoke to Alain Spireaux for the June '68 edition of *Noir & Blanc*: Eddy Mitchell complained about the cancellation of his concerts, France Gall chafed that the release of her latest disc had been affected (but was happy that things had at last "returned to normal"), while Sheila was just keen to put the whole thing behind her.

A very different attitude shines through when speaking to musicians from the French underground. Almost all view May '68 as a defining moment, something that would influence them for years to come. In many cases it was the catalyst steeling their determination to devote their lives to music.

> Alain Roux *(Maajun)*:
> "Most of the musicians involved in the underground movement at the beginning of the '70s were around twenty years old in May '68. Obviously at that age, such an experience is formative and structuring. I was a political activist and in '68 I was a student in sociology at the Sorbonne in Paris, the right place *(laughs)*. I took part in the events of '68, and was wounded on the barricades. I was blind for three weeks, with tear gas directly in the eyes."

> Michel Peteau *(Cheval Fou/Nyl)*:
> "I was fourteen, living in Paris, it felt like I was seeing a world turn from black and white to colour. It was the demolition of an outmoded society. The feeling of freedom that floated in the air spurred me on to quit my studies and inevitably head towards music."

> Christian Tritsch *(Gong)*:
> "For me, at the beginning, being a musician was a job like any other. I played behind Claude François alongside musicians like François Jeanneau, Mimi Lorenzini, and Rachid Houari. May '68 changed everything. We all left the roles we'd assumed before then. Rock and roll became the music of revolution. After May '68 I played with Jacques Thollot, Eddie Gaumont, and Barney Wilen."

Didier Malherbe *(Gong)*:
"I did participate in the events. I didn't throw *pavés* at the cops, but my friends and I were sticking posters on the walls, and taking part in actions. I participated without being violent. I was even caught by the cops one morning, arrested, put in a bus, and taken to the Town Hall of the 14th Arrondissement. They threatened me, saying, 'We recognise you, we saw you running between barricades'. So I went to the chief cop, looked him in the eyes and said 'Look I'm very ill, and you'll have trouble if you keep me'. So he let me go."

Klaus Blasquiz *(Magma)*:
"In May I worked at the Beaux Arts. I even slept there, while constantly making silkscreen posters by hand. My clothes and shoes had traces of ink on them for ages. Sometimes I delivered bundles of posters on my bicycle. Public transport was on strike, so I lugged them around to the suburbs, to supply schools and universities far away from the Latin Quarter."

Dominique Lentin *(Dagon)*:
"I was thirteen years old in May '68. At Lycée Buffon in Paris we burned our report cards in the middle of the courtyard. My parents and my two older brothers went to the demonstrations. I came back home at 7pm (it was too dangerous after that)... May '68 provoked me to reject the [accepted] model of society."

Cyrille Verdeaux *(Clearlight)*:
"I was in hospital for weeks recovering from the 'migraine' that some hate-filled CRS had given me with their rifle butts... apart from a musician and a protester, I don't really see what I could have been."

Patrick Fontaine *(Bananamoon/Ame Son/Cheval Fou/Nyl)*:
"The student riots paralysed the Latin Quarter where we were. Before going onto the street, we had to make sure that the CRS weren't charging at groups of students. Garbage was piling up on the streets, transport was at a standstill, there was a shortage of petrol, but discussions took place on every

subject, irrespective of generation. It was a new hope, we had to reinvent life."

Olivier Zdrzalik *(Komintern)*:
"There was an incredible atmosphere! The barricades in the streets, the smoke, the tear gas and these extraordinary situations: everyone talking to each other from the youngest to the oldest... We thought that the world was about to topple over and that we'd be the ones to make it happen. What a feeling!"

Guigou Chenevier *(Etron Fou Leloublan)*:
"You have to understand that at the time, everybody (I mean the majority of young people between sixteen and thirty) was absolutely sure that the revolution would be happening in the very near future! And of course this idea, this 'utopia' had a very big influence on the general atmosphere including art, and specifically on the music scene. In my opinion, the French musical underground scene was the most creative one in Europe between '68 and '75, and there is necessarily a historical connection with the political events in France in '68..."

Dominique Grimaud *(Camizole)*:
"May 1968 was a very intense moment, socially and politically. It is a symbolic and significant event in France. But changes in the way of thinking didn't come suddenly, as if by magic, following a month of student protests, strikes, and factory occupations... In fact, the changes occurred little by little in French society over the years that followed this spring of revolt and protests."

As Grimaud points out, while May '68 had been a social and political explosion, musically it was the ignition of a slow fuse. The musical explosion would come at the end of the next year, with a new wave of highly-politicised bands like Red Noise at the vanguard.

actuel

JAZZ
MUSIQUE
CONTEMPORAINE
THEATRE
POÉSIE

"ils ont sondé mon opinion"
WOLINSKI

NUMERO 2
NOVEMBRE 1968
3,50 F

JACQUES
COURSIL

A BRIEF HISTORY OF FRENCH UNDERGROUND MUSIC
Part 1: 1968-69

> In the fallout of '68, plenty of groups spring up like Patrick Vian's Red Noise and Barricades *(sic)*. There's the feeling that a movement is being born - a real rock movement that isn't satisfied with copying the English... the French underground really emerges in '69. It's a scene that doesn't imitate (that isn't *yé-yé*) and whose goal isn't to get a single into the charts, but to play music, to play their own music.
>
> *Philippe Thieyre*

> The era after May '68 was like a bottle of champagne whose cork had popped.
>
> *Didier Malherbe, Gong*

In Britain and America '68 was the year the underground turned political, with growing opposition to the Vietnam war and support for Civil Rights as the catalysts. The events of May proved that French youth suffered from no lack of political militancy, what *was* lacking was a strong cultural and musical underground. The alternative scene remained a small, very loose collection of artists, film-makers, and musicians centred on the Parisian Left Bank.

The Anglo-American counter-culture began to make real inroads into France in the aftermath of May '68. Underground culture and music streamed in from the English-speaking countries to meet a surging French political youth movement, creating a local underground with very different priorities to that in the UK and USA. A radical leftist outlook was basically a given, with some of the very first underground bands as focused on their politics as on their music.

In mid-'68 local French rock acts were very thin on the ground, and underground bands even more so. Daevid Allen's Bananamoon had been active since the beginning of the year, and Red Noise had unleashed its free-form noise-rock in May. Apart from these isolated examples almost all activity would be positively subterranean until the second half of '69, when the first wave of new bands bubbled to the surface.

The first influx of these new groups displayed a great diversity of sound. Gong and Ame Son carried a late-psychedelic tinge, Barricade (from Marseille) were aligned more with Captain Beefheart, Moving Gelatine Plates and Magma displayed distinct jazz influences, while Art Zoyd began to plough their own avant-rock path.

The lack of support for home-grown rock music hindered the development of the underground scene. At the end of the '60s the French media's coverage of any kind of rock was still incredibly sparse. However a few avenues of exposure on radio, television, and in print began to emerge in '68/'69.

A few precious hours of pop and rock programming appeared on the radio in late '68. The most important was José Artur's *Pop Club* on France Inter, which started its run in October '68. *Pop Club* would become an important advocate for French rock bands when Patrice Blanc-Francard became host in '69. Other programmes of note were *Campus* (on Europe 1) and *Poste Restante* (on RTL).

The *yé-yé* flagship *Salut les copains* finally ended its tenure in '69, by which time even Johnny Hallyday celebrated its demise. Nevertheless, it has to be acknowledged that even while *Salut les copains*' programming was anodyne, it *was* firmly focused on French-produced music. On the new rock music programmes French acts were competing for airtime with British and American music on the ascent.

Television was even more of a wasteland than radio. With the surprise cancellation of *Bouton Rouge* in May '68 there was no pop programming at all until *Tous en Scene* emerged in late '68. This was a variety show mixing comedy sketches, mimed appearances by *variétés* artists, and live performances from pop and rock acts. British groups like Pink Floyd, Yes, and Led Zeppelin appeared alongside the mainstream French acts Martin Circus and Les Variations

Two new music magazines had been launched at the end of '68. *Best* arrived in September as a direct competitor to *Rock & Folk*, differentiating itself with a greater willingness to let its readers' tastes set the agenda. Consequently *Best* gave precious coverage to the emerging local rock scene, which *Rock & Folk* had virtually ignored. Nothing helps focus the attention like competition, and by mid-'69 *Rock & Folk* had begun to give serious attention to the music bubbling up from the underground. Philippe Paringaux and Paul Alessandrini became particularly vocal in their advocacy for the first wave of bands.

October saw the arrival of *Actuel*, created by jazz drummer and writer Claude Delcloo to give a voice to alternative culture. Its masthead declared the magazine's major concerns as "Jazz, Contemporary Music, Theatre, Poetry".

The biggest story of '69 was the development of a joint venture between *Actuel* and the record label BYG. Together they created a new label (BYG/Actuel) that would be the first to record the new underground bands, and would organise the very first French rock festival. They had an extraordinary year, releasing more than twenty albums from acts including Gong, Don Cherry, Art Ensemble of Chicago, Archie Shepp, and Sunny Murray. They had also recorded, and would later release, albums by Ame Son and Alan Jack Civilization.

UNE EXCLUSIVITÉ RTL

JEAN GEORGAKARAKOS   JEAN LUC YOUNG
PRÉSENTENT
THE FIRST PARIS MUSIC FESTIVAL
actuel
24/28 OCTOBRE

ORGANISÉ PAR **BYG RECORDS** ET **RICARD** ANISETTE

PELOUSE DE REUILLY (VINCENNES)

60 HEURES DE MUSIQUE · 60 FRANCS

PRÉSENTÉ PAR FRANK ZAPPA & PIERRE LATTES

VEN. 24 (SOIR)
POP MUSIC
TEN YEARS AFTER
COLOSSEUM
AYNSLEY DUNBAR RETALIATION
ALAN JACK CIVILIZATION
FREE JAZZ
ART ENSEMBLE OF CHICAGO
SUNNY MURRAY
BURTON GREENE
360 DEGREE MUSIC EXPERIENCE
NEW MUSIC
FREE MUSIC GROUP

SAM. 25 (SOIR)
POP MUSIC
PINK FLOYD
FREEDOM
KEITH RELF'S RENAISSANCE
ALEXIS KORNER & THE NEW CHURCH
BLUES CONVENTION
FREE JAZZ
GRACHAN MONCUR III
ARTHUR JONES
JOACHIM KUHN
DON CHERRY

DIM. 26 (APRES MIDI)
FRENCH POP GROUPS
MARTIN CIRCUS
ALAN JACK CIVILIZATION
TRIANGLE
WE FREE
CRUCIFERIUS
INDESCRIPTIBLE CHAOS RAMPANT

DIM. 26 (SOIR)
POP MUSIC
NICE
CARAVAN
BLOSSOM TOES
AME SON
FREE JAZZ
ARCHIE SHEPP
KENNETH TERROADE
ANTHONY BRAXTON
NEW MUSIC
GERM (P. MARIETAN)

LUN. 27 (SOIR)
POP MUSIC
YES
PRETTY THINGS
CHICKEN SHACK
SAM APPLE PIE
FROGEATERS
DAVID ALLEN GROUP
KEITH TIPPETT GROUP
FREE JAZZ
PHAROAH SANDERS
DAVE BURRELL
JOHN SURMAN
CLIFFORD THORNTON
SONNY SHARROCK
NEW MUSIC
ACTING TRIO

MAR. 28 (SOIR)
POP MUSIC
SOFT MACHINE
CAPTAIN BEEFHEART
EAST OF EDEN
FAT MATTRESS
ZOO
FREE JAZZ
ALAN SILVA
ROBIN KENYATTA
CHRIS MACGREGOR
STEVE LACEY
DAVE BURRELL BIG BAND
NEW MUSIC
MUSICA ELETTRONICA VIVA

SONORISATION : STANDEL
(INTERIM SPECTACLE:
MAX AUER & CLAUDIA SAUMADE)

DIRECTEUR DE L'ENVIRONNEMENT :
JACQUES CHERIX

COORDINATION : BRIGITTE GUICHARD

LOCATION
80 RUE DE ROME, PARIS 8°, LAB 74 03
LIDO MUSIQUE, CHAMPS ELYSEES, PARIS 8°, 225 30 86
DREAM STORE, 4 PLACE SAINT MICHEL, PARIS 6°
FNAC CHATELET, BOULEVARD DE SEBASTOPOL, PARIS 1°, 887 29 49
FNAC WAGRAM, AVENUE DE WAGRAM, PARIS 17°, 267 02 50

OCTOBER '69:
The Amougies Festival

> The most renowned French bands played at Amougies. For the first time they were able to play in front of a large audience, and therefore the Amougies Festival marks the starting point for French pop. Martin Circus signed to Vogue, Triangle to Pathé, Gong and Ame Son to BYG, and Blues Convention to Vogue.
>
> Victor & Regoli, "Vingt ans de Rock Français"

The Amougies Festival, one of the most important events in French rock music history, took place at the end of '69. The team behind the BYG/Actuel label (Jean Karakos and Claude Delcloo) decided the time was ripe to organise the first French pop music festival, and showed remarkable tenacity in the torturous battle to stage the event.

The First Paris Music Festival was arranged to dovetail with the '69 Pan-African Cultural Festival in Algeria, which had already attracted a large number of American jazz players. Delcloo invited these musicians to travel on to Paris, record albums for BYG/Actuel, and play a series of concerts throughout the summer. The culmination would be the first large-scale French music festival - giving equal billing to rock, free jazz, and avant-garde acts. The mix of genres reflected the musical backgrounds of the organisers, and foreshadowed the direction taken by French underground music in the early '70s.

The beating heart of Paris (or as Zola had dubbed it, the *belly* of Paris) was selected as the perfect site: the Les Halles markets. Delcloo and Karakos set out to secure the necessary permissions without suspecting the drama that was about to unfold.

In the aftermath of May '68 the authorities were terrified by the prospect of any mass gathering of youth, and worked hard to quash them. Pompidou had replaced de Gaulle as President in June '69, but hard-liner Raymond Marcellin (who'd earned the nickname Raymond the Matraque* in '68) remained as Minister of the Interior. As Delcloo and Karakos were to discover, it would be next to impossible to secure a site for a major rock music festival while he was around.

Their proposal to hold the festival at Les Halles was summarily rejected. Undaunted, they secured another venue, the Bois De Vincennes to the east of Paris, and printed up posters promoting "The First Paris Music Festival" to be held between 24-28 October '69. However it didn't take long for the authorities to decide that the Vincennes site was unviable. A scramble for a new venue ensued. They settled on Parc de Saint-Cloud in the west of Paris. New posters were printed, this time with no mention of a "Paris Music Festival", but rather the "First Continental Festival". Had the promoters' ambition grown, or did they have an inkling of what would happen next?

All too predictably another pretext was found to make the new site unavailable. Karakos and Delcloo looked farther and farther outside Paris, until they finally found a small town named Amougies willing to host their festival. While its name was French, Amougies was not actually inside the country. To hold "The First Paris Music Festival" the organisers were forced to look not only outside the capital, but over the French border. The first "French" music festival was to be held in Belgium.

This farce had been played out in full public view, and Amougies had won the name *Le Festival Maudit* (The Cursed Festival) before a note had been played. Thankfully when the festival proper kicked off, on 24 October as originally scheduled, the curse appeared to be lifted. Yes, it was held in a foreign country, but the headline acts were all present, and a healthy crowd of 80,000 people braved the cold, wet weather to trek to the small Belgian town.

A marquee had been erected as protection from the elements, with two stages underneath to allow for a continuous flow of music over five days. Soft Machine, Pink Floyd, Captain Beefheart, and Frank Zappa were the big international draw-cards. However, the recent break up of The Mothers of Invention meant that Zappa would only appear as compère - with his musical involvement reduced to on-stage jams (most famously with Pink Floyd).

The innovation of the Amougies Festival was to programme bands

---

* The *matraque* was a particularly nasty flexible leather truncheon used by the French police.

like Ten Years After, Yes, and The Pretty Things side-by-side with acts like Archie Shepp, The Art Ensemble of Chicago, and Musica Elettronica Viva.

In his review for *Best* Jean-Noël Coghe praised this decision: "The festival was a huge survey of the different musical trends of today: progressive rock, free jazz, electronic music. It was the first festival in the world that dared to blend the sounds of our era, bringing together the audience for three different kinds of music... And the gamble paid off."

According to musician Jean-Jacques Birgé his exposure to new musical styles at Amougies was formative: "The shock for me was discovering free jazz, from the first night with the Art Ensemble of Chicago. Seeing Joseph Jarman, totally naked on electric guitar imitating the rockers, but better than them! I was blown away."

While Amougies brought a cornucopia of diverse international acts to the French audience, it also served as an invaluable launchpad for local acts. These included Martin Circus, Ame Son, Gong, Triangle, Alan Jack Civilization, Blues Convention, We Free, Cruciferius and Zoo. It was an essential step forward for the French underground, helping to accelerate the development of the musical hybrids that would characterise it.

The festival's curse had been lifted for its duration, but the fate of a documentary film made by Jérôme Laperrousaz and Jean-Noël Roy suggests that it lingered afterwards. In May '70 a 3½ hour film titled *Amougies (Music Power - European Music Revolution)* opened in French cinemas. Almost immediately a number of artists (most notably Pink Floyd) served injunctions to stop screenings. The directors had been assured that filming permissions were in place, but to their chagrin Karakos hadn't secured them. Within weeks the film was withdrawn from distribution, and has remained in legal limbo ever since. Perhaps a fitting postscript for such a troubled venture

A BRIEF HISTORY OF FRENCH UNDERGROUND MUSIC
Part 2: 1970

> It was the start of a unique French rock movement and I was mightily impressed by their gung-ho stylistic scattergun approach. Nothing was sacred. For variety, invention, and originality, these French bands were miles ahead of the complacent English style-queens... We connected strongly with them... Gong was now being treated as big brothersister to the new music. It was a difficult projection to resist. So I didn't.
>
> *Daevid Allen, Gong*

Rock & Folk's Readers' Poll gave a good indication of the state of the contemporary French rock scene at the beginning of 1970. The Best French Group category (which actually hadn't existed the year before) held no surprises in the Top Five: Martin Circus, Zoo, Triangle, Les Variations, and Cruciferius were all mainstream artists. However four bands from the underground also earned a spot - even though only one (Gong) had released a record. Two were placed in the Top Ten (Ame Son at #8 and Gong at #10) and two just outside (Red Noise at #12 and We Three at #13).

The year was heralded in with an event right in the heart (or belly) of the capital - at Les Halles. It's something of a mystery as to how permission was obtained, since only months earlier the site had been denied to the organisers of Amougies. Whatever the background, for three days at the very beginning of January a selection of British and French bands played at the first rock festival held inside Paris.

Ame Son were on the bill, and drummer Marc Blanc recalls the importance of the occasion: "The Halles Festival was organised to protest against the demolition of Les Halles and the Pavillon Baltard. It was a great event with several light shows, The Pretty Things, and

Deep Purple's first appearance in France. Having the chance to play a few nights there was a real confirmation of our new status as an important French group."

Other underground acts that featured on the bill included Red Noise, Jacques Dudon (aka Guilain), Alan Jack Civilization, and We Three (who were billed as We Free).

In March the Festival Musique Evolution was held in an aircraft hanger at the Le Bourget airport on the outskirts of Paris. Bizarrely the authorities had insisted that the word "pop" wasn't used by the event, explaining its rather vague name. Most acts on the bill were British (Edgar Broughton Band, Hawkwind, Kevin Ayers, Pink Floyd, Procol Harum) with only a few French bands programmed (the most significant being Moving Gelatine Plates).

A rather different event was held over five days in May. The Open Circus was organised by circus director Madona Bouglione as a multi-media happening under a tent with seating for 5,000. It brought together circus acts, theatre groups (incl. The Living Theatre), light shows, and rock music. The British contingent of bands included Pink Floyd, Deep Purple, and East of Eden, while France was represented by Gong, Magma, and Red Noise.

The highlight of 1970 came in August with a run of major festivals in the South of France (see next chapter). While this proved to be the story of the year there were also some very important developments in the support system for underground music.

A major step forward was the arrival of the TV programme *Pop 2* in April '70. It was hosted by Patrice Blanc-Francard who had already proved to be a strong advocate for the new French rock scene during his tenure on *Pop Club*. *Pop 2* would have a long and influential life, running regularly until the end of '73.

The format was a free-wheeling and innovative mix of shorter segments that culminated in a major extract from a live performance (often 20-30 minutes long). The segments included documentary reports (e.g. a visit to the *Actuel* office, Komintern in rehearsal, an interview with illustrator/animator Roland Topor), record reviews, and a rundown of the news from the local and overseas music press. The live performances were drawn from a broad selection of bands (Soft Machine, Genesis, James Brown, The Grateful Dead, Aretha Franklin, MC5, Can, and Amon Düül II all appeared) with a surprising number of French acts. Magma, Gong, Komintern, Lard Free, Total Issue, Zao, Catherine Ribeiro + Alpes, Valérie Lagrange, and Alice were all given extensive air-time. There were also special episodes devoted to the Biot and Auvers-sur-Oise Festivals.

Blanc-Francard had high hopes that the exposure *Pop 2* gave to French groups would have some impact, but was disappointed by a lack of support from the local music business: "French rock has always had a serious problem leaving behind its ersatz role... None of the French groups we interviewed were simply mimicking something invented by the English... but the music business just wasn't capable of giving them financial, intellectual, or structural support. So nothing happened."

Three new music magazines appeared in 1970: the weekly *Pop Music* (April '70 to April '73), the monthly *Extra* (Dec '70 to Dec '75), and the short lived *Music Maker*. More important to the counter-culture was the emergence of a number of homegrown underground press titles during the year.

The first was *Le Pop*, launched by Max Peteau in March. As the title suggests it was initially focused on the music of the underground, but quickly expanded to cover every aspect of the counter-culture: communal living, drugs, art, ecology, women's liberation, etc. The magazine was produced by a community gathered around Peteau, so its editorial position and derisive, ironic style reflected the lived reality of the "freak" scene.

While *Le Pop* beat it to the punch, it was the new series of *Actuel* that would take the crown as the underground's magazine of choice. Journalist Jean-François Bizot had been working towards the launch of a new magazine since early in the year. His working title was *Acide*, an obvious nod to the underground readership he was angling for. While the team he had gathered was more inclined towards a political magazine, Bizot insisted: "Rock! It's rock! That's the new mass media, the medium of the new culture."

After months of making little progress fate lent a hand when Claude Delcloo declared he was looking to sell his interest in *Actuel*. The original series of *Actuel* had gradually embraced elements of the counter-culture, but under Bizot's editorship it became the underground press title *par excellence*. Launched in October '70, for the next five years the new series of *Actuel* would be a lightning rod for the concerns of the counter-culture, becoming one of its most important proponents.

The psychedelic aesthetic of the magazine, with multicolured page layouts and the integration of illustrations and comic strips gave it an iconic look. Editorially it actively advocated alternative ways of life, publishing major features on communities, drugs, sexual liberation, and the "hippy trail" to the East.

Jean-Pierre Lentin, Dagon's bass player, was *Actuel*'s music editor, and unsurprisingly priority was given to the underground music scene. While music certainly wasn't its main focus, *Actuel* was instrumental in promoting and publicising the music coming out of the French underground.

Another musician, Henri-Jean Enu, launched the magazine *Le Parapluie* in November '70. Enu's background as an artist fed into both the radical collage aesthetic of the magazine and its concern with all forms of art, literature, theatre, and music. *Le Parapluie*'s stance was highly libertarian and stridently anti-authoritarian, championing freedom in every aspect of life. Former Lettrist Jean-Louis Brau contributed articles on drugs, while Gilles Yeprémian (who would go on to manage Lard Free and Komintern) was music correspondent.

The underground music scene had developed rapidly during '70. While only Gong and Magma had released LPs, a number of other bands had recorded during the year. As a result Ame Son, Maajun, and Red Noise were scheduled to release albums early in the new year. Many more would make recordings over the next twelve months (including Moving Gelatine Plates, Komintern, Fille Qui Mousse, and Chico Magnetic Band).

Of course not every band in the underground had the desire or the means to record. Cheval Fou, Barricade, and Dagon continued to play live shows for many years, but none would issue a record in their lifetimes. Others like Lard Free and Camizole had to bide their time for several years before entering the studio.

Best's end-of-year Readers' Poll for 1970 confirmed the significant shift that French rock had undergone during the year. Of the twenty groups listed only six had made an appearance in the previous year's poll. The Top Five was still dominated by the mainstream (represented by Triangle, Les Variations, and Zoo), but it now included Magma and Alice (formed by two members of We Three/We Free). There was also a very decent showing of bands from the underground with Gong (#7), Ame Son (#8), Catherine Ribeiro + Alpes (#10), Chico Magnetic Band (#12), and Moving Gelatine Plates (#15) all taking their places. As the year ended the first wave of French underground bands was gathering strength.

SUMMER '70:
L'été Pop

> What happened this week in Aix-en-Provence is serious. Young people have not been allowed to listen to their music because it isn't permitted by the society in which they live. It's as if everything that accompanies this music puts the established order in danger. We don't like hippies, and we prove it, just as we don't like our conscience when it points out our faults. What a terrible admission that we were afraid of music! When did this country begin to fear the arts? Pop music in Aix, the theatrical creations of young Avignon companies, have they become vehicles so dangerous that they absolutely have to be suffocated under the tawdry rags of traditions?
>
> *Christian Colombani, Le Monde (10/8/70)*

August '69 saw festivals on both sides of the Atlantic draw hundreds of thousands to multi-day gatherings of the tribes. The successes of Woodstock and the Isle of Wight cemented the open-air festival as a bedrock of youth culture, and led to an explosion in the number and size of music festivals.

The French were keen to participate in this new phenomenon, but there were some specifically French problems to overcome. The first was highlighted by the fate of the Amougies Festival, forced by the spectre of May '68 to relocate time and time again (until it was finally outside the country). In the authorities' eyes every mass gathering of youth was a powder-keg. Obtaining the permits needed to stage a large-scale music festival would prove to be virtually impossible.

The second challenge came from the political left, which held a very strong position post-May '68. An essential part of their platform was that culture belonged to *the people*, and that concrete action must be taken to return it to them. This led to demands that all cultural events, including rock festivals, be free-of-charge and open to all. Similar appeals were made in the USA and UK, but there they were raised by disorganised fringe groups. In France it was the active policy of a large militant left which, when motivated, had the resources to enforce it.

Different combinations of these two factors would lead to a series of thwarted music festivals that the music press would again dub *Festivals Maudits* (Cursed Festivals). As events progressed precious few would avoid taking on the mantle as the latest *Festival Maudit*.

After the difficult gestation, but ultimate success, of Amougies, many were inspired to follow its example. The summer of '70 was christened *L'été Pop* (the Summer of Pop) in anticipation of the events planned. All too predictably the French authorities played havoc with the organisation of festivals by withholding permissions or imposing outright bans. This led to an early demise for many. In the end the fortnight between 23 July and 5 August would see three festivals taking place in the South of France. Of the three only one was held without the cloud of an official ban hanging over it.

L'été Pop happened to coincide with a political campaign organised by the Maoist group Gauche Prolétarienne, dubbed *L'été Chaud* (The Hot Summer). The organisation had been declared illegal in May '70, and planned to flex its muscles during the summer to demonstrate that it could still act against the ruling classes. A series of actions was organised to make the traditional July/August holiday as uncomfortable as possible for the moneyed classes vacationing in the resorts of Southern France. The slogan of *L'été Chaud* was "*Pas de vacances pour les riches*" - "No holidays for the rich".

Throughout July and August a number of resorts, private beaches and villas were vandalised by Gauche Prolétarienne activists. To show that "liberty and joy can be seized" they "liberated" leisure items and luxury goods and redistributed them in working class areas. They also took actions to liberate cultural events, in a bid to give culture directly back to the people. As all three rock festivals were held in the South of France, a collision course was inexorably set between *L'été Pop* and *L'été Chaud*.

The organisers of each festival would be caught up in an attack from at least one of two sides: the reactionary national and municipal authorities on the right, and the radical Maoists on the left.

Riviera Festival, Valbonne (23-25 July)

The first event of *L'été Pop* was the Riviera Festival held in Valbonne (near Cannes). It was organised by Claude Rousseau who had run the Le Bourget Festival in March. Three days of music were promised with international draw-cards like Iron Butterfly, Amon Düül II, and Frank Zappa sharing the stage with a swathe of the new French bands.

The authorities banned the event at the last minute citing a "serious and on-going risk of forest fires" and "the insufficiency of the organiser's planned health and security measures." The injunction arrived after the festival had been extensively promoted and part-fees had been paid to some of the international artists. This left Rousseau with little choice but to carry on in defiance of the ban.

The authorities did nothing to stop the festival itself, but the combination of uncertainty created by their injunction and the blocking of roads by the local *gendarmerie* had the desired effect of keeping numbers low. Only an estimated 1800 attended. This was bad enough, but the killer blow came with the levelling of the fences (in this case by punters who simply refused to pay, rather than Maoist agitators). Valbonne was forced to become a de-facto "free festival".

Faced with the prospect of being unable to pay the artists, Rousseau appealed to them for help. From the international contingent Amon Düül II, Frank Zappa, and Country Joe all agreed to perform (Zappa went so far as to refuse any payment). The large selection of French acts (Red Noise, Komintern, Barricade, Fille Qui Mousse, Maajun, Moving Gelatine Plates, Ame Son, Jacques Dudon, Gong, and Total Issue) also performed as scheduled.

Paul Alessandrini's report for *Rock & Folk* had a strong focus on the French acts, and was generally quite positive. While noting the occasional chaotic or failed performance, Alessandrini made the point that the Valbonne Festival heralded the arrival of an authentically French music scene.

Progressive Music Festival, Aix-en-Provence (1-3 August)

Aix-en-Provence was the site of the next event. It featured a more mainstream line-up than the other summer festivals, with Leonard Cohen, Johnny Winter, Colosseum, and Mungo Jerry heading the bill. They were joined by local acts Triangle, Chico Magnetic Band,

Komintern, Catherine Ribeiro + Alpes, and Dynastie Crisis.

The festival was organised by a curious figure: Claude Clément. He was a retired army general infamous for his right-wing affiliations during the Algerian War. Nevertheless he viewed himself as a man of the arts, attracted to the humanist values of rock music. Joan Baez was unconvinced, and refused to play when she learned of his past.

Félix Ciccolini, the mayor of Aix-en-Provence, was equally unimpressed with the idea of a rock festival in his municipality, especially as it coincided with the city's annual International Music Festival of classical music. He served an injunction on the Progressive Music Festival in order to protect "the security of people and property."

Clément wasn't temperamentally inclined to go down without a fight, and contested the legality of the ban. He also ensured that his fight would be reported in the pages of *Le Monde*. There he invoked "the right of the French to gather together and listen to the music they like", warning that the banning of music festivals "isn't the way we open a dialogue with the youth. In my opinion we are preparing the way for a new May 1968."

He decided to disregard the injunction, but in a show of compromise reduced the duration from three to two days (dropping scheduled performances from Magma, Family, Deep Purple, Flock, and Renaissance). However, as at Valbonne a week earlier, the well-publicised conflict created confusion, and the number of attendees (estimated at 20,000 by *Rock & Folk*) was much less than anticipated. Even so the festival went comparatively well.[1]

Despite some misgivings Jacques Vassal of *Rock & Folk* reported that in his opinion this was the best organised festival of *L'été Pop*. His report also alluded to an event that signalled the first collision of the *Été Pop* with the *Été Chaud*.

In a bid to return "pop to the people" a Maoist group had forced its way onto the site demanding that Clément declare it to be a free festival. In the on-stage debate that followed, Clément and the Maoists made appeals to the crowd, each claiming to be the true representative of the festival-goers' interests. The crowd was unmoved by the Maoists, and the festival continued. A few days later it would be made clear that this was merely a prelude...

Popanalia, Biot (5 August)

The last festival of the summer, Popanalia held at Biot[2], was organised by the veteran of Amougies, Jean Karakos. He was joined by Jean-François Bizot and the staff of *Actuel*. As expected the acts advertised on the bill were of the highest calibre: Joan Baez, Pink Floyd, Eric Clapton, Soft Machine, Traffic, Plastic Ono Band, King Crimson, Moody Blues, Archie Shepp, Art Ensemble of Chicago, Kevin Ayers, and Gong.

While the authorities hadn't given their authorisation for the festival to go ahead, neither had they taken any action to ban it, so Popanalia was able to proceed without that particular cloud hanging over its head. Another cloud, however, loomed large.

The appearance of Maoist agitators at Aix a few days earlier had given rise to rumours that a larger contingent was making its way to Biot. Although forewarned, the scale of the intervention caught the organisers totally off-guard. In their book *Generation 2* authors Hamon & Rotman paint a vivid picture of what unfolded:

"On the road, a growing cloud of dust. Bizot craned his neck, shading his eyes with his hand. He made out a small band walking at a good pace with banners unfurled, heard distant chants, and spotted a red flag. Maoists! It was the Maoists... 'Pop to the people! Down with the merchants of pop!'... The procession drew near, raising a pale cloud of dust; with at least a thousand shouting in unison: 'Pop to the people!'. Amongst the organisers the panic grew: how to stop them? Discussions? Negotiations? Explain that the festival hadn't made a penny? The phalanx enters without blinking an eye. And without paying..."

The group immediately demolished the fences, ensuring that their demand for a free festival was met. From this moment financial doom was assured (of the 25,000 in the crowd only 4,000 had paid). Knowing he was totally reliant on ticket sales to pay the artists, Jean Karakos rushed on stage while Ame Son were setting up. His appeal to the crowd was drowned out by chants of "Pop to the people!"

Then counter-cultural icon Aguigui Mouna took the microphone and made an appeal of his own: "Comrades, despite the repression, here we have shown the strength of the youth, and it's been great... But, comrades, the bands haven't all been paid. Let's pass the hat around." A collection was taken, raising a derisory 11,000 Francs (the equivalent of less than 400 ticket sales).[3] The die was cast.

Serge Loupien reports on the denouement: "With Gong's set barely finished Soft Machine's manager rushed on stage to announce that the band refused to play because they hadn't been paid. This time it was the ire of the paying audience that was provoked: 'Bastards! Give us our money back!' Meanwhile a chant of 'Organisers, exploiters of the people!' started up again, even louder..."

The festival degenerated into a shambles, not even making it to the end of the first day. Joan Baez, Frank Zappa, Country Joe, Ame Son, Gong, Komintern, and Barricade had all managed to perform, but Biot went into the annals of French music history as the greatest *Festival Maudit* of all.

The Aftermath

In spite of the litany of disasters that this "Summer of Pop" left in its wake, the French rock festival *did* have a future, but not as a commercial proposition. When interviewed for *Pop Music* magazine, the organisers all agreed that free festivals were the only possible way forward in the short term.

Indeed Jean Bouquin (who had run the Aix Festival with Claude Clément) organised a free festival the next year. However, the Auvers-sur-Oise Festival, held in June '71, was an even greater disaster than Biot. This time it wasn't Maoist militants or anxious authorities that provided the death blow - but a sustained downpour of Biblical proportions. Just hours into the first day the unprotected stage was flooded, the sound system destroyed, and the site transformed into a quagmire.

Auvers-sur-Oise was the final attempt by the French to emulate the major British and American festivals. For the remainder of the '70s, festivals were much less ambitious in scope, with French acts as the main draw-cards. The Bièvres Festival was one notable success. In '73 it attracted more than 50,000 people, culminating in a concert featuring Crium Delirium and Gong. Naturally, entry to the festival was free...

Notes

1   The festival was documented in a film shot by Daniel Szuster: *Guitare au poing/À cause du pop*.

2   A report on the Biot festival is included in the *Pop 2* programme broadcast on 20/8/70 - with footage of Country Joe, Joan Baez, and Aguigui Mouna.

3   *Le Monde* quoted Karakos as saying this figure was actually much less: 3100 francs!

A BRIEF HISTORY OF FRENCH UNDERGROUND MUSIC
Part 3: 1971-73

> It's interesting to see a particular style of French pop gradually emerge, both on Maajun's album and from bands like Magma, Komintern, Dagon, Red Noise, Planétarium, Ame Son, etc... It's a disjointed style of music, filled with ruptures and unexpected breaks, wilful and sarcastic... with half-political, half-surrealistic lyrics.
>
> *Jean-Pierre Lentin*, Actuel *Feb '71*

1971 was shaping up to be a major year for the French underground music scene. However, a survey of the musical state of the nation, published in *Rock & Folk*'s first issue of the year, highlighted the difficult situation that bands were facing. Participants drawn from the underground (Komintern, Red Noise) and the mainstream (Dynastie Crisis, Les Variations, Triangle) all bemoaned their lack of access to radio and TV, lacklustre support from the print media, and the aversion of the music business to anything more challenging than *yé-yé* or *chanson*.

A small report in the same magazine highlighted an additional problem faced by the underground. A rock and free-jazz concert (featuring musicians from Red Noise, Crouille Marteau, and Planétarium) had been canceled at short notice "under pressure from the police... Yet again due to fear of a political demonstration".

Nevertheless, the next twelve months would see a slew of albums released. Major labels would even take the odd punt on underground acts with CBS (Moving Gelatine Plates), Pathé-Marconi (Komintern), Vogue (Maajun, Chico Magnetic Band), and Philips (Magma) all in the game. Prior to '71 the most important record label for the underground had been BYG, but they were soon eclipsed by Gérard Terronès's Futura Records. Terronès began recording underground acts for his rock-based RED series (Red Noise, Mahogany Brain, Triode, Fille Qui Mousse, and Travelling) and esoteric SON series (Horde Catalytique Pour La Fin, Jean Guérin, Jac Berrocal, and Semool).

This explosion of activity proved to be unsustainable. More than a dozen underground acts released a debut album in '71, however only two of them (Catharsis and Moving Gelatine Plates) would release a follow-up. There were no debut albums released in '72, only a smattering of albums from Brigitte Fontaine, Catherine Ribeiro + Alpes, Magma (under the name Univeria Zekt), and Moving Gelatine Plates. The first wave of French underground bands had prematurely crested.

There were some developments in the media between '71 and '73. On television the weekly *Point Chaud* and the monthly *Rock en stock* began their runs. However they paid little attention to French acts, and the print media were left to champion the local scene. In Jan '72 a significant advocate arrived when *Pop 2000* began publication.

The twin disasters of Biot and Auvers thankfully hadn't sounded the death knell of the pop festival in France, but the festival as a commercial proposition was mortally wounded. Ambitions had been tempered, leading to a number of free-festivals appearing over the next few years. These were more locally-focused, with few major international acts. One upside of this changed orientation was the increased exposure given to underground bands. In '71 festivals were held at St Gratien and Seloncourt, and in June '72 the Epone and Bièvres festivals were staged near Paris with Komintern, Gong, Magma, Crium Delirium, Lard Free, Catharsis, Herbe Rouge, and Dagon featured on the bills. The Bagas Cheap Festival, held near Bordeaux in August '72, saw Magma, Lard Free, Gong, Barricade, and Catherine Ribeiro + Alps play beside Matching Mole and the Pretty Things.

The '73 Bièvres Festival built on the success of the first iteration, becoming one of the few free-festivals of the '70s to be celebrated as an unmitigated success. An audience of over 50,000 attended, with Crium Delirium and Gong as headline acts.

Canadian music magazine *Mainmise* published an overview of the French rock scene in April '73, giving coverage to a dozen underground acts. However, by the time of publication six were already defunct (Ame Son, Red Noise, Jacques Dudon, Moving Gelatine Plates, Maajun, Fille Qui Mousse) and another (Komintern) would be gone within months.

It was a sobering state of affairs. At the end of '72 *Actuel* had commented: "Moving Gelatine Plates, Ergo Sum, Le Poing and even Zoo are dead. Gong, Magma, and Komintern have weathered storms, crises, and the loss of musicians... Dagon, Lard Free, and Herbe Rouge are all trying out different players... Why do musicians persevere? Masochism, madness, or fanaticism? Or do they just not know how to do anything else?"

By the end of '73 Dagon and Cheval Fou were added to the list of the fallen. The first wave of underground bands was well and truly receding. Of the original contingent only Magma, Gong, Barricade, Lard Free, and Contrepoint were still standing, with Art Zoyd bubbling along under the surface.

Precious few new acts had emerged to replace them. The short-lived Schizo arrived in '71, with Crium Delirium following in '72. It wasn't until '73 that a second wave begin to build with Etron Fou Leloublan, Clearlight, Jac Berrocal, Zao, Heldon, and Nyl all arriving on the scene. Camizole also roused itself from almost two years of hibernation to take their place in this new wave.

While '73 wasn't a huge improvement in terms of records released, it was much more significant than the previous year with debut albums from Lard Free, Travelling, Jac Berrocal, Mahjun, and Zao. It also saw definitive releases from both Gong and Magma.

1971:
The MJC Circuit

> At the beginning of the '70s, rock concerts were a rare commodity in France. There weren't a great number of clubs and theatres... and the majority didn't accept rock bands: their audience was dirty and noisy, and their music had neither significance nor a future. Theatre and *varieté* acts had monopolised the touring network for decades, so there wasn't even one hall with a real sound system.
>
> *Klaus Blasquiz, Magma*

From the outset France's underground music scene was faced with a major problem: a total lack of any infrastructure. The local music business was set up solely to create and support *varieté* and *yé-yé* stars. Rock music, underground or not, was barely an afterthought.

When Robert Wood moved to Paris from the UK in 1970 he was immediately struck by the stark differences between their music scenes: "The only 'system' that existed in France was the old *varieté* management system. To get regular gigs a band needed a hit record, and to get a hit they had to write a *varieté*-style pop song. To get a recording contract they needed an agent, and to get the agent they needed contacts with the right people.

"There were no rock managers, and those that became active in the early '70s, such as Benamou, Yeprémian, Daniel Bornet, Dominique Mouyeaux etc., had to create their own style and methods. The concept of a management company with a stable of bands never caught on in France. In the UK the managers ran the show, and they could and would take from twenty to seventy-five per cent of all the band's takings. In France the bands tried to run things, and discussions were rife as to whether it was acceptable for a manager to take five to fifteen per cent."

While the UK system allowed unscrupulous managers to exploit their bands, it provided an established structure with a highly-organised touring circuit.

Wood: "In the UK it was the norm to go to a club or venue every week to drink, socialise, and listen to whatever bands were playing. This meant that even lesser known bands played to full venues. There were several well-established concert circuits: small gigs in clubs and pubs, a tech-college and university circuit, then large concerts, and festivals. The idea was to start at the bottom, work up to the university circuit, then hope for festival spots. It was very organised and there was the assumption that a band that reached a certain level wouldn't go back to playing the 'lower' circuits. This gave the UK a fantastic platform for underground music.

"France did have music halls, large theatres, and jazz clubs, but there was no circuit whatsoever for rock. There were only small, improvised gigs in clubs, museums, or art galleries, with occasional shows at universities. Large theatre concerts were reserved for French *varieté* stars and well-known international bands. The local rock bands just didn't have the structure the UK bands could fall back on to build their careers."

The only other option for new French bands was to compete in battle-of-the-band competitions, *tremplins*, held at clubs like Golf Drouot, to win whatever prize was on offer, and more importantly score a few precious lines in the music press.

This was the environment that Magma's manager, Giorgio Gomelsky, was confronted with in '71. Coming from managing The Yardbirds he was stunned by the lack of organisation, and quickly realised he would have to build a touring circuit from scratch. While searching out suitable venues he happened upon one of the youth cultural centres (Maisons des Jeunes et de la Culture, or MJCs) dotted across France.

Gomelsky: "One afternoon I went to pick up Klaus Blasquiz, Magma's lead singer, to take him to a rehearsal. He was teaching comic strip drawing in a youth centre outside Paris. I was early, so I walked around the place and, behold, discovered there was a small theatre at the back of the centre. I guess it could hold around 200. [I asked] the centre's director what kind of events they were holding there. 'None', he answered, 'we can't afford to book people…' Wow!

I had a flash! It dawned on me there was a solution here, so I asked him if he would agree for Magma to play there... We would promote the show ourselves, use his Xerox machine and the young kids to distribute fliers and give him fifteen percent of the door. He thought that was a good deal...

"This got my juices going, so I enquired how many of these MJCs there were and I found out there were some 200 around the country. Every political party seemed to have a 'chain' of them... Well, that was it! I got a list of them and for a month I drove around Paris convincing them to go along with my plan... To cut a long story short, a couple of weeks later, Magma did their first MJC tour. Five weeks, five concerts a week, a total of twenty-five shows... From there I started to work on the rest of the country. Within a few months we had more than 120 venues, a complete circuit!"

This MJC circuit finally gave rock bands the ability to organise decent nationwide tours. Despite very basic touring conditions it was a huge step forward. Gomelsky joined forces with the managers of Crium Delirium and Gong (Jacques Pasquier and Bob Benamou) to create the Rock Pas Gaga agency. They set about extending the touring circuit by encouraging small, independent promoters in regional towns.

Michel Carvallo had set up Annecy Jazz Action in '69 to bring national and international acts to his small town. This became the model for a grassroots movement, encouraged by Rock Pas Gaga, to bring concerts to the regions. A multitude of local initiatives were launched throughout France, and by '73 there was an informal network that stretched from Lille, Rouen, and Rennes in the north to Toulouse and Marseille in the south. It was essential to the development of French acts like Crium Delirium, Zao, and Brigitte Fontaine, and it also enabled bands like Can and Tangerine Dream to tour France for the first time.

Daevid Allen: "It was an extraordinary flowering... an intelligent circuit of young, inexperienced, but ingenious fans who were fast learning unorthodox ways to be promoters. Gong and Magma were the icebreaker bands for this giant experiment and the result was a cycle of enormously successful concerts..."

kevin coyne▫obscure records▫malicorne

atem

entretiens avec magma

N° 2   15 Janvier 76   3 F

A BRIEF HISTORY OF FRENCH UNDERGROUND MUSIC
Part 4: 1974-78

> It's a socio-economic, rather than a musical, phenomenon that has dominated French musical life since 1975: groups have been forced to self-produce and even self-distribute, diverting their time and energy into non-musical activity... This seems to be the only possible alternative for groups to survive and get beyond their first [and often only] release.
>
> *Grosse & Gueffier, "La Discographie du rock français"*

The second wave of underground bands began to make its mark in '74 and '75. There were debut albums from Heldon, Birgé Gorgé Shiroc, Philippe Besombes, Pôle, Ariel Kalma, Albert Marcoeur, Clearlight, Fluence (Pascal Comelade), Pataphonie, and Henri Roger. The majority of them were released on independent labels, a movement spearheaded by Richard Pinhas's Disjuncta Records.

While this new wave of bands built momentum, more of the originators of the scene went under: Crium Delirium, Barricade, Gong, and Dagon all called time by the end of '75. The end of an era was even more conclusively signalled with the scuppering of *Actuel* magazine in October of that year. A number of its writers took up positions at *Libération*, encouraging the newspaper to expand its coverage of music. In the years that followed, *Libération* gave important national exposure to bands like Camizole, Etron Fou Leloublan, ZNR, and Urban Sax. The arrival of the fanzine *Atem* in December '75 also helped to compensate for the loss of *Actuel*. In early '77 it was joined by *Rock'n'Roll Musique* and *Rock en Stock*.

While many things had changed for the better since the beginning of the decade, French bands were still forced to compete with Anglo-Saxon acts for press coverage, radio airplay, and live bookings. In October '76 the Manifeste des Bas Rock (Manifesto of Low Rock) was published in *Libération*. Over a hundred musicians, journalists, record labels, and record stores signed the manifesto, demanding greater access to the media, proper promotion of French acts by record companies, and the recognition of rock music by public institutions. A Festival Bas Rock was held on 6 November '76 with Etron Fou Leloublan, Urban Sax, Stinky Toys, Angel Face, Steve Hillage, and Kevin Coyne. However, like every previous initiative, Bas Rock had little or no lasting impact.

The Festival Bas Rock tipped a hat to the emergence of punk rock by including Stinky Toys and Angel Face on the bill. However, the underground developed no real association with the punk movement, which they viewed as insufficiently radical, both musically and politically. Between '76 and '79 the underground and punk scenes ran in parallel, with little interaction.

It wasn't until post-punk emerged that the underground found a movement with which they could engage both musically and philosophically. Indeed Ilitch, Etron Fou Leloublan, and Heldon* were already making music that anticipated this style, and after '78 musicians from the underground began to form new bands with post-punk sensibilities. Jac Berrocal was one of the first: "What really blew us away was PiL... The first PiL record is amazing. Punk was a hot music, The Pistols were hot, but PiL was coooold. A glacial universe." Inspired, he formed Catalogue with Gilbert Artman. Other underground musicians who followed suit included Pascal Comelade (Fall of Saigon), Dominique Grimaud (Vidéo-Aventures), Dominique Lentin (Les i), and Michel Peteau (Pierrot Le Fou).

Between '76-'78 the first wave of the underground was played out: the demise of Contrepoint, Lard Free, and Camizole left only Magma and Art Zoyd III still standing alongside stalwarts Brigitte Fontaine and Catherine Ribeiro. However, the next wave had established itself with debuts from Etron Fou Leloublan, Nyl, Potemkine, Verto, Robert Wood & Vibrarock, ZNR, Plat du Jour, Urban Sax, Patrick Vian, Christian Boulé, Ilitch, Spacecraft, and Weidorje.

---

* Two early punk bands, Metal Urbain and Asphalt Jungle, displayed their appreciation of Heldon by asking Richard Pinhas to produce their debut singles.

DISJUNCTA RECORD

HELDON

FACE A
"GUERILLA ELECTRONIQUE"
WILLIAM BURROUGHS

D.R.
DISJUNCTA
Intensité $= \sqrt{2}/13$
GU

1. ZIND
2. BACK TO HELDON
3. NORTHERNLAND LADY
(Richard Pinhas)

PRODUCTION : PARANO'S LIMITED

MADE IN FRANCE

TOUS DROITS DU PRODUCTEUR PHONOGRAPHIQUE ET DU PROPRIÉTAIRE DE L'ŒUVRE ENREGISTRÉE RÉSERVÉS . DUPLICATION EXECUTION PUBLIQUE RADIODIFFUSION INTERDITES

1974:
Independent Record Labels

> No-one had started an independent label before... It was a real innovation, a step forward in the battle against the system of stupid consumerism and the society of the spectacle. There was a real desire to make records available to the maximum number of people, sell them at half the price, and break the regular channels of distribution.
>
> *Richard Pinhas, Disjuncta Records*

As the '70s dawned, two French record labels dominated the music business: Vogue and Barclay. While they were genuinely interested in discovering local talent, theirs was a search for sure-fire hits with little concern for developing unknown acts. The other major labels (Philips, CBS, RCA, Pathé-Marconi) were subsidiaries of international companies, and focused mainly on selling their American and British catalogue to the French audience. In the early '70s these labels punted on signing a few underground acts (Komintern, Magma, and Moving Gelatine Plates) but the only lasting relationship was between Catherine Ribeiro and Philips (with seven albums released in as many years).

On the whole it was left to smaller labels to foster the underground scene, with Saravah, BYG, and Futura taking on that role in the early years. Saravah, founded by actor and singer Pierre Barouh, became the first to recognise the underground by signing Brigitte Fontaine in '68. BYG/Actuel had a strong focus on jazz, but signed both Gong and Ame Son in '69. Gérard Terronès's Futura was another jazz-oriented label that became the major supporter of the underground scene. Futura recorded albums by Mahogany Brain, Red Noise, Jac Berrocal, Fille Qui Mousse, Triode, Travelling, Semool, Jean Guérin, Bernard Vitet, and Horde Catalytique Pour La Fin.

After promising beginnings, both BYG/Actuel and Futura were defunct by '73, leaving a dearth of underground-oriented labels in France. This was the landscape that confronted Richard Pinhas as he completed the first Heldon album in '74. Unable to see any other way forward, he took the bold step of creating his own record label: Disjuncta Records.

Disjuncta was set up as a non-profit organisation, run by Pinhas and Alain Renaud. It became an exemplar of the "do it yourself" ethos well before punk came on the scene. Pinhas: "People had the aim of releasing whatever they wanted, but at that time, if you didn't sing in French, it was almost unthinkable... After going to the factories we realized that [even by] selling discs at half the price of other record companies, we could earn twice as much money."

Pinhas released four of his own albums on Disjuncta, but also opened it up to other artists: "What was important about the label is that we made about ten other albums, even some Balinese and Brazilian music. If something was good, we tried to release it." The label produced records by Zao, Nyl, Alain Renaud, and the German band Exmagma.

When Heldon attracted support from the music press and radio, Disjuncta became a surprise success. "[In] fifteen months we sold 19,000 records, with only about six points of sale. There were maybe three or four [stores] in Paris... One store, Gérard Nguyen's Atem in Nancy, even sold 600 albums on its own."

Its very success forced Pinhas to divest himself of the label: "Alain and I had been run off our feet, we had to supervise the recordings, ... act as travelling salesmen, package the discs, everything... I couldn't manage Disjuncta at the same time as Heldon." He found a buyer who took over the catalogue, and rebranded the label as Urus Records.

Although it operated for just over a year, Disjuncta had provided a model that inspired many others. Ariel Kalma was directly encouraged by Pinhas to self-release his '75 debut: "I'd told Richard I thought it was great that he produced his record himself, and he said 'Well, you can do it, too'. When I said, 'Whoa, that's expensive!', he told me, 'No, no, no, do it yourself.' So he gave me advice, and that's what I did. I'm eternally grateful."

Jean-Jacques Birgé took the same route in '75 when a deal to release Birgé Gorgé Shiroc's debut album fell through. His GRRR

Records was originally intended to be a one-off solution, but became permanent when Un Drame Musical Instantané's debut encountered similar problems a few years later. Birgé: "We were waiting for producers who couldn't make up their minds and kept giving us the run-around, so we released *Trop d'adrenaline nuit* on GRRR... After that we preferred to remain free and independent by releasing all our records ourselves...We didn't have to put up with the nonsense of producers who wanted to put in their two cents about what we were doing without understanding our motivations, and who didn't respect their contractual commitments."

Another important early independent label was Pôle, started by Paul Putti in '75 to release his own music. Putti: "We sold 3500 copies of *Kotrill* in three months. But the income was relatively unimportant to us, the goal was to create something without the financial support of the 'big companies', and we achieved it." After the success of the first album Putti used the income from sales to fund his next record, then as Pinhas had done with Disjuncta, he opened up the label to other acts. Over the next two years Pôle released albums from Philippe Besombes, Pataphonie, Henri Roger, Fluence (Pascal Comelade), Verto, Potemkine, and Mahogany Brain.

Disjuncta, Pôle, and other early artist-run labels provided an important model of self-sufficiency that would inspire the underground music scene well into the next decade.

A NOTE ON THE CATEGORIES USED IN THIS BOOK

Each of the bands discussed in this book has been placed into one of five categories: Political Underground, Lysergic Underground, Jazz Underground, Electronic Underground, and Avant Underground. This has been done to give structure to the text, but in the end these designations are quite arbitrary. None of this music can be so readily pigeonholed.

The 'Political Underground' is the only category that has a solid foundation, as each of these bands explicitly declared the political dimension of their music. However, all of them could just as easily fit into other categories. For example, Barricade were certainly as 'avant-garde' as Etron Fou Leloublan, and their heroic drug consumption may even warrant a filing under 'lysergic'...

To underscore the knowing folly of this categorisation, Lard Free is highlighted as a counterexample. Over its lifespan this band managed to fall within the boundary of every one of the categories used, with the possible exception of 'lysergic'. On their first demos in mid-'71, Lard Free were playing a style of jazz-inflected rock, with influences from both Soft Machine and Pink Floyd. Less than a year later, when they recorded an ill-fated album for Saravah, their music blurred the boundaries of free jazz and the avant-garde. By '73, synthesiser had become (and would remain) an essential element of their sound. They were also most definitely politically aligned, publicly declaring their leftist leanings when Lard Free II became a signatory to the manifesto of the Rock-Music Liberation Front.

It's hoped that the decision to structure the text in this way doesn't lead to any misunderstandings regarding the character of these bands. The French underground produced highly idiosyncratic music, which defies easy categorisation.

part two:
the exception that proves the rule

LARD FREE

> Like the mythical sea serpent, Lard Free surfaces, dives, then resurfaces just when people have (almost) forgotten it exists. It's a group, a style of music, but above all it's an individual: Gilbert Artman. Bearded and taciturn, this composer and multi-instrumentalist (drums, vibes, organ, piano, saxophone) - *he* is Lard Free."
>
> Rock & Roll Musique no.2, February '77

Lard Free is usually referred to as the artistic vehicle of one man: Gilbert Artman. While it's true that Artman was the one constant member of the group, for the majority of its existence Lard Free was most definitely a *band*. It wasn't until the recording of their second album, *I'm Around About Midnight*, that this band identity gave way to that of a musical collective centred around Artman. In the last few years of its existence it may have seemed that Gilbert Artman was, and always had been, the crux of Lard Free - but the reality is much more complex and interesting.

The original core of the group came together in Saint-Maur to the east of Paris, almost a year before Artman's arrival. The early driver of the band was guitarist François Mativet. As Jean-Jacques Miette recalls: "He really invested his whole life into the creation of the group. François took a job at the Post Office so he could afford a Gibson and a Marshall, and he was the one who bought a van to transport the very impressive Marshall and Carlsbro stacks."

Mativet's introduction to guitar came at the dawn of the '60s: "I'm completely self-taught. I got my first (acoustic) guitar at the age of eleven. I listened to lots of records from every genre: Johnny Hallyday, Django Reinhardt, a lot of rock... I was a fan of The Rolling Stones and The Beatles from the beginning of '62/'63... In '67/'68 I was influenced by guitarists like Clapton, Jeff Beck, and Hendrix. Then in '69 I bought a Gibson SG Standard, and worked on developing a more individualistic, jazzy style."

In late '69 Mativet asked his neighbour Jean-Jacques Miette to join him in a group. Miette: "François lived in the same building and played guitar much more seriously than me. We spent days in his room listening to rock records, and to guitarists like Wes Montgomery, Larry Coryell, and Sonny Sharrock. François had the idea to start a band, it was all very amateurish and amusing - except to the neighbours."

The next recruit to the embryonic band was Jacques Chantrier. Miette: "Jacky was François's sister's boyfriend. He loved everything about sound, and started making loudspeakers so we could listen to our music louder, to the neighbours' chagrin."

Saxophonist Philippe Bolliet was brought into the band by Miette: "I met Philippe at a private school in Paris. I went up to talk to him because he looked different from the other students with his long hair, and he told me he played saxophone and flute."

Bolliet: "I was a big fan of Ray Charles, rhythm and blues, and of course jazz. Jean-Jacques introduced me to François Mativet. François lived with his parents, and we rehearsed in his room. At the same time I got to know Jacques Chantrier who would become our sound engineer. By the end of '69 we had a rehearsal room that Jacques had fitted out in Montreuil sous Bois. We were playing covers of English blues-rock bands. Rehearsals were starting to get relatively serious. We started looking for other musicians, especially a drummer."

It was after playing an early gig as a trio, with Jean-Jacques Miette playing electric bass, that the band stepped up their search. Miette: "We played at an event in Montreuil - it wasn't too bad but we lacked a drum's rhythm. There were a lot of try-outs until we found a very loud rock drummer with a huge drum kit."

This drummer (only known as Gerald) didn't really gel, so the search continued until the band came across Gilbert Artman in the second half of '70. Bolliet: "One day, a drummer with an impressive kit came to practise at the room. We got in touch and asked if he wanted to play with us."

Miette: "He was very different from us... His playing style was much more jazzy and he had excellent technique. We decided he was the man we needed. We were different from the musicians he'd played with, and he was interested in a new experience."

Artman: "Mativet, Bolliet and Miette were looking for a drummer, and I'd just decided to give myself a year off work. They were playing 'prog' music that I wasn't familiar with: covers of Blodwyn Pig and

Keef Hartley Band. But first and foremost, they were characters."

Artman was born in Livarot near the port of Le Havre. He was another self-taught musician, who had gained his musical education listening to jazz on the radio and American R&B singles brought back from Paris by his brother. He quickly made the jump from drumming on the kitchen table to sitting in with the house band at a dingy jazz club in Le Havre.

In the mid-'60s Artman moved to Paris and immersed himself in the booming jazz scene, where he cut his teeth backing the likes of Don Cherry and Steve Lacy. Free-jazz was a revelation to the young drummer: "It allowed you to break all the codes, all the shackles... the music seemed to invent itself in the reflex, the gesture, the emotion, and in the collective... everything seemed to become possible."

His conversion to rock came later, when he was exposed to the music of Van der Graaf Generator, Black Sabbath, and the MC5. His epiphany came during an early Captain Beefheart concert: "The music was unrestrained and creative, the audience was more festive, much less serious, less [apparently] intellectual... I found the cocktail explosive! It was around this time that I met up with the musicians who were to become Lard Free."

The last piece of the puzzle arrived in December '70 in the form of Dominique Triloff. Miette: "We worked for several months, but something was missing. We decided we needed an organist, so we placed an advertisement in a music newspaper, and met Dominique. He was studying music at the Rachmaninov conservatory in Paris and he brought new musical possibilities with more harmonic playing. We were very happy to play together, life was good."

Artman highlights the diversity of musical backgrounds in the band: "François Mativet was definitely the most iconoclastic - he could just as easily play in a Gypsy style as be influenced by John McLaughlin or Jimi Hendrix. He was also studying classical guitar and appreciated Indian music. His playing was steeped in a mix of all these things... I still think of him as an exceptional guitarist and person. Philippe Bolliet was infinitely calmer... but the moment he put both his alto and tenor saxophones to his lips (somewhat like Roland Kirk) he became very militant. He was the lynchpin of the group. Dominique Triloff was very immersed in the Canterbury Scene, his playing was rather influenced by Soft Machine. Jean-Jacques Miette was a proud Corsican who played his bass parts with style, and not without a touch of humour. And we shouldn't forget the amazing, explosive Jacky Chantrier, our favourite sound engineer."

With the line-up complete the band took on the name Lard Free and set to work. Bolliet: "The name was coined by François Mativet and Jean-Jacques Miette, we put together a repertoire with our own compositions, and we were ready to play live."

Artman organised their first concerts, including a spot at the *Tremplin* battle-of-bands held at the legendary Golf Drouot, which they won. Jacques Chabiron, who was on the jury, wrote in *Rock & Folk*: "Lard Free is a band absolutely without equal in France, miles ahead of everyone who struggles to synthesise jazz, rock, and free pop... They offer music that's difficult to play, difficult to write, but that gets ovations... They are a very important group."

Their prize was a four-hour demo session at Chappell Publishing's studio. Two of the tracks recorded that day ('Cochonailles' and 'Petit Tripou du Matin')[1] were released on the posthumous *Unnamed* album. While these early tracks display influences from Soft Machine (and to lesser extent Pink Floyd) the stunning interplay between musicians makes it easy to understand Chabiron's enthusiasm.

Artman: "The music on the first recording is a good reflection of this era and of the disparate approaches of the members of the group. It was this diversity that allowed us to find the way through to new territories."

Apart from this recording the only other documentation of the original line-up is a TV appearance on *Pop 2*, filmed in June '71 at the Jamboree Pop Français festival.[2] This TV debut was impressive enough to land the band a place at the Paris Biennale that October.

By the end of the year Lard Free's music had progressed, incorporating more influences from modern jazz. Miette: "Pop music was getting boring, and we were turning more and more to John Coltrane, Miles Davis, Herbie Hancock, Sun Ra, and The Art Ensemble of Chicago - more radical music that corresponded to the spirit of the time."

Early in '72 Dominique Triloff left to return to the world of classical music. Bolliet explains that his departure and changed circumstances accelerated the band's move towards a freer kind of music: "In addition to Dominique Triloff leaving, we no longer had a rehearsal room. So we hardly practised anymore and concerts were actually improvisations."

The musical transition was sealed when English jazz vibraphonist Robert Wood was added to the line-up in March '72.

Wood already had a long association with France before he moved to Paris in 1970 to dive headlong into the local jazz scene. On the release of his debut album, *Tarot*, he'd been surprised by an invitation to perform on *Pop Club*. Wood: "I was a jazz musician, and it was a very popular mainstream radio programme, so I didn't quite understand why..." By March '72 he had played several sessions on the programme.

The night after one of these broadcasts Wood heard a commotion in his building's courtyard. "A female voice called out to tell me a man was on the street and wished to speak to me, but the concierge wasn't going to let him in. I went down and saw Gilbert Artman through the grille in the door.

"He introduced himself, said he'd heard my concert on *Pop Club* and asked if I'd like to come and do a session with his band Lard Free? I was totally caught up with the Paris jazz scene, and hadn't heard of them, but Gilbert's demeanour and communicative nature woke my immediate interest. I decided to go for it on the spot. I just knew the adventure would be worthwhile.

"We got my acoustic vibes into his car and drove off.... to the Ecole d'Architecture. I actually arrived on stage with my vibraphone minutes before the band started playing. So my first conversation with François, Philippe and Jean-Jacques took place after the concert was over!"

Wood was immediately impressed by the band: "As soon as I started playing I found there was space for me to fit in. I wasn't playing on top or beside the music but was weaving in and out the same as the others. Lard Free didn't treat me as anything special, I was simply in and part of the music. They wouldn't wait respectfully for me to finish whatever I was playing, they just swept in and carried the music forward. I really liked that."

While Wood never considered himself a full member of the band, he played at most of their concerts from this point on. He quickly discovered the extent of their reputation: "When I was hanging out where rock musicians, music fans and journalists would meet (the record store at Gibert Jeune, the music shops in Pigalle, the cafés and bars of Saint Denis) I realised that every Lard Free concert was seen as a special event. There would be a lot of talk about them for some time afterwards." [3]

During the band's next appearance at the Ecole d'Architecture Wood recalls taking part in Gilbert Artman's first experiment with spatialised live performance: "Gilbert, with his drums, and I, with my vibes, played the whole gig suspended from the ceiling on swaying metal structures, above a packed crowd. It caused quite a stir. We were unable to come down until the end of the proceedings! A first indication of what Gilbert would later develop with Urban Sax."

The band's experimentation extended to the creation of unusual sonic ambiences, well before they had access to synthesisers. Miette: "We didn't have electronic instruments, but we had Jacky. Thanks to his overflowing imagination we had access to effects using Revox [tape machines] and other oddities. There was even a piano we'd found on the side of the road, that we completely dismantled, keeping only the frame with the strings attached which was used as a percussion instrument or as a kind of harp."

Artman: "We would start concerts with the curtain closed, playing a bugle into the strings, scraping and hitting it. We'd placed the piano frame on four stools, and when the curtain opened, we sent it crashing to the ground."[4]

Around the time Wood joined the band, Lard Free also took on a manager: Gilles Yeprémian, the music columnist at *Le Parapluie*. He would become the only other constant alongside Artman throughout Lard Free's career.

Lard Free's growing reputation enabled Yeprémian to secure Saravah Records' interest in recording the band. A session was organised with Hervé Bergerat, who had produced Catharsis's debut album. Catharsis were much more restrained, but had something of a family resemblance to Lard Free, as both played expanded compositions in a "rock" format. At least that had been true when Lard Free recorded their demos in mid-'71. The Lard Free that entered the studio in Spring '72 was a very different proposition, however. Miette: "When we recorded with Saravah our music was becoming more and more radical and less and less based on harmony. All the rage of the time and a certain violence against consumer society came out in our interpretation."

The recording session started well enough. Artman: "We set up the piano frame, the rest of the band, and started...We spent a long part of the session playing the basic parts... So we knew roughly where we wanted to go. Then Bergerat arrived late in the morning or early afternoon."

Bolliet: "Hervé Bergerat was stunned by the music we were making, he didn't seem to like it at all." Artman: "When he came in and realised the kind of music we were going to make, he paid for the sessions, thanked everyone, and left!" The band never saw the producer again.[5]

Artman: "When we knew we weren't going any further we wanted to record as much as possible. So that afternoon we recorded four or five tracks live."

Between the morning and afternoon sessions Artman visited Robert Wood. "Gilbert invited me to lunch. During lunch we chatted about music, dance and theatre. Then Gilbert mentioned Lard Free had a recording session booked. He asked me if I was interested in joining in the venture. 'Ok', I said, 'it depends when the session is and if I am free that day.' 'Well, that's no problem', says Gilbert, 'the session is now and the guys are already in the studio ready to start. Let's go over and check it out, it's just around the corner."

When Wood protested that he didn't have access to his vibraphone, he was told there was one already set up in the studio: "I started playing notes and chords to hear how the vibraphone sounded. I hardly had time to say hello to the other members of the band when the engineer's voice comes over the talkback: 'Are we ready to begin?' The first number was called out and off we go."

The afternoon session went smoothly, but Bergerat's reaction led to Saravah shelving the project. Bolliet: "We were able to finish the recording session, but the tape remained in Saravah's vaults until Gilbert recovered it in 1994."

When the session was finally released on the *Unnamed* album in 1997, it was a revelation. Rather than evoking Soft Machine or Pink Floyd like the mid-'71 demos, Lard Free were exploring similar territory to British free-improvising bands like AMM. The new version of Triloff's composition 'Cochonailles' (renamed 'Choconailles') gives the best indication of the changes. Months earlier the debt to Soft Machine had been obvious, but the ghostly glissandos of Wood's vibraphone and lack of any chordal foundation pulls the new interpretation into the realm of free improvisation. The one remnant from the earlier version is the bass riff, but when it arrives, Bolliet's sax and Mativet's guitar push the piece towards the freest jazz fusion. It's an excellent piece, but its relation to the previous version seems almost incidental.

While the release of *Unnamed* finally allowed Lard Free's early music to be heard, the story of the twelve months following the thwarted recorded session at Saravah remains obscured. The failure of the session seems to have totally knocked the wind out of the band. They would play only a handful of gigs afterwards, with the last on 16 June '72. The decisive blow was Gilbert Artman's departure.

Most of those involved will discuss the period only in the vaguest of terms. Mativet: "After some differences between us and a certain weariness, the group stopped temporarily." Artman: "After these unfinished productions, the group had effectively ceased to exist." Of the original members only Miette is more forthcoming about events: "We continued for a while, then broke up. François, Philippe, Jacky and I looked for a new drummer. We played a few gigs with a very good drummer, Hector Barthélémy, still under the name of Lard Free." The first performance of this line-up was at the Bièvres Festival less than two weeks after their last performance with Artman.[6]

Meanwhile Gilbert Artman put together a new band, named Lard Free II. Artman: "There was a rift in the group. And just as there was Barricade I and Barricade II at that time, there was Lard Free I and Lard Free II." Artman was joined in Lard Free II by Alain Audat (sax), Bernard Weber (bass), and Bernard Poyaut (drums). With Poyaut on drums Artman was freed up to play keyboards and vibraphone.

Neither Lard Free nor Lard Free II made it to the end of '72. Lard Free played their last concert in Essen, Germany in October, and effectively disbanded when Philippe Bolliet was called up for his national service in December. The details of Lard Free II's dissolution are unknown, however the band was a signatory to the Rock Music Liberation Front manifesto in October '72, so it must have been some time after that. Whatever the details, by the beginning of '73 Lard Free didn't exist in *any* form whatsoever.

Then in April '73 a flurry of events prompted the band's reformation.

Robert Wood had invited Gilbert Artman to join him in a trio for an ORTF radio broadcast on 7 April '73. After the performance Artman was introduced to the manager of Disques Motors, Francis Dreyfus. Artman: "A few days later he invited me to a meeting where I was offered a recording session at Island Studios... [for] a new label, Vamp Records, within the Motors group...

"Gilles Yeprémian suggested I do something with Maurice Lemaître, a contemporary Letterist poet, which was an exciting project. But at that time, I preferred to work in continuity with François and Philippe. I really wanted us to make this album together, it was important for me to concretise our work and friendship... I also really wanted to work with Hervé Elhyani, anticipating a great collaboration. Elhyani had mastered the ARP 2600, and its deep, repetitive bass made it possible to envisage a more linear music, based on sound and its modulations. Philippe and François would bring the ruptures...the fractal."

Why did Artman choose to return to the line-up he had left almost twelve months earlier, rather than calling on his bandmates from Lard Free II? The answer seems to lie in the level of musical excitement the original Lard Free could generate. Robert Wood's description of playing with the original Lard Free line-up is striking: "The band really knew what they were doing. No matter how wild the overall impression could be to the first time listener, their performance was based on a solid structure and each of the 'moving parts' of the band had its specific place and role. For example, there was no moment, as there sometimes is in jazz, when one soloist slowly wound down indicating to the next soloist to take over. Philippe Bolliet would be going full blast, then suddenly I'd realise that in fact François Mativet had been soloing for at least a minute already...

"Playing on stage with Lard Free was similar to being in a powerful car, racing at high speed down an unfamiliar country road with rapidly changing weather. Sometimes you think you are driving, only to discover that you are bouncing about on the back seat. Then you land in the front passenger seat before being behind the steering wheel again... for a moment..." This level of musical excitement was obviously something Artman valued, and wanted to experience again.

The band was assembled in lightning speed. Artman: "We had ten days to get the group back together to go and record at Island Studio.

We were expected in England for three days of recording. Mixing included!"

The inclusion of Hervé Elhyani seems to have been based on the perception that Jean-Jacques Miette had already sidelined the band, coupled with excitement at the possibilities that Elhyani offered by doubling on bass and synth.[7] Both Mativet and Bolliet agree that the synthesiser would prove to be an important element in the reformed Lard Free. Bolliet: "Hervé introduced the synth into Lard Free. It, and the person who knew how to use it, were essential for this recording."

Hervé Elhyani was a young bassplayer who had realised playing in groups wasn't putting food on the table: "At twenty-one I started looking for a real job. I heard about a position in the Gaffarel Musique store - they were the importer for Marshall, Fender and other prestigious brands. It was good work: meeting other musicians, getting better knowledge of equipment, etc. After summer '72 my boss told me about a new import: the ARP, that along with the Moog was the top synth of the time. I was very quickly seduced, and discovered its vast, new potential...

"Gilbert was a customer and was also at the Gibus Club. So there were jam sessions at Gibus, and meetings at Gaffarel. He told me about his recording project with Vamp Records, and his concept of a style of jazz-rock well-removed from the traditional blues-rock cliches. Of course I was attracted.

"There were a few practices. I got to know the rest of the group, Philippe Bolliet was an amazing sax player full of ideas, the guitarist François was a little crazy, and Gilbert was a very interesting character, a good drummer and percussionist with unconventional ideas about music, painting, theatre. The rehearsals were more like jams than the arrangement of pieces. But everyone thought it was very good and Gilbert was delighted."

Elhyani was able to get time off from his job (and borrow Gaffarel's ARP synth), but the French army wasn't so flexible when it came to Bolliet: "To make this record I had to go AWOL. On returning to the barracks, I was sentenced to one month in prison." François Mativet's participation was also problematic, as he was suffering from a bout of depression.

Nevertheless the full complement made the trek to London's Island Studios, with Frank Owen engineering. Artman: "We set up and got the sound we wanted. There were no pre-conceptions about what we were going to do... There was a good listening environment and the atmosphere was pleasant and relaxed...But the guitarist was unwell, so we put the framework of the album together while he was still absent... we weren't all recording at the same time, so at least that wasn't a concern."

Bolliet: "François was ill with depression, and all of his interventions were recorded in one go, which is very representative of the mood of the album."

Artman: "Mativet is the musician who most impressed me with his musical brilliance. He has breathtaking technique, but also the idea of gesture and an essential understanding of the moment... For the first two days the guitarist couldn't take part, but on the third day he played all the songs brilliantly in one take!"

The music recorded in April '73 reveals a stunning progression from the sessions for the aborted first album. It's not that the band had improved, but rather their approach had changed beyond all recognition. The first two tracks on the album illustrate the change. 'Warinobaril' kicks off with Artman and Elhyani laying down a relaxed groove that straddles German Motorik and jazz-fusion. Bolliet's sax adds a melodic stasis that brings Faust and Neu to mind, then Mativet crashes in on guitar with absolutely no sense of style or decorum, slashing straight across the groove. His (controlled) carnage recalls John McLaughlin's and Pete Cosey's playing with Miles Davis.

'12 ou 13 juillet que je sais d'elle Pt 1' changes mood totally, with a wonderfully throbbing ARP sequence overlaid with gorgeous long sax lines from Bolliet. Elhyani shows his talent by constantly morphing the timbre of the ARP - as the sequence relentlessly chugs along the sound never stops evolving. This ability to make highly repetitive synth lines constantly evolve is something that Richard Pinhas from Heldon would also master. It's a totally different approach from the German and British synthesists of the time, and is one of the hallmarks of the French underground sound. The seeds of European techno are being sown in tracks like '12 ou 13 juillet que je sais d'elle Pt 1'.

The album was launched by a concert at L'Olympia on 7 May. Exactly why the recording and release was so hurried is a mystery. However what *is* clear is that the rushed decisions made in the process affected relations in the band. The most obvious being the choice of album title: *Gilbert Artman's Lard Free*.

Artman: "Things were done in a hurry. I'd hoped that the cover would be created by Dominique Mulhem, a hyperrealist painter who was a friend (he was creator of the fanzine *Vanille Free Press*). But Dreyfus chose the cover and title, which I found out about when the album was released. At that time we didn't really have a say in the matter, the producers decided.[8]"

Bolliet: "The disc came out quite quickly after the recording. I was in the army under close arrest, François was in a depressed state, and Hervé had returned to his work. Regarding the cover, the credits, etc. - Gilbert, the producers, and Dreyfus Publishing acted without ever seeking the views of the other musicians. The first time I saw the album was in the record department of the Drugstore des Champs Elysées. What a surprise! Lard Free had become 'Gilbert Artman's Lard Free'. We were faced with a *fait accompli*."

Elhyani: "Everyone trusted Gilbert, so he took care of signing the contracts with Vamp for us. It's true that recording an album in London's Island studio was enough for me - I was on cloud nine. Then Gilbert registered the pieces in the name of 'Gilbert Artman's Lard Free'. That had never been anticipated. But at that time, trust reigned." Whatever the intention behind them, the credits on the album cover would remain a thorn in the side of the band for the next twelve months.

The album generally received a positive reception in the media. *Actuel* was impressed by Lard Free's ambition, singling out "the use of the synthesiser to the most unsettling effect... [and] a guitarist at war with his instrument. There is enough electric violence here to make you prick up your ears." *Pop Club* also chose the album as their 'sélection pop' for two weeks in a row.

Due to Bolliet's army service there were few opportunities for Lard Free to perform in the remainder of the year, apart from a short tour on the Côte d'Azur. Artman recalls that it was during a stop in Menton, near Monaco, that the concept for Urban Sax crystallised. He was inspired to submit a proposal for a performance: "The cathedral square was like a kind of open-air Italian theatre. The plan was to place four sound generators in the little alleyways leading to the square, and have four musicians on a merry-go-round in the middle of Place St Michel, with another four on the balconies surrounding it. The idea was to form a spiral of continuous sound, with very minimalist loops. Naturally the project was rejected!" Nevertheless, the concept would continue to develop in Artman's mind until Urban Sax was finally realised in '76.

In December '73 Bolliet was released from military service, and the band was finally free to perform regularly. However their next concert, in Grenoble, was to be the last for this line-up, as Hervé Elhyani departed soon afterwards: "We released the record, played a few concerts and my first disagreements with Gilbert followed: over clothing, the choice of music, the contract with Vamp... I left Lard Free, somewhat with Gilbert's blessing."

François Mativet followed at the beginning of '74: "After the record, tours became scarce, there was the lack of money, the expenses of the group... we separated on good terms and I continued to play with Philippe Bolliet and some of the others until the end of the '70s."

Alain Audat, who had been part of Lard Free II, joined the band on synthesiser and saxophone. Bolliet: "Alain Audat joined us to play concerts and for the second album. Most concerts were done by the three of us: Gilbert, Alain and myself." They were occasionally joined by another saxophonist, Antoine Duvernet.

In late '74 Vamp began talking about a second album. Bolliet and Artman contacted Mativet to see if he would return for the recording. When he declined, Artman approached Heldon's Richard Pinhas to play guitar on the session. Artman: "I'd met Richard Pinhas several times, and I'd been to a very good concert where he opened for Nico... It seemed like an interesting idea to ask him to join us for the recording."

Pinhas agreed to appear on the album, and would play at some concerts afterwards, but he points out that he was never part of Lard Free: "I wasn't a member of the band. I had my own band, and being in several bands at the same time is difficult. We were friends, and at this time musicians played for each other for free."

The sessions for the album were booked for October '74. Just before they entered the studio Philippe Bolliet left Lard Free: "We had a rehearsal with Richard Pinhas two days before the recording. There was a small, non-musical dispute between Richard and myself. Being rather temperamental, I decided not to go to the recording sessions..."

Artman: "I would have liked lifelong companion Philippe Bolliet to join us, but it couldn't be done which I regret... three saxes would have given another [dimension] to this recording!"

With Bolliet's shock departure Lard Free entered Studio Ferber to record *I'm Around About Midnight* with Gilbert Artman as the only original member present. During the recording Artman played drums, percussion, vibraphone, organ and tenor sax, with Alain Audat on AKS synth and tenor sax, Antoine Duvernet on alto sax and flute, and Richard Pinhas playing guitar, bass and additional synth.

Artman: "Again we had only three days to make this album, including the mix. The main problem was that the sound engineer wanted to record us as a live free-jazz band. At this point I knew the potential of the studio, and had envisioned structuring the pieces into one sequence per side. I wanted to record the different parts on separate tracks to give space and consistency to the pieces.

"I used up a whole morning explaining why I wanted to work with the instruments on separate tracks! The sound engineer declared the idea suicidal, but we were able to wrap it up in three days and part as friends. Even so the label let us have an extra half day for the mix."

Artman told *Atem* that the intention on this album had been to dial back on the ruptures that had been contributed by Bolliet and Mativet in the past: "The second disc is calmer... the aggressiveness is no longer wilful, but more surreptitiously taut, indirect, incantatory."

On its release, *Actuel* was positive but equivocal about the album: "Lard Free resurface with a new incarnation touched by the charm of 'cosmic music'... This second album still doesn't generate the ecstasy of great discoveries, but... the marriage of minimalism and strident rock shoots out encouraging sparks."

Rock & Folk's Hervé Muller was much more positive, believing that the new album made up for what he had felt was an uncohesive debut: "The first album... dated from a time when Lard Free was still trying to be a band, and the result was rather confused. There are still some incongruities on this album, but it is infinitely superior as it has an obvious musical unity: it is Artman's trip, and that's a very good thing."

This is one of the earliest references to Lard Free as Gilbert Artman's vehicle, something that would become more and more common over time. Muller actually went further earlier in the piece, stating: "Lard Free *is* Gilbert Artman (drums, vibraphone, organ, piano, sax, writer of every piece) just as Heldon *is* Richard Pinhas..."

According to Alain Audat this group dynamic had played out in the studio during the creation of *I'm Around About Midnight*. He left Lard Free immediately after the sessions: "Without doubt it was this, among other things, that led me to leave Studio Ferber and reform Lard Free II - to pay homage to the original artistic, ideological and political commitment."[9]

Richard Pinhas confirms that during his involvement with Lard Free, he saw Gilbert Artman as the band's leader: "He was the head when I knew them. Lard Free was Gilbert's band, like Urban Sax was afterwards."

For the remainder of Lard Free's existence it operated as a loose collective of musicians gathered around Artman, rather than as a "band". His conception of musical creation suggests this was Artman's preferred set-up: "Coming more from free and jazz music, the notion of a group wasn't very familiar to me. I was more eager for musical adventures where each musician can bring his own colour... Music is a journey made of encounters, every musician brings different scenery to it... This was a time when the experiences and interchange of musicians multiplied. This gave the possibility of encounters, not only with musicians, but also with poetry (Angeline Neveu, Dialy Karam), painting, and light shows."

Jean-Jacques Birgé was involved with Lard Free at this point: "I was part of the group for a few months... At the time Gilbert Artman played more vibraphone than drums, and I helmed my ARP 2600. I remember Lard Free as a group that didn't exist really. Gilbert was always there, but the group around him changed. Some concerts sounded very rock, some very jazz, some very minimalist - it depended on what he wanted to do."

Among the musicians who performed with Lard Free in '75/'76 were Peter Varady, Jean-Jacques Leurion (Alpes), Phil Le Pieux, Jean-Pierre Thirault (Mahjun), and Christian Boulé (Clearlight). The flux in the line-up created challenges, but Artman also viewed it as a positive. He told *Rock en Stock*: "I've never believed in the notion of a group. Friction between musicians is more interesting than stagnation; if needed there should be new people at every concert, as, for example, in free-jazz... We must demystify the 'sacred' image of the group."

The opportunities for new encounters reached a peak in '76,

with Artman widening his circle of musical collaborators. He points to François Tusques' big-band project as an important part of the process: "Operation Rhino allowed me to reconnect with free-jazz and play with the free musicians I appreciated: François Tusques, Daniel Deshays, Pierre Bastien, etc. It's probably not insignificant that it was at this concert I met Dominique Grimaud [from Camizole] and Monique Alba [of Vidéo-Aventures] who, although more extreme in their thinking, were gravitating towards this kind of performance, where the gesture becomes music. This meeting gave rise to a number of collaborations and exchanges."

A year of new encounters and musical exchanges culminated in the realisation of the Urban Sax project, based on the notion Artman had landed on back in '73: "The idea of spatialising the stage, putting an end to the head-on spectacle: theatrical, cinematographic, political or religious... The idea that the empirical gesture must be extended to work in 360 degrees (vertically and horizontally)...

"[Urban Sax is] the unitary sound *par excellence*, aiming to create a continuous sound somewhere other than on stage, and to rotate this... very constant, very incantatory, and very cyclical sound around the audience."

Urban Sax played for the first time at the Bas-Rock Festival in Paris on 4 November '76. Guigou Chenevier from Etron Fou was in the audience: "Sixteen saxophonists lined up on the stage. They didn't yet wear the white overalls that would become the Urban's trademark. [The performance] was powerful."[10]

Urban Sax would operate in parallel with Lard Free for the next two years, with the stories of the two bands intertwining, and members floating between bands. Artman: "It was an ill-defined, but very friendly ensemble. This period was an unlikely adventure, made up of paths crossing, encounters, creativity, activism!"

By the time Lard Free was ready to record its third, and last, album it had crystallised into a core trio of musicians. Artman "I worked a lot with Christian Boulé at the time. He introduced me to Xavier Baulleret who'd been in Kool Gool, and had played live with Cyrille Verdeaux (Clearlight). Xavier introduced me to Yves Lanes."

Artman explained to *Rock en Stock* that this combination of musicians drove the music in a new direction: "All of the current musicians play keyboards, and that suggests a certain approach.

Everything is always based on the sound, and the sonics have more importance than the notes."

The trio went into Studio Hautefeuille in January '77 to record *Lard Free* accompanied by Jean-Pierre Thirault from Mahjun on clarinet. Artmen told *Atem*: "The previous two discs were a little held back by lack of preparation, lack of time (three days of recording for each of them), and by the quality of the studios... This third disc achieved what we hadn't really succeeded in doing before... the second side is beginning to move towards what we would like to strive for."

Artman based the album on the idea of a musical spiral, employing available studio effects and techniques to the fullest: "We created spiral motifs, and time-shifted everything to accentuate the permanent rotational movement. Then we added phasing that ran against the movement of the music."

Lard Free is made up of two side-long pieces with repetitive motifs weaving in and out of a heavily-effected musical bed with resonances of industrial machinery. It is an ambitious album, combining minimalist motifs, *kosmische* atmospheres, pounding drums, and heavy guitar riffs into an otherworldly mix.

Today Artman expresses the desire to revisit the album to spatialise it in accordance with the original intention: "The ideal would of course have been to release it in [surround sound]. I haven't given up hope of being able to remix it one day with this in mind." At the time the compromise was to rely on the immersiveness of headphone listening: "I had the idea of saying on the cover, 'Must be listened to on headphones', but that wasn't commercially acceptable..."

On its release *Lard Free* split the critics. *Atem*'s Xavier Beal was perplexed by Lard Free's sudden change of style: "This third disc has lost the sonic coherence that was the strength of their second... There is a bias towards improvisation on rather vague themes... this desire to be 'free' leads to no instrument being foregrounded in the mix. Artman's unusual drumming, which gave interesting colour to the other two albums, is lost..."

In *Le Matin* Hervé Muller praised the album, noting its similarity to the music of Urban Sax: "It shares an extremely dense atmosphere evoking anxiety and dread, with strange, repetitive sonorities to test the nerves, but which is too moving not to be captivating... Artman creates a resounding, distorted jungle from which mad organs, wild pianos and solitary and despairing clarinets emerge."

Meanwhile *Rock en Stock* favourably compared the album to Heldon's recently-released *Interface*: "Lard Free produces something both very similar and very different. There is less sense of urgency, allowing the mind to roam more. More risks are taken, especially in the mixing... It heads in a more futuristic direction."

The *Lard Free* album was released on the Cobra label, which would also record Urban Sax's debut. Artman: "There were people from Cobra... who were truly open-minded, letting us do whatever took our fancy. To make the last album with Lard Free I had [struck] a deal, 'I'm [happy to] make this album, but I insist on working on a project that includes sixteen saxophonists', and they agreed to it."

The first Urban Sax album was recorded in the same studio and with the same sound engineers as *Lard Free*. Among the saxophonists featured were a number known from significant underground bands: Chris Chanet (Etron Fou/Camizole), Antoine Duvernet (Lard Free), Alain Potier (Plat du Jour), Patrice Quentin (Crium Delirium/Nyl), and Jean-Pierre Thiraut (Mahjun).

Artman had intended this album to be the first of four: "The Urban Sax project represents a suite of three hours of music. We would have preferred [to release it on] tape as that would capture the spirit of uninterrupted music more completely... The first album is like a preface, a beginning, the rise of a progression with the saxes and metallic resonances... In the following records there will be voices added, then something else entirely, other non-instrumental noises."

Only two of the proposed quadrilogy of LPs would see the light of day, and *Urban Sax 2* (released in '78) did indeed include a chorus of voices. *Urban Sax* was released by Cobra at around the same time as the third Lard Free album, to a unanimously positive response.

Le Matin: "In *Urban Sax* the saxophone is used more as a vehicle for sound than as an instrument in itself, and is at times barely recognisable... The result is a heightened atmosphere, where changes are barely perceptible but incessant, to the point of creating a... disturbing urban nightmare... that it is absolutely contemporary."

Rock & Folk: "The atmosphere created is imposing: intense, and quite often harrowing. The comparison to Philip Glass is unavoidable... but the approach is individual."

It is interesting to compare the *Lard Free* and *Urban Sax* albums, as they both show different aspects of the same musical vision. Artman: "It is quite similar music, if you listen to both albums they border on being able to be blended into one another. All the tracks are in minor keys and have linear structures.

"Indeed, even if the means and the result are very different, [they share] this concept of spatialisation and the spiral. This also finds an echo in 'Les Noces chymiques', a collaboration with Pierre Henry for the Paris Opera."[11]

In his review of the last Lard Free album *Atem*'s Xavier Beal had pondered whether its lack of coherence compared to Urban Sax signalled Artman's desire to devote himself to his newest project. This may have been a fanciful notion at that time, but by late '78 Lard Free would be gone, and Urban Sax would indeed be Artman's primary focus.

At the beginning of '78 Lard Free's original saxophonist, Philippe Bolliet, had returned, and for the rest of its existence he and Artman would be the band's core. Dominique Grimaud (Camizole): "In '78, Lard Free's membership was very changeable. It always had been, but now it was at its height... For this concert Gilbert Artman would recruit this musician, for the next another. I think he wanted to experiment with as many combinations and possibilities as possible."

The final experiment involved the merging of Lard Free with Camizole in May '78. The resulting six-piece would perform four times between May and August. Grimaud: "These were the very last concerts of Camizole and Lard Free. Gilbert was about to devote all his time to Urban Sax." [12]

Gilbert Artman continues to lead Urban Sax, which has become internationally known for its large-scale immersive events. He was also a member of Jac Berrocal's band Catalogue in the '80s.

Philippe Bolliet continues to play music, and was until recently involved with Urban Sax and its off-shoot projects Quad Sax and Urbi Flat. He runs a small recording studio with Lard Free's original sound engineer, Jacques Chantrier.

Françoise Mativet and Jean-Jacques Miette remained active in live performance on the underground music scene throughout the '70s, though neither pursued careers as recording artists.

Hervé Elhyani continued to work as a musician through the '70s, playing synthesiser with film composer Michel Magne, notably on the LP Elements N° 1 "La Terre".

Robert Wood released four solo albums in the '70s, and continues to make music.

Notes

1 In *Actuel* the band had drolly stated: "Our name already shows several influences, we wish to speak of pork products and liberty.". The track titles illustrated this purported influence of pork: 'Cochonailles' is a purposeful misspelling of the French word for 'Pork Products' and 'Petit Tripou du Matin' translates to 'Little Tripe of the Morning'.

2 The programme can be viewed on-line at INA Madelen.

3 One of these events was an appearance at the Evry Festival in May '72. Wood: "We were told to get ready to play on the second stage. Word got around and a spontaneous demonstration demanded that Lard Free play on the main stage. There was a bit of a scuffle with a well-known pop band... Our performance was greeted enthusiastically with anarchistic chants and militant left-wing slogans. Lard Free was the subject of both enthusiasm and contention yet again."

4 "This marvellous instrument had a poetic end: splash, gurgle... thrown into the Marne to my great regret." *(Artman)*

5 Artman admits that there was another factor to Bergerat's exit: "The mic was open while the band was making fun of a group the producer had previously worked with - let's call it a *faux pas*. This precipitated the halt of the recording session."

6 Gilbert Artman was also at the Bièvres Festival playing in a trio with Robert Wood.

7 Miette has a different recollection of events: "We reconnected with Gilbert with the intention of re-founding the band. He told us that he agreed to come back and play with us and that there was even a record in preparation, but that there was a condition. And that's when he told me I wasn't part of this new adventure without really giving me an explanation. I was shocked, and left very distraught. That's how my story with Lard Free ended." Miette stated his suspicion that Artman's desire to explore synthesiser led to his being replaced by Hervé Elhyani. Artman is adamant that this wasn't the case: "I don't remember this episode... I don't think (except for an incident at the Bièvres festival) that there was the slightest problem with Jean-Jacques, I really appreciated his humour and his playing. At no point was there the idea of replacing him with Hervé Elhyani."

8 The cover was actually designed by the brother of one of the producers: Jean-Louis Guinochet.

9 Lard Free II was indeed revived by Audat. It played only infrequently over the next few years. Robert Wood recalls playing bass in a line-up that included Bolliet, Mativet, and drummer Richard Rougier at the Essen Festival in '75.

10 Artman told *Atem* that he regretted that this first performance hadn't allowed for the spatialisation of sound so fundamental to the project: "it wasn't possible to arrange the sixteen saxes in four angles. The principle of four groups of saxes is that it gives a continuous movement... three groups play while the fourth group takes a breath in a circular, rotating movement, where the motifs appear little by little. The goal is to cause something like a hypnotic state in the people who are in the middle of the four independent points of sound."

11 'Noces chymiques' was a Pierre Henry work staged with Urban Sax at the Paris Opera in June '80 (a version was recorded for Radio France in '81). Artman and Henry would collaborate again on the *Paradise Lost* album released in '82.

12 In 2018 a recording of the penultimate Lard Free concert from 30 July '78 was released under the title *Camizole + Lard Free*.

part three:

the political underground

INTRODUCTION

> In France, Pop equals helmets, truncheons, cops, iron bars, riots, repression, and free concerts... Since May '68, the youth movement has been severely repressed, militants locked up, political actions broken up...
>
> Apart from the factory or the workplace, young people have only one place of their own where they can meet: the pop concert. Nothing else offers a large forum for underlying ideas, suppressed ideologies, and shared questions. This is a good reason to ban them, to restrict the number attending, to try to clamp down on the phenomenon...
>
> *"Free, pop et politique"*, Actuel n° 6, March '71

There has been much discussion among English-speaking music critics about the influence of the French avant-political group the Situationist International (SI) on the development of British punk rock. While some threads of influence can be unraveled (e.g. Malcolm McLaren and Jamie Reid *had* been introduced to some of the SI's ideas in their art school days), it was a diluted and garbled version of SI theory that was incorporated into the punk ethos.

What these critics have overlooked is that in post-'68 France there was a movement of homegrown bands *totally committed* to the radical politics of groups like the Situationists. These groups dedicated themselves to expressing their political stance on stage and on record. This flowering of highly-politicised music was often accompanied by an incredibly similar attitude to that shown by British punk almost a decade later. The guard-dogs of the music establishment, and sometimes the audience themselves, weren't safe from subversive attack.

In addition to their political commitment these groups (like their contemporaries in Germany) were fierce in asserting their *own* identity. They broke with the modes of music inherited from Britain and the USA, and as an early survey of French rock[1] points out, they were the first to do so: "These bands were committed to the ideas of

May '68 and its aftermath and weren't afraid to assert themselves as French... With them the era of embarrassment at not having been born in San Francisco, at not having an Anglo-American coolness, ended... Red Noise, Maajun and their kin were eventually ground down, but they left behind inklings of what could be done in France, apart from imitating Americans."

These bands differentiated themselves from those from the British and American undergrounds by focussing on the concrete political potential of rock music. Writing in '73, Alain Roux (of Maajun) pointed out that in contrast to an Anglo-American underground that "dreams and contemplates itself... the originality of the French youth movement is the awareness that action must be the goal... French pop is political, or is at the very least forced to take a political position."

Heldon's Richard Pinhas also notes the influence of contemporary political struggles on the French music scene of the early '70s: "We were in the fallout from May '68 and the Vietnam War, and music became an effective way of calling for a radical challenge to the established order... Political motivations were present at all levels: music, production, distribution, discourse. Life itself was becoming a kind of politics, a revolution (both individual and social) was on the horizon..." [2]

The Valbonne and Biot Festivals (held in August '70) were major coming-out events for the politically committed groups.[3] Coming together for the first time fostered a sense that they were part of a wider movement. The first concrete outcome of this new sense of identity grew from the bond Komintern and Maajun had forged after meeting at Valbonne. These bands joined forces to create the FLIP (Force for the Liberation of and Intervention in Pop).[4] As was tradition for all French art and political movements the creation of the group was announced in the form of a manifesto.

Michel Muzac of Komintern: "The idea to create the FLIP was mainly at the initiative of Maajun's Alain Roux, and sympathisers from the Maoist/spontaneist group Vive La Révolution (VLR). After some joint meetings Alain wrote the manifesto/tract that we signed, along with Fille Qui Mousse and Dagon. It was a Situationist-inspired text that was published or mentioned in several left-wing publications, and in the music newspapers and magazines." The political journal *Tout!* published the complete manifesto in October '70:

APPEAL OF THE FLIP

We are a group of people in the Pop scene who want to draw lessons from the 1970 Summer of 'Pop'. While the festivals were 'cursed' (banned, tolerated, or scuttled) they demonstrated the strength of the Pop movement among the young. The obvious fiasco of these bourgeoisie-style spectacular-market festivals doesn't signal the failure of Pop in France. What it highlights is what young people no longer want. Pop is something more than a marketplace to them, it's a new way of life that inevitably involves questioning bourgeoise society, its laws, and the alienation it produces (which, like a hydra with a thousand heads, suppresses us all). Pop is freedom.

Therefore we've decided to take the initiative: from now on Pop will not simply be a product of greater or lesser quality, it will be the vehicle of our revolt against the old world. It will be a subversive weapon to change life and transform the world right here, right now, everywhere that struggles are carried out: in offices, workers hostels, suburbs, council estates, schools, universities etc... From now on we'll choose the time and place to take action, we'll create situations ourselves. We will be, we already are, the FLIP: Force for the Liberation of and Intervention in Pop.

We'll fight on two fronts. We'll use the current system to communicate what we want to say through our music, turning the weapon of mass media against those who wield it. We will also remain in contact with the different revolutionary organisations and grass-root groups, to allow us to take stock of opportunities to step onto the field of struggle.

The first concrete action of the FLIP was a joint concert at Faculté Dauphine on 5 February '71. The bands on the bill were Fille Qui Mousse, Dagon, Komintern, Maajun, and Musica Elettronica Viva.

Other events organised by the FLIP were explicitly political, such as the guerilla-style concert organised on 18 March '71 at Saint-Ouen flea-market to celebrate the centennial of the Paris Commune.[5] A band composed of members of Komintern, Red Noise, and Fille Qui Mousse played on a moving flat-bed truck at the centre of a wild demonstration. The performance lasted only fifteen minutes before being brought to an abrupt end by a mass of police.[6]

Pop Music ran a report from François Joffra: "The FLIP brought musicians to the Marché au Puces to celebrate the centenary of the Commune. The dream was music in the streets, free of charge, with the participation of onlookers. Sadly the police shattered the spell. Those responsible for the crackdown showed a fear of the instinctive need for artistic freedom. Quite rightly. The storming of the Bastille, a couple of centuries later, would've taken place to the rhythms of rock and roll."

To the dismay of the bands involved it quickly became obvious that radical leftist groups were determined to take over the FLIP. Alain Roux wrote, "Various groups (from the Ligue Communiste to the VLR) weren't able to tolerate an autonomous movement that'd developed apart from them. Every time the FLIP concretely intervened, its activity was co-opted. This quickly led to it being scuttled."

The groups involved in the FLIP continued to play together after its dissolution, but without any official affiliation. A new attempt to create a united front was made by the Rock-Music Liberation Front. Their manifesto of October '72 read (in part):

"Rock-Music smashes the glacial apathy of urban systems. It's the scream of those who fear suffocating or starving to death in concentration camps of mediocrity. The scream of those who have realised the "pathetic poverty of reality" (as one of Marx brothers put it) and have decided to liquidate it...

"The many paths leading to authenticity run through a wilderness of market-relations, ambivalent relationships where death rules over life, where the parade of ghosts has no magic, and where one encounters only a jumble of ossified cadavers. Rock-Music struggles in this dense jungle, and in the end remains its prisoner. Through the spectacular relationship it maintains with the media, Rock-Music allows a new alienated image to be projected onto people, the stereotype of which is the 'pop-star'... In the end, the 'pop-star' is nothing more than a celebrity with access to every consumer product...

"It's obvious to the Rock-Music Liberation Front that the liberation of rock (and of music generally, and of all art) will come only with the revolution. Music as a separate form will be dissolved into the lived experience of everyone: 'PLAY THE MUSIC OF LIFE AND LIVE THE LIFE OF MUSIC' "

The text was drafted by Michel Muzac, and signed by Komintern, Lard Free II[7], Robert Wood's Tarot, Herbe Rouge, Barricade I (Crève Vite Charogne), Alpha du Centaure, and Barricade II (Roquet et ses Lévriers Basanés).

Like the FLIP before it, the Rock-Music Liberation Front ended up more notable for its ideas than for any concrete results. Nevertheless, Dominique Grimaud points out that these groupings and the bands they brought together were essential to the development of the French underground music scene: "It was a rather brief era, beginning in '68 and coming to an end quite early in the '70s. But it leaves traces. It explains a lot of the behaviour and the decisions made by most groups in the following years."

Notes

1   Victor & Regoli, *20 ans de Rock Français*

2   Elsewhere Pinhas warns against viewing the politically-engaged groups as representing a widespread popular movement: "To be realistic, the politically committed groups reached four to five thousand people at the most. It was a movement at the fringe of the fringe."

3   Paul Alessandrini reported in *Rock & Folk*: "Rushing through the breach opened by Red Noise, a whole batch of 'politicised' groups played on stage for the first time: Barricades *(sic)*, Fille Qui Mousse, Maajum *(sic)*."

4   Note that "to flip" *(flipper)* was also Parisian slang for getting high.

5   The Paris Commune holds a key place in France's revolutionary history. Its participants, known as the Communards, governed Paris from March to May 1871. A counter-revolutionary attack by the army known as "The Bloody Week" ended the Commune. The fighting left 15,000 Communards dead, many believed to have been summarily executed.

6   The photo on the cover of this book shows Patrick Vian of Red Noise being arrested at this event (it featured on the front page of *Tout!* n° 11, 29 March '71).

7   Lard Free II was a short-lived band formed by Gilbert Artman that ran in parallel to Lard Free when the group split in mid-'72.

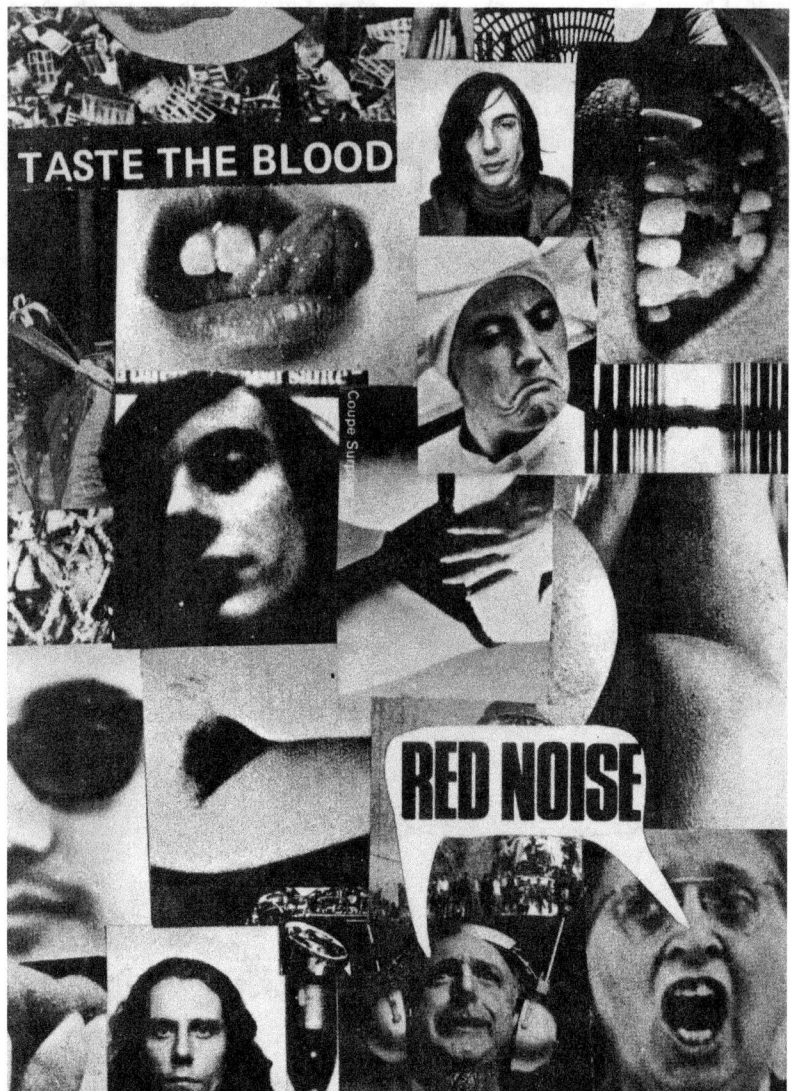

RED NOISE

> I wanted our music to be a kind of rubbish bin: we threw in scraps of popular songs, noises, anything, stirred it all up, and dished it out as it came. We wanted to demolish, to throw everything away. If others want to reconstruct afterwards, that's their job, not ours.
>
> *Patrick Vian*

While many of the French musicians of the early '70s claimed May '68 as a pivotal moment, only one band was actually forged in the white heat of the *événements*. They were an amalgam of anarchist and communist musicians that played their very first gig at May '68's ground-zero: the courtyard of the occupied Sorbonne.

Thierry Lewin recalled that moment a few years later: "May 1968. The students occupy the Sorbonne. An atmosphere of festival and freedom is spontaneously created. The old university becomes a small-scale model of the society of the future. To bolster the festival some young people bring their instruments, set up and play... Spring 1968 ends, but the band continue playing their music, keeping the ideas of the May movement alive. The band is called Red Noise."

With such auspicious beginnings it's hardly surprising that Red Noise would go on to become one of the most legendary bands of the era. Writing in '72, Jean-Pierre Lentin (himself a member of the band Dagon) called it "the first underground band... a symbol, the unrivalled reference for a whole new generation of groups."

Red Noise was both band name and manifesto; its music a sonic explosion of insurgency. Guitarist and instigator Patrick Vian was joined by Daniel Geoffroy (bass), Serge Cattalano (drums), and Francis Lemonnier (sax). Vian was son of the notorious Boris Vian (an accomplished jazz trumpeter, writer, and doyen of '50s bohemian Paris), and while the rest of the band were practised musicians he was defiantly amateur. In a 2013 interview Vian made it very clear that it was attitude and not any sense of musical "quality" that mattered to him at the time: "I wanted to show that to make music it was enough to take an instrument and go on stage. It was just a question of nerve. We're called pre-punk and it's true that the one thing we did was to thoroughly fuck with the sound."

The band's *laissez faire* attitude to their own music prefigured some of punk's anti-music ethos. Likewise Red Noise presaged punk attitude with their audience provocation. According to Vian they were determined to make music "that doesn't try to make people forget their little day-to-day problems, but makes them realise that their problems are bigger than they ever imagined.

"In the beginning, a good Red Noise concert only ended when the cops intervened. We started the only group that was able to say: anyone can go stage and play, no-one will notice anyway. And that didn't bother us."

While the band's sound and attitude was transgressive, its members were aware that Red Noise could hardly be called a "revolutionary" band in the political sense, even though radical politics informed their music and performance. The tension between the band's politics and music-making was made manifest on stage, as Vian was at pains to point out:

"Instinctively you want to be appealing, or rather cause a reaction. There's always an immense fear of indifference. Whatever happens, the audience has to respond. People will like what we play on stage to the extent that we exteriorise their internal rebellion. They'll come to see a violent act... I'm for a music that's disturbing, I don't like music with a 'message'. I'm against music as the 'opium of the people' but I'm aware that as far as our music has appeal we'll also become the opium of the people."

Red Noise also knew that the incendiary device of their music ran the risk of being defused by the music business, but as Vian stated: "Revolutionary songs have been sung for a thousand years, and the revolution doesn't look like it's coming closer. We have to try something else... I don't believe in pop music's revolutionary influence. Bands just want to become an advertising medium: to sell toothpaste and clothes. I don't believe in the undermining of values, and that kind of thing: we've been talking about that for the last decade. My old man told me that the same thing happened in the be-bop era, it's always the same shit."

The reaction the band elicited from audiences and the press suggested that their attempt to do something revolutionary was at least partially effective. An article in *Rock & Folk* testifies to the visceral impact of the band at their peak: "There's no respite. Red Noise set off a blinding explosion... a noise that crushes your innards, that blows minds to pieces... It is raw violence, constant aggression. These long screams, this sonic madness, are possibly unique in pop music. The guitar is no longer a musical instrument, but a wooden object emitting sonic shocks with the aid of echo chambers, distortion, effects, and wah pedals. The audience is initially bewildered, then riled up."

Musician and writer Dominique Grimaud was in the audience at an early Red Noise concert, and described the epiphany of their performance: "A scream. Slogans. Almost continuous electric guitar feedback from beginning to end. Patrick Vian left the stage with his guitar howling against his amp... I was in heaven."

Red Noise made a surprising first appearance on vinyl backing ingenue Marie-Blanche Vergne on her single *La Veuve du Hibou* (released by Columbia in February '70).[1] The song is a strangely beautiful collision of Red Noise's free-jazz-freakout with Vergne's jaunty acoustic ditty, sounding for all the world as if the recording engineer was tuning between two adjacent radio stations with radically different programming policies.

In May '70, just months before making its only album, Red Noise was rent in two, when Serge Cattalano and Francis Lemonnier left to form Komintern. Olivier Zdrzalik (one of their new bandmates) explained the situation: "Patrick Vian considered music to be revolutionary in itself, with its shattering of structures, and that was enough. Francis Lemonnier, who was really the thinker of the group, didn't agree. He thought it should be based on a discourse and, in the literal sense of the term, say something."[2] (This would be the path taken by Komintern.) To fill the vacancies left by the schism Jean-Claude Cenci was drafted in on sax and Philip Barry on drums.[3]

It was this new line-up that recorded the album *Sarcelles-Lochères*, produced in a single-day session on 28 November '70, and released by Futura in January '71.[4]

The album title appears mysterious until you lay eyes on a photo of the Lochères district of Sarcelles (a satellite town of Paris). In the '50s and '60s high-density housing projects held the same appeal to the authorities in France as elsewhere, and had pretty much the same end result. The liner notes of *Sarcelles-Lochères* bluntly states: "There are more suicides here than anywhere else." Obviously Red Noise had a point to make.

But, there are two sides to every record - and it isn't until the second that the significance of the title becomes clear.

The first side of *Sarcelles-Lochères* seems to reveal a band in thrall to Frank Zappa. Constructed from a collage of skits and musical sketches (a significant number written by Phil Barry, Red Noise's new scatology-loving English drummer[5]), it veers from the sublime to the ridiculous. There is toilet humour ('Cosmic Toilet Ditty', the introduction to 'Galactic Sewer Song'), rock'n'roll pastiche ('Caka Slow/Vertebrate Twist', 'À la mémoire du rockeur inconnu'), free jazz ('Obsession Sexuelle'), and some surprisingly funky grooves ('20 Mirror Mozarts Composing On Tea Bag And ½ Cup Bra', 'Galactic Sewer Song'). *Rock & Folk* praised this side of the record: "Its structure, its form, its approach... is unique in France, and possibly in pop music... a cinematic montage, with scenarios, breaks, sped-up sequences, and collages." Fine as it is, Side One is really only an interesting *amuse-bouche* to the coming feast.

Side Two opens with yet another skit, however 'Petit precis d'instruction civique' (Little Handbook of Civic Education) serves up something completely different to Barry's toilet humour. Its call-and-response chant unmistakably conjures up the spirit of May '68: "The police: *they're shit!* The army: *it's shit!* The law, members of the jury: *it's shit!* Religion: *it's shit!* Patriotism: *it's shit!* Capital: *it's shit!*" One reviewer described this as "a rock thrown through a window" to prepare the listener for the coming sonic blast.

On 'Sarcelles C'est L'avenir' (Sarcelles is the Future), Red Noise finally unleash. Extra heft is loaned by the addition of organist John Livengood (of Planétarium, a band that frequently shared the stage with Red Noise) and percussionist Austin Blue Warner. *Actuel* lauded the track for approximating the intensity of the band on stage: "a completely free improvisation where the sound intensifies to a scream. The approach is close to free jazz without being an imitation of it. Red Noise have arrived at this fury by exploring the potential of pop music's electrification, and screams from *banlieus* and grey cities raging against day-to-day boredom and alienation."

Indeed 'Sarcelles C'est L'avenir' does scream, and it bruises; it ebbs and flows in squalls and deluges like a massive storm raging against the brutalist tower blocks that made Sarcelles such an oppressively drab symbol of modern life. Sarcelles might be the future, but it's not a future that Red Noise are going to accept without a fight. Reworking and re-contextualising Vian's opening quote: "We want to demolish, to throw it away. If others want to reconstruct afterwards, that's their job, not ours."

In *Rock & Folk* Philippe Paringaux praised the nihilistic beauty of the track: "You immediately sense their real desire and pleasure in smashing music open, making it into a feast, bursting out in every sense, breaking out through every crack, exploring every horizon... In the eighteen minutes of 'Sarcelles' there is a real sense of music and of beauty, a smashed, violent, dramatic, and joyous beauty."

'Sarcelles C'est L'avenir' is one of the pinnacles of recorded free improvisation: jazz but not jazz, rock but not rock... After sixteen minutes of combative extemporisation a kind of equilibrium is reached, which is then gradually breached by screams before building to a final crescendo. Vian's promised demolition is completed.

Nevertheless, those who actually witnessed the band live consider 'Sarcelles' to be but a shadow of the sonic fury they unleashed on stage. In his book *L'underground musical en France* Dominique Grimaud describes the album as "a half-success or a half-failure, whichever you prefer; still far from the sonic molotov cocktail they presented live." [6]

Unfortunately, like many of the first wave of underground bands, the release of their only album would prove to be the apogee of Red Noise's career. Phil Barry left not long after the recording session. His initial replacement was Austin Blue Warner (the percussionist on the album session). He was followed by Marc Blanc (ex-Ame Son) in mid '71. Blanc was already in the band's circle, in fact it's *his* toilet that makes an appearance on 'Cosmic Toilet Ditty'.[7] He confirms that after he joined Red Noise they continued to play in their free-wheeling experimental style ("we never rehearsed, and played free with no restrictions") but recalls only a handful of concerts in and around Paris during his ten month tenure.

The remainder of '71 saw Red Noise continuing to lose ground. There was an attempt to create some momentum at the beginning of '72, with *Rock & Folk* reporting that a second album was in preparation.

In February Vian spruiked the band's new musical direction in *Actuel*: "Today our music is built on sonic experimentation. We want to improvise, but also create four or five very short, fastidiously-rehearsed pieces. Above everything else it has to shun categories... the important thing is to make music that has some *effect*." However nothing was ever recorded, and a few months later Red Noise dissolved.

In a 2013 interview Vian took some of the responsibility for the band's downward spiral: "I lacked that Napoleonic side needed to lead a band. At one point with Red Noise, we almost managed to make music *(laughs)*. We came to understand each other, things were going well. After that, everyone had to be directed... I hated that."

Red Noise may not have been able to maintain their explosive promise, but they do remain an important totem of the French underground. Their very existence encouraged many of the second wave of underground bands to take up arms and continue the fight they had begun.

After Red Noise dissolved, Patrick Vian joined Dagon. He then discovered the sonic potential of synthesisers, and went on to record a solo electronic album in 1976. He died in 2023, at the age of 80.

Komintern was founded by Serge Cattalano and Francis Lemonnier immediately after leaving Red Noise in May '70. Its story is recounted in Chapter 16.

Notes

1 Michel Musac (of Komintern) sheds light on how this collaboration came about: "The connection was made by the lyricist Étienne Roda-Gil, who knew Francis Lemonnier from May '68. Gérard Pompougnac, who wrote the music, played guitar so Patrick Vian didn't take part in the recording."

2 In a TV interview on *Pop 2* Lemonnier himself explained: "There was a political and musical disagreement... [Vian] didn't agree with the idea of having texts over the music, thinking that music was revolutionary in itself and that was enough. We were in favour of integrating texts into the music."

3 Apart from their guest appearance on Marie-Blanche Vergne's single, the only other documentation of Red Noise's first lineup is in a short interview and music clip shown on French TV (available on YouTube).

4 Futura's Gérard Terronès was particularly proud of Red Noise's record: "The toughest record, the most politically anarchistic, was Patrick Vian's. That well and truly took a crap on the face of music." *(La France Underground, p.85)*

5 Barry was also a guitarist. It was actually his guitar playing that features on the first side of the album.

6 Marc Blanc (of Ame Son) also highlighted the difference between the record and live performances: "On stage Red Noise played completely free, noisy and free; nothing like the record, which is more 'normal'."

7 "I met Red Noise through Paul Alessandrini who was sort of their manager... At the beginning of '70 they came to my place because I had a Revox tape machine, and recorded a few things like the toilet and the tune 'tout ça c'est de la merde'. I was impressed because Patrick was the son of Boris Vian who was kind of a legend for our generation." *(Marc Blanc)*

BARRICADE

> This time it's just too much, there are groups being political on stage! ... for almost an hour a lamentable band named Barricade, scaled the summit of mediocrity: with insults and incoherent music. Worst of all, the audience seemed to like it! You have to condemn this decadent "popularisation" without delay.
> *Letter to the Editor (sent by Barricade themselves),*
> Best, *Sept '70*

As noted previously, a flood of ink has been spilled discussing the influence of the Situationist International on the development of British punk rock (with Malcolm McLaren's machinations behind the Sex Pistols touted as exhibit one). Amp McLaren's provocations up to eleven and you get some idea of Barricade's *modus operandi*. Fist-fights with the audience? *Check!* Using and abusing the press? *Check!* Charges of petty larceny? *Check!* Music deemed to be barely listenable? *Check!* Blagging a contract with Virgin Records?... well... almost... However, unlike McLaren and co., Barricade (particularly founding member François Billard) were fully steeped in Situationist ideas.

On stage the band wilfully subverted the relationship between audience and performer. Billard: "Every concert was provocation first and foremost. Anything could happen; the audience was gleefully insulted, the organisers even more so." To help this process along, a variety of second-rate artists and undesirables they had just met were routinely invited to join Barricade on stage.

The commingling of trained musicians and absolute beginners illustrated one of Barricade's few guiding principles: membership was never to be based on musical ability, but on adherence to an ethos. A musician wanting to join would be instructed to take on a household chore for a few days rather than show off their musical chops. If they were deemed to have the Barricadian spirit they were inducted.

The spirit was key, and breaking with it could lead to a speedy exit even for erstwhile leaders. "Many people were able to be part of

Barricade... It was easy to 'get in', but very few were able to stay. There were no membership cards, but expulsions were very quick." By the time Barricade finally called it a day in late '74, dozens of musicians (and non-musicians) had passed through their ranks.[1] Among the most celebrated of the Barricade "alumni" are Hector Zazou[*] and Joseph Racaille of ZNR, and Cyrille Verdeaux of Clearlight.

Musically Barricade took their inspiration from Captain Beefheart, Dr John, and free jazz. Socially and politically it was a particularly anarchic and acidic reading of the Situationists. Billard confesses: "I was the initiator of that. The spirit was maintained and adapted in the 'anti-spectacular' practice of the different Barricades, without the need to resort to the Situ bible. There could be no relation to the Situationists other than total independence. The Situationists would probably have hated a pro-Situ band.

"We weren't politicised in the classical sense, we weren't militants. We were concerned that our lives bore witness to *something else*. We were the poorest and led the most 'dissipated' life which, for some of us, involved the almost daily use of hallucinogens."

Rather than take on society as a whole, Barricade aimed their actions squarely against their own subculture. The band's strange and convoluted career was one long art-attack on the vacuity of the music business and its self-deluded "rebel rockers".

"We were pretty clear-eyed about our limitations. As musicians we couldn't claim to be 'revolutionaries'... We could only take action in our little domain: denouncing the totally reactionary character of the rock scene."[2]

It was in their chaotic stage performances that the Barricadian spirit was made flesh. "The goal was to shake up the audience and to highlight the difference with the usual behaviour of musicians (underground or otherwise). The majority of our audience were drop-outs we managed to find everywhere we played. It was people like these who followed our 'advice' and attacked the closest supermarket after our first concert."

---

[*] Pierre Job (who was known as Roquet-Belles-Oreilles in Barricade) would gain fame afterwards under the pseudonym Hector Zazou.

Barricade began life as a duo in '69, with François Billard on saxophone and vocals, and Gérard Lapeyre playing violin and harmonica. "At the very beginning it was just Gérard Lapeyre and myself playing in dingy bars around Marseille. At that time my influences were mainly Captain Beefheart and free jazz, with The Rolling Stones and blues harp for Lapeyre."

After a few months the duo expanded to become a quintet. Bass-player Pierre Job would become the other hub of the band, balancing Billard's anarchic energy with his desire for order. It was Job who found Barricade a rehearsal space and a drummer (Thierry Gazeux a.k.a. Kühl the Clown). The line-up was completed by Simon Dahan, a guitarist who had played with Billard earlier in the '60s.

Billard: "When the group became a quintet Job came with his Black Sabbath-era hard rock background. Gazeux was probably in the same waters as Job, and Simon had a great knowledge of blues and blues rock."

Barricade's first public performance was at the Festival de Port Leucate in July '70, billed alongside Ame Son, Red Noise, and the UK's East of Eden. Their performance in front of a stunned audience was deemed a success. However, it was the aftermath that was most significant. Barricade used the event as a springboard to launch the first in a series of audacious press offensives.

Friends from all over France were encouraged to send letters, in turn eulogising and vilifying the band, to the music magazines. A surprising number were published:

> "I want to mention a band whose music and ideas left quite a few people speechless. They are Barricades *(sic)*, who it seems were making their French debut." (*Best*)

> "I had a laugh at some clowns called Red Noise, and even better (wait for it) Barricade... Little politicised jerks who want to play music even though they're incapable." (*Rock & Folk*)

> "For the first time I witnessed the audience's desire to transcend the stage of musical consumption... the catalyst mounted the stage, a group whose name doesn't attempt to hide their politics... and 3,000 people stood, raising black flags. The cloud of dust kicked up by the dancing crowd made me dream of the smoke of revolutions." (*Rock & Folk*)

There followed an appearance at the Biot Festival in August. Billard: "Lester Bowie and Roscoe Mitchell spontaneously joined us on stage, so did Marc Hollander and Paolo Radoni (the leaders of [Belgian band] Here and Now). Festivals are where we found our 'true' audience."

In September '70 Barricade appeared at Festival Rock des Biscuits Belin[3] near Marseille. The group entered the afternoon "battle of the bands" multiple times, under a variety of fanciful names. Each time they were immediately eliminated. That evening the competition's organisers were astonished to see the same band (this time under their own name) playing on the main stage just before Magma.[4]

As intended, the band polarised opinion. Jean Tronchot of *Rock & Folk* wasn't impressed with what he witnessed that night: "Barricade creates an atmosphere of apocalypse with a certain sense of humour. At least I hope they do. Because if they take themselves seriously... Anti-conformism? Sure. The singer, with a litre of red in his jacket pocket, screams: 'Down with culture'. OK. Getting high, madness, the anti-bourgeois scream? Why not. But musical oblivion in the service of hysterics and paroxysm? Ah, no."

While some, like Tronchot, just couldn't see the appeal of Barricade, the rock press as a whole couldn't resist the allure of such a perverse band. Only too happy to oblige, Barricade took the opportunity to increase the flow of provocative missives and pure disinformation. The press carried reports of Barricade performances at fake art exhibitions, bogus conferences, and ultimately the news that they were to be the first western band *ever* to tour behind the Iron Curtain.[5]

Barricade continued to play concerts at festivals and universities in the south of France into '71. Goading the audience became *de rigueur*. Billard: "We mostly played in front of an uninformed audience who couldn't believe their ears. La Gloute, Barricade's fake manager, would spend ten minutes on stage trying to auction off photos of his dog, infuriating the audience. Then they'd scream demanding that Barricade finally take the stage."

It was April '71 when the band made its first foray to the capital. Their appearance at the Festival de St Gratien to the north of Paris was briefly reviewed in *Superhebdo Pop Music*: "Barricade are the anti-spectacle, an outrageous provocation intended to incite reaction. They make strange music, closely related to the musical explorations of John Cage and Captain Beefheart. It's just a shame that the late hour and weary audience didn't allow for the confrontation the musicians were expecting."

Returning to the south of France, Barricade began to experiment with the idea of living in community. The impetus was a lack of financial resources rather than political idealism. In the process they squatted in a number of buildings - including one with incredible musical provenance.

Billard: "We moved into a magnificent house in the countryside, near Aix. It belonged to Pierre Schaeffer, the great pioneer of contemporary music. We rented part of it, then squatted in the rest. Schaeffer had thought that he was leasing the house to decent law students from Aix." When Pierre Schaeffer travelled south for his August vacation, he found himself cohabiting with a horde of intransigents, until he was finally able to force their eviction.

In September the band relocated to another country property outside Aix, next to a psychiatric hospital. Billard: "La Rigoutière was an open house. Sometimes we'd run into a nutcase; one day a hitch-hiker we'd picked up put a razor to the driver's neck, which luckily didn't go any further... There were very pretty girls, a rare few musicians passing though, drug dealers, the toughest hitch-hikers and *michetonneuses* ('independent prostitutes') who came from Marseille to change their ideas in the countryside. In short it was an ideal place for people reputed to be disreputable." It was during this period that Jean-Louis Tixier (who would become central to the later history of the band) joined Barricade.

Not long after setting up at La Rigoutière the tensions between the anarchic Billard and the more controlling Job began to create fault-lines in Barricade. Billard: "The question of leadership was quite complex. Like it or not, there were kind of two 'leaders'. Pierre Job often played the main man, but participated little in daily life, with its playful side and daily excesses. On the other hand, he did organise most of the rehearsals at La Rigoutière. As for me, I often slipped away to see this or that girlfriend in Marseille or Aix-en-Provence, or to play with L'Ecole des Caillols.[6]

"There was a total incompatibility between Pierre Job's vision and my own (which was much more utopian regarding the running of the community). A free culture wasn't very compatible with the post-Satie-in-the-making."

Job wrote about the inevitable split in an unpublished article for *Actuel*: "Barricade followed the path of 'political music' up to its split in '72, which was the fruit of its first experiment (read: of its failure) in living in community. The two powers who complemented each other in the creation of the group confronted each other in everyday life. They divided up their troops and separated."

The outcome of the split was the creation of two new bands: Barricade I - Crève Vite Charogne (CVC), and Barricade II - Roquet et ses Lévriers Basanés. Barricade I ("Die Quickly Bastard") was centred around François Billard (sax), with Gilbert Gambus (drums), Francis Montesinos (guitar), and Jean-Louis Tixier (sax) following him from Barricade. Barricade II ("Roquet & His Swarthy Hounds") was composed of Pierre Job (bass), Fanfan Belles-Cuisses (keys), Pépée Minègue (flute, vocals), Manfred Kovacic (sax), and Thierry Gazeux (drums).

A retrospective piece in *Actuel* described the differences between the two bands: "From Barricade have come two groups who share the same resounding aggressiveness towards everything conformist. Crève Vite Charogne (Barricade I) practise free improvisation on various instruments, and numerous blunt, metallic or utilitarian objects that few have dared to bang together on stage. Roquet et ses Lévriers Basanés (Barricade II) are more organised but make noises that are just as astonishing, seasoned with grotesque choruses and incongruous interjections."

Barricade I viewed itself as the most explicitly radical of the two bands. With Billard at the helm it attempted to retain the pro-Situationist orientation and loose organisation of the original band. Their musical style drifted more towards free jazz, with a heavy emphasis on brass.

Billard: "I had the feeling that rock was suffering the effect of banalisation from the overuse of the guitar, not to mention from the reign of the guitar hero. CVC's musical orientation was very brass-based, let's say in an attempt to replace the guitar in rock. It was about keeping rock's energy and trying to invent a slightly new sonic arsenal by *detourn*ing instruments, combining a trumpet with a saxophone mouthpiece, for example.

"Relations with Barricade II were very good, although 'cool' with Job. At concerts (we were booked at the same festivals a number of times) we occasionally found ourselves on the same stage. We displayed a similar, let's say complementary, attitude to provocation. Otherwise, in everyday life we didn't join together. The fundamental opposition between Job and myself remained."

Barricade I survived for only a matter of months after the scission of the original band. Their last concert was on 18 July '72 when they shared the bill with Gong in La Ciotat. Just before the final dissolution they did, however, manage to orchestrate a last Barricadian provocation at the Bièvres Festival (held near Paris in June '72). The Dominique Gaumont trio had found themselves without a drummer, so were unable to play a planned tribute to Jimi Hendrix. Barricade I came to the rescue, offering their own drummer to step into the breach. It soon became apparent to Gaumont that accepting the offer had been a terrible mistake. The borrowed "drummer" was actually Billard, a saxophonist, who unleashed an apocalyptic "free jazz" drum solo forcing Gaumont to make a hasty exit. Happily this allowed Barricade I to begin their own set earlier than expected.

When Barricade I wrapped up, several of its members simply moved across to Barricade II. One of these was saxophonist Jean-Louis Tixier: "I stayed with François when he started Barricade I. But after a few months Barricade I ended and I went to Barricade II with some of the other musicians... There was really very little difference between Barricade I and Barricade II."

At around the time that Tixier joined Barricade II, Joseph Racaille was also recruited. "In the Autumn of '72 I saw an ad in the Aix-en-Provence university restaurant for an electric piano. It was being sold by Barricade, and I eventually bought it. They suggested that I play with them (without having any idea how well I played). So they kept the piano, got some money, and a new member.

"It was fantastic, there were seven or eight of us, with two girls (and I was strongly in favour of diversity). We could play music all day and all night. I didn't really know how to play piano, but nobody gave a damn. It was a big open workshop, you just had to come up with something worthwhile, and I had a lot of ideas. I had good experience in collective musical work and even some practical experience of concerts, but in Barricade I really felt that I was fully embracing the dream I'd pursued for years... I wasn't even 19 and I was already in Heaven!"

Racaille's description of his first performance with Barricade II proves that it continued the spirit of provocation found in the original band: "A friend who was a restaurant chef cooked a goose which we ate on stage around a table, like 'The Last Supper' by Leonardo da Vinci. The concert was scheduled to start at 9:30 p.m. and the audience arrived to find us in the middle of our Christmas meal.

"Finally, at about 10 p.m. we took our places one after the other. Roquet[7] grabbed his bass, gave the table a huge kick that knocked it down, and we started to play. It was my first concert with Barricade and, as the poet said, 'nothing ever looked the same again'. At the end of the concert, Roquet began to insult the audience and a free-for-all fight ensued, a custom it didn't take long for me to become familiar with. I tried to participate in that as little as possible, but it wasn't always easy."

Racaille's captures so much of the Barricadian spirit in his description of everyday life in the band that it's well-worth quoting in full.

> "We lived in a small house, named 'Campagne Bianco', about five or six kilometres outside town. The permanent residents at that time were Roquet-Belles-Oreilles (later Hector Zazou, his real name being Pierre Job), his wife Fanfan Belles-Cuisses (pregnant, at the time), Pépée (Fanfan's sister), Manfred Kovacic, and myself.
>
> "Roquet played bass, Fanfan played piano and organ (but I took the piano, so she only played organ after I arrived), Pépée sang and played the Pakistani flute, and Manfred played clarinet and alto sax.
>
> "There was also Thierry dit Kühl le Clown, a very nice guy who couldn't stand Roquet's authority. He was a brilliant drummer who made thunderous entries, like a sack of potatoes rolling down the cellar stairs. He left not long after I arrived, having just had a little girl and needing to feed his family.
>
> "Speaking about Roquet-Belles-Oreilles (in case you didn't

know, that's the French name for the blue dog in the Hannah-Barbera cartoons: Huckleberry Hound) is complicated for me because the image of Hector Zazou has practically replaced that of his previous avatar.

"He was very much the leader in the band, and even more so in the community. I didn't like leaders at all, but when I arrived I was very keen to fit in. So for a while I was happy to follow local customs and habits. I could see that the others obeyed him without question. Later his authority weakened a bit.

"He was always quite extravagant (except when he had administrative or other meetings). Tall with rather long, curly hair, he was already sporting a moustache and round glasses.[8] He had a tic (or OCD, I don't know which): when he was thinking or listening to someone speak (which didn't happen often) he tapped his top incisors with a bent thumb. You can't really say he was thin, rather that he was cylindrical.

"Pépée sang with a powerful, husky voice and incredibly inventive phrasing which, even if it didn't actually sound like it, was absolutely Beefheartian in spirit. She wrote some of the lyrics, less intellectual than Roquet, but more singable of course. She went so far as to parody Catherine Ribeiro, who at the time was one of the most well-known underground singers.

"She was also the one who found nicknames for the musicians. I never asked the historic Barricadians about it, but I guess the custom came from the Magic Band. I don't know how much an Anglo-Saxon can appreciate the acerbic humour of nicknames like Thierry dit Kühl le Clown or Gérard Manvu...

"For my part, I was given the name Allah Tienne, which would perhaps nowadays earn us a fatwa, but at the time it was an amusing pun on my christian name (Etienne) and to my inclination, already proven and still present, to 'bend the elbow'. Later, the name was developed through *i)* reference to the percussionist who played with Ravi Shankar, Alla Rakha and *ii)* the grumbling of the whole group about Roquet, the 'boss', who always accorded himself special treatment compared to the other members. 'It's really Roquet and the riff-raff (*racaille*)!', Pépée exclaimed one day, and suddenly my name was Allah Racaille. But no-one can be known as a deity for too long, and one fine day Pépée suggested that I rename myself Joseph. What a gift!

"Manfred was of Yugoslav origin, I believe he was born in Dubrovnik, but he had spent his entire childhood in Longwy, (not very far from Reims, where I come from myself). He studied clarinet at the conservatory of Marseille. He was, musically in any case, gifted. He left the conservatory at 15 with a first prize for clarinet which, even for Marseille, was a great achievement. He was a bit like the Ian Underwood of Barricade II, he knew how to do everything, and did everything well. His Barricadian name was Armand Talot.

"During concerts he had a hilarious ethnic routine. He'd unexpectedly come up to the microphone and start speaking in pseudo-Slavic (but maybe it was real Serbo-Croatian, which I think he spoke). Then he'd shout with a thick accent: 'I'm *biiig* socialist spy!'

"When I arrived Fanfan seemed quite enigmatic to me. She was 5 months pregnant and she spent almost all of her time in her room. I think she read, but above all else she slept a lot (that's what she liked to do, even when she wasn't pregnant). Pretty quickly, she stopped coming to rehearsals and, especially, concerts. She knew how to take advantage of her status as 'the boss's wife' but at the same time she wasn't at all submissive and could stand up to him. She was tall and beautiful, with a more classical, less wild, beauty than her sister, but didn't seem to take much interest in the commotion she created in the boys around her. She was built like a swimmer, with broad shoulders, a huge chest, hips that weren't very wide, and long, slender legs - hence her nickname Fanfan Belles Cuisses.

"Thierry dit Kühl le Clown was eventually replaced by Fernand Le Salé d'Arlès (Luc Heller), a psychotic and devilishly effective drummer. When he was very young he'd had a serious neurological disease (I think it was Huntington's Chorea, which killed Woody Guthrie) that you usually don't recover from. He'd done well, thanks to an iron will and his practice of drumming. He was regularly shaken by rather dramatic nervous tics, often accompanied by terrible cries, but the practice of his art calmed him for several hours.

"He was a great drummer, very powerful and consistent. Having joined the group, Fernand was taken care of by Pépée who even put him in her bed, to the chagrin of Roquet who, for hierarchical reasons, would have preferred that she sleep with me (he reproached her for it in my presence).

"There was also Mario Branlo (J-L Tixier) and Marcel Morabito, previously associated with Barricade I, who had just returned to Barricade II. Mario Branlo played amateur sax and barked post-Situationist slogans and Marcel Morabito played electric guitar.

"Not long after Mario brought his comrade from the sanatorium where they'd both been treated for tuberculosis. Daniel Barbetti seemed likeable enough to be integrated into the group, but didn't know how to play anything. We thought about it and agreed that he was the right person to play the violin. So we bought him a violin and a reverb unit and he became our violinist under the name of Gato Montauban.

"Also in the 'gang' was our roadie Dédé la Frite, a guy from the North of France. He was a kind of vagabond, basically homeless, very strong, and almost illiterate. Every now and then he'd crack up, climb into a police van, and fight the cops. He'd do a few weeks or months of jail time. Then he'd keep a low profile until one day it was too much for him, and he'd do it all again. I think it was a kind of self-regulation, his stays on the inside must have helped him dry out. He treated his stomach and liver complaints by drinking pure pastis, without water. So, inevitably..."

While it's clear from his recollections that Racaille fully embraced the Barricadian spirit, one of the band's most celebrated alumni found it much too nihilistic for his liking. Cyrille Verdeaux would go on to attain success with his own band Clearlight, but in Spring '73 he found himself a member of Barricade II. "I don't remember how the first contact was made, but I knew they were looking for a keyboard player. So I went to their house near Marseille with all my gear: Wurlitzer piano, Leslie cabinet, echo chamber, etc.

"There was Hector Zazou, a violin player nicknamed Paganini, a drummer with a neurological disorder, who couldn't control his moves, except when he was drumming... very strange. A roadie that I knew from before... A few girls also...I forget their names (it was a long time ago!) I also invited a guitarist, Fred le Vicomte Electrique, to join me in Barricade. We'd previous played together in a band. [9]

"Basically, I don't have very fond memories of these few months spent with them. Nobody had money. They were stealing a lot of stuff from stores, including an electric guitar. Because they called themselves 'anarchists' they had no problem with robbing people. Including me...

"All of my gear disappeared from my home in Paris a few weeks after I left their house in Marseille. I was in London negotiating my contract with Virgin... One of Barricade's roadies knew where I lived, we were friends... the door hadn't been broken, and I have no evidence, but...

"The other problem I had was that the music they were playing on stage had nothing to do with the music we were working on at home. On stage it was mainly noise and meaningless sounds. The concerts were also pathetically organised with very low pay. I was disappointed, and realised that there was no hope of a glorious future with them!"

Verdeaux had left by Summer '73. Shortly after his departure, Barricade traveled north to Paris in an attempt to earn enough money to fund urgently needed repairs to their southern base.

To make cash quickly the band came up with an eminently Barricadian scheme. They simply "borrowed" the identity of the American band Bulldog, and armed with copies of their LP, fake business cards, and posters, secured a good run of gigs. By the time each venue finally twigged that this American band only seemed able to speak French, it was too late, and the show had to go on. Barricade continued this lucrative ruse until the real Bulldog scored a minor hit in France, and it was deemed too risky to carry on.

It was around this time that the band broke with a long-held tenet, entering a recording studio for the first and only time. Jean-Louis Tixier: "We weren't in the habit of recording. In two years we hadn't *ever* recorded. For us it was always about improvisation and we didn't want to set the music in stone. But when I went looking for work around France people told me that I needed a demo of the band. So we had to record some songs." [10]

Armed with the new demo tape Tixier scored a prestigious booking at a new Paris nightclub. "A big nightclub was opening. It was around the time of David Bowie and they wanted unusual music. So they chose Barricade. First up was a drag show, then us.

"In the first week a lot of the Parisian musicians came to listen, and wanted to jam with us. The week went so well that we signed a contract for another month. This was fantastic because we could get enough money to go back to the south and repair the roof! But the police came to the nightclub and found that their papers weren't in order, so it was shut down."

Thinking it would only be a matter of weeks before the nightclub reopened, the members of the band fanned out around Paris to bide their time. To make ends meet they performed in smaller groupings in the neighbouring towns, but never as Barricade.

After a month or two it became obvious that the nightclub was not reopening any time soon (in the end it took a year) and the band drifted back to the south.

While this Parisian interlude had been draining, *Actuel*'s review of a March '74 concert proves that the band hadn't lost their anarchic spirit:

"Barricade II is practically the only survivor of a generation of non-conformist groups created in the wake of May '68... Imagine dreadful hairy creatures, of both sexes, making an unbearable cacophony with their huge, filthy amps at maximum volume. Red Noise you tell me. Yes, but there were four in Red Noise, there are eight in Barricade II. The outcome: it's even more unbearable than Red Noise, and therefore enjoyable enough provided you have a psychopathic and bloodthirsty disposition.

"They start with 'Mekanik Depannajh Desvoitürh', a wicked parody of Magma.[11] They continue with a terrible racket and pounding of unprecedented brutality. A considerable volume of red wine is downed, and they quickly reach a more bestial state. The violinist draws pitiful groans of agony from his unfortunate instrument... The drummer thrashes with manic delight..."

While the spirit was still strong, Job's authoritarian behaviour had been creating tension within the band for quite some time. In fact Joseph Racaille left Barricade not long before this concert because of it.[12] However, if he'd bided his time Racaille would have seen Job himself deposed just months later.

Tixier: "Pierre was probably the most creative musician, but he was difficult to live with. There was a clash in the group, and he was thrown out because he'd hidden the supply of chocolate! It was an absurd pretext, but for Barricade it was for the best. It was in the spirit, and it was the opportunity to do it. So we continued Barricade, but without Pierre."

Shortly after Job's exit Barricade's already storied career took possibly its most bizarre turn.

The band's attitude to recording was, in line with its general ethos, totally scornful. Only once had they begrudgingly entered a studio to record the demo that booking agents had demanded.

Joseph Racaille: "To us music was something that was living, there was no question of stuffing and mounting it, of fixing it permanently...Barricade was really a live band. In addition we mistrusted record companies from a political point of view, to us they were the lackeys of big capital (and still are, probably even more so).

"I remember a meeting where we discussed the possibility of releasing a Barricade LP. We were trying to work out the best way to make it unplayable: a blank disc, scratched, sticky, or putrid, with a hole right through it to break the stylus, or with frequencies that would destroy the stereo, etc."

This attitude remained uncontested until the band received a surprise offer, with the real proposition of recording an album.

Jean-Louis Tixier traveled to the UK in August '74 to visit guitarist Chris Wiley (who had briefly played in Barricade, before returning to finish his studies). Wiley had a meeting arranged with Virgin's Richard Branson, and invited Tixier to come along.

During the meeting Wiley speculatively passed Barricade's demo tape to Branson. Tixier still sounds surprised when he relates what happened next: "Branson listened and got in touch. He told us that he thought it was great, that we were the new Captain Beefheart!" The Virgin boss offered Barricade a six-date tour of UK universities, followed by a recording session at The Manor.

"So we decided to get together in September to rehearse, before going on the university tour and making the record in November. At the time we had a very good guitarist, a very good drummer and a very good sax player. But we needed a good bass player.

"I was the worst musician, but I was the catalyst of the group. I was organising everything, being the mediator, and I was getting tired of it all. So I suggested that we do the tour, make the recording, then stop. After that everyone would have their freedom.

"Because I wanted the disc to be a powerful memento of this great adventure I decided, against the opinion of the others, to ask Pierre to play bass again. Pierre had a lot of the spirit of the group, and we wanted to finish all together in a spirit of friendship."

Among the musicians brought back into the fold for the project was François Billard. Job wrote of this period: "The two survivors of this sad tale, who had laid claim to the name Barricade planned to reform the group, gathering together all of its ex-members. Around ten of them accepted the idea to meet... But the Barricadian mystique returned, with its confusionism and contradictions. Once again everyone began to believe that their power was independent of their, sometimes stormy, relations with the others... The bad faith and misunderstanding of the past five years returned..."

Tixier's recollection differs markedly, and his account is disarmingly blunt: "When we started to practise together again, Pierre started to break our balls again! *(laughs)* He was being difficult, and there was a difference of opinion. Pierre wanted to play different music, somewhat in the style of Erik Satie (like he did afterwards with ZNR). The rest of the group wanted to finish by recording a disc that was faithful to what we'd played for the past four or five years.

"So when that began, it just became too complicated. There were lots of questions, and no answers. There was no fight, I just got bored of it. I was at the beginning of a relationship that was important to me, and I just wanted it all to stop. So we broke up."

In retrospect Billard believes that this project was doomed from the start: "The result was predictable: the group never signed the contract, and this episode led almost immediately to our breaking up... It can always be said that submitting the recordings marked a backwards step with regards to the group's radical attitude to the media. Barricade were far too extreme to honour that kind of commitment. Its attitude could be considered to be suicidal... it was hard to see Barricade calmly pursuing a career on a label like that."

During their existence Barricade often told the press that they would only ever consider releasing an album after the year 2000. Of course, in the early '70s that was shorthand for *never*. But in 2005, to the surprise of anyone who still remembered the band, a Barricade CD (*Le rire des Camisoles*) appeared.

Jean-Louis Tixier had stumbled across a treasure trove of recordings, including the legendary demo tape that had attracted Branson's attention.

"I'd made a few recordings when we played different concerts at Maisons de Jeunes and universities. I put all the tapes in a suitcase, stored it in my parents' cellar, and totally forgot about them. Twenty-five years later my parents told me they'd found a case full of tapes and that I should listen to them."

Tixier contacted François Billard and Manfred Kovacic (who by now was the owner of his own recording studio).

"I took the tapes to the studio, not expecting anything to be on them after all this time. And all the tapes were good! They'd kept like good wine in my father's cellar!

"So we were listening to this music that we hadn't heard for twenty-five years. Listening to them was like having acid flashbacks. We put together a selection on CD to give to everyone in the group.

"A few weeks later Manfred, who had music contacts, mentioned Terronès, the legendary label owner. I called him on the phone and told him that I was listening to Barricade's music. 'What, you have songs by Barricade! I'll release it!' "

Billard points out that all but one of the recordings on *Le rire des Camisoles* are from Barricade II.[13] "Zazou must have destroyed a good number of tapes, apart from those that actually involved Barricade II. Nothing that CVC played was recorded.

"All the same, some live recordings of Barricade II testify to the spirit of Barricade (e.g. 'Dubble Pépée Blues'). I'd call it the Beefheartian aesthetic, which was even more present in CVC. The recording most representative of Barricade's live spirit is "Lorient Express" (a long extract from a concert). Paradoxically it's from when Zazou was no longer in the group! I would have been proud to have been!"

François Billard continues to play music, but is today better known as a jazz critic and writer. Since the mid-'80s he has authored over a dozen books and published articles in Guitar Magazine, Musician, *and* Jazz Magazine.

Pierre Job (Roquet-Belles-Oreilles) changed his name to Hector Zazou and formed ZNR with Joseph Racaille and Harvey Néneux in '75. Néneux left before the recording of their first album and went on to teach classical guitar at the Marseille conservatory.

After ZNR came to an end in '80 Zazou went on to international renown as a composer. He released sixteen albums before his death at age 60 in 2008. Joseph Racaille went on to release eight albums of his own compositions.

Manfred Kovacik (Armand Talot) played saxophone and keyboards in the bands of Alain Bashung, Jaques Higelin, and Sapho. He currently runs his own recording studio.

Jean-Louis Tixier (Mario Branlo) became a lawyer and still has his own practice. He is also currently deputy mayor of La Ciotat.

Luc Heller (Fernand Le Salé d'Arlès) drummed and recorded with Mama Bea, Jacques Loussier, and Jo Corbeau.

François Billard gave a partial account of some of the rest of Barricade's large cast of characters: "The multi-instrumentalist, Francis "le baron des grottes" leads a salsa orchestra. Gilbert "Sulma Pontoise" played drums with Paul Mauriat before becoming a sound engineer at major sporting events, including the Olympic Games. Fred "le vicomte électrique" has led several groups particularly in England."

Notes

1   Twenty-two musicians are listed as contributing to the compilation CD 'Barricade 1969-1974' - and this was not the full roster by any means!

2   Elsewhere Billard has commented that Barricade "was originally built on a number of very simple ideas: that the rock scene wasn't characterised by wit or intelligence, and that the subversive character of music was often over-exaggerated... We had the material means and a particular desire to attack the rock scene, not to 'make the revolution'." *(Fuzzine Blog)*

3   Belin, a famous brand of French biscuits, sponsored the event.

4   Barricade's performance that night was an hour-long collective improvisation (with extemporised lyrics by Billard) entitled 'I Owe My Most Beautiful Nights of Passion to Belin Biscuits'.

5   Barricade II's concocted tour of Yugoslavia purportedly took place in January '73. A member with relatives in Yugoslavia had primed them to send both pro- and anti-Barricade reports to the French music press. Joseph Racaille: "*Actuel* was very interested. They asked us to write an article on rock in the East, and we did! We wrote about our tour, invented Yugoslav groups that we'd played with, etc. It was quite believable, because Manfred took care of the geographical and linguistic details. But *Actuel* didn't accept the article, because they found it too anecdotal, it wasn't general enough!"

6   Billard: "L'école des Caillols, which some of the musicians from Barricade played in, was the true radical matrix of Barricade. It was much more concerned with free jazz. Pieces lasted some fifteen minutes, or even more." Two of the musicians from l'école des Caillols had joined Barricade on-stage at the Biscuits Belin festival in September '70.

7   As mentioned previously Pierre Job was known as Roquet-Belles-Oreilles in his Barricade years.

8   When he took on the name Hector Zazou, Job also adopted many of the affectations of a classical composer. His round glasses and moustache became an important part of the Zazou persona. Job's road-to-Damascus conversion to "serious" music occurred when Racaille introduced him to the work of Erik Satie: "Inevitably his enthusiasm was a bit overbearing, and every morning we found ourselves listening to France-Musique, a radio station that broadcast mostly scholarly music. Manfred (who had a 'classical' education) almost got a going over by Pierre because he knew all of this music but he'd never mentioned it!" *(Racaille)*

9   Verdeaux doesn't recall meeting Joseph Racaille. It's unclear why their paths didn't cross in these few months.

10   The band at the time of the recording of the demo tape were Pepée Minégue (vocals), Pierre Job (bass), Luc Heller (drums), Fred the Vicomte

Electrique (guitar), Jean-Louis Tixier (sax/vocals), and Charly Bidineux (sax). The keyboard was credited to Cyrille Verdeaux, but as he can't recall ever recording with the band, it is most likely Joseph Racaille.

11   This title (based on Magma's 'Mëkanïk Dëstruktïẁ Kömmandöh') is a fine example of French wordplay. It is phonetically identical to 'Mécanique dépannage des voitures': 'Car Repair Mechanics'!

12   Nevertheless, only a year later Racaille would team up with Job (by now known as Hector Zazou) in ZNR.

13   The only recording of the original Barricade on the CD is 'Ah qu'elle est triste cette soirée!'

MAAJUN

> The label told us, "You can record whatever you want to." They never had the notion that it would sell at all... They pressed 545 copies of our album. Well, you don't run the risk of cultural revolution with that!
>
> *Jean-Louis Lefèbvre*

While Red Noise was France's first political rock band, Maajun was the first to record and release an album. Curiously their LP was released on Vogue, a major French label. Inevitably this marriage of radical politics to commercial interests would not lead to a lasting and happy union.

Maajun came together in Autumn '69 when Jean-Pierre Arnoux (drums, sax, vibes), Cyril Lefèbvre (guitar, organ), Jean-Louis Lefèbvre (bass, violin, vocals)[1], Alain-Noël Roux (sax, flute, harmonica), and Roger Scaglia (guitar, vocals) joined forces. Unlike the majority of underground groups Maajun was made up of relatively seasoned musicians.

Alain Roux and Cyril Lefèbvre had played as an acoustic blues duo for more than five years. As Roux explains, "Cyril and I were in the same *lycée* when we were young. We began to play blues around 1963/64, copying Sonny Terry & Brownie McGee... Cyril played a 12-string guitar with a bottleneck slide, and I played harmonica. Our duo existed *long* before Maajun."

Jean-Louis Lefèbvre and Roger Scaglia met while on national service in Germany. Their first performance together was a Christmas concert of Beatles songs in their barracks at the end of '66. Scaglia: "We rehearsed for months getting that together, it was quite serious. When they saw what we were capable of we became involved in cultural relations, going around Germany playing as the French military band."

On leaving the army and returning to Paris, Jean-Louis Lefèbvre introduced Scaglia to his musical circle, and they formed a vocal group, Les 5 Apôtres. Scaglia: "I'd say we were like a French version of Crosby, Stills, Nash & Young. Doing beautiful harmonies, playing poppy, but intelligent music... nothing heavy or avant-garde like Maajun."

Keen to succeed, the band sought out Christian Fechner, the manager of Antoine and Les Charlots. He took them on, changed their name to Le Musical College, added a drummer, and brokered a recording contract with Disques Vogue.

An EP recorded at the beginning of '68 was scheduled to be released mid-year but was delayed by the aftershocks of May '68. J-L Lefèbvre: "The disc was due out in June, but then came the general strike. I was furious (I was a student at Censier but couldn't have cared less about the demonstrations). It came out too late, right in the middle of releases from the Vogue stars... so it was a flop."

The catalyst for the formation of Maajun came when Jean-Louis Lefèbvre met Jean-Pierre Arnoux, a drummer with a background in free jazz. "In '69 I went to work in my old high school, supervising students. The school was only a hundred metres from Jean-Pierre's place, and we became friends. Together we discovered Vanilla Fudge, King Crimson, Hendrix, The Mothers of Invention, Pink Floyd, etc. And hash, of course..."

Arnoux had a connection to Cyril Lefèbvre, and invited him along to play guitar. Alain Roux was away travelling through Palestine, but when he returned he was recruited: "Cyril had started playing blues with Jean-Pierre on drums and Jean-Louis on bass and violin. He told me, 'You've got to come along'. So we had a combo, called The Blues Unit. When I joined I was playing harmonica and guitar."

Roger Scaglia had also been out of Paris for a few months, and on his return he was integrated into the group. At that point Roux made the brave decision to switch instruments: "There were too many guitarists *(laughs)*. I'd never played saxophone or flute before. So Jean-Pierre lent me his saxophone, and I learned. Then Jean-Louis said it'd be good to have flute in one number, and I said 'OK, I'll do it'. So I went and bought a flute."

Jean-Louis Lefèbvre's prior connection with Disques Vogue landed Maajun a recording contract at the beginning of '70. The home of stars Françoise Hardy, Antoine, and Jacques Dutronc seems an odd fit for a revolutionary rock band. According to Scaglia the label seemed oblivious to the fact that Maajun was a very different proposition to Le Musical College: "The musical director was a very nice guy, very professional, but he didn't truly understand what we were about, who we were. He was thinking: it's not my cup of tea, but they're good, they could make some money these guys." Roux concurs: "He came to see us at a concert and said 'OK, it's good. Let's try.' But I'm quite sure he didn't understand the lyrics!"

Roux had been a sociology student at the Sorbonne when May '68 hit, and became heavily involved in the protests ("I was wounded on the barricades, blinded for three weeks, with tear gas directly in the eyes"). He brought a strong political angle to Maajun's lyrics.

The other members had been affected by May '68 to varying degrees. Roux: "The period was *hot* you know. Leftist ideas influenced everybody. The rest of the band followed the movement... to a *certain* point *(laughs)*." Jean-Louis Lefèbvre: "There was tension between a Situationist orientation, represented by Alain Roux, and the Zen orientation of Cyril Lefèbvre. I swayed between the two leanings, then later on we definitively chose the leftist inclination."

This political edge was balanced by another important lyrical influence on the band. Roux explains that there was actually a *sixth* member of Maajun: "Gérald Escot-Bocanegra wrote a lot of the lyrics. I wrote leftist, engaged texts, and he wrote poetry influenced by Rimbaud and Lautreamont. I was a political activist, he was an activist poet, and I think our two energies drove the band. There was a sort of fusion between my ideas, Gérald's poetry, and a foundation of blues. If you look at Maajun's lyrics they're a kind of mix of poetry and politics."

Roux credits Escot-Bocanegra's contribution with giving Maajun the opportunity to widen their musical palette beyond blues to take in free jazz, rock'n'roll, traditional French songs, as well as Indian and Middle Eastern music.

According to Scaglia, it was he and Jean-Louis Lefèbvre that brought the more exotic folk influences into the band: "Indian modal music, electronics... I would have loved to bring that kind of music more into Maajun, but no... They accepted *some*, so there is a bit of Indian raga on *Vivre la mort du vieux monde*." Scaglia also highlights another important influence on the band: "We knew Gong very well, we went to parties with them. We had a lot of respect for them - they were right at the edge. Gong was the biggest inspiration, and I loved them because they weren't political."

In Maajun's early days there were very few live performances, and certainly none with any major public exposure.[2] The emphasis was on writing and rehearsing. Roux: "We rehearsed a lot, about three or four times every week. At that time everyone in the band wanted to express himself, nobody was in the background, everybody wanted to bring something. It was a really intense time."

The roles that each member played in the band seems to have been somewhat contested at the time.

Scaglia: "From the beginning Jean-Louis and I wanted to make it in music, we wanted to be musicians. Together we were the driving force. Jean-Louis was the leader technically. I had a very good relationship with him, but he had the biggest ego in the world. I'm not saying that in a bad way - he *was* very good, but he said so! I accepted it because he taught me a lot music-wise."

Roux: "Jean-Louis wasn't the leader - but he was kind of a reference... because he knew how to write musical scores. I can't read music, neither could Jean-Pierre or Roger. Cyril played piano when he was young so he knew music theory. When we had an idea Jean-Louis tried to quickly write it down. For the arrangements we all worked together."

J-L Lefèbvre: "I wrote everything on the record that is 'written' ('L'Orgasme' etc.) while I was at work supervising (!) students. The improvised tracks (like 'La chanson du boulot') were created in the moment around the lyrics. Cyril wrote the 'Comptines'. Afterwards we shared the credits in the interests of egalitarianism."

Scaglia: "We tried to share the writing. Jean-Louis wrote the most. I think two of the band weren't writing at all. I wrote three or four of the pieces on the album: the music for two and the lyrics for two."

The band took on the name Maajun just before they entered the studio to record their album. The choice was explained in an interview with *Actuel*: "Maajun is a hashish confectionery you find in Morocco. It was totally by chance that we took it as our name. One of us came back from Morocco and we were talking about maajun. We liked the name and gave it to the group."

When the newly-christened Maajun entered the historic Studio

Vogue in Spring '70 they were well-drilled and ready for action. Roux: "When we came into the studio we knew exactly what we wanted to do, the whole album was ready. We were very proud to be in that studio. Sidney Bechet, Miles Davis, and Françoise Hardy had all recorded there." Scaglia: "It was one of the best times of my life... a very exciting time for all of us. It was intense work, no fucking around, but still very relaxed."

The five-day session went smoothly, with most tracks captured in live takes. Roux: "I think we made the album in five days, four days recording and one day to mix. It wasn't difficult to mix because it was only four channels, just like The Beatles *(laughs)*."

J-L Lefèbvre: "Four tracks! All the songs had been rehearsed, and everything, except for the vocals, was recorded at the same time. The mix was transferred to two tracks and vocals and effects were added - I turned the tape over on 'La chanson du boulot' so the echo came before Roger's voice!"

While most of the songs on the album were completely composed, there were also moments of improvisation on the record. Roux points out that the opening track, 'Avertissement' was completely improvised.

Scaglia also highlights this free element as essential to the spirit of Maajun's music. "There's a bit of free jazz in some parts, completely freestyle. Jean-Louis was saying 'Play these notes', and I said, 'Let's be free-form, let's not try to organise this too much, we'll begin to lose the essence.' There are sections on the album where we go three to four measures with Alain playing whatever he feels like on saxophone and me doing the same on guitar. But then *'boom'!* You can do all the shit you want, but when you all arrive at a point precisely together, that chaos is going to become *divine*, because organised chaos is divine."

The sessions at Studio Vogue produced *Vivre la mort du vieux monde*, an album that traverses blues-rock, heavy psychedelia, and folk, with leavening from Indian and Latin influences, a smattering of free jazz wildness, and even the odd wry blast of accordion.

According to Roux the flow of the album was carefully planned: "It was a concept album from beginning to end. For us it was logical. We wanted to explain all the questions, all the problems, all the contradictions we were living at that time. We began by saying: 'Okay, pay attention, we're taking the time to tell you about things that are important'.[3] Then we went through a sort of review of love, relationships, and political demands. Then if they understand, normally the crowd applauds *(laughs)*. That's it!" [4]

While the music may have been somewhat confronting to a label like Vogue, in the end it was lyrics infused with revolutionary politics and libertine poetry (song titles like 'The Long March' and 'The Orgasm' are indicative) that shocked them. The label point-blank refused to release the record. Scaglia: "The people at Vogue said 'What the fuck is that shit!... Are they on drugs or what? This is *horrible!*' "

Roux: "So we recorded the LP and Vogue said: *we cannot issue that! (laughs)* First, it's not in the mood, it's not trendy... It's breaking with the rules and we *knew* that - it was too *new*, you know. Then we had discussions with our producer and we said, we want to play free concerts. And Vogue said, '*What!*' *(laughs).*" [5]

J-L Lefèbvre: "The artistic director told us that the bosses didn't give a damn about the success of this kind of LP."

A piece published in *Actuel* explained the predicament the band found themselves in:

"When the company's management heard the tape a new problem arose: tracks called 'L'Orgasme' and 'Choeur du peuple las' ['The Weary Peoples' Chorus'] that spoke of *"Travail Famille Patrie"* * over an ironic Marseillaise, of 'The brigade of pleasures forbidden by the law...' and of '[taking] up arms to transform the old world'...

"It was far from the diverting and inoffensive music needed to take over from a *yé-yé* in decline; this music had the sulphurous scent of stormy festivals and ever-present protest. Thus the disc was judged 'unmarketable' and locked in a vault."

Indeed the album would remain in Vogue's vaults for almost a year. Had it been released in early summer '70 as scheduled, Maajun's position at the forefront of the French underground scene would have been secured. Instead the band had to engage in a long guerrilla campaign to force their own label's hand.

Roux: "To get the album issued, we did a few things. First, in July we went to the Valbonne Festival in the South of France. We played

---

* This phrase ('Work, Family, Motherland') replaced the French national motto of *Liberté, Egalité, Fraternité* ('Liberty, Equality, Brotherhood') during the reign of the despised, German-backed Vichy government from 1940-44.

on the same stage as Country Joe McDonald and Gong, so it couldn't be ignored. And we had good press."

Surprisingly their appearance at Valbonne was Maajun's first major public performance. Their second was two weeks later at the Biot Festival. It was at Valbonne that the band met Komintern and developed the connections that led to the formation of the FLIP.[6]

Maajun were encouraged by the strong reactions they received at these festivals: "There were people screaming 'Go back to Peking, Maoists' and there were people dancing everywhere. It was great."

The success of their festival appearances gave Maajun a platform in the music press, allowing them to agitate for the album's release. In an interview with *Rock & Folk* they took the opportunity to publicise their plight: "We recorded a disc at Vogue that's still in their vaults. They were frightened by the lyrics. So we were blocked by the authorities, their police, and their impresarios... stopped from expressing ourselves."

In another interview the band spelled out their motivation in making such a provocative record: "We recorded this disc above everything else to be able to express what we feel in the gut. Even if the simple act of releasing a record goes against our ideas about exploitation in the world of the spectacle, we decided to do it anyway. It seems more important to us to take full advantage of the system we're fighting against to express our ideas; in fact, we're fighting against society by turning its own means against itself."

An appearance on the renowned *Pop Club* radio show was what finally tipped the balance. Roux: "We played three songs live on *Pop Club*, and it was a hit. I mean, phone calls, things like that. On the programme we said that the album was being held back, and people phoned Vogue to say, 'You *must* issue the record!' "

The label finally relented and released the album in January '71. No cuts were made to the record itself, but Vogue refused to print any lyrics on the cover. They also ensured that the record was buried by pressing a ludicrously small number of discs: less than 2000 ("You know, for France that's *nothing!*" comments Roux).[7] Vogue's publicity machine was also conspicuously absent in any promotion of the album: "They completely forgot us after they issued the record, there was no relationship with Vogue afterwards."

Just as *Vivre la mort du vieux monde* was finally being readied for release, pressures within the band came to a head. One of the last concerts Maajun would play was in Gagny, in the east of Paris in late '70.[8] Although it was a success, the police had turned up in force and tried (but failed) to stop it. According to Roux the events of that night caused Jean-Pierre Arnoux and Cyril Lefèbvre to rethink their positions within the band.

"I think at one moment Jean-Pierre and Cyril were afraid, because it was dangerous. They didn't want to be involved in any more political concerts. It had become too much, they couldn't bear the weight. And they felt that they weren't in control of the evolution of the band.

"They wanted to make a musical career, but Vogue didn't want to make any effort for us. There were no bad feelings, it was a gentleman's agreement. What's funny is that the record was issued one or two weeks before we split... That's the story of Maajun! *(laughs)*"

Jean-Pierre Arnoux and Cyril Lefèbvre had left Maajun by the end of January '71. The band had been booked to appear at Faculté Dauphine on 5 February '71 (with Komintern, Fille Qui Mousse, and Dagon); a review in *Rock & Folk* tersely reported, "Maajun didn't play, as some line-up problems were still unresolved."

These problems remained unresolved for several months. Roux: "Jean-Louis, Roger, and I were looking for another drummer and lead guitarist, but without hope. We tried to go on with the band until Spring '71. And there was a disagreement between Jean-Louis and me politically. He was also afraid to go too far, because he was thinking about his musical career, which wasn't a problem for me."

Of this final period J-L Lefèbvre simply states: "I don't recall a sudden break-up, there was a lassitude, and no concerts. I don't remember anything else."

In Autumn '71 Jean-Louis Lefèbvre and Jean-Pierre Arnoux would regroup as Mahjun with the addition of Pierre Rigaux (sax) and Philippe Beaupoil (bass). However in the interim Maajun had something of an afterlife.

Shortly after Alain Roux had left, Arnoux rejoined J-L Lefèbvre and Scaglia to take on a major project scheduled for June '71. "Gisele Today" was a re-imagining of the classical ballet as a multimedia event, which ran for two weeks at the American Center in Paris (from 7-21 June '71).

Scaglia remembers these shows as one of the musical highpoints of his time in the band: "It was one of the best concerts we'd ever done. The show was truly extraordinary. We performed with a group of French dancers, about thirty beautiful girls inside a huge covered swimming pool emptied of water. The stage was at the deep end, and the ballet dancers were in the rest of the pool. The audience was above on wooden bleachers all the way to the ceiling.

"The music was completely new, we put in some of the stuff that we'd been working on, but we had to make new music for the play, a tango for example. We rehearsed two months for that show. There were flyers, spots on television and on radio. For us it was a big deal."

Unfortunately while Scaglia remembers the event as a career highlight, an event during the two-week run led to his own forced departure from the band.

"In the middle of the run I came on stage, and I was tripping... I don't exactly know what happened, but when I came to play I was tripping. And that didn't go very well with the other members. I couldn't find my guitar! *(laughs)* I played very well that night by the way, but I was too high, I shouldn't have done that. That started a very bad vibe..."

When another, more personal, conflict arose between Scaglia and Arnoux the writing was on the wall for the guitarist.

"I had to leave because Jean-Pierre made an alliance with Jean-Louis, and they basically told me to go. They thought I wasn't serious, I was using drugs, I couldn't be trusted: we'd always said we'd never trip on stage - and I did."

With Scaglia's departure Maajun was definitively finished.

Jean-Louis Lefèbvre and Jean-Pierre Arnoux created a new band, named Mahjun, in Autumn '71. The name may have been almost identical, but the musical direction was markedly different from Maajun - with a strong folk influence, touches of jazz, and even a splash of circus music. Mahjun released three albums between '73 and '77.

In '79 Jean-Louis Lefèbvre started on a successful solo career under the name Jean-Louis Mahjun. He continues performing to this day.

Jean-Pierre Arnoux played in folk-rock band Malicorne for many years, as well as playing in the first line-up of Catalogue with Jac Berrocal and Jean-François Pauvros. He died in 2002.

Cyril Lefèbvre went on to release three solo albums between '76 and '79, featuring his own idiosyncratic take on left-field acoustic folk and blues. He died in 2012.

Alain Roux played on Cyril Lefèbvre's first solo record, then formed the group Lapins Bleus des Îles with Michel Muzac and Olivier Zdrzalik (both ex-Komintern). In '80 his final band released the eponymous album Bluesdeluxe.

Roger Scaglia played in duos and trios around Paris until '72 when he left France for India. He travelled the world for many years, before settling in Australia.

Notes

1 Cyril and Jean-Louis Lefèbvre were not related. When Jean-Louis Lefèbvre launched his solo career in the late '70s he changed his name to Jean-Louis Mahjun (as he is still known today).

2 Roux was only able to recall one early performance that wasn't a low-key event for friends: "The first appearance of Maajun as a band was at Espace Lovecraft in the American Center in Paris, in Autumn '69. But it wasn't a concert, it was a kind of happening with other groups: Crium Delirium, Ame Son maybe, and Bashful Beats (a real underground band! I think they lasted 6 months)."

3 The opening track of the album is titled 'Avertissement'. Note that this French word can refer to either the foreword of a book, or to a warning sign. Both meanings seem to be invoked in this case.

4 Indeed the last sound heard on *Vivre la mort du vieux monde* is a crowd shouting. Roux states, "That was the sound engineer's idea. We took ideas from every side, if it was good for the music, for the feeling."

5 "During the autumn, we played some free concerts around Paris - political interventions in Nanterre, in the faculty, things like that. That did *not* please Vogue! *(laughs)*" *(Alain Roux)*

6 See *Introduction* to this section for the story of the FLIP.

7 Jean-Louis Lefèbvre believes the pressing may have been as small as 500 copies.

8 In the book *Musique et vie quotidienne*, Roux gives a full description of Maajun's performance that night: "We organised a small festival at Gagny... several groups played, with a light show, slideshows of May '68 etc. During the show, there were some 'interventions'... It started very violently, then we played a fanfare, 'Le grande méchant loup'. People laughed. There were a few gentle pieces: 'Les alchemistes', with very poetic words. Then the whole suite 'La longe marche': a Tibetan piece with chanted words, a little bit of violin, very Brechtian, and a kind of very serious march, with very harsh words, another shot of Brecht, followed by a Samba, 'La chanson du bulot'. Then the people danced, it was very, very good. We had tried it out once in a school. The 14-15 year olds danced like crazy, with fists in the air. The last piece 'Vivre la mort du vieux monde' was the most climactic thing we could play, a kind of very hard rock, with really intense free passages. We played for one and a half hours with no encore." (p. 134)

KOMINTERN

> We wanted to interrupt the ball, to stop it dead with two spoken texts that put the record directly in question, by totally discrediting it. The momentary negation of the music would allow the eruption of a significant new whole giving the album a totally different impact... Little of the "ball" as we conceived it remains, the "dead rats" are everywhere, swarming under our feet, above our heads, the filthy beasts.
>
> *Komintern*

Cousins Michel Muzac and Olivier Zdrzalik began listening to music together as teens in the early '60s, developing a shared interest in British R&B. By the end of the decade they were both playing guitar and harbouring the vague notion of forming a group. A chance meeting with another Parisian guitarist, Pascal Chassin, during a summer '69 holiday in Majorca and Ibiza spurred them on. By year's end the three musicians were rehearsing together.

They experimented with a variety of styles, but according to Zdrzalik couldn't really settle on any one. This continued until the very end of April '70 when they finally ran an advert in *Le Pop* seeking "a saxophonist and drummer to form a Free-Pop group."

The unknown trio were stunned to receive a call from Red Noise's Francis Lemonnier (who along with Serge Cattalano had just split from Patrick Vian over musical and political differences). Zdrzalik: "We knew the name, we'd even seen them in concert. It was too good to be true... beyond even our greatest hopes." They had been looking for a sax player and drummer to play free-rock, and here were arguably the most experienced musicians playing in the genre! Lemonnier and Cattalano urgently needed musicians for a tour that was already booked supporting the UK's East of Eden.

Muzac: "We had a try-out together. Francis played a free, wild, violent, parodic, and ironic music with influences from Albert Ayler, Eric Dolphy, and John Coltrane. Serge was a particularly explosive drummer whose model was Elvin Jones. Pascal, Olivier, and I were very inspired by Captain Beefheart, The Mothers of Invention, and Soft Machine. After a totally wild free-rock jam, we decided to form a band."

Zdrzalik switched to bass, and Red Noise was reconstituted as a five-piece with two guitarists. However it transpired that Patrick Vian intended to keep the Red Noise moniker, so the search was on for a new name.[1] If the name of their previous band needed little interpretation, Komintern, the name Cattalano and Lemonnier chose for their new band, left no doubt as to their politics.[2]

The newly-christened band had only a matter of weeks to source gear and put together a set for their upcoming tour. East of Eden was at the peak of its popularity in France, meaning Komintern would be playing their very first concerts to expectant crowds in large venues.

Muzac: "We left on tour, heroically or suicidally according to your point of view, and found ourselves thrown onto the big stages of the Maisons de la Culture after very few rehearsals, without any sound-check whatsoever, and with just one long piece inspired by the free-rock jam from our first rehearsal..."

The tour proved to be a baptism of fire, with Komintern receiving "a mixed, even hostile reception" according to Muzac. However Philippe Constantin, managing the tour on behalf of East of Eden's French record label, could see potential in the new band. He had befriended Cattalano and Lemonnier in their Red Noise days (hence the offer to support East of Eden) and would remain a close confidante of the band, helping them to find gigs and advocating for them within his record label.

After this whirlwind period Komintern took a quick breather to flesh out their musical and political intentions. Cattalano and Lemonnier had split from Patrick Vian because they wanted their music to have a more overtly political voice - this would clearly be a major element in their new band.

Muzac: "Olivier, Pascal and I had obviously been engaged by the explosion of speech and revolutionary creativity of May 1968, by its libertarian and festive side. But we didn't adhere to the dogma and sectarianism of the 'classic' leftist groups... Serge was very involved with the militants and was close to the Trotskyist Ligue Communiste.

At that time Francis largely supported his ideas... In the early days the atmosphere was a little tense, and discussions were impassioned."

Zdrzalik: "We weren't really politicised at the time but this idea interested us and through [Cattalano and Lemonnier] we made contact with the Ligue Communiste... So we started to meet people, to think about what we wanted to say."

At the same time their musical canvas was broadened when Jean-Michel Berté (tenor sax and flute) was brought into the band by Pascal Chassin. This expanded line-up took time out to write and rehearse in the run up to the festivals of *L'été Pop*.

Muzac: "By the time of the 1970 summer festivals we were already playing more intricate music. Texts had also been added, which Francis or Olivier declaimed, haranguing the festival-goers. Olivier wore a grotesque mask that looked a bit like a skull.[3] All of this added a theatrical aspect to the concerts."

Komintern played at the three most important festivals of '70: Valbonne, Aix, and Biot. *Rock & Folk* featured two reports on their appearance at Aix: a positive assessment from Paul Alessandrini ("The subversive aspect, the reading of political tracts by a musician in a ridiculously grotesque Nixon-Pompidou mask, was challenged by the lyricism of the saxophone and the beauty of the melodies") balanced by a more ambivalent Jacques Vassal ("Is this group in the process of making the first 'Leftist co-option of pop'?... While waiting for the answer, they aren't as bad as is claimed").

At Valbonne Komintern met and befriended Maajun. At the end of the festival season the two bands arranged to share equipment and a rehearsal space in the cellar of Maajun's house.[4]

Now they finally had a permanent base, Komintern took the opportunity to refine their sound. Muzac: "The time had come for us to seriously rehearse and structure our free-pop musical agitation. Our system of musical collage came naturally and spontaneously, and we put together the long suite mixing revolutionary songs and free-pop sections that became 'Bal pour un Rat Vivant' ['Ball for a Living Rat']."

By the end of '70 Jean-Michel Berté (who had never really integrated into the band according to Muzac) had left, and in January '71 Richard Aubert was recruited.[5] Aubert's violin added folk and classical touches to Komintern's music. According to Muzac it was only after his arrival that the 'Bal pour un Rat Vivant' suite took on its definitive form.

One of the first performances with this new line-up was at Faculté Dauphine on 5 February '71. Yves Adrien from *Rock & Folk* was there: "The music of Komintern can seem austere and cold at first, but listen more carefully and you'll discover a whole jungle seething there. Judging by the number who dance at the group's concerts, it would appear the Parisian audience has overcome their initial distrust of this 'difficult' music."

In March '71 the band took part in the events organised by the FLIP to celebrate the centenary of the Paris Commune. Just two days after the ill-fated concert/demonstration at the Marché au Puces, Komintern took part in an even wilder event at the Ecole Normale Supérieure playing alongside Red Noise, Gong, and Barney Wilen.

Muzac: "It was a totally frenzied party where the intoxication of the audience reached new heights after the school's cellar of vintage wines was looted… The police intervened at dawn, but we'd already left. The next day there was a huge scandal raised in the media."

By the end of March Philippe Constantin was finally in the position to offer the band a recording contract with Pathé-Marconi. Within the company he had the support of Etienne Roda-Gil, the famous French lyricist, who according to Muzac "was won over by the idea of a group like Komintern with its provocative and anti-establishment aspect." As for Constantin he was attracted to both their music and politics ("He was in league with us, subverting the system from within seemed to appeal to him").

The first fruit of the association was a ten-minute feature on *Pop 2* filmed during rehearsals.[6] The depth of Constantin's involvement can be gauged by his support for Komintern's political goals voiced during an interview on the programme.

In July '71 the band entered the rather staid environment of the Pathé-Marconi studios to record their debut album (as part of EMI, Pathé-Marconi's studio shared some of the quaint customs of the UK's Abbey Road). Zdrzalik remembers, "The recording process was quite extraordinary for us. Think about it: we were six far-left musicians with long hair and flares mixing with sound engineers dressed in white coats working from 9 to 5!"

In spite of the potential culture clash the recording session went smoothly. The budget even allowed Lemonnier to augment his saxophone with brass arrangements provided by Jean Morlier (a popular band leader and multi-instrumentalist).

Muzac: "The recording went very well, the conditions at Pathé-Marconi were excellent. We had the large recording studio, and all the time we needed. The technicians were very knowledgeable and professional, as were the arranger Jean Morlier and the other additional musicians. Recording on a 'major label' obviously provided a lot of advantages."

Le Bal du Rat Mort (The Dead Rat's Ball)[7] is split into two complementary sides. The first, titled 'Bal pour un Rat Vivant', is taken up by the long, dazzlingly ambitious suite written at the beginning of the year. This freely traverses accordion-driven *bal musette*, fanfares, progressive rock, free jazz, and revolutionary songs.[8] Muzac: "It was a joyful and festive piece of music dedicated to all those who fought for the revolution against the dominant ideology, with a dramatic intensity in the evolution of the theme to end on a bright and optimistic note."

The second side, titled 'Le Bal du Rat mort', portrays the old, decadent bourgeois world. It features the very first piece the band wrote ('Petite musique pour un blockhaus' - born from the improvisations on their first tour) and a completely new song written in the studio.

Muzac: "One morning, when Olivier and I arrived at the studios we saw a beautiful black Gibson Les Paul. Tempted to try it out, Olivier played a chord progression, and I improvised lead guitar over it. That's how 'Fou, Roi, Pantin' was born. Olivier and I decided to make it into a vocal piece. Olivier found an Arthur Rimbaud poem about the Paris Commune[9], and Etienne Roda-Gil contributed to the final lyric."

While Cattalano and Lemonnier initially baulked at the idea of including a more traditional song on the album (even one with strong revolutionary imagery), Pathé-Marconi were enthused, seeing 'Fou, Roi, Pantin' as the obvious choice for a single.

The band left the studio happy with what had been committed to tape. However this was only half the story, because almost everything else to do with the album had been a bone of contention.

To mark the centenary of the Paris Commune, Komintern had included many musical allusions on the album. Pathé Marconi were fine with that, but the album cover submitted by the band was another matter. Muzac: "We put forward a draft cover created by a friend who was at art school. From a joint idea he'd *detourned* the cover of a US underground magazine drawn by Robert Crumb: a little rat with a bomb in his hand threatening to blow everything up, yelling 'The Commune was party time!'" This cover was rejected as too confrontational, and replaced with a painting by the revolutionary Mexican artist Diego Rivera.

With the cover already compromised, salt was rubbed into the wound by the sleeve-notes written by Philippe Constantin. Believing that the text badly misrepresented their politics, it was rejected by the band. Pathé-Marconi printed it anyway, so Komintern's album would come wrapped in a sleeve that significantly negated their own stance.

In an interview with *Actuel* the band bluntly expressed their displeasure: "The text on the sleeve is completely unrepresentative of the orientation of the group. It was inspired by a Leninist analysis that we totally object to. We demanded some lines underneath to state that we disapproved, but didn't have the right to say why."

In the same interview they spoke of an even more contentious intervention from their label. "We wanted to put entirely spoken passages on the album that challenged the status and function of the record, and of music itself. This was rejected... Our album is a huge compromise." The intention had been to bring the music to a crashing halt with a long speech attacking "work and commodities", that went so far as to critique their own record as a simple commercial product. For Komintern this was essential to the album's statement - daring to stare down the contradictions inherent in releasing "revolutionary" music into the capitalist marketplace.

It was Constantin, as their producer, who had refused to let Komintern record the two spoken-word passages. While the text of the main intervention has been lost, a shorter text that was to open the second side is preserved in the rehearsal footage broadcast on *Pop 2*. Just before launching into 'Hommage Au Maire De Tours' Cattalano and Lemonnier are seen declaiming a sardonic "capitalist creed":

> "I believe in private property, the fruit of the work of others, that will endure to the end of time.

I believe in the need for poverty: the supplier of workers, the mother of surplus labour.

I believe in an eternity of paid labour that relieves the worker of all the burdens of property.

I believe in the extension of the working day, the reduction of wages, and the falsification of products.

And I believe in the sacred dogma: 'buy low, sell high'.

I also believe in the eternal principles of our most holy Church: the official political-economic system.

Amen."

Only the "amen" was retained to incongruously open the album's second side. With the band's incendiary intention already defused in so many ways, Komintern had entered the studio to record what in their eyes was already a compromised album.

Today Muzac is sympathetic to the position Constantin had found himself in: "He was in a tricky situation vis-à-vis the label. On one hand he had free rein, but only in theory because, as Pathé-Marconi's employee, he obviously had to take into account what would or wouldn't be accepted by the label."

Le Bal du Rat Mort was released on EMI's prestigious Harvest imprint in November '71. Even if it had been artistically compromised, the album was very well-received by the music press and is still considered to be one of the most important French records of the early '70s.

Pop Music-Superhebdo: "Without ever falling into the musical jumble that was offered by the Red Noise album... Komintern suggests that a popular and political pop music could thrive in France."

Best: "Above all else this politically motivated band plays the card of musical derision, of provocation through a hyper-irony that even strikes some traditional revolutionary songs... 'Fou, Roi, Pantin', a successful adaptation of Rimbaud, isn't far from being the best French title of the year."

Even the UK's John Peel heaped praise on the album (which he also featured on his radio programme): "One of the LPs I bought was by a band called Komintern. They are, I imagine, French. Their LP is released on French Harvest and it is quite superb. Articulate, witty, played with remarkable skill and precision..."

The critical praise was capped by 'Fou, Roi, Pantin' being made

Single of the Week on José Artur's highly influential *Pop Club* radio show.

Despite the promising reception, the label's lack of energy in promoting the album suggests they believed Komintern had been let off the leash too much. "Pathé-Marconi's managers weren't happy when they discovered the content of the disc, no doubt thinking that our producer hadn't censored us enough, so they restricted the album's distribution." This effectively negated the momentum generated by the press and radio support.

Nevertheless, Komintern's growing reputation led to a number of offers to take part in prestigious events, one being the '71 Paris Biennale. For this event the band decided to stage an intervention rather than a concert. Muzac: "After a totally free improvisation and a text criticising commercial art written and read by Francis, we put our guitars against the amps, creating an enormous amount of feedback. Then we sat down amongst the stunned audience… watching an empty stage for the (rather long) time it took a Biennale technician to cut the sound." [10]

Soon after this "non-concert" Komintern took up an offer to take part in the production of Fernando Arrabal's play *Bella Ciao: la guerre de mille ans*. It would be a full-time proposition for the band, keeping them occupied for the first three months of '72. This meant there would be no more concerts in the crucial period following the release of their album. When asked about this decision in a contemporary interview they replied: "We're basically doing this to secure the survival of the group: to buy a van, a sound system, pay the rent…"

The production of *Bella Ciao* was a fraught process. Inspired by the events of '68, Arrabal attempted to write the play collaboratively with the entire production team, but this quickly led to divisions between those who saw the play as primarily artistic or political. The vagueness of Arrabal's instructions also created a situation where no-one in the production could actually understand the play's structure. Muzac: "After two or three weeks of gruelling rehearsals, the director, Jorge Lavelli, had lost any control over the situation in the face of the troupe's protests. As a result, we and part of the troupe decided to go on strike. Incredible for a play supposedly communicating revolutionary ideas! This went on for ten days, then, after some compromises were made rehearsals resumed."

After three months of preparation *Bella Ciao* began a four week run in February/March '72, on the main stage of the Palais de Chaillot.

Pathé-Marconi had encouraged Komintern's involvement, and afterwards saw an opportunity to release a song from the play as a single. Muzac: "It was to be released under the name of Komintern but neither the lyrics nor the music were ours, and the song was to be performed by the actress who'd sung it in the play."

Cattalano and Lemonnier refused to take part in the recording, believing it to be a totally commercial project far from the original spirit of Komintern. Despite their opposition the rest of the band entered the Pathé-Marconi studios with other musicians from the production. However the recording was a failure, and the project was abandoned.

The whole *Bella Ciao* episode had put a strain on Komintern and, with their motivation waning, they decided to take a break. It was at this point that Cattalano announced his intention to leave. There were several factors behind his decision: the internal dynamics of Komintern had been altered by working on the play so intensively, and the disagreement over the recording certainly played a part, but for Cattalano a major problem was the changing political orientation of the band. While he remained firmly aligned with the Ligue Communiste, Lemmonier and the others were increasingly embracing Situationist ideas.

The remainder of '72 would see Komintern maintain their high profile, but Cattalano's departure signalled the beginning of the slow disintegration of the original line-up. Lemmonier would take a leave of absence for several months in the middle of the year, and Pascal Chassin would be gone by year's end.

In the meantime the search was on for a new drummer. The cooler relationship with Constantin (who had reduced his involvement since the release of the album) and changes in the music scene meant the band also needed to find a manager. The solution to both problems arrived in the person of Gilles Yéprémian, manager of Lard Free. "Gilles offered to manage us and introduced us to Gilbert Artman, Lard Free's drummer. Gilbert played free in the spirit of Serge, so he joined the group and Gilles became our manager.

"Because of our participation in *Bella Ciao*, we hadn't had the chance to perform the album on stage since it was released. The concerts Gilles found for us gave us the opportunity. We'd developed more ease and confidence on stage by then, which *Bella Ciao* certainly had something to do with, and the performance aspect also took on more importance for us."

The band played several high profile gigs during '72, including some in support of Magma and Gong, but as for many bands of the era, finances had become a real problem. While their involvement in *Bella Ciao* had been fraught, the wages it garnered had been a godsend. Now they were back to living hand to mouth.

This was particularly difficult for Pascal Chassin, who had just become a father. He found himself having to leave the band in October '72. Muzac: "Pascal needed a more regular job... but he continued his interest in the group, coming to some of our concerts and taking photos for us. We've always remained friends."

After Chassin's departure, Zdrzalik was keen to add a second drummer to the line-up. Gilbert Artman agreed and introduced André Ghozland to the band, who in turn brought in Michel Bourzeix (a fellow drummer) to be Komintern's sound engineer. After a few weeks Ghozland and Bourzeix switched roles. Bourzeix's straight rock playing combined with Artman's freer jazz style to open up the rhythmic possibilities of Komintern's music.

Lemonnier was the next casualty of the band's continuing financial woes. He left in the spring of '73 after playing major concerts at the Biennale of Bologna and the Palais des Sports in Paris.[11]

Lemonnier's sax had always been a major voice in the band, and his departure led to a musical reorientation. Aubert's violin came to the fore, along with his predilection for a more "progressive" musical style. "After Francis left, Richard began to play a more prominent role in the group... Komintern started to play more progressive and less free jazz rock, based more around violin and guitar."

An article published in *Actuel* in March '73 suggests that the political leanings of the band were beginning to alter in tandem with the change in music: "Komintern has changed since its 'leftist' period, giving more time to instrumental research, but keeping a penchant for vocal eccentricities and theatre."

While Komintern continued to perform until the end of '73, the loss of so many of its old guard led to an erosion of the band's original spirit and vitality. Muzac: "After the departure of Serge, Pascal and Francis the group found itself emptied of a good part of its substance. Without them the band's fire gradually faded, we lacked motivation and inspiration to write new songs. We all agreed it was time to stop, and broke up at the end of '73."

The story doesn't quite end there however. According to Muzac, at the dinner after Francis Lemonnier's last concert some Situationist friends had spoken at length about a "project of *detourned* songs" which particularly interested the saxophonist. This resulted in a project parallel to Komintern involving Lemonnier, Muzac, Zdrzalik, Jacques Le Glou, and Jean-Louis Rançon. During '73 they entered Pierre Barouh's Saravah Studios to record four tracks (including two with music composed by Lemmonier).[12]

After Komintern dissolved its members remained on friendly terms, so it's not too surprising that Lemonnier approached Muzac and Zdrzalik again in '75 asking them to play on recordings for another project of *detourned* songs he had been working on with lyricist Guy Peterman. Peterman had taken some well-known songs and altered their lyrics, transforming them into revolutionary anthems. Rehearsals were held with vocalist Olivier Lorquin and drummer Marcel Bel[13], and a recording was made, again at Saravah Studios.

Muzac: "The music was very different from Komintern's album. It was performed in the spirit of original titles from the '30s/'40s, '50s and '60s. It was quite varied: there was a French song from 1935, an Eddie Cochran song from 1958, and one by The Troggs from 1966... I presented this rather violent music to Philippe Constantin and Etienne Roda-Gil to see if Pathé-Marconi would be interested, but that wasn't the case. I also approached other labels, but to no avail."

For decades these two sets of recordings made at Saravah Studios were thought to have been lost, but recently surfaced on the internet. It's certainly fitting that the last music produced by three of the five original members of Komintern would be made with such unambiguously revolutionary intent.

In the mid-'70s Serge Cattalano and Francis Lemonnier collaborated on a Situationist-inspired art project, producing a booklet of postcards depicting well-known Parisian sites with all monuments removed. Francis Lemmonier taught music until he tragically died in the late '70s. Unfortunately it is not known what became of Serge Cattalano.

After Komintern, Michel Muzac and Olivier Zdrzalik joined with Alain Roux from Maajun to form the band Les Lapins Bleus des Îles. When this band broke up in '76, Zdrzalik became the bassist for the folk-rock band Malicorne. In '81 he recorded a solo album, Photocopies, *for Virgin Records under the name Olivier Kowalski. With the end of Malicorne in '82, Zdrzalik turned his hand to record production. In '87 he become manager of Paris's famed Davout Studios.*

In '77 Michel Muzac joined The Partners (a Paris-based new-wave band), then in '80 formed the neo-rockabilly Macadam Cowboy with Eric Rice (ex-Rockin' Rebels). Muzac also took part in the sessions for Olivier Zdrzalik's solo album.

Pascal Chassin became a photographer after leaving Komintern, but continued to play music. In '79 he recorded a single, 'La Nouvelle Européenne' for Ballon Noir. On the recording he is backed by Muzac and Zdrzalik, with Jean-Pierre Arnoux of Maajun on drums.

Violinist Richard Aubert played in a number of short-lived groups (Violon d'Ingres, Divodorum) before joining the progressive rock band Atoll in '75. He appears on their album L'Araignée-Mal. *Aubert remained active as a musician into the '80s under the moniker Klassik.*

Gilbert Artman recorded three albums with Lard Free between '73 and '77. As Lard Free wound down in '78, he devoted most of his energy to his unique Urban Sax project. In the '80s Artman teamed up with Jac Berrocal and Jean-François Pauvros to create avant-rock trio Catalogue. Urban Sax continues to be active, more than forty years after it was founded.

Notes

1   Muzac: "Olivier, Pascal and I hadn't thought it would be possible to keep the name because of Patrick Vian; it was disappointing because we were excited about the prospect of calling ourselves Red Noise!"

2   The Comintern (The *Communist Intern*ational) was created in Moscow in 1919 to: "struggle by all available means, including armed force, for the overthrow of the international bourgeoisie." Musac: "For a 'politicised' rock group born out of their split from Red Noise (the Comintern being born out of a scission) the name wasn't lacking in humour."

3   Zdrzalik had tried to find a mask depicting the face of a "decadent bourgeois", and failing to find one had decided to make do with a skull.

4   Komintern also joined Maajun in the FLIP (see *Introduction* to this section).

5   Between Berté's departure and Aubert's arrival, Komintern made their first TV appearance on *Pop 2* (filmed supporting Kevin Ayers at la Mutualité). Interestingly none of the three pieces performed on this broadcast are included on Komintern's album.

6   The segment was filmed on 23 March '71.

7   According to Pascal Chassin, "The title was chosen by Philippe Constantin, and refers to a wild Belgian ball/carnival, that in turn referred to a popular 19th Century Parisian café-bar named Le Rat Mort."

8   These include the Italian song 'Bandiera Rossa' and 'Los Cuatros Generales' from the Spanish Civil War.

9   The chorus of 'Fou, Roi, Pantin' is taken from Rimbaud's poem 'L'orgie parisienne ou Paris se repeuple' in which he denounces the massacre that ended the Paris Commune in 1871: "Syphilitics, madmen, kings, puppets, ventriloquists / Why would Paris, that old whore, care / About your bodies and souls, your poisons and rags? / She's well rid of you, you rabble!"

10   This was the last intervention Komintern took as members of FLIP.

11   Their appearance at the Bologna Biennale, on 20 January '73, was Komintern's only performance outside of France.

12   Jacques Le Glou later brought in Michel Devy and Jean Morlier (who had worked on the brass arrangements for *Le Bal du Rat Mort*). The trio created more traditional *chanson* arrangements for the songs, and an album, *Pour En Finir Avec Le Travail - Chansons Du Prolétariat Révolutionnaire - Vol:1*, was released in '74.

13   Bel had played with Jacques Dudon, Robert Wood, and French-based US folk-singer Roger Mason.

FILLE QUI MOUSSE

> From its birth Fille Qui Mousse was a group that travelled in the opposite direction to the normal musical path. One of its distinguishing features was to be an illusory group, that's to say ephemeral, in a tradition found in the plastic arts. Indeed, the musical concept was greatly inspired by a blank book created by Pierre Restany, with nothing written on the front, back, or spine...
>
> *Henri-Jean Enu*

Of all the bands that emerged from the French underground, Fille Qui Mousse is by far the most enigmatic. Its main protagonist, Henri-Jean Enu, was an experimental artist who had founded the underground journal *Le Parapluie*. Already a major figure in the artistic counter-culture, *Actuel* called him "the pontiff of the Parisian underground." His vision for Fille Qui Mousse was as an extension of his work in the plastic arts, and as a consequence he speaks about his music in artistic and poetic terms. The opening quotation gives a flavour of this inclination, which serves to intensify the air of mystery surrounding the group.

Henri-Jean Enu was deeply entrenched in the artistic and political milieu of '60s France. Through friendships with Jean-Louis Brau and Jacques Spacagna he'd been drawn into the orbit of the Lettristes, attracted by their fusion of the artistic and the political - a central theme in his own art practice.

"As a painter at the beginning of the '60s I worked on the reverse of stencils that had been used in the printing of political tracts. They were impregnated with ink during the printing process, producing forms that wavered between the *informel* and the abstract, while retaining the memory of social struggles."

For Enu art was necessarily political; he intended his radical use of collage to be an expression of both artistic and political rupture. Inevitably he became involved in the May '68 uprising.

"Involvement in the events of '68 was just the logical continuation of an approach. At its core this phenomenon carries elements inseparable from the counter-culture and the underground. It birthed a set of cultural concerns that were the source of the themes of *Le Parapluie*. Music was also conceived as a bearer of values that had to contribute to the yearning for change, for social equality... Fille Qui Mousse was mobilised in this atmosphere of rupture and social struggle..."

* * *

In French music journalism there are a great many groups described as *"mythique"*. The literal meaning is "mythical", but what is really meant is "legendary" (although a surprising number of translations do insist on referring to "mythical" French bands!). In the case of Fille Qui Mousse, it's easy to argue that *both* translations are equally valid.

In its lifetime the band enjoyed legendary status within the French underground (aided and abetted by Enu's editorship of *Le Parapluie*). Posthumously Fille Qui Mousse also achieved quasi-legendary status in the English-speaking world, courtesy of its inclusion on the infamous Nurse With Wound List.

However, for decades there was virtually no information available about the band and absolutely no trace of an album purportedly recorded in '71. This led many to believe that Fille Qui Mousse had been added to the Nurse With Wound List as a hoax, as a truly "mythical" band. That was until 1994, when the fabled album finally surfaced.

The quasi-mythical nature of the band was even invoked during its existence. A contemporary article in *Actuel* commented: "Fille Qui Mousse embodies the ego-trip of Henri-Jean Enu... an ideal mythical group that belongs as much in the fantasies of its founder as on the concert stage." In recent interviews, those who had been close to the band also emphasised its virtual non-existence.

Alain Roux (Maajun): "Fille Qui Mousse was just a name. I knew the people, but I didn't hear of too many concerts by them. They were trying to build up a band but, you know, there was no realisation."

Dominique Lentin (Dagon): "First and foremost the group was

a concept for Henri-Jean Enu's album. It wasn't really a group that rehearsed much. There were five or six Fille Qui Mousse concerts? I actually never saw them play." [1]

Enu insists that the intention was always to create something ephemeral, saying: "Fille Qui Mousse was conceived as a bottle thrown on the waves of an ocean. Without any real will to endure." However the band *did* have a corporeal existence.

It was in the middle of '70 that Enu found a group of willing companions in his musical quest. The first to be recruited was Benjamin Legrand.

"I met Henri-Jean Enu through friends. He ran an excellent underground newspaper. I gave him a hand selling it, and even came up with a slogan that we'd shout out before concerts or at festivals: '*Le Parapluie*, sex, drugs, revolution: the lot! 3 Francs!' Henri-Jean was a pretty good guitarist - but completely crazy(!) and wanted to start a band."

Benjamin Legrand was from *that* Legrand family; the son of composer Raymond Legrand (who had worked with Maurice Chevalier) and half-brother of Michel Legrand (winner of three Oscars and five Grammys).

"I was glued to the piano from the age of six. With a father who was an orchestral conductor, a half-sister who was a jazz singer, and a half-brother who was becoming more and more famous in the '60s, I told myself that I probably wasn't going to have a career in music! There wasn't much room for another Legrand!

"My little brother Olivier was sixteen and had become an excellent young drummer. He'd taken lessons from the famous jazz drummer Kenny Clarke, who was teaching in Paris at the time. We recruited bassist Stéphane Korb, (who was also sixteen) and a friend of Henri-Jean (whose name I have unfortunately forgotten) who was a fantastic young violinist." [2]

Korb was from another famous musical family, son of renowned songwriter and *chansonnier* Francis Lemarque.

"My father met and worked with Michel Legrand in the '60s, and I met Benjamin and Olivier through Michel. We spent holidays together in a house my father owned in the Alps, and I would spend time at their house. Little by little we started to do things together, playing music. Olivier was very talented, he played drums and piano, and Benjamin played piano as well. They were two very creative men."

While Legrand senior was very dubious about his sons' involvement in an underground rock band, Korb's father was fully supportive of the endeavour, and even expressed an interest in producing their album.

"There was a brief relationship between my father and Fille Qui Mousse. Of course I told my father I played with the group, and my father, who was a very kind man, said 'I'd like to produce them.' He had a music publishing company called Éditions Francis Lemarque. So I told Henri-Jean, and we met with my father.

"But my father and Henri-Jean were from two different worlds. I don't think my father understood Henri-Jean. So when they met, he said 'Oh no, no, no! I never said that!' Henri-Jean was a bit angry with me, telling me that it had just been a fantasy in my mind."

This first line-up of Henri-Jean Enu (guitar), Benjamin Legrand (keyboard), Olivier Legrand (drums), and Stéphane Korb (bass) began rehearsing in the offices of *Le Parapluie* after business hours. The band was originally to be named Supermarket (Warhol's pop art was an acknowledged influence) before Enu settled on the more enigmatic Fille Qui Mousse.

From the outset improvisation was at the core of their music. While there would be a few more structured pieces on the album, live performances were always unplanned and unpredictable. As Korb describes it: "It was a little bit chaotic, but not *bad* chaos. It was experimental music. We just played - plugged in and played. Totally improvised."

Enu took Captain Beefheart as a model for their on-stage improvisations: "These could be compared to a session by the group around Captain Beefheart. We'd begin with an evolving beat, a melody line, and a sequence of a few chords. Everyone came out of themselves little by little, having random encounters, shooting out exploding fragments; every musician in tune with an improvisation that becomes so collective it reaches a convergence full of surprise and the unexpected."

Benjamin Legrand's description of this process is a little more prosaic: "On stage we didn't really know what we were doing... especially as we never planned what we were going to play. We started improvising, and at times that produced stuff that was really good. Everything depended on the state of decrepitude and dope that the different characters found themselves in."

This side of Fille Qui Mousse is highlighted by Legrand's description of the band's early concerts.

"One was at the Dauphine Faculty in Paris, with lots of different groups, some of them very militant, like Komintern... We were all high on different things and it was a kind of soup of intertwined improvisations which I remember only very vaguely..."[3]

"The next concert took place at the Ranelagh theatre. The sound was really terrible. Henri-Jean was completely stoned and fell behind the amps after ten minutes, Stéphane Korb also dropped out... (I can't remember if the violinist was still with us...)

"The person in charge of the theatre came up asking us to stop making this unlistenable 'noise'... So my brother and I began an organ-drums duet based on 'Light My Fire' by The Doors. We kept going for half an hour... it wasn't so experimental anymore, just rock'n'roll! When we stopped the audience gave us an ovation and wanted us to continue, but we just couldn't keep going!"

This would be the last appearance of the original line-up. Stéphane Korb was the first to leave: "I wasn't comfortable on stage... it was too much for me. As a young man I was very, very shy."

Korb rues the fact that no documentation of this original incarnation of the band remains, especially because he knows that a recording *was* made. "I told a friend who was at film school that I played with a group, and he said why don't you come to the studio and I'll shoot some footage. We did, but he never showed me the film. I asked him several times, but I never got to see it. I'm very upset about that, because there aren't even any *photos* of myself with Fille Qui Mousse."

Not long after Korb left the band, Benjamin Legrand also departed, "I met the mother of my son and went back to working as an assistant director, translator, etc..." His brother Oliver also seems to have left at around the same time.

Up to the departure of Korb and the Legrand brothers the story of

Fille Qui Mousse has a flow, but from this point it becomes a montage of vignettes linked by jump-cuts. While this creates problems for a narrator, it fully aligns with Enu's aesthetic of rupture and collage.

The first scenario takes place on 18 March '71 at the FLIP-organised demonstration/concert to celebrate the centenary of the Paris Commune. Enu: "I found myself on a truck with Red Noise and Bernard Gilson[4] with a generator powering the instruments so we could play while travelling through the streets of Paris. The adventure ended with arrests."

Enu recalls another event which must have taken place in this period. "The group went to Corrèze with its gear in a Citroen truck. We rented a secluded house so we would avoid possible noise problems and complaints from neighbours. This refuge allowed everyone to get to know each other musically. Through a programme of improvisation, compositions took shape with a particular insistence on a series of rhythmic breaks prefiguring those that I was preparing for the upcoming recording."

The last episode took place at the ill-fated Auvers-sur-Oise Festival in June '71. Benjamin Legrand recalls being at this festival with the band, so presumably he'd been called back for this performance. "I remember being backstage, but the rain was so heavy that they cancelled that day... After a few hours I gave up and drove back to Paris." Their non-appearance at this disastrous festival was the inauspicious end to Fille Qui Mousse's live performance career. Nevertheless, less than a month later Fille Qui Mousse was in the studio recording an album for Gérard Terronès' Futura label.

When Henri-Jean Enu entered Studio Wagram on 8 July '71 he was the only person from the live incarnation of the band present. The other musicians on the session had been drafted in just for the day: the members of Dagon (Dominique Lentin, Jean-Pierre Lentin, and Daniel Hoffman) as the rhythm section, along with guitarist François Guildon and violinist Léo Sab.

According to Dominique Lentin, his band's involvement was organised at the very last minute: "Henri-Jean Enu invited us to the recording not long before the session. We arrived in the morning and were there for only three hours." Dagon's contribution resulted in the long groove-based improvisation that bookends *Trixie Stapelton 291 - Se taire pour une femme trop belle*. The opening half ('Cantate Disparate') is driven by François Guildon's guitar while the closing section ('L'eau Etait Vitage') features Léo Sab's violin. Together the two parts of this improvisation account for a full fourteen of the album's thirty-five minute running time.

Dominique Lentin also played some percussion to be used in the sound collages that make up the remainder of the album (the drum groove for 'Quatrieme Episode' and the detuned tom rolls on 'Fraîcheur Et Amalgame').

These collage pieces were central to Enu's musical concept, and corresponded to his *modus operandi* as a visual artist. "The idea of collage is the foundation of my compositions... My musical conceptions aren't far from my paintings. Above all else I apply the idea of transversality to both painting and music. I can recall a desire to build a collage of elements from different cultural spheres to generate an unexpected sound."

A head-on collision of disparate elements was the desired outcome in these collages. "Mixing two, or more, antagonising structures... all struggling together; working and creating with contradiction. It was like an inner fight in the music..."

Some of the elements used in the musical collages were recorded before the July session, meaning that a single day in the studio was sufficient to record, edit, and mix the entire album. These pre-recorded passages include the contributions by Benjamin Legrand, who wasn't aware of his involvement on the album until after the fact. "I wasn't there at the recording sessions. The pieces used on the disc were test recordings performed at the request of Denis Gheerbrandt, who was making short films."

As Enu intended, the album creates unexpected juxtapositions, the apogee being on 'Esplanade' when Barbara Lowengreen's poetic recitation over a background of barking dogs is cut short by a drone of unidentifiable origin.[5]

In the final analysis *Trixie Stapelton 291 - Se taire pour une femme trop belle* shares a remarkable family resemblance to Faust's debut album. It is looser, and less tightly-edited, but so similar in concept and execution that it's stunning to discover that both records were recorded at almost exactly the same time - with no possibility of influence having flowed in either direction.[6]

The story of Fille Qui Mousse becomes occluded after the album session, and it seems that by the end of '71 the band had ceased to exist in all but name. Nevertheless, in December '71, *Actuel* reported: "Futura will soon release an album from Fille Qui Mousse, which promises to serve up the most bizarre sounds."

Actuel followed up by interviewing Enu in February '72. In the piece he took the opportunity to describe the band's musical approach in typically enigmatic terms: "When the Spanish invaders arrived in Latin America the Indians welcomed them in a very peaceful way: they surrounded them and played their musical instruments day and night. Hundreds of the Spanish soldiers committed suicide. Fille Qui Mousse is a little like that."

He also shed some light on the album title: "Trixie Stapelton is a friend of ours, she was part of the Exploding Galaxy...[7] She lived with us for a long time. Something very curious happened to her before being interned in a psychiatric institution: in Piccadilly Circus she was able to immobilise two to three hundred people by the power of her mind. An act that's symbolic of our musical position." This interview appears to be the last time that Fille Qui Mousse had any kind of existence, even in the mind of Enu.

A handful of test pressings of the album were made in anticipation of an early '72 release. However, due to financial problems at Futura the album never appeared. Untroubled, Enu simply returned to his visual art: "I was trapped by my visual conception. I liked working alone, and I split up with everything.... I was busy painting, with exhibitions and so on, and just forgot [the album]... Fille Qui Mousse disappeared, I did too, and the record disappeared!"

Fille Qui Mousse's reputation as an illusory, truly mythological group seemed sealed. Enu confirms that this fully conformed with his initial vision, "I paid no attention to these affairs. I devised this disc as a Rimbaudian work[8], then farewell - a bottle in the ocean."

The bottle floated on its way until the early '80s when Steven Stapleton of Nurse With Wound became involved in the album's convoluted tale. Stapleton had been mystified by a gap in the Futura catalogue: the mysterious, missing RED 04 and 05.[9] When Enu told him that RED 04 was actually the Fille Qui Mousse LP, he was intrigued, and became determined to give corporeal form to this phantom disc. With Enu's agreement *Trixie Stapelton 291 - Se taire pour une femme trop belle* was readied for release on his United Dairies label. Stapleton worked with Enu preparing the logistics, and a cover was designed... but Gérard Terronès, Futura's owner, refused to hand over the master tapes.

The bottle was cast back into the ocean.

More than a decade passed. In the mid-'90s Enu received some surprising news: "One day Gilles Yéprémian called me, suggesting that I go to FNAC, where they had one of my works for sale. I hurried down, but they were all gone. That's how I found out about the pirate release."

Evidently one of Futura's test pressings had washed ashore in Italy. An Italian collector had reportedly paid quite a tidy sum to acquire this rare copy of *Trixie Stapelton 291 - Se taire pour une femme trop belle*. It would go on to be used as the source for the 1994 Mellow Records CD Yéprémain had discovered in the local record hypermarket.

There have been a number of both official and unofficial releases since 1994.[10] However it was Mellow Record's pirate CD that finally released *Trixie Stapelton 291 - Se taire pour une femme trop belle* from limbo. With that the ephemeral and illusory nature of Fille Qui Mousse was put to rest, and the myth gave way to the legend.

Henri-Jean Enu continues his practice as an artist, creating work in his Paris studio.

Benjamin Legrand is an author and scriptwriter. He is most well-known for co-authoring the graphic novel Snowpiercer, *made into an award-winning film directed by Bong Joon-ho.*

Stéphane Korb started a successful career as a music photographer in the early '70s. In '78 he turned to photojournalism, working with the Magnum agency. His photographs have been published in Paris-Match, l'Express, Rock & Folk, Life, *and* Newsweek. *Korb has also published a number of books of his photography.*

NOTE ON TRACK TITLES

The 2002 Fractal/Futura release of *Trixie Stapelton 291 - Se taire pour une femme trop belle* is the version currently available on streaming platforms. This CD was issued by Gérard Terronès without Enu's consent and uses track names (repeated on Spotify etc.) chosen by Terronès that bear no relationship to Enu's original titles.

To assist, here is a comparison of Enu's correct titles to Terronès's:

Enu's Title	**Terronès's Title**
1 Cantate Disparate	Barbara Lowengreen Speed-Way
2 Transcription Interrompue	Mirroir Nagait dans Le Lac du Bois de Boulogne
3 Fraîcheur Et Amalgame	Princesse Nuage
4 Esplanade	Amour-Gel + Derrière Le Paravent
5 Résistance Instinctive	Bubble Gun A Jacqueline Prothèse + Tibhora-Parissalla
6 Quatrième Épisode	Magic-Bag
7 Transplantation	Untitled/Composition Fille Qui Mousse
8 Antinomique	Gibet-Jasmin Ordination
9 L'eau Était Vitale	Annal-Mandreke-Cool Non Imperial News

Notes

1 Note that Dominique Lentin actually participated in the recording of the Fille Qui Mousse album.

2 It's quite likely that Legrand is here referring to Richard Aubert, who occasionally played with Fille Qui Mousse before joining Komintern.

3 This was the "Free Fuck" concert held on 5 February '71 which also featured Komintern, Dagon, Musica Elettronica Viva, and Flat.

4 Guitarist Bernard Gilson must have joined Fille Qui Mousse after Korb and the Legrand brothers had departed, as they can't remember playing with him during their time in the band. Oddly, Gilson was also absent from the July '71 recording session.

5 The last five minutes of 'Esplanade' is either mesmerising or simply incessant depending on your disposition. Enu certainly missed a trick by not closing the side in a locked-groove, ensuring that the sonic stasis he conjures could potentially last for eternity.

6 When asked if Faust had contact with any other bands while living at their rural commune/studio, Jean-Hervé Peron reply was emphatic: "No! We didn't want to have any contact with the rest of the world. We didn't have a TV, no newspapers, I think we had a radio somewhere but we didn't use it. We weren't looking to communicate with other bands. We knew they existed, but let them do what they want - we've got our music in *our* heads."

7 The Exploding Galaxy were an English experimental performance art collective.

8 Here Enu is probably referring to Rimbaud's poem 'Le bateau ivre' (The Drunken Boat).

9 The Futura RED series jumps from RED 03 (Triode's *On n'a pas fini d'avoir tout vu* from '71) to RED 06 (Travelling's *Voici la nuit tombée* from '73).

10 There have been three unofficial CD releases of the album: on Mellow Records, Fractal/Futura, and Bichon Records. There are only two releases authorised by Enu: the CD by Spalax and the vinyl LP by Monster Melodies.

DAGON

> Dagon mesmerised a generation of French pot-heads with live performances of music that was essentially instrumental, more unsettling than soothing, scorning the simple backbeat, seeking out the most original sounds - achieved in the pre-synthesiser era by the linking of effects pedals and echo units. Part of the repertoire was composed, but most was left open to improvisation; frenzied, and either inspired or interminable according to the mood, the ambience, and the quality of dope consumed.
>
> *Jean-Pierre Lentin*

Like so many French bands formed in the late '60s, Dagon began as a gathering of high-school friends inspired by the British blues boom. In their case the group was made up of young blues enthusiasts who studied together at Lycée Buffon in Paris.

The drummer, Dominique Lentin, was from a politically active family. His father, the Algerian-born journalist Albert-Paul Lentin, advocated for anti-colonialist causes in *Libération*, *Nouvel Observateur*, *Esprit*, and Jean-Paul Sartre's *Les Temps Modernes*. Dominique Lentin: "Our house had been bombed by the OAS[1] at the beginning of the '60s because of my father's commitment to Algerian independence... For me May '68 was part of a process that had started before and would continue after."

'68 was also the year that Lentin began to play drums and formed Crossroad Blues with guitarist Jean-Paul Pillot.[2] Their schoolmates Daniel Hoffmann and Fabien "Loupi" Poutignat came along to listen to the fledgling group's rehearsals, with the vague notion of creating a light show. Hoffmann: "The rehearsals were in a small cellar under a music store, equipped with a drum kit and two small amps. The rent was ten francs an hour. Loupi and I would go begging in the neighbouring streets to get enough to pay for an extra hour…"

In summer '69 the trio's bassist announced he was leaving[3], so

Lentin approached his older brother Jean-Pierre to take over. Jean-Pierre Lentin: "None of them knew how to play, and they were looking for a bass player. At the time I was already studying at Sciences Po, but when they asked I said, why not? It seemed like fun to me."

Crossroad Blues became a five-piece when Daniel Hoffmann took on rhythm guitar and Fabien Poutignat added flute. The band began to play at venues around Paris. Dominique Lentin: "We played at *tremplins* (competitions for young groups) with other musicians who were better than us, and occasional concerts. Along the way we progressed from playing blues to writing our own compositions."

Jean-Pierre Lentin: "We started listening to English psychedelic groups like Soft Machine, and realised that was what we wanted to play. Since we really couldn't sing we became an instrumental band... We were looking for another name, and came across Lovecraft's 'Dagon' - an ancient monster. Dagon was also a divinity in the Bible, the God of the Philistines, directly opposed to the biblical God... That really appealed to us, so it's the name we chose!"

Jean-Pierre Lentin became *Actuel*'s music correspondent in 1970, and his musical influence would loom large in Dagon through introducing his younger band-mates to Captain Beefheart, Frank Zappa, and Can.[4] His father would also become important in the band's destiny.

Hoffmann: "Albert-Paul knew a lot of people from very diverse backgrounds. He introduced us to one of his acquaintances, a man named Audibert, who was director of the Musée d'Art Moderne de la Ville de Paris. He was very interested to discover a group of young, modern musicians to spice up exhibition openings.

"He invited us to play at an opening, and allowed us to rehearse in the museum building... Suddenly we had opportunities to perform in a prestigious place right in the heart of Paris, to an open-minded audience. We also had a place to rehearse and store our gear that was secured by uniformed museum guards paid by the City of Paris..."

At the end of Spring '70 Lentin senior pulled another rabbit from the hat. Hoffmann: "One of his acquaintances ran a travel agency and was looking for musicians to play in Tunisia that Summer. We played every night for tourists and got transport, accommodation, and food for two months. It was very poorly paid, but was the perfect opportunity to have a holiday while working on our music... So off we went to North Africa, with all our gear."

Jean-Paul Pillot left Tunisia and the band after only a fortnight, returning to Paris with his new love Nadia (a tourist he'd just met). The others saw the contract through and took the chance to work on a totally new repertoire.

Soon after returning to Paris, Dagon was back up to five members with the addition of another Lycée Buffon alumni. Hoffmann: "Denis Martignon became Dagon's singer in autumn. I wasn't really in favour, but wasn't in a position to object since the rest of the band was unanimous. He was a little older than us, intelligent, overbearing, and manipulative. But, he was clever enough not to risk offending Jean-Pierre, who was almost the same age.

"Denis was stylish, a bit of a dandy who always wore a long, Gestapo-style leather coat. His singing talents were rather limited, even non-existent, but almost continuous use of an echo chamber made it possible to stun everyone and cover up any vocal shortcomings."

Dagon had already started looking for opportunities to apply their aural and visual assault to political ends, staging interventions to disrupt events they considered regressive (e.g. the Congress of Sociology). So it's unsurprising that they joined the FLIP in October '70, although Dominique Lentin confesses they weren't very active members: "I remember going to one or two meetings at the Faculté de Jussieu, but we didn't put a lot into it... We gradually moved away from the political side of things while keeping our convictions."

Around this time Dagon also briefly become a six-piece. Hoffmann: "I met François Aubert[5], a parliamentarian's son, whose bourgeois upbringing included learning violin. I invited him to one of our rehearsals, and his virtuosity left us all speechless. He played with Dagon for two or three weeks, then during a meeting of the FLIP, he met someone from Komintern and left to join them. Komintern were much better known than us and played more concerts."

Denis Martignon displayed something of an entrepreneurial streak when he hatched an extra-musical scheme to make some money. He had connections that could supply "low-quality Moroccan hashish"[6] and convinced the others that selling it would allow them to buy better equipment. Hoffmann: "The small business prospered for a few weeks, and Dominique, Denis, and I went to London to buy a sound system, an echo chamber (very important), a drum kit, and an amp. It was around Christmas and freezing cold, with Denis as tyrannical as ever. Of all my stays in London this was hands down the most unpleasant."

In addition to hash Martignon brought two more significant influences into the band: The Velvet Underground and hard drugs. Hoffmann: "Before Denis imposed himself as 'leader' none of us had ever tried hard drugs like morphine, heroin, opium, amphetamines. Since the small business was flourishing, the boss-singer suddenly had a lot more means, and was meeting unsavoury people, junkies and petty crooks who were basically high all the time. One day he announced that it was time for us to move on to 'serious things': namely, heroin."

Martignon's infatuation with the Velvet Underground and heroin radically changed Dagon's public persona. Hoffmann: "The rest of us produced little or no lyrics, so his limited talent for writing fundamentally changed the image of the group. His lyrics were mainly inspired by heroin and its use: 'Son, what are you doing? I'm heating my spoon / Son, what are you doing? I'm filling my syringe...' We made a giant syringe painted in gold which was part of the show. It was laughable and ridiculous, but spectacular. The image projected by the group could only make one think of the Velvet Underground. As for the music, it was nothing like the Velvet Underground: they weren't very good, and we were even worse." [7]

In December '70 the Velvet Underground connection was bolstered when the band played at the opening of Andy Warhol's exhibition at the Paris Museum of Modern Art.[8] In an homage to 'Venus in Furs' they were joined on stage by a leather-clad guest fondling a whip and spitting at the crowd.

According to Dominique Lentin, visual and physical provocation was essential to a Dagon performance: "We mixed a happening with a concert, preparing a different visual element each time. There were non-musicians who performed on stage: a butler on roller-skates, a hairdresser, and quite a few others. We were into a thing of psychedelic provocation...

"I remember lying in a tub full of detergent and meat, then throwing it all over the audience. Jean-Jacques Birgé, who was doing our light show, was soaked through."

Pop 2000 wrote about this period: "They had a highly individual vision expressed in a strong appetite for theatrical extravagance and dramatic delirium... Their musical world owed a lot to a grating, demented singer who delivered surrealist lyrics distorted by electronics. Dagon always provoked violent reactions, you either loved them or hated them. They couldn't be ignored, or leave you indifferent!"

It was this aspect of Dagon that led some later music writers to refer to them as "precursors to punk". Hoffmann: "Of course we were! Well before taking on Denis as 'singer' and obviously well before 'punk' existed."

Dominique Lentin: "I think calling Dagon a precursor of punk is going a bit too far. We did provocative things like spitting on stage, but we were probably closer to Frank Zappa's happenings than punk. We were into more complex music like Zappa, Beefheart, Soft Machine, Can, etc... Our music wasn't just raw energy - even if we weren't very good technically."

In the first half of '71 the band played gigs at university faculties, venues like Golf Drouot and the Bus Palladium, and were booked to play at the ill-fated Auvers-sur-Oise Festival. Hoffmann: "We arrived to find everything cancelled, the site laid waste by a storm, and the sad spectacle of hundreds of sodden, muddy people tramping out."

In July Dagon entered a recording studio for the first time, although not to record their own music. Henri-Jean Enu had asked the rhythm section to join him at Studio Wagram to play on the Fille Qui Mousse album. Dominique Lentin: "Henri-Jean Enu invited us to the recording not long before the session. It was the first time in my life that I'd set foot in a recording studio." Unfortunately it would also be the last time during Dagon's career.

In August the band travelled south for what was intended to be a summer of beach-side holidaying and relaxed music-making. Hoffmann: "We had found a vacation rental in a small resort about ten kilometres west of Cannes. The whole group piled into a recently purchased truck, and headed to the Côte d'Azur.

"The tensions between the singer and myself intensified during the trip. Once at the seaside, I refused to participate in any attempt to rehearse, and methodically applied myself to making everyone's lives a misery. Jean-Pierre returned to Paris in disgust after a week. A week later, Denis and Loupi (who'd decided to support him no matter what) left in the truck with all the equipment."

Dagon had split, but not before playing one final concert - perhaps the most unusual in the story of the French underground scene.

Hoffmann: "An American warship, the USS Mitchell, dropped anchor a hundred metres from our house. The sailors landed on a small pontoon fifty meters from our house, and my girlfriend Julie, a Canadian, took me with her to meet the 'boys'. They'd come straight from Vietnam, for the commemoration of the Provence landings in August 1944.

"That night our house was invaded by more than fifty sailors. They arrived in twos or threes with cases of beer. I spent a lot of the evening making sautéed potatoes for everyone and listening to their stories - things like: 'I haven't been able to sleep for a week, since we bombed the coast... we killed a lot of civilians'.

"The military police came to thank us because our reception had headed off most of the fights and incidents that happen when sailors are let loose in town. A very friendly officer asked us to play on the destroyer and we accepted. It was Denis's last concert as Dagon's singer." [9]

When the dust settled the Lentin brothers and Daniel Hoffmann decided to reform Dagon as a trio. Dominique Lentin: "Daniel began to play the organ (a big Farfisa). Musically this was the most interesting period for me. There was a little more influence from Soft Machine because of the organ."

They also decided to leave Paris to set up a community house in the countryside. So, in early '72, the band moved to a house christened "La Dagondiére" at Montigny-le-Gannelon, 150km outside Paris.[10] There they began working on a new style, putting aside theatricality and searching for more musical complexity. Jean-Pierre Lentin led the process.

Hoffmann: "In a way Jean-Pierre was the musical authority of the group. He was the only one of us able to arrange our music, to build coherent pieces from the different themes."

Jean-Pierre Lentin: "We'd smoke joints, everyone would take their instruments and we'd improvise - it could last one, two, three hours. We recorded everything on a little crappy tape recorder, and I'd listen back and note the passages that seemed interesting. I'd say 'we should redo this passage here, it's really good, then that one'... Little by little they were given structure... they evolved and finally became quite long instrumental suites, pieces around twenty minutes long. We wrote three or four 'suites' like that."

Pop 2000 noted the change in the band's priorities: "Their music lost the surrealism and imagery their singer had contributed, but gained an undeniable technical maturity. From this point [their repertoire] was made up of long instrumental pieces with many twists and turns, featuring complex rhythms and strange electronic sounds."

Dagon spent the first months of '72 developing their new style, then began to play small towns in the local area like Cloyes and Vendôme. In March they performed at the St. Gratien Festival in Troyes, and in June played at the Bièvres Festival near Paris.

The arrival of an underground band attracted attention from the regional press. Gerald Moenner from *La Nouvelle République* became something of a champion of the band after reviewing a performance concert at Cloyes: "Dagon was able to captivate the audience from the very beginning of the concert with a piece in which the drummer uttered little cries into the microphone that sounded like chirping birds. Dagon's music is very reminiscent of overseas groups like Pink Floyd, Iron Butterfly, and Soft Machine, and could be referred to as "free pop". Let's hope for great success for this group."

While Dagon still made occasional visits to the capital, most of their performances were in the regions, often to a somewhat stunned audience. Dominique Lentin: "The majority of the time the people who came to our concerts had never seen or heard us, but in Paris there was an underground scene that could appreciate our music. Although we played at a festival in Nantes once to a crowd of 1500 people, and it went really well."[11]

In the second half of '72 another drummer, Mike Freitag, was added to the group. Frietag had previously played with Contrepoint. Dominique Lentin: "Mike was a better technical player than me; having him in the line-up gave the group more power." Unfortunately he was only with Dagon for a short time.

At the end of '72 Hoffmann returned to live in the capital while remaining part of the group. In Paris he managed to recruit two new members. The first was guitarist Roman Sienkiewicz, and the second was none-other than Patrick Vian, ex-Red Noise. Hoffmann also asked Fabien Poutignat to rejoin on flute and sax.

The new six-piece Dagon was equally split between Paris and Montigny-le-Gannelon. Hoffmann: "Patrick and his partner Emilie had a Ford Transit. The people from Paris piled into it and we travelled to the Dagondière, where we'd stay for a little under a week at a time."

Vian's influence steered the band towards free improvisation. Dominique Lentin: "The final era of the band with Patrick Vian involved total improvisation, although we'd sometimes incorporate themes." The line-up only survived for a few months, and there were only rare live performances. Hoffmann: "I remember a concert in Chateaudun, and another in Orléans. All of the music was improvised, with nothing composed or developed in rehearsals."

A few months into '73, Dagon began to break up in a surprisingly common scenario for French bands of the era, involving both drugs and sexual impropriety... Hoffmann: "One day we all took mescaline together, and an affair between Emilie and Roman came to light... Patrick and Emilie hastily returned to Paris. They stopped coming to La Dagondière, That was the end of Dagon, at least in this form."

After Vian's departure they struggled on for a month or two. Hoffmann can only recall the group playing one or two more times: "I believe Dagon's last concert was in Roanne. It was totally improvised. Loupi, who was very drunk, let loose a long sequence of bellows and grunts, then fell asleep on the stage."

Gerald Moenner wrote one last article about Dagon in May '73 where he notes the Roanne performance (although the flautist's unorthodox performance is glossed over). The journalist's enthusiasm is undiminished, and he seems unaware that the group had just sung its swansong: "Dagon's music is a continual search for original sounds... They make spellbinding and almost surreal music, and are a group who understand the meaning of pop music."

Dominique Lentin continues to play music. He drummed in the bands Empire des Soins, Ferinand et les Philosophes, Zov, and in a duo with Takum Fukushima. In addition to making experimental music he writes music for theatre and teaches drumming.

Daniel Hoffmann continued to play music through the '70s, including a stint with Patrick Vian in the short-lived three-piece Einstein. Today he makes sets for cinema, advertising and theatre.

Jean-Pierre Lentin became a well-known journalist, writer, radio producer, and documentary maker with a passion for music, cinema, and alternative science. He published three books and made a series of documentaries for Arte, on scientific subjects. He died in 2009, aged 58.

Fabien Poutignat has become one of the main specialists in LED lighting in Paris.

Denis Martignon moved to New York in the '80s. In 1984 he opened Midnight Records and started a record label of the same name. Both the store and the label became notorious in the US garage-rock and punk scene. He died in 2016.

Roman Sientiewicks studied at Berkeley School and became a guitar and music teacher.

Patrick Vian recorded a solo electronic album for Egg Records in 1976. Little was seen of him after that point, except for his occasional appearance at events organised to celebrate the life of his father, Boris Vian. He died in 2023, aged 80.

Notes

1   The OAS (Organisation armée secrète) was a right-wing paramiliary group that waged a campaign of terrorism during the Algerian War, which included the assassination of pro-independence figures.

2   Pillot had previously played in a trio with Gabriel Yacoub, another Lyceé Buffon student. Yacoub would go on to form the seminal folk-rock band Malicorne.

3   "At the beginning of Summer, Loupi, Jean-Paul, François (the bass player) and I went to London for four weeks. We stayed with Gabriel Yacoub in a cheap bed & breakfast, and at night went to clubs to listen to blues and rock…When we got back François told us he was leaving the group," *(Hoffman)*

4   "Jean-Pierre was one of the first, if not the very first, journalist to write about German Rock." *(Dominique Lentin)*

5   François Aubert performed as Richard Aubert in Komintern and afterwards. Aubert had also briefly played in Fille Qui Mousse.

6   In his Foreword Jean-Jacques Birge recalls that hashish sold by Dagon was of much better quality than Hoffman remembers!

7   A live review in *Rock & Folk* commented: "Their grimy sound creates a noxious atmosphere reminiscent of the Velvet Underground."

8   "Warhol walked right in front of us while we were playing, He didn't even look in our direction." *(Hoffman)*

9   The photograph at the beginning of this chapter was taken at the concert on the USS Mitchell.

10   "Crium Delirium lived thirty kilometres away, so we'd meet up with them now and then." *(Dominique Lentin)*

11   "There is a live cassette of a Dagon concert at Nantes (that I recorded, if my memory is correct). The piece on the [*30 Years of Musical Insurrection in France*] box-set comes from that tape" *(Gilles Yéprémian)*

part four:

the lysergic underground

INTRODUCTION

> There is just a great tradition in France of listening to music and dealing with the arts that is completely conducive to the creation of, and the appreciation of, the sort of avant-garde set ups that we dealt in... You could really stretch out in front of a French audience, you almost had to apologise for it in England... Fucking paradise as far as I was concerned...
>
> Robert Wyatt, *Soft Machine*

An English band, Soft Machine, and an Australian musician, Daevid Allen, had a surprisingly influential role in the birth of the French music underground.

Soft Machine arrived in France at the beginning of July '67 with a booking to play all summer long at a "psychedelic discotheque" near St. Tropez. When "all summer long" turned into "for five nights only" the band found themselves stranded in paradise with a truck full of gear and no money.[1] However a chance encounter with Parisian antique dealer Bob Benamou would quickly turn things around.

"They were playing on the beach at a Beer Festival, it was a horrible place and nobody was there. I told them, 'You can't stay here', so I took the whole group, and installed them in a villa in St Tropez. We became friends. I became very close to Daevid Allen who was so creative, so poetic, and so surrealistic. Really an amazing person."

Benamou was in the area with underground artist Jean-Jacques Lebel organising a series of happenings for the Parisian artistic elite who'd flocked to the Côte d'Azur for Summer. Lebel offered Soft Machine the opportunity to perform during a staging of Picasso's play *Desire Caught by the Tail*. The band leapt at the chance, immersing themselves in the Dadaist production for three weeks.[2]

Soft Machine also scored an invitation to play at a party organised by the owner of Barclay Records, where they impressed a large crowd of movers-and-shakers with a 40-minute rendition of 'We Did It Again'.

The strong reaction to these performances gave the band a solid foothold in France. As Daevid Allen related: "People like Brigitte Bardot were there and lots of film producers and directors. It was the event that really gave us the standing in Paris that led to Soft Machine being that favourite band in the land..." They would consolidate this position by returning to the country every month for the remainder of '67, developing an influence on the nascent French underground that was only rivalled by that of Frank Zappa.

However, Soft Machine would make these return trips as a three-piece. An expired visa saw Allen turned back at Dover, and worse yet, banned from entering the UK for three years. Not wanting to return to Australia, Allen had little choice but to install himself in Paris. His time in Soft Machine was cut brutally short, but he quickly became a strong presence on the local scene.

By the end of '67 psychedelic culture and music was beginning to make further inroads into France. Jean-Jacques Lebel was inspired by London's 14 Hour Technicolor Dream to stage his country's first psychedelic all-nighter, La Fenêtre Rose, on 17 November '67. 1500 people attended the event which featured Soft Machine, Spencer Davis Group, Tomorrow, Dantalion's Chariot, and Cat Stevens.[3]

With the seed already planted, Daevid Allen's presence in Paris worked to accelerate the growth of psychedelia in France. His band Bananamoon was the first real exponent of psychedelic music on the scene. However, it was soon joined by some local adepts.

Guitarist Jacques Dudon had begun '68 touted as the Gallic Eric Clapton. He was the leader of Blues Bag, one of the premier blues-rock bands in France. However, in the wake of May '68 he suddenly changed course, steering his band into very different musical waters.

Dudon: "Very quickly the group took a turn towards much more innovative and creative music, inspired by Californian 'acid rock', improvisation, and traditional music. At the same time I was trying more and more experimentation - trying to get deep inside the sound."

The radical change in direction and Dudon's contentious decision to add François Breton to the line up led to the break-up of Blues Bag.[4] Three of the band (Dudon, Breton, and drummer Roland Tuder) carried on under the name L'Assemblée. The short-lived band released only one single, but it would become an underground classic. While 'Le Chien', released in '69 on Pathé Marconi[5], was not the first home-grown psychedelic record[6] it can credibly claim to be the first example of an authentically *French* psychedelia. This stunning slice of sound shows almost no discernible Anglo-American influence - its pounding polyrhythms and keening traditional pipes send 'Le Chien' plunging headlong into the heart of North African trance.

L'Assemblée came to a premature end when François Breton refused to sign with Pathé ("he was too much of an anarchist to sign a contract with them" according to Dudon) and Roland Tuder was called up for military service.

Jacques Dudon carried on as a soloist, and was still heading deep into psychedelic territory when he had an encounter that sealed his commitment.

In October '70 the surprise appearance of a traveling commune of American hippies created a sensation in Paris' growing underground. When the Hog Farm arrived they brought undiluted US counter-culture directly into the heart of the city.

Led by Wavy Gravy (Hugh Romney), the Hog Farm's history stretched back to the Merry Pranksters' Acid Tests in '64. Romney and his comrades had created a live-in community at an *actual* hog farm outside Los Angeles in the mid-'60s, before taking to the road in '67. The Hog Farm travelled across the US in converted school buses spreading a gospel of peace, love, and dope. They became famous for their involvement at Woodstock in '69 where they kept order as the "Please Force" and ran the festival's free kitchen.

In '70 the Hog Farm took their road-trip international. They had travelled through the UK and were on their way to India when they hit Paris. The forty-strong group arrived in the middle of a happening staged by Lionel Magal at the American Center.

Magal recalls: "I was holding a billhook in one hand and a chicken in the other, and I was preparing myself to cut its head off. Then this horde of *freaks* came into the hall: some old, some young, some tall, some short, some fat, some scrawny, along with babies and animals. It was something that we'd never seen before. They all began to take the audience's hands. The Hog Farm had landed."

With their sudden arrival the performance was transformed (and the life of a hapless chicken was saved). Magal suggested that the commune move into his studio space, where there was already a large creative community domiciled. The Hog Farm would stay for several months, before heading off to India with a second bus-load of French adherents including Lionel Magal and Jacques Dudon.

The encounter was pivotal not only for Magal and Dudon, but for many of the Parisian underground, especially those who would go on to play psychedelically-inspired music. These included the members of Cheval Fou, who were encouraged by the Hog Farm's example to embark on their own psychedelic road-trip with the *Le Pop* Tribe.

With seeds from both sides of the Atlantic firmly planted, the French psychedelic scene ripened quickly. By the end of '69 Ame Son and Gong (possibly the most iconic psychedelic band of the '70s) had both recorded albums, and Chico Magnetic Band were creating their own brand of psychedelic mayhem in Lyon.

With the end of his stay in India, Lionel Magal returned to Paris in '72. Almost immediately he and his brother Thierry created Crium Delirium. Along with Cheval Fou and Gong the Magal brothers would keep the freak flag flying high in France for the next few years.

Notes

1 Daevid Allen: "We only played there about five times. They found that the music was too loud and there were a lot of complaints from people around, and a lot of unfavourable publicity."

2 Lebel told writer Aymeric Leroy, "Daevid and Kevin [Ayers] said to me several times afterwards that this experience had really allowed them to 'bloom' as artists, to differentiate themselves from what was around them." Soft Machine also played at a happening organised by Lebel, footage of which (although without audio) is included in his film *Sun Love*.

3 La Fenêtre Rose also featured a performance by The Exploding Galaxy dance troupe and the first light show to grace Paris. The audience included luminaries like film-makers Jean-Luc Godard and Claude Lelouch. A four minute clip of Soft Machine's performance was aired on *Bouton Rouge*, 9 Dec '67.

4 Breton was a traveling folk musician whose main instrument was traditional pipes. When Blues Bag split he quickly learned bass guitar. Dudon: "I taught François to play bass in fifteen days so we could perform at our upcoming concerts."

5 The connection between Pathé Marconi and Dudon was already established, he was signed to them as a solo artist, under the name Claude Guilain.

6 Of all the contenders the most unambiguously lysergic must be Les 5 Gentlemen's 'LSD 25 ou les métamorphoses de Margaret Steinway' from '66.

A TALE OF TWO MOONS:
Gong Full Moon Fantastickal & Bananamoon

> At the beginning of 1968 Marc and I had the unbelievable good luck to meet Daevid Allen. He was looking to start a new group to play his compositions. Marc and I had the "look." We were among the very first in Paris to have long hair and wear Carnaby Street gear, and we were developing in the same musical vein as Daevid. There was good chemistry immediately. It was the start of a real Odyssey.
>
> *Patrick Fontaine*

When Daevid Allen found himself barred from England he installed himself in Paris.[1] There he leapt into action, quickly gathering a collective of improvising musicians around himself. They included his long-term collaborator and partner Gilli Smyth, vocalist Ziska Baum, and flautist Loren Standlee. For their first show they took the name Gong Full Moon Fantastickal.[2] Within weeks Allen had landed the group a ten-week residency at La Vieille Grille, located near the Sorbonne in the Latin Quarter.

Along with La Coupole in Montparnasse, La Vieille Grille was one of the hubs of Paris's nascent counter-culture. Since the early '60s the venue had played host to the radical new wave of *chanson* (represented by Jacques Higelin, Colette Magny, and Brigitte Fontaine), free jazz (Archie Shepp and Ornette Coleman had played there), and happenings organised by artist, and doyen of the underground, Jean-Jacques Lebel.

The atmosphere of improvisation and exploration at La Vieille Grille gave Allen and Smyth free rein to develop the idiosyncratic styles that would later become fundamental to Gong's music: Allen's "glissando" guitar technique and Smyth's "spacewhisper" vocals.

Allen has always given Pink Floyd's Syd Barrett full credit for inspiring his glissando guitar style. "I saw Syd playing a curious sort of slide guitar with the Floyd at the Ally Pally in 1967 and he looked rather embarrassed by it. But out front it sounded spectacularly Wagnerian! I was impressed. [In Paris] I stayed with a black American lady-friend whose absent husband was an antiquarian. Here I discovered a stainless steel box of 19th Century gynaecological surgical instruments and inspired by the sound of Syd I set to work on a guitar." Armed with these unorthodox implements Allen learned to coax constellations of sound from his Telecaster.[3]

Although able to explain the origin of his own style, Allen was at a loss when it came to the genesis of Smyth's "spacewhisper" vocals: "it didn't come from any outside influence that I know of. She just immediately began to sing like that... Ziska Baum [and Gilli] were magical together. The two of them just created that style together out of thin air."

Taner Celensu provided the final element needed to craft the group's sound: a Semprini Eco 6-channel mixer/echo chamber. Rather than simply adding effects to the instruments, Celensu used the device to meld the individual elements into a cosmic symphony.

The music this protozoan Gong produced was akin to the more floating passages of Pink Floyd, but pushed to the extreme in both duration and abstraction. In many ways it anticipated the German *kosmische* music that bands like Tangerine Dream would explore.

Through the winter of '67 and into early '68 their improvised performances in the cellar of La Vieille Grille caused something of a stir in the Parisian underground. Allen: "No one had heard music like that because nobody had done it before; with gliss guitar, spacewhisper by both Gilli and Ziska Baum, and flute by Loren Stanlee, all being heavily processed by Taner Celensu."

The impact of these performances (along with an insight into the celestial sound of the group) can be gauged from an almost seven-minute segment broadcast on the French television programme *Le Petit Dimanche Illustré*.[4] Allen had hit Paris with a bang.

While this period of free-form musical exploration had been a welcome interlude, by the beginning of '68 Allen was writing traditionally-structured songs again, and he began looking for a group to give them voice. A chance meeting with a Parisian film-maker would put Allen in contact with the players he needed.

"I was introduced to a young filmmaker named Jérôme Laperrousaz. A prodigy at 18 years of age, he was already making award winning programmes for French TV, and he had a plan. He knew of a bassist and a drummer who he felt could back me, and his proposal was to make us a TV clip. Well, why not?"

The musicians Laperrousaz had in mind were Marc Blanc and Patrick Fontaine, who had been the rhythm section of the band Expression. As fate would have it, Blanc and Fontaine had seen Soft Machine perform and were already ardent fans of Allen's old band.

Blanc was stunned by Laperrousaz's proposition: "One morning Jérôme asked me if I wanted to play with Daevid Allen, the founder of Soft Machine. And of course I was completely enthusiastic, but I was a little embarrassed because I said maybe he won't want to play with French beginners. But he said, 'No, no, he's in Paris, he's looking for people'.

"David came to my place... we improvised and he said, 'Yeah, it's okay, it's okay. Why not?' Expression had a gig three weeks later, and he said, 'Let's do it'."

Allen saw the promise in the rhythm section: "Mark Blanc the drummer was a ready-made Gallic rock image, suave and pretty; while bassist Patrice LaFontaine *(sic)* was tall, tawny, and boyish blonde. As musicians they were about a quarter ripe, but they had *'le look'* and with a few rehearsals, some coaxing and a couple of long guitar solos we had four of my songs down, and could fill about half an hour."

Allen is selling his bandmates short here - the demos the group would record show that while Blanc was not quite the equal of Robert Wyatt he was a very capable drummer, and Fontaine's bass playing was every bit as supple and flowing as Kevin Ayers.

The new three-piece played their first gig in January '68, under the name Expression. Blanc: "We had just enough time to rehearse two tracks ('Why are we Sleeping' and 'We did it Again'). The three sets we were scheduled to play were basically made up of freak-outs. The audience was stunned, but enjoyed it, without realising that it was Soft Machine's guitarist who was playing."

Allen quickly christened the new band Bananamoon. While they would only play a score of gigs and record a handful of demos, they helped to shape the country's emerging musical underground, spawned the bands Gong and Ame Son, and brought the first flush of homegrown psychedelia to France.

Jérôme Laperrousaz continued his association, becoming Bananamoon's de-facto manager. In addition to filming them as promised, he approached record labels on their behalf and organised demo recordings.

Laperrousaz had a day job filming segments for the TV series *Bouton Rouge*, and in February '68 he produced the first to feature Bananamoon. Blanc describes it as "a horror film, shot in Normandy, where we played a kind of rock'n'roll sect, kidnapping a tramp to torture him with music... Daevid, Patrick and I played completely mad music in the film, 100 percent underground, and very psychedelic." [5]

Bouton Rouge was presented by Pierre Lattès, who also hosted France Inter's *Pop Club*. In April Bananamoon appeared on the nation-wide radio broadcast playing several songs live to air (a booking presumably organised by Laperrousaz).

Another film shoot for *Bouton Rouge* was organised for the second week of May. Allen and Blanc had been in Rome attending a music festival, and had to rush back for the filming. As they drove into Paris they were stunned to find it in complete turmoil. It was the very beginning of the May '68 *événements*.

Laperrousaz met the band the next day to film the clip for their version of 'Why are we Sleeping?'. Bravely or foolishly, he couldn't resist filming Bananamoon against the backdrop of a Latin Quarter reeling in the aftermath of the Night of the Barricades. When they arrived they were greeted by the acrid smell of smoke and tear gas as a scene of carnage was revealed: entire roads stripped of the famous Parisian paving stones, hastily erected barricades, burned-out vehicles, and uprooted trees. CRS riot police were everywhere, and the air was electric with tension. The only thing protecting the band and film crew from the attention of the massed police force was that Laperrousaz was filming for the national broadcaster, the ORTF.

Fontaine: "The shoot included a sequence at the corner of Rue Gay-Lussac and Boulevard Saint-Michel where we were filmed climbing the barricades with our instruments, against a background of total chaos." [6]

Pushing his luck, Laperrousaz took the opportunity to create something of a happening right in the middle of this tense scene of destruction. Allen: "Followed by the cameras, I wandered down a block to find a menacing black battle-truck full of super tough para-commandos. From somewhere Jérôme miraculously conjured up a large paper bag full of toy teddy bears. So I danced up to the wagon, and bowed to the stone-faced paratroopers...

" 'Les compliments de Winnie le Pooh' I cried solemnly and handed each of them a wee teddy bear. Stern jaw-lines cracked open with amazement and then delight. They'd all abruptly turned into little boys. I left behind a truckload of human laughter..."

The paras may have been laughing, but once news of this filmed escapade reached the authorities they were not amused. Laperrousaz was fired by the ORTF the next day, but worse was potentially in store for Allen: "A friend of ours was arrested in some kind of raid and was released and told us he saw Gilli's and my photographs on top of the file on the desk where he was arrested." Both Allen and Smyth had been designated "undesirable aliens" and were facing probable arrest and deportation.

They grabbed everything that would fit into their Volkswagen van and headed to Spain. They owned a property in Deya on the island of Majorca that would serve them now as a refuge from the French authorities, and would in later days become a haven from the pressures of the music business.

Fontaine and Blanc had been left behind in Paris, but in July they joined Allen and Smyth in Deya. Fontaine: "Deya was an intense period of sunshine, total freedom, extraordinary encounters, discoveries, and dreams. It wasn't just the music that brought us closer together. As children of the Baby Boom and the hippie generation, we yearned for more freedoms and rejected material comfort as our only goal. We couldn't conceive of playing together without sharing the other moments of life. There was a family spirit in our little community with Gilli and her daughter Tasmin representing the feminine aspect."

While living together in Deya, Bananamoon took the chance to rehearse intensively and began to document their new songs on a Revox tape recorder. They performed at several parties and notably at the Sergeant Pepper club in Palma. Allen: "I was running a lot of creative fire over this gig... I don't think I have ever felt I had so much to prove. I played with an intensity and fury that lasted until the last number... The gig ended just before it climaxed. The surprised audience loved it but I was left feeling like a goosestep looking for a landmine. I had to get moving. Get back to the real world and away from Majorcan tourists."

Blanc and Fontaine returned to Paris in October '68, but stayed in close contact with Allen. Jérôme Laperrousaz had been speaking to record labels on the band's behalf and in December Allen and Smyth clandestinely returned to the French capital to record demos for those that showed some interest. The band spent two days in Bernard Estardy's CBE studio recording for Barclay, and one day in Studios Pathé recording for Pathé-Marconi.[7]

Some of the experiments that Allen and Gilli Smyth had been working on at La Vieille Grille, and would go on to refine in Gong, can be heard making their mark on these demos. Smyth's spacewhisper features on 'Enough for You'/'An Oeuf for You', and the intro to 'My Mother's Gone to India' is pure proto-Gong with spacewhisper vocals and glissando guitar.

It's actually surprising to hear how important Smyth's contribution is to the Bananamoon recordings, given that Allen usually described the band as a trio. Fontaine explains: "Gilli's place in Bananamoon, then in Gong, was vital. She was much more than Daevid's partner, she was also his inspiration, and our muse in a way. She made brief interventions at our concerts but had a much more active role in the recordings."

A few of the songs from these sessions would be re-recorded by Allen later. 'Pretty Miss Titty' was included on *Magick Brother*, while 'Enough for You'/'An Oeuf for You' formed the basis of 'Stoned Innocent Frankenstein' from Allen's *Banana Moon* solo LP.

After making these recordings, the whole band relocated to relative safety in the South of France, far from the reach of the Parisian police. Fontaine: "We went down to Montaulieu, where Bob Benamou owned a house overlooking the valley." Both Benamou and Montaulieu would remain important in Daevid Allen's life: Benamou would become Gong's manager, and Montaulieu would be the birthplace of the Gong community.

When the demos failed to secure the interest of Barclay or Pathé Marconi, Allen turned his hand to writing new material. Unfortunately

Marc Blanc was finding less inspiration in this new music, and his thoughts turned to creating his own. So while Allen was working on the songs that would form the core of his *Magick Brother* album, Blanc began to work on the first tracks that would give voice to Ame Son.

When Expression's former guitarist, Bernard Lavialle, returned from Army service in April '69, Blanc began to seriously consider reconvening the old band. He made the final decision on the evening of 25 June '69: "We had invitations to this concert at the Bataclan. Soft Machine were headlining and the supports were all French. There was someone I knew in almost every group! I thought we'd missed the boat, we were playing with one of Soft Machine's founders and we weren't on stage! I said to myself that we had to put our own group together, because we were going to miss this wave."

When they returned to Drôme, Blanc and Fontaine discussed their future. Fontaine: "It was Marc's idea to form Ame Son. Personally, I was more inclined to stay with Daevid, but it was hard for me to imagine continuing on alone with Daevid and Gilli." Blanc had no such inclination: "I thought, we've got to do something, we've got to start our own group again. So, we had a conversation with Daevid, and I said 'We want to do our own thing now' and he told me he had the same feeling, because he had the dream of Gong at that time."

They parted amicably, and Bananamoon was no more. From this point things moved very quickly; within months both Ame Son and Daevid Allen had signed to BYG Records, recorded their debut albums, and were sharing the stage at the legendary Amougies Festival.

Notes

1   See the Introduction to this section for more on Daevid Allen becoming stranded in France.

2   Gong Full Moon Fantastickal changed name regularly in the short time it existed. Allen often referred to it afterwards as "proto-Gong".

3   Allen appeared on the television programme *Au risque de vous plaire* in September '67. This segment was the public debut of the "glissando guitar" technique.

4   This segment was broadcast on 21 April '68. It is available to view on YouTube.

5   This piece was never broadcast on *Bouton Rouge*, but it is likely to be the film shown under the title 'Nightmares Of Mr. Respectable' at Gong's 'Kouhoutek Comet Party' at the London Lyceum in '73.

6   Fontaine added: "I've never seen this clip which, to my knowledge, was never broadcast." *Bouton Rouge*'s run was brought to an end when the ORTF joined the May '68 general strike on 25 May (the final episode was broadcast on 18 May '68). The Bananamoon footage, shot on 12 May, was never aired.
In an interview with Udi Koomran, Allen mentions that this footage was shown at Gong's 'Kouhoutek Comet Party' in '73: "During the interval, a film shot during the Paris street riots was projected on a large screen."

7   These demos (along with other recordings made in Deya during the summer of '68) were eventually released on the CD *Je Ne Fum' Pas Des Bananes* (Legend, 1992) and the LP *Bananamoon Band* (Monster Melodies, 2014). See the Discography for more details.

AME SON

> Aborted projects, that's the story of Ame Son. Brigitte Fontaine suggested she was willing to make a record with us. We turned it down. So she recorded with the Art Ensemble of Chicago. Dashiell Hedayat also got in touch. He wanted us to help out with what became the album *Obsolete*. The problem was that he made obscene propositions to François... "No way I'm making a record with that guy"... It was really tricky.
>
> *Marc Blanc*

The story of the '70s French underground is filled with bands never given the chance to live up to their obvious potential. For every Magma, Gong, or Heldon there were dozens of equally talented groups that failed to produce anything beyond a debut release (and many more who didn't make it that far). While there was a plethora of reasons, the most common was the French music business's almost complete disinterest in home-grown rock. For Ame Son it was different - opportunities seemingly threw themselves at the band, but through a series of missteps and spurned chances they too were lost to history.

In the middle of '70 that just didn't seem to be possible. Ame Son had been the first band from the French underground to record an album, and had appeared on the bill of almost every important French music festival. Their pedigree was strong too: Marc Blanc (drums) and Patrick Fontaine (bass) having played with Daevid Allen in Bananamoon.

Blanc and Fontaine had met at school and began playing music together in the mid-'60s with a fellow-student, guitarist Bernard Lavialle. 1966 saw the trio embark on their first serious musical venture with Bernard Stisi (vocals and guitar) and Michel Fillon (vocals) as Les Primitiv's. The band took its cue from the British R&B of The Yardbirds and The Pretty Things, and like most bands of the era their repertoire was cover-versions of English-language songs.

Les Primitiv's played semi-professionally at society balls[1] and in the smaller Paris clubs, before taking up a three-month residency in a Corsican holiday resort during the summer of '67. This was to be their swan song. On returning to Paris in September, Stisi and Fillon announced they were leaving to continue their studies.

The remaining members decided to carry on as a three-piece, but were desperate to change musical direction. As luck would have it, Blanc would have a musical encounter that decisively changed the band's orientation.

At the end of summer Blanc travelled on to London, keen to see what was new on the music scene. He was on his way to the Marquee Club (an obvious choice for a fan of British R&B) when a chance meeting changed his plans: "a girl on the underground told me that the Marquee was finished, the new hot spot was UFO, where a group called Soft Machine was playing." [2] What he witnessed at the UFO club that evening converted him to the freer, psychedelic rock that Soft Machine pioneered. When he returned to Paris he encouraged his own band to explore this new sound.

Patrick Fontaine: "Our music developed under the influence of groups like The Mothers of Invention, Syd Barrett-era Pink Floyd, and especially Soft Machine, who we were unreserved fans of... we experimented with music halfway between rock and improvisation." To signal the change in direction the band changed their name to Expression.

One of their first gigs after this re-orientation was at Le Damier, a club where Les Primitiv's had been resident before their summer sojourn. Blanc: "We went there and we decided just to play free rock: no songs, no tunes just free, free, free! We smoked a little (it was the beginning of hashish) then played for an hour, completely free. And the owner came down to the cellar and said: 'It's not possible. You have to stop. It's not my Primitiv's! I don't want you anymore!' "

While Expression had failed to win over the owner with their new direction, there was someone in the club that night who *was* impressed, and who would become central to Ame Son's story: the young film-maker Jérôme Laperrousaz.[3]

Blanc: "We were a little disappointed, but Jérôme said to us: 'Come and have a drink. I really like what you are doing - it's very, very interesting.' He was very important for us because he was the first person to say, 'I like what you're doing'. We took a lot of risks in '67, it was really revolutionary to play like this: free rock. Free jazz was okay, but free rock was really strange. I don't know how we had the courage to do it, but we did."

Patrick Fontaine believes that they were the first Parisian band to play this style of music, "Without being fully aware of it and without seeking it out, we really were an underground band. I didn't know of any others in Paris."

Expression was only able to explore their new direction for three months before Bernard Lavialle was called up for national service. Nevertheless it was a very productive period: they held a residency at a Saint-Germain-des-Prés club, played a radio session with jazz drummer Jacques Thollot, and recorded a fifteen-minute tape to be played as in-store music at the Dorothée Bis boutique.[4] Fontaine notes that in December '67 Expression played fifteen concerts.

With the forced departure of Lavialle at the end of '67 (he would be gone for eighteen months) Blanc and Fontaine were left as a rhythm section without a guitarist. Just when it looked like they were dead in the water Blanc received the phone call from Jérôme Laperrousaz that led to the duo joining Daevid Allen in Bananamoon. In an incredible stroke of good fortune they would spend the next year and a half playing with a founding member of the band that had inspired their radical change in direction.

It may be tempting to see Blanc and Fontaine's time in Bananamoon as serving a psychedelic apprenticeship under one of its doyens. However Expression had found a voice in its brief existence; Blanc notes that he had already written pieces that would later feature on the Ame Son album. So when Lavialle returned from his Army service in mid-'69 it was natural that the trio decided to take up where they had left off.

Ame Son was born in July '69 when Blanc, Fontaine, and Lavialle were joined by François Garrel on flute.[5] Blanc: "For a short period we were rehearsing with Bananamoon and Ame Son at the same time, but Daevid had his great vision of Gong and we had our dream of Ame Son."

The new quartet remained in the south of France for the remainder of the summer before returning to Paris. A three-week residency at a holiday resort near Saint-Tropez gave them the chance to rehearse every day and play every night, allowing them to develop musical ideas and road-test a new repertoire.

When the band returned to Paris in September '69 Blanc contacted Jérôme Laperrousaz. "I called Jérôme, and he said 'Go to BYG records, they're signing everybody. Pierre Lattès is artistic director, he'll sign you for sure!' And that's what happened. So one more time, it was Jérôme. We went to BYG records, they listened to a few tunes, then said 'You go to London in fifteen days. We're putting out twenty records and we want you in!' "

From the south of France, to Paris and on to London all within weeks - things were moving very fast for the band. Ame Son found themselves forced to make the leap from writing new material and working up a live set to recording a debut album in mere months.

Fontaine: "Everything happened pretty quickly. We went to Tangerine Studios for the recording. It was our first recording in the world of London, the heart of pop music... it all went well, the sound engineers were cooperative and in two days the album was finished. At night we wandered around London a bit, I think I remember seeing Spooky Tooth at the Marquee club. The next morning we walked up King's Road then returned to Paris."

Blanc: "We had two days in the studio to do all of the backing tracks for *Catalyse*. It was a good studio with an eight-track recorder... Pierre Lattès was there to supervise. We were given a lot of freedom. We'd prepared pieces of six to eight minutes each which included improvisations, some fairly free jazz intros, and poems... It was recorded in one take... no editing, no special effects."

Two days in London wasn't quite enough time to complete the recording, so another run of sessions was organised at Paris's Europa Sonor studio. There the band put down extra backing tracks (for 'Unity' and 'A coup de hache'), recorded the vocals, and produced the final mixes.

The resulting album displays an undeniable influence from the first two Soft Machine albums along with a sprinkling of early Gong, hardly surprising given the band's background. However Ame Son bring a little more rock muscle to their music than that might imply, a legacy from their R&B roots.

Catalyse is composed of six short suites which lead the listener through a variety of moods, revealing Ame Son's musical ambition along the way. The album flies out of the stalls with a bracingly frenetic instrumental ('Seventh Time Key') that morphs into the song 'I Just Want to Say'. Both feature intense fuzz guitar work from Lavialle.

The most impressive track on the album is 'Coeur fou'. It begins with an almost industrial ambience before the drums lead into an improvisation with touches of Barrett-era Pink Floyd. There is a seamless transition into Fontaine's instrumental 'La globule', then the song 'Le mal sonne'. The range of moods and the supple flow of the music is surprisingly mature for a band that had only been together for a matter of months.

Musically *Catalyse* is a very successful debut, featuring ambitious music with playing to match. Unfortunately the quality of the music is undercut by surprisingly muted and undynamic mixes. It's hard to fathom exactly why this is the case. It's unlikely that London's Tangerine Studio was the weak link; at around the same time albums for Caravan, East of Eden, and Rory Gallagher were recorded there. Instead it seems that something went terribly wrong during the mixing sessions in Paris. As it stands *Catalyse* has the misfortune to be an album of classic music compromised by lacklustre production. This deficiency would soon lead to problems.

Just weeks after the London recording session Ame Son were playing their first major concert at the Amougies Festival. The association with BYG had assured them a prestigious spot on the bill. Blanc admits that the band were terrified when they took the stage, having no idea how they'd be received by the huge crowd. Thankfully the performance went very well, "We got a great ovation, and our first reviews in magazines. It opened Ame Son's career." [6]

Paul Alessandrini, writing for *Rock & Folk*, was impressed by the young band's performance: "If everything doesn't yet seem to be perfect, if there still seems to be some inconsistency and weakness, the approach appears definitive. Their use of the French language... transfigured, and amplified is exciting. So is the contribution of electric flute and the use of sound effects from the guitar. A group to watch." Jean-Noël Coghe, in *Best*, was taciturn, but positive: "Ame Son are French and full of promise."

After their success at early festivals like Amougies and Les Halles the band were becoming hot property. Blanc: "After Amougies, it suddenly happened, like we were beginning to be, not really stars, but... Wow! You know a lot of newspapers speaking about us, television..." All they needed to do was release an album to capitalise on the buzz generated by their live performances. BYG had *Catalyse* ready to go, but as we'll see, it wouldn't be seeing the light of day for quite some time yet.

In recognition of their success a surprising number of opportunities to collaborate with established artists started coming their way. Unfortunately, for a variety of reasons, none would come to fruition.

The first came through François Garrel's film-making brother, Philippe. He had contracted Nico, the former Velvet Underground singer, to star in his next film (eventually released in '72 under the title *La Cicatrice Intérieure*), and gave Ame Son the opportunity to work on the soundtrack.

Blanc: "At the end of the Amougies Festival, François Garrel and I flew to Positano in the south of Italy, to work on music for Philippe's film... Philippe booked the Davout Studio in Paris. He played a theme on 12-string guitar that François and I improvised over in a completely free style... He was very happy with the music and initially incorporated it into the film. But Nico was the star, and she wanted to release an album of the music that she sang and played in the film. For her there was no question of there being any music other than her own." [7]

The next opportunity came through the music journalist Paul Alessandrini. The poet and writer Dashiell Hedayat (who had already released an album, *La Devanture Des Ivresses*, under the name Melmoth) was looking for musicians to back him on his next record. Blanc: "After Les Halles, around January or February, we were introduced to Dashiell by Alessandrini... He had this project to make a more rock'n'roll record with us. We met up with him once or twice."

The record that Hedayat was about to make (*Obsolete*) would go on to be acknowledged as an underground classic, but rather than being recorded with Ame Son, it was recorded with Gong a year later. Blanc explains what happened: "One night Dashiell called François making humorous sexual proposals to him, François was quite shocked and told us that he didn't want to work with him... It's a shame because the record he made with Gong is a great record and he had a lot of talent as a writer. We missed out on an opportunity."

Lastly, Brigitte Fontaine intimated that she wished to make her next record with the band. But once again, François Garrell nixed the idea. Blanc: "With Brigitte Fontaine it was much more vague. Through BYG we found out that she wanted to make a record with a rock band and was looking to meet up with us. But it didn't go any further... So it was really fine that François said no. All his life François was a bit like this, he wasn't open to do other projects... We were kind of successful and we wanted to champion our own music... But it's a pity because we should have done *all* of these projects."

These missed opportunities shouldn't have been too concerning; Ame Son's star was on the rise. They were voted the 6th most popular French group in *Best*'s 1969 end-of-year poll, and their own LP was due to be released within months. However this is where the Ame Son story takes a surprising turn. The band themselves *insisted* that BYG didn't release the album.[8]

Blanc explains: "After we played in Amougies in October, and in Les Halles in December we realised that we were playing much better on stage than we did in the studio... the songs were so much better after a few months of performance...That's why we asked BYG not to release the album."

Having grown increasingly disappointed with the results of the September '69 sessions, the band had begun to view the outcome as a demo recording rather than a defining statement. Blanc: "We wanted to do something like Pink Floyd, really perfect, really great. But we were young, and we were inexperienced... we didn't realise all the money that was involved... We were too young, we were crazy. We thought they can pay to record the same album a second time."

BYG responded to the band's demand by sending them a registered letter stating that they would have to repay the 40,000F* recording costs if they didn't want the record to be released. Obviously this was never going to happen, so it's a mystery why BYG honoured the band's wish to keep the record under wraps (at least for the time being).

In the midst of ongoing drama with BYG, Ame Son continued to move forward musically. They undertook an experiment in March '70, holding a writing session where the whole band was under the influence of LSD. Blanc: "We were a little blocked on *Catalyse*... we wanted to find new inspiration and said, 'yeah, let's try new

---

* Approximately 30,000€ today.

experiences to do it'." The experiment didn't yield much material, but it did catch the attention of Jacques Dudon, one of France's leading rock guitarists. Blanc: "Our manager played the tape to Jacques... and Jacques told him 'I want to play with them.' I was very flattered. And, so we played together for two days. I liked it, but the other members of the group didn't. I was disappointed, because I admired him a lot."

Although Dudon didn't end up joining Ame Son, he became a regular feature at their concerts, often opening for them with a solo set.

The impasse with BYG was eased when it was agreed that two of the songs from the album sessions could be re-recorded and released as a single. Blanc: "BYG had a project for summer '70 for four bands to do a promotion around the country... We were free to do what we wanted, so we decided to record a French version of 'I Just Want to Say' ('Je veux juste dire') with a new arrangement, and an acoustic, psychedelic version of 'Unity' with different sounds like bowed guitar etc..."[9]

The recording session was held in Paris' Studio Patay, and the result confirms that Ame Son's reservations about the recordings on *Catalyse* weren't unfounded. The new version of 'I Just Want to Say' not only features a more confident band performance, but more importantly has a much more powerful and dynamic mix. It's interesting to speculate what the reaction to *Catalyse* would have been if it *had* been released in '70 in a form that had this much punch and energy.[10]

'Je veux juste dire'/'Unity' was released in June '70, just before the festivals of *L'Été Pop*. The single and a good run of festival appearances raised the band's profile yet again. Blanc: "I think we are one of the only French groups to have played the Grand Slam of festivals: We played at Amougies, Les Halles, Le Bourget, Biot ... all of them."

Fontaine: "The group was beginning to be well-known... We gave a joint concert with Gong in Dieulefit at the end of August '70 (it was the great family reunion)... At the end of September, we appeared on Jacques Martin and Danielle Gilbert's *Midi Magazine* television show."

An October concert at the Théâtre de la musique in Paris was reviewed by Philippe Paringaux for *Rock & Folk*: "Ame Son express some snatches of plastic beauty in the style of Pink Floyd, but fortunately hasten to lay waste to this beauty with great blows of edgy stridency and fierce screams... these torn, delirious passages were the best moments of the night. When the sweat and the cry are real... the band undeniably have something to say."

The year closed with Ame Son once again making it into the Top 10 most popular French bands in *Best*'s end of year poll - (at 8th, they were just one position behind Gong). However there was disquiet in the band. Fontaine: "We had achieved some form of success. We had the sense that a *commercial* career could be opening before us, which could be seductive and worrying at the same time."

There doesn't appear to have been any major issue that was dividing the band, but rather a number of smaller ones. Fontaine mentions "a rivalry between Marc and François that I had trouble explaining and understanding. And for myself, my partner at the time was expecting our child and I anticipated that it might be difficult to combine music and fatherhood."

The internal turmoil continued, and led to a meeting at their manager's home to come to some kind of resolution. Fontaine: "Everyone had their say without anything being decided. At the end of the discussion our manager asked one of us to formulate the break-up that we'd been talking about all evening. No one wanted to speak, so it was finally me (even though I hadn't been arguing for it) that did. I don't think I've ever regretted it."

Today Blanc expresses his belief that their manager mishandled the situation, and rues the decision to call it a day: "We could have easily carried on like Magma and Gong. It would have been enough for a slightly determined manager to advise us not to throw in the towel, instead he was the first to persuade us to stop." [11]

Ame Son would play their last concert at the Paris Museum of Modern Art on 27 January '71, which according to Fontaine was one of their best.[12]

At some point in mid-'71 BYG finally released the *Catalyse* album.[13] According to Blanc the band was never informed: "I suppose they released it in the [rest of the] world, but not in France during our existence. In '72 Jérôme came back from the US and told me, 'Hey, Marc, I saw your record in the supermarket in San Francisco.' So I knew that they'd put it out there."

Today Blanc is able to see that *Catalyse* has appeal, and is glad that it finally saw the light of day after the band split. "It was a great period, fast and intense, with so many experiences. Fortunately BYG did release the album as a witness to our dreams and poetry. It's good that it was put out because it became like a sort of cult, which is great. Even if it's not perfect, it exists! Anyway, I can feel the energy we had at that time."

Marc Blanc went on to join Patrick Vian in Red Noise, followed in '72 by a short-lived project with his old Les Primitiv's bandmate Bernard Stisi (the recordings they made were released as Eclosion *by Monster Melodies in 2015). In '73 he unsuccessfully attempted to relaunch Ame Son with Jacques Dudon, and Jean-Louis Aubert (who would go on to found Téléphone).*

Patrick Fontaine played in a number of bands after Ame Son. He joined the Peteau brothers in Cheval Fou at the end of '72 (he would also play on the Nyl *record in '75), Robert Wood's Woodlands in '73, Mahjun in '74 ,and toured with Graeme Allwright in '76.*

Bernard Lavialle played guitar on albums by Nyl and Patrick Vian. He died in 2024.

A NOTE ON THE TWO VERSIONS OF *CATALYSE*

All references to *Catalyse* are to the pressing released on BYG. In mastering it was discovered that Side Two ran longer than the maximum duration allowed for vinyl. Blanc relates that the band were present when the mastering engineer physically cut the tape (removing the song 'Unity') as a result.

This excision means that on the original BYG issue the suite 'Reborn This Morning On The Way Of ...' is reduced to a flute-based instrumental.

The German mastering engineer responsible for the Metronome release of the album was able to include 'Unity' by rearranging the track order.

Thankfully the track 'Unity' has been reinstated on all of the subsequent reissues of *Catalyse*. Most have followed the original BYG running order, but a few have used the altered Metronome running order.

Notes

1   "We had a manager whose only possessions were a tuxedo and a modicum of nobility. This gave him access to society balls - evenings whose sole purpose is for young people from noble and rich families to meet in order to avoid any mismatch." *(Patrick Fontaine)*

2   Blanc saw Soft Machine perform *just* after they had returned from France and Daevid Allen had been turned back at the UK border.

3   Laperrousaz would also be important in the story of Bananamoon and the beginnings of Gong.

4   Unfortunately this recording has been lost.

5   Garrel had been Blanc's close friend since the end of '67. He was already living in the Montaulieu community where Bananamoon were based.

6   Jérôme Laperrousaz's film of the festival, *Music Power - European Music Revolution*, includes 'Marie aux quatre vents' from Ame Son's performance. A clip is available to view on YouTube.

7   The piece recorded for this film, 'Le grand cirque de la lune', was included on the posthumously released *Primitive Expression* album (see Discography).

8   This decision must have been made at quite a late stage, because the vinyl master had already been created, with the band present.

9   Blanc points out that 'I Just Want to Say' was originally written in French; their producer had asked them to record an English version for the album.

10   There is a live film clip for 'Hein quant à toi' shot by Jean-Noel Roy that confirms the maturation in Ame Son's sound. The band's playing is more muscular and confident than on *Catalyse*. Blanc states that it gives a very good indication of the band's live sound at the time. The sound recording is included on the *Primitive Expression* album (see Discography).

11   Fontaine disagrees with this characterisation of Ame Son's manager, Adrien Nataff: "If he truly didn't put all of his energy into convincing us to continue, he simply wasn't able to diffuse the latent rivalry between Marc and François, which I see as the real cause for the group's break-up."

12   Fontaine mentioned that he knew that this concert had been recorded on cassette, but that the recording had since been lost.

13   A BYG advert in *Rock & Folk* #50 (March '71) includes Gong's *Magick Brother* and Alice's self-titled albums (both released on BYG) but not *Catalyse* - so presumably it was released some time after that date.

GONG

> At various times in France, Gong was a revolutionary band - a flat-out anarchist, student's revolutionary band. Then, for a while, when we did *Continental Circus*, we became a biker's band... that was outrageous! And from there, it went on to the flower-power, hippie thing... it would never have happened like that in England. We would have been confined to a certain style of playing and would have stayed much less interesting, much less of a smorgasbord than it could be in France.
>
> *Daevid Allen*

Gong's genesis can be traced back to one of several events. Daevid Allen himself refers to the "seed vision" he experienced over Easter '66 while in Deya on the island of Majorca. Another, more prosaic possibility is the residency at La Vieille Grille in late '67 where Allen explored his "glissando" guitar technique while Gilli Smyth birthed her "spacewhisper" vocals.[1] However, a good case can also be made that Gong was conceived on Boulevard Saint-Germain. It was there, outside the famed Café de Flore, that Allen had a chance meeting with a saxophonist named Didier Malherbe.

Just a few weeks later, over 1000 km away, they would encounter each other for a second time. Their relationship developed, and it was Malherbe that Allen called on to be at the core of his new venture. Along with Gilli Smyth, Malherbe would be a constant presence at Allen's side for the next five years. According to Bob Benamou: "Didier Malherbe is a great, great musician; he was the most important person in Gong after Daevid."

Before the Beginning

Malherbe was already an experienced jazz musician when he met Allen: "I started playing saxophone when I was fourteen. At seventeen I was playing bebop (Johnny Griffin, Coltrane, Rollins) with gigs at Le

Chat Qui Pêche in Paris. My background was totally in jazz: bebop, then free-jazz. Then I went to India when I was nineteen, and became interested in modal music. I started playing bamboo flute and drifted away from jazz a little - dropping saxophone, just playing flute."

In '66 Malherbe performed in the play *Les Idoles*[2] alongside singer Valérie Lagrange and actors Pierre Clémenti and Jean-Pierre Kalfon. He was cast as a member of the on-stage band Les Rollsticks.

At the end of '67 Malherbe saw Soft Machine's performance at La Fenêtre Rose: "I was fascinated, they were playing a good fusion of elements of jazz and pop... There was also a harmonic originality that was different from American jazz. In a way it decided a lot of things for me."

A few months later he had a fortuitous encounter with their ex-guitarist: "A German actor from the Living Theatre introduced me to Daevid near the famous cafés de Flore and Deux Magots. That night we spent quite a few hours together. Daevid told all his funny stories about pot head pixies. I had my flute so we played together. I was impressed."

Malherbe was surprised to meet Allen in Spain only a few weeks later: "I spent the summer of '68 in Deya. It was pretty amazing... one of the best times I've had in my life. Some people had come from France after the events of May... And Daevid was there! He had his house on the top of the hill next to the church. Robert Graves, an incredible man, lent me a little shepherd's cave not far from Daevid's house... We saw a lot of each other, played music, and eventually we kind of decided to set up Gong. Not just like that... it came little by little."

At the end of summer Malherbe returned to Paris. He teamed up with an English singer/guitarist and an American violinist in '69 to busk outside the underground hot-spot, La Coupole. "I met... Leo Gillespie [and] Gerry Field, an excellent young violin player from Chicago. We played in the streets of Montparnasse for a couple of months, just before the founding of Gong."

According to Field the trio attracted support from both a future star and a mysterious benefactor: "Patti Smith had started hanging out with us, and she passed the hat. She didn't let us know she could sing or that she was writing poetry!... Then one day, a guy came up and said, 'Would you like to make a record? I'm with Decca in Paris and I have access to the studio.' So the three of us went and made this impromptu recording. It was just a jam session, but the guy turned it into a record - he called the group 'Morning Calm' and the album *Song Under a Tree*." [3]

Magick Brother, Amougies, and the Birth of Gong

In August '69 Daevid Allen was in limbo. His band Bananamoon had just split, but the idea of Gong kept growing stronger. He was kicked into action when Jean Karakos appeared out of the blue with an offer.[4] BYG Records wanted him to make an album, quickly! Allen immediately contacted Didier Malherbe.

Malherbe is quick to stress that this first album for BYG was a Daevid Allen solo LP, not a Gong record. While future members of Gong were featured (himself, Gilli Smyth, and drummer Rachid Houari) there was an equally important contingent of American jazzmen. "That first [album] was a mix of Daevid's songs and free-jazz, completely free stuff. Jazz musicians like Earl Freeman, Burton Greene, and Barre Philips were on the record."

The sessions took place at Studio ETA and Studio Europa Sonor in September/October '69 with Pierre Lattès producing. The resulting album, *Magick Brother,* is a fine set of psychedelic pop songs leavened with flourishes of free jazz. Most significant in foreshadowing the sound of Gong-to-come are the bookending tracks: 'Mystic Sister' highlights the interweaving of Allen's glissando-guitar and Smyth's spacewhisper-vocal, while 'Cos You Got Green Hair' serves as a more earthy taster of the floating stoned-ambient interludes of the Radio Gnome trilogy.

Bassist Christian Tritsch had been brought into the group alongside Rachid Houari[5], but due to time constraints Allen had played the bass parts on *Magick Brother* himself. Immediately after the recording, violinists Gerry Field and Dieter Gewissler[6], along with the wildcard figure of Daniel Laloux (on vocals, hunting horn, and marching drum), were enlisted into the band. This was the line-up that took the stage at the Amougies festival in October '69.[7] Gerry Field notes that they were billed as The Daevid Allen Group, and can't recall the name Gong being used during his short tenure.

Because of Allen's relationship with BYG, the band had a feature slot at the festival, headlining the Sunday night line-up of French bands. However a series of delays and over-runs pushed their appearance into the wee hours of Monday morning. When they finally took the stage at 5am, shock tactics were needed to energise a fading audience. Malherbe: "People were lying like corpses, half asleep. Daniel Laloux played a military drum from the Napoleonic period. So Daniel pounded on his drum, and recited a famous Victor Hugo poem about Napoleon and Waterloo[8] (which was only a couple of kilometres away)." The crowd responded enthusiastically.

The remainder of the set featured songs from *Magick Brother* interspersed with a good deal of free improvisation. Pierre Lattès wrote in *Best*: "You could sense the real freshness, intelligence, and notion of a totally new music... Some talents make the world move a little, and it's time for Daevid Allen to make it move... It was probably worth freezing for five days if only for the rendition of 'Waterloo'." In his review for *Rock & Folk* Paul Alessandrini lauded the band's balance of "musical delirium" and "devastating humour", labelling their performance an "indisputable success".

Allen's friend Jérôme Laperrousaz had filmed the set for his festival movie, but the sound recording proved unusable. To allow them to recreate the music for the sequence, he offered his family's Normandy chateau as a temporary base for the band. Château du Thiel would be their home for the next five months.

The Gong Community: The Haunted Chateau & Montaulieu

While Allen has stated that Gong was born at Amougies, Malherbe notes that it was during their stay at the "haunted chateau" that Gong became a community. An important member was added to this nascent community in February '70 when Allen asked Bob Benamou to become Gong's manager.

The recordings made at Château du Thiel[9] reveal a progression from the psychedelic pop of *Magick Brother* towards a hard-edged, free-flowing psych-rock. Allen almost dismissed his first album in an early interview: "It doesn't represent the current group. It was a kind of masturbation, or rather the result of massive constipation. In short I relieved myself."

A 7" record that *did* represent the current group was released hot on the heels of *Magick Brother*. 'Garçon Ou Fille' exhibited a new-found aggression, with Allen's fuzzed-out guitar and violently delirious vocal giving it an almost punk energy. However this only revealed part of Gong's evolution. A performance of 'Dreaming It' filmed at the same time puts the spotlight on Malherbe and Gewissler, foregrounding the more esoteric, improvisational side of their music.

Paul Alessandrini was clearly biased towards this era's divergent, but oddly cohesive melange of music. In his survey of the band for *Rock & Folk* he described it as "sonic madness, a kind of violence, with so many original components asserted to excess, without any search for formal perfection." He singled out Daniel Laloux's contribution to Gong's "comedic and derisive theatricality."

Bob Benamou also praised Laloux's work with Gong: "He didn't stay long, less than a year, but he was great, completely surrealistic, a fantastic artist." This early era of Gong was brought to a close when Laloux and Gewissler played their last concert at the Open Circus in May '70.

With Château du Thiel no longer available to them, the band spent two months in Paris before heading south to their new home base: Benamou's property in Montaulieu. The catalyst needed for the next stage of Gong's evolution was discovered just before they left Paris: in the person of Francis Linon, aka Venux De Luxe.

Linon: "I was living at a friend's flat in Les Halles. One night Daevid appeared saying that Bob Benamou had sent him, and could he stay? Ok great! After a cup of coffee, we started an exchange half in English half in French, inventing words, smoking joints. I had no clue who he was, and it took me some time to understand his position... he was a musician, part of a band rehearsing in Mr. Benamou's basement, who were on their way to the south. They needed people to help with the equipment, and without any knowledge at all on what was required, I said 'I'm the man you're looking for'.

"In the middle of the night I called George Vidon, a Vietnamese guy I'd met a few days before - a photographer and a sound engineer. He came straight around, tried to understand the situation and told us he was in. At the end of the night Daevid told me I was coming from Venus and he welcomes me to the Planet Gong. He had the revelation of my name 'Venux De Luxe' and my whole life suddenly changed: my first close encounter of the third kind."

A few days later, Linon and Vidon were in Montaulieu with the rest of the band. "It was a typical small village at the end of the road on top of a hill. Bob owned practically the entire village, which he was rumoured to have bought at a very low price. There was even a church in the square, but I don't know if it was part of the deal... Daevid had an old mill further down the valley.

"Bob owned an ancient sheepfold in the wilderness behind the village. The electricity had just been connected, and this is where we moved in with the equipment. It took us more than a week to clean up the goat droppings that covered the floor. We put rugs all over, the gear in the middle, and some mattresses separated by stretched fabric for a little privacy. A stove in a corner, the toilets outside, the bathroom in the river... The Gong community was born."

In the three months Gong spent there, Montaulieu became their spiritual home, and communal living became an essential part of their lives. It was during their stay in Montaulieu that Gong's music made a quantum leap - as Linon massaged their sound through his effects processors, a truly cosmic music emerged.

"Christian Tritsch taught George and I every aspect of the equipment. We spent our time making music and experimenting with the gear, and Daevid and Gilli joined us in the evening to rehearse. One evening I was playing around with their Semprini echo chambers during the long improvisations, and seeing Daevid's satisfied look I realised that I'd found my way. My name was lengthened to become Venux De Luxe Semprini Fingertips."

Winter was approaching, and life in the sheepfold was becoming harder and harder. The band began the search for a permanent base, and found it when Gilli Smyth randomly placed her finger on a map. Pavillon du Hay, an abandoned twelve-room hunting lodge near Voisines and Sens, 120km south-east of Paris, which would be their home for the next three years. It would also be the birthplace of much of the Gong mythology that would inform their later albums.

Linon: "The development occurred during long nights at the Pavillon du Hay with whoever was present around the table after dinner. At the end of a big delirium, Daevid went back to his room to put it together. So nothing took us by surprise, it was Daevid's story evolving night after night."

Malherbe: "Before Gong Daevid had told stories about the Pot

Head Pixies, the Submarine Captain, the Octave Doctors, and all that. He already had all that in his head. It was mainly Daevid's thing to be honest, but I played along with the game. Everyone had a nickname*, so I chose my own: Bloomdido, the title of a tune by Charlie Parker, the first guy I really wanted to imitate on the saxophone. Then the Anglo-Saxon people translated my name Malherbe into Bad de Grasse. And Daevid added Count. So I was Count Bloomdido Bad de Grasse and became this character in the Gong mythology."

Camembert Electrique, Continental Circus, Obselete

1970 had been a formative year for Gong. They'd honed an idiosyncratic musical style and developed a strong community ethos. The foundations had been laid for an incredible creative explosion.

The first order of business in the new year was the recording of Daevid Allen's sophomore solo album. BYG wanted to capitalise on Soft Machine's fame by having Allen record with some of his former band-mates. Allen's visa ban had finally ended[10], allowing him to return to London and do just that. He entered Marquee Studios with Robert Wyatt in February '71 to record the *Banana Moon* LP. Other players on the session included violinist Gerry Field (from the Amougies band), Archie Leggett, and drummer Pip Pyle.

During the sessions Allen met a young sound engineer named Tim Blake. "I did an apprenticeship in a studio... When I met Daevid he was having trouble completing his record, so I helped them with the mixing. I believe we finished *Banana Moon* on 22 March, and Daevid invited me to go back with him to France the next day"

Blake moved in to Pavillon du Hay. "I came into Gong to do the sound. When I arrived Venux De Luxe was already doing it, and it was good, so there was no reason to change anything. I think he was very important to Gong... So I stayed with the band and when we

---

* Daevid Allen named himself "Dingo Virgin/Bert Camembert", Christian Tritsch was "The Submarine Captain", and Gilli Allen was "Shakti Yoni". Drummers seemed to miss out on colourful alter-egos (Pip Pyle was simply "The Heap" and Pierre Moerlen was "Pierre de Stasbourg". As new members joined characters were recycled or created: Steve Hillage was "Steve Hillside Village" briefly before taking over as "The Submarine Captain", Tim Blake was "High T Moonweed", and Mike Howlett was "Mista T Being".

went to record the *Continental Circus* soundtrack, Pip came to join."

Rachid Houari's wife had never felt at ease in the Gong community, and the drummer finally made the decision to leave the band in spring '71.[11] Allen called Pip Pyle from the *Banana Moon* sessions to take over. In an interview with *Rock & Folk* Allen praised their new drummer, "He brings a new energy to Gong… he plays so hard that he doesn't have to be amplified. He forces all of us to play harder as well."

Pyle and Blake had history: "Pip and I knew each other, but I don't think we liked each other very much! By the time he arrived I'd already gotten rid of all my sound equipment, and bought synthesisers." Pyle hated Blake's synthesisers, claiming they sounded "like a flock of deranged psychedelic chaffinches." He put his foot down saying it was either him or Blake. Exit Tim Blake (at least for now).

Pyle's first few months in Gong were a blur of activity. The band entered the Chateau d'Hérouville studio (Elton John's "Honky Chateau") in May '71 to record two albums in quick succession. The first was the soundtrack to Jerôme Laperrousaz's film *Continental Circus*. For Allen this was an important opportunity to acknowledge his support. In *Gong Dreaming 2* he writes: "We went into the studio clean and clear. With Pip on drums and no rehearsal whatsoever, we completed the soundtrack/album in a series of perfect first takes…"[12] This was recorded, overdubbed and mixed in two days. Jérôme was delighted. He had supported Gilli and I, and Bananamoon and Gong with his considerable enthusiasm and material resourcefulness for three years. This was the kiss of good Karma."

It was Francis Linon's first time in a recording studio: "Everything was done almost live, so no big difference for me. I was operating the echo chambers like in a concert. Everything went very quickly and everyone was pleased with the result."

Almost immediately Gong were back at Hérouville to play on Dashiell Hedayat's album *Obsolete*. Allen was a fan of Hedayat's poetry, so was very happy to provide the music for his songs and poems. The album, now recognised as a classic of the French underground scene, was wrapped up in another whirlwind two-day session.

While these albums are overshadowed by *Camembert Electrique*, they are essential to Gong's discography. The longer tracks on both records allow the band to stretch out, showcasing their improvisational skill.

Gong entered Hérouville studios yet again in June '71 for the main event: a ten-day session to track their debut album. According to Linon the band were primed to bring the past twelve months to its culmination: "The recording of *Camembert Electrique* was the concretisation of everything that happened before, the perfect way of life we were in at Montaulieu, and Pavillon du Hay."

Allen was satisfied with the result: "The band was right on its own cutting edge... Within ten days we had completed the backing tracks and most instrumental overdubs, so we left it there 'til the Autumn...".

Between the recording and mixing sessions Daevid Allen led the band across the channel to the '71 Glastonbury Festival. Francis Linon's account of the event is striking: "Glastonbury was like a vortex. No one could stop us. We went through customs without any papers, just a smile on our faces and Gilli driving. We were real aliens, not speaking the same language, going home to this magic place. Arriving on the site we saw a bunch of people building a huge Pyramid. An incredible energy was happening there, you could feel it, you could touch it..."

The next day was to be Gong's UK debut, an afternoon concert on the Pyramid Stage. "Everybody was enjoying themselves except poor Pip who was very ill, living a complete nightmare. We were due to go any minute but the festival was running late giving Pip more of a chance to recover."

The band had just kicked off when disaster struck: "As soon as we started, in a climax going up, the generator broke down." The apparent setback was actually a godsend. "When the electricity came back it was evening and that changed everything. The Pyramid came out of the dark, Pip was on his feet, and while the band played loud and clear, people came rushing down the hill dancing. Pure magic."

Allen picks up the story: "By the time we resumed it was that magic sunset time... We had barely started when I looked up to see a pied piper line of a thousand or so dancing people snaking down the hill to gather at the front of the stage, cavorting and rejoicing to the music of this odd French band... This was the kind of audience that Gong had been created for, and the gathering awareness of this was running both ways at once. This was our English Spiritual family."

Gong returned to Hérouville in September to add the finishing touches to *Camembert Electrique*. Allen: "We'd been listening to the rough mixes for two months and we knew what we had to do. The September full moon was due in the middle of the recording period and we used the extra creative juice available to work on the most sensitive inspiration based music... The guitar glissando and space-whisper parts, Bloomdido's solos, and vocals..."

Camembert Electrique was released in October '71; in an interview with *Rock & Folk* Allen expressed satisfaction: "This record shows the development of the group over the last six months, it represents the music of the group as it is right now." [13] *Actuel*'s review went further: "*Camembert Electrique* meets all expectations. A gust of madness finally sweeps through French pop, as frenzied rhythms couple with crazy humor in 45 minutes of cosmic and pataphysical coitus."

Between the recording and release of the album Kevin Ayers had moved into Pavillon du Hay and become a semi-permanent member of Gong. Thus, when the band returned to the UK in October for their first major tour, half of the original Soft Machine was on-stage. Ayers would remain with Gong for the next four months.

Linon: "Daevid was happy to be back in England. The Roundhouse was the peak and it established Gong as a major act for the years to come. At the end of the tour Daevid told me something I'll never forget: 'Venux you've brought a totally new sound to England'. That first tour was very important, it gave Daevid confidence in what he was doing and that was good for all of us."

Allen: "What a difference to France! Suddenly I could communicate in my own language and was astonished by the level of acceptance..."

A fortnight after appearing at The Roundhouse Gong were featured on John Peel's BBC radio programme[14], further cementing their place on the British scene.

At the beginning of the tour Pip Pyle had told the band he intended to leave, and suggested Robert Wyatt as his replacement. This raised the tantalising prospect of a Gong line-up featuring three-quarters of the original Soft Machine. Rehearsals were held, and Wyatt joined the band on-stage at a few concerts, but in the end he opted out in favour of starting his own band, Matching Mole.

Pyle stayed on until Laurie Allen was able to take over in late December. His jazzier style and light touch delighted Daevid Allen: "He carried a lithe dancing cowboy jazz style that protected itself with a detached laconic laugh... if I sneezed he would play my sneeze back to me. He lived on the edge of the instant. Bloomdido loved him. So did I. A true alien."

As '71 drew to a close Gong could look back on a year of milestones. Their real debut as a band had been released, another two albums had been recorded, and they had opened the way into the UK. With these foundations in place '72 looked like it would be Gong's year.

Instead '72 was the year of the rotating drum stool - with no less than four changes of drummer. When the *Continental Circus* album was released in March '72, Laurie Allen had already departed.

Didier Malherbe considers the constant turnover of drummers to be the main challenge Gong faced over its lifetime: "In the '70s we had no less than ten drummers. The thing was people would come to stay with us for a few months, or a year or so, and then feel like going back to England. Some of the drummers were from jazz like Rachid Houari and Laurie Allen, but others were very rock.

"Every time their styles alternated. A jazzy drummer would be followed by a rock drummer, who'd be followed by a light drummer, then a woodchopper..."

To support the launch of *Continental Circus* Gong was contracted to play a thirty minute live set in a selection of cinemas across France. The drummer on this tour was Mac Poole, who according to Malherbe "played as if he was deaf." Allen: "It was creative frustration for Shakti Yoni and the crimson face of the overblow for Bloomdido... I had no longer any idea if I was singing in tune. But French audiences rose in uproar as Mac the Poole laboured manfully to eclipse Vander's[15] legendary drum solos and added to his own display by spectacularly juggling his sticks at the crucial moment on climax."

Poole's rock shtick worked to Gong's advantage on this tour, which saw them play to audiences of bikers attracted by the subject matter of the *Continental Circus* film. When he was finally convinced to rein in the volume, the on-stage problems were resolved. Nevertheless Poole left in June, to be replaced by avant-rock drummer Charles Hayward.

Gong had begun to gain widespread exposure in France thanks to the *Continental Circus* soundtrack and through touring on the new circuit set up by Bob Benamou and Magma's manager Giorgio Gomelsky. However the continuing instability in the rhythm section was a constant problem, and it came to a head when bass-player Christian Tritsch announced that he was intending to leave.[16]

Near Death & Rebirth

Only a few weeks earlier Daevid Allen's and Gilli Smyth's first child, Taliesin, had been born. The confluence of events precipitated a major crisis for Allen: "Every time a new drummer had come it was Christian and I who taught them the set... The prospect of teaching well worn Gong arrangements to a new drummer and bassist at the same time as keeping my music tribe and my own physical family happy put me into overwhelm."

The situation reached critical mass in August '72 when Allen announced that *he* was leaving Gong. He discussed this decision in a later interview: "It was a moment, a crisis, of splittingness... at the end of the band that had made *Camembert Electrique*. I *really* wanted to split, but I just couldn't do it... we stopped playing, and I went into retirement. Giorgio Gomelsky and Bob Benamou both came down one day, cornered me, and talked me into going to London."

Allen expands in *Gong Dreaming 2*: "They were sympathetic and proposed to finance a trip to London to audition a new rhythm section. At the same time, Giorgio produced two aces from his pack. Firstly, Francis Moze, my favourite Magma bassist would be happy to join Gong. Secondly, there was a new progressive label starting up in London. They had heard of Gong and were keen to sign us. A faint glimmer of hope winked seductively."

Allen was encouraged to take a few weeks to travel with Smyth and their new child to their Deya property, settle the family there, then fly on to London. When he arrived in October Virgin came through, giving him access to The Manor Studio for auditions. There were also discussions about recording Gong's next album there, with Virgin interested in handling its UK release. Allen was able to return to France with Rob Tait as Gong's new drummer, and the prospect of consolidating the band's position in the UK.

Just before leaving to resolve the drummer issue, Allen had asked Tim Blake to return to the Gong fold. After leaving Pavillon du Hay Blake had settled in Paris, continuing his synthesiser experimentation.

Tim Blake: "The phone rang, and it was Daevid saying I hear you've been playing gigs... He said, 'We're going to make *Flying Teapot*. You should come and play with the band a bit, and then we should make the record. So I moved up to the Pavillon du Hay, this time as the synthesiser player. Pip had bailed... so we didn't have his objections to synthesiser."

For Didier Malherbe the addition of Tim Blake was crucial to the development of Gong: "Synthesiser was a brand new sound in Gong. The cosmic aspect of Planet Gong needed strange sounds, so his synthesisers fit very well... When Tim came Gong became complete."

Didier Thibault (ex-Moving Gelatine Plates) was called in as the new bass player, but as he explains: "Working with Christian Tritsch proved to be impossible. He wanted to leave bass for the guitar, but he wanted me to copy his bass parts exactly. So I left." [17]

Shortly afterwards Francis Moze arrived. While he was happy to play bass on Gong's next album, he had no intention of remaining with the band afterwards.[18] According to Allen his personal and musical aggression brought a matching air of tension: "Francis came from a heady mix of Apache and French blood. He was a master of his instrument and an extravagant musical talent. The result was a potent technical ability and a fiery disdain for musicians who sank below his own perceived waterline of artistic perfection."

The endless drummer-go-round continued when Rob Tait left for Africa in December. Laurie Allen was called back as a temporary replacement for the recording. For a short period Rachid Houari also returned (he contributed percussion on *Flying Teapot*).

Gong managed to add another key member just before decamping to the UK for the recording. They had gone to see Kevin Ayers perform and had been stunned by his new guitarist.

Steve Hillage continues the story: "Kevin invited Didier Malherbe to jam and we had this really fantastic musical communication on the stage. I thought, 'Wow!' After that, Daevid invited me down to their house for a couple of days and while I was there he asked me if I'd like to join the band. And, y'know, it was a 'Is the Pope a Catholic?' moment! *(laughs)* I often compare joining Gong to taking the red pill in The Matrix. Once you're in, everything sort of goes a bit different!"

At the close of a turbulent year a brand new Gong had been assembled around the original core of Allen, Smyth, and Malherbe -

with newcomers Tim Blake and Steve Hillage as permanent members, and Laurie Allen and Francis Moze as the temporary rhythm section. It was this line-up that would record their next album - the first of the Radio Gnome trilogy.

'Keep Calm and Carry Gong' (*Flying Teapot*)

While previous records had alluded to pot head pixies and the Planet Gong, *Flying Teapot* would begin to fully explore the cosmology of the Gong universe. Allen: "It was my idea that this would be the first of a three album concept sequence to be called the Gong Trilogy. It would tell the story of Zero the Hero... a sort of hippy prodigal son who would leave his familiar surrounds for a trip to an unknown planet in a mythical universe."

Didier Malherbe views the Gong mythology as a light-hearted way of exploring deeper truths: "It began as an imaginative game to explain the rapport Daevid, Gilli and I felt. Everybody is driven by some unexplainable force and we tried to explain the almost telepathic understanding we had. But it reached the point that the thing in our imagination was in reality the thing that was imagining us!"

The stories and characters were all new to Steve Hillage: "Daevid had the fully developed Gong cosmology and I was happy to embrace it and become part of it. When I popped out at the other end of the intense Gong experience a few years later, and resumed my solo career, my ideas had been strongly infected by the deep spirituality of Daevid's vision... I was always fond of Daevid's Gong mythology. It gave the band something really special and unique."

Gong arrived in the UK at the start of '73 ready to commit *Flying Teapot* to tape with Giorgio Gormelsky as producer.

Allen: "We arrived at The Manor on New Years Day '73 in time for a new years dinner with Richard [Branson]... on Jan 2nd we began working with Simon Heyworth afternoons and into the late nights, whereupon Mike Oldfield would emerge from under the kitchen table... then work the red eye shift on *Tubular Bells*.

"Compared to Hérouville where we made *Camembert Electrique*, Manor Studios was third world. The overall sound of the band came off tape in the odd shaped upstairs control room without weight or presence... We had played the music with much feeling. It simply didn't sound like we had."

Gomelsky had taken to the role of producer with great gusto, imparting his vision to Simon Heyworth in poetic terms. If the results didn't match what he heard so clearly in his own head he would rain insults on Heyworth. Francis Moze was equally opinionated, and he and Gomelsky would have impassioned arguments in French over the bewildered engineer's head.

Allen: "Simon Heyworth was practically driven to a nervous breakdown by the Gong group production method... Finally the band was banned and Simon mixed alone."

Members of the band were also subject to the extremes of Moze's temperament. Hillage: "Francis Moze was somewhat bemused and a bit disdainful, giving the impression that he thought we were just a bunch of silly hippies. We found his attitude hilarious."

Steve Hillage's own involvement on his first Gong album was quite low-key: "Since the songs on *Flying Teapot* were all pretty much formed... I participated in all the recordings in a mostly rhythm guitar role, locking in with the bass and drums."

While Gomelsky's and Moze's behaviour had made the atmosphere at The Manor combustible, it became explosive when terrible news arrived in the middle of the sessions: Gong's record label had collapsed.

Mike Howlett: "BYG had booked The Manor studio to make *Flying Teapot*, but couldn't pay the bill. In January '73 Virgin and Daevid tried to call BYG in Paris, but no-one answered the phone. So they sent somebody around who told them, 'The building's stripped bare, the office is empty, no-one's there'. As far as anybody knew they'd been left in the shit." [19]

By rights Virgin could have turfed the band out of The Manor, but they allowed the recording session to continue.

Hillage: "Despite the chaos and the problems the recording of the album was still going on. I was one of those in the band, like Didier Malherbe and Laurie Allan, who were happy to continue recording and overdubbing in a fairly jolly spirit that you could describe as 'Keep Calm and Carry Gong'...

"Daevid, of course, was distraught some of the time, and had bouts of rage, arguing with manager Bob Benamou... But despite his despair Daevid also spent a bit of time in the studio finishing his parts.

I think we all wanted to get the album to a kind of finished pre-mixing state, although we had no clear idea what was going to happen with it. It was a surreal state of affairs but it was well imbued with Gongish 'Floating Anarchy'."

At the end of January the *Flying Teapot* line-up of Gong returned to France to play their final gig on 27 January '73: the last hurrah for Christian Tritsch, Francis Moze, and Laurie Allen. It looked like the months of hard work rebuilding the band could have been for nothing. What was to become of the newly-recorded album? Where were they going to find another bass player, and yet another new drummer?

Recollections differ, but it was either at this gig, or just after it, that a solution to one of those problems presented itself in the person of Pierre Moerlen.

According to Steve Hillage: "It was at the last of these gigs in Malakoff, a suburb of Paris, that Pierre Moerlen introduced himself to Didier and confidently proclaimed that he was going to be Gong's next drummer. A few days after this he came down to Sens, and Didier and I gave him a try-out." [20]

Tim Blake remembers things differently: "Didier and I returned from The Manor, next gig 6th of February! And when we got to the house there was this guy unloading drums from a battered old car. And I said 'Who the fuck are you?' He said, 'Don't worry about me man, I'm the new drummer'. And this was Pierre!"

Whatever the circumstances everyone agrees that Moerlen was key to the next stage of Gong's evolution.

Tim Blake: "I really do believe that the day we found Pierre I was looking at the best drummer I'd ever seen or heard. When you meet up with people like Pierre you get to such a height in your playing that perhaps you don't want to go back down."

Steve Hillage: "He's a key element of the Gong sound in the '70s. He was a very tortured guy. It wasn't an easy musical relationship with him, but he was brilliant because of his uniqueness. He was a classically-trained percussionist from a family of classical percussionists, who were involved in the famous ensemble Les Percussions de Strasbourg. Pierre was the rebel of that crew. He wanted to play rock drums as well, but he was always a bit schizoid about it. He never quite decided if he wanted to be a classical percussionist or a rock drummer. He was yo-yoing between the two quite a lot."

Just when some of the uncertainty had been resolved, Daevid Allen had a musical crisis of confidence. He had assembled a brilliant band, but now he had difficulty seeing how *he* fitted into it.

"My guitar sound seemed crude and clumsy beside the silken floating elegance of the Hillage gossamer. And it was. My vocals sounded nasal and forced. They were. Was there still a place left for an inspired amateur bereft of inspiration?... In rehearsal the band would jam ecstatically for hours yet I could find no point of entry. I would stand poised unable to start. Acutely self-conscious I was worried that the new musicians were rapidly losing respect for me..."

"The final straw was the collapse of my personal and working relationship with Bob Bananamou... With his departure a healthy chunk of Gong died forever."

Six months of crisis after crisis had strained the relationship between band leader and manager, and it finally broke down.

Benamou: "One day, we had an argument over some futile pretext – a mistake I'd made about dates I'd booked, or something - and we clashed.... I quit, no bad blood or hard feelings. I returned to my antiques business and never looked back."

Allen had reached breaking point himself. A few days later he assembled the others: "I announced to the band that I wanted to leave but before I finally decided, I would take a sabbatical in Deya to consider the ramifications. Bloomdido was upset and Steve was nonplussed. Moonweed... and Moerlen were unimpressed."

While some in the band believed Allen really would leave this time, Francis Linon was convinced he would return: "Daevid didn't go straight away, it was as if he wanted to make sure we understood that he wasn't leaving, but was planning the next stage. After convincing Steve that Daevid would return, it was now up to us to create a new sound while we waited. We had everything to continue. We were the guardians of the Temple."

'Paragong'

Daevid Allen remained at Pavillon du Hay while the new line-up (often referred to as Paragong) rehearsed and played their first few gigs.

Didier Thibault came back to try out on bass: "Didier Malherbe called to tell me that a new line-up was coming together, with the excellent Steve Hillage on guitar, Tim Blake on keyboards, Pierre Moerlen on drums, Didier Malherbe and myself." Over time it became clear that his distinctive bass style wasn't gelling with the rest of the band. And according to Tim Blake: "Didier Thibault was finding it difficult to blend in with such an excessively 'hippy' band of stoned psychedelic musicians."

Nevertheless Thibault played a handful of gigs with the Daevid Allen-less Gong. The first was on 6 February '73, after just one week of rehearsals. Tim Blake recalls it as a disappointment: "We hadn't written any music so we had to improvise. It was pretty awful, but it was the first outing of Gong without Daevid so it was very interesting."

In March Allen left to travel to Deya via London. In London he was able to check out a new bass player. A girl staying at Pavillon du Hay had insisted that her ex-boyfriend would be the perfect bass player for Gong.

Mike Howlett: "She rang me from France and said I must come immediately because they had a Leo guitarist (Steve), Aquarius sax and synth (Didier and Tim) and a Scorpio drummer (Pierre) - with a Taurus bass player they would have the four fixed signs - Fire, Air, Water and Earth. Being a Taurus I was the obvious choice. *(laughs)*

"I insisted they must at least hear me play. As it happened, Daevid was coming through London... He turned up at the Pheasantry Club in the King's Road, where I played at a regular Monday night jam. Before he even heard me play he said: 'You're perfect, mate! Just go!' During my set I remember him leaping about on the dance floor not really taking much notice, but he still insisted afterwards, so a couple of days later I arrived at the Pavillon du Hay with all my earthly possessions - my bass guitar, a change of underwear and a second shirt."

According to Tim Blake, Howlett was the final piece of the puzzle: "Mike came out to us, and then it was done! We had the perfect band, no doubt about that."

Howlett did, however, have some early misgivings about Moerlen's drumming: "My first jam with Pierre was frustrating. I came from a background of funk, soul and rock, whereas Pierre's schooling was still heavily influenced by his classical education... But I think we grew to respect each other's position and moved towards a mutually satisfying balance of heart and mind - emotion and technique."

Their new bass player found it easy to relax into life in the Gong community: "The atmosphere was magical at the Pavillon du Hay. It was a big ramshackle 19th century hunting lodge with around a dozen or so stoned hippies from a mix of countries... I slotted right in. It also felt like a sort of modern mystical monastery with everyone into alchemy and astrology..."

Hillage agrees that Gong's days at Pavillon du Hay were special: "Definitely magical, because as well as making music we were immersing ourselves in deeply esoteric subjects. For me it was a highly creative time, where I defined my musical style. I would say quite unequivocally that the 'Paragong' lineup was the best band I've ever had the privilege to play in."

Howlett: "A lot happened over the next few months, a lot of jamming and somehow (because I had no idea who was organising anything) a ten date mini-tour of France. We put together a set with material from *Camembert Electrique* and *Flying Teapot*, Steve had written the basics of 'I Never Glid Before' and 'Oily Way', and I'd sketched out 'Sold to the Highest Buddha'."

Hillage: "We were enjoying playing together, and things started to sound really good... We began to get more bookings, so some people were definitely enjoying it. We were being booked as Gong, and we all wished to make music in the spirit of Gong... But at the same time we were players with our own individual styles, being ourselves and coming up with our own ideas..."

Meanwhile, in Deya, Daevid Allen had been able to carefully think through his position in Gong: "I had time and space to meditate on a new direction for Gong. I saw myself playing less lead guitar & leaving this to Steve while concentrating on vocals, audience connection, and ritual theatrics. We returned invigorated three weeks later..."

The Prodigal Returns

The majority of the band welcomed Daevid Allen's and Gilli Smyth's return at the end of April with open arms, but Tim Blake and Pierre Moerlen appeared to harbour reservations.

Howlett: "As far as I knew Daevid and Gilli were always going to be coming back, and I fully expected them to carry on as before I joined. I wasn't aware of any of the tension that Tim has ranted about. That wasn't my perception, and I saw no conflict with Steve or Didier either."

Hillage confirms that he was glad to see Allen and Smyth return: "Personally I was happy with the way they reintegrated into the band - after all my original attraction had been to play with a Gong that included Daevid and Gilli, and now my wish was achieved. I was content to withstand the regular bouts of turbulence..."

While the musical future of the band was being forged at Pavillon du Hay, there was movement across the Channel. Virgin had decided to release *Flying Teapot* in the label's first batch of albums, and Giorgio Gomelsky supervised the mixing sessions at The Manor and George Martin's Air studio.[21] Virgin also expressed their interest in recording Gong's next record. The ongoing silence from BYG, and the uncertainty over the legal status of Gong's contract with them was a real concern. Branson and co. decided to test the waters by signing Daevid Allen individually. If this didn't draw a legal challenge from the presumably defunct BYG the entire band would be signed.

The year had opened with a plethora of crises, but now Gong were not merely back on track, they had reached a creative peak and had the backing of a UK label. *Flying Teapot* was released on 25 May '73 in Virgin's first batch of records - alongside Mike Oldfield's *Tubular Bells*, and Faust's *The Faust Tapes*.

With a new album assured, the band got to work structuring the compositions written over the last few months, as well as writing new material with Allen and Smyth.

Hillage: "These songs were almost entirely created in Spring 1973... before Daevid and Gilli rejoined the band: 'Other Side of the Sky', '6/8 tune' (the instrumental intro to 'Sold to the Highest Buddha'), 'Oily Way', 'Flute Salad', 'Inner Temple', 'Outer Temple', and 'I Never Glid Before'. Gilli of course added spacewhisper, and Daevid added his glissando guitar... Daevid rewrote the lyrics for 'Oily Way', leaving just the chorus line and the title (which Bloom had come up with). He added the great counterpoint vocal melody in the middle stops section.

"The other tracks came together after Daevid and Gilli's return. Of particular note were the two percussion based pieces written by

Pierre Moerlen: 'Percolations' and 'Love is How U Make It' which added a great new dimension to Gong's sound."

To promote the release of *Flying Teapot* Virgin organised a UK tour in June '73 - a combination of appearances in Virgin stores, club dates, and major concerts (often supporting Faust).

Malherbe: "We did a first tour of some pretty big places, like Newcastle City Hall, Birmingham Town Hall, Manchester Free Trade Hall... And in fact, I have to say that we completely out-staged Faust. We were really bursting with energy!"

Hillage: "I vividly remember the free show we played at the 'Magic Roundabout', a patch of open space under the flyover at the end of the newly-built Westway. It was a particularly great gig in front of quite a pretty big crowd, and at one point Richard Branson and the Virgin Records crew got onto the overhead roadway and sent down a rain of hundreds of flying paper plates. Some in the band were somewhat fuelled by LSD for the show and as we hadn't been told this was planned it was definitely a very 'trippy' moment. The plates had some mad blurb on them about flying teapots."

Angel's Egg

After the tour, the band returned to Pavillon du Hay, and spent the next month readying themselves to record *Angel's Egg*. Instead of having to travel to The Manor studio, this time it was coming to them... Howlett: "Virgin sent the Virgin Manor mobile, the first 24-track machine in Europe to that fabulous old house. It was fantastic to have it there."

Simon Heyworth was again at the helm, and took the opportunity to use Pavillon du Hay and its surrounds as an expanded recording studio. Francis Linon: "Simon made good use of the space and the surrounding forest. We wired up the whole house. The musicians were recorded in their rooms, the rhythm section in the rehearsal room, and Gilli in the forest. It was spectacular!"

It wasn't just the technical set-up that created the perfect conditions for the recording. Allen: "There was a lot of good acid available at this point as well as Datura so we were well away on our group shamanic journey by the time recording began. It was close to the ideal circumstances for us... The house was alive with inspiration. Everybody was writing something and there was a lot of joy in the air."

The "good acid" Allen refers to fueled an extraordinary nighttime recording session for 'The Other Side of the Sky'. "The sun was setting as we gathered in the dining room to take the acid together. We ate lightly and wandered out under the cool clear night sky to watch the full moon rise over the forest..."

Howlett: "Steve, Pierre and I played in the music hall. Didier asked if he could play out in the forest, and Gilli asked to be recorded in another part of the woods. The Virgin Mobile crew were very helpful, and even put up with Tim's demand to be recorded in yet another part of the forest - because synthesisers are so organic, right?"

The two week session at Pavillon du Hay produced one of the highlights of Gong's output, with Allen's patented whimsy seamlessly integrated into the musical muscle of what is now recognised as the classic Gong line-up. Although many view *You* as Gong's *magnum opus*, there is a very good case to be made for *Angel's Egg*. Tim Blake sums up its appeal well: "*Angel's Egg* has some pure innocence to it. It probably sounds just like us, while *You* might sound *better* than we did."

In September Gong returned to the UK. After mixing the album at The Manor they went out on tour for a third time. They had just set off when Pierre Moerlen announced he was leaving the band - immediately! He was eventually convinced to see out his commitments, playing his last show in Sheffield on 8 October '73.[22]

Moerlen's tenure in Gong would be peppered with explosive departures, followed by reconciliation a few months later. Howlett: "Pierre was quite arrogant. He thought we weren't up to his level of musicianship, which is why he left several times. He was a classically trained percussionist who'd graduated top of his year at the Strasbourg Conservatoire and had worked with Stockhausen... But three times he came to see us and said he would like to come back, having seen that we were actually quite good *(laughs)*."

Moerlen seems to have been torn between a career as a classical percussionist and as a rock drummer. According to Howlett and Blake he would often blame his dissatisfaction on the esoteric and whimsical Gong mythology expressed in Daevid Allen's lyrics.

Blake: "Every time Pierre would finish making a record with us he'd have the words translated and say 'Fuck this! I'm going back to the orchestra. This is ridiculous.' Of course next time we were ready to start writing he'd rock up. *(laughs)* He knew we were doing something good, but couldn't consider the shame of it, which is weird..."

Steve Hillage believes that was simply a justification for a more fundamental issue: "I don't think it's plausible to think Pierre always had these kind of misgivings. After all, he came to Gong and requested to join... he'd seen Gong with Daevid in full flight, so what on earth was he expecting? I think Pierre's instability about staying in Gong or leaving was essentially a personal psychological issue of his own, and his attempting to blame things on Daevid's contributions was a flimsy scapegoat, and also, if I may say, rather unfair on Daevid."

In a 1995 interview with Aymeric Leroy, Moerlen commented: "There were indeed some problems between me and Daevid, but not so many. It was actually him who had problems with the evolution we were taking, we the musicians. He felt marginalised, but in my opinion he was not. Our styles were definitely compatible... cosmic and complex go very well together, don't you think?"

A French Band on English Soil

Another major upheaval took place in October '73, when Gong uprooted themselves and relocated to the UK. Steve Hillage: "We lost the house at the end of '73 sadly, and ended up moving the whole operation to England... We kept the band going and we still kept producing great stuff, but I felt we lost something when we left France. For me that was the best period of Gong. It was *really* special in France."

Rob Tait, who had been auditioned by Allen back in October '72 finally took his place on the drum stool. His girlfriend Di Bond also joined the band as backing vocalist.[23]

With *Flying Teapot* already in the shops, and *Angel's Egg* scheduled to be released in December, Gong's first few months in the UK were focused solely on touring. Between November '73 and February '74 the band played over sixty gigs.

Another major change came just after the tour. Gilli Smyth had given birth to Orlando Allen in January: she'd tried juggling parenting with touring, but it was proving too much. In February she knew it was time to choose: "I finished up in the Milkweg in Amsterdam, where I had an important dream. It was a revelation that I would soon leave the band both because of the babies, and because I wanted to explore my own lyrical/musical ideas... But there were also Gong musics bubbling, which eventually became the *You* album, which I stayed to help finish." Smyth pulled back her involvement in live performances and Di Bond took over her on-stage role.

Unfortunately for Rob Tait, during his tenure a faction in the band were fixated on bringing Pierre Moerlen back into the band. Allen: "Pierre's ghost was ever present and rumours abounded that he would return. The band divided as it mostly did into two fields of opinion. Each of us freely swapped back and forth according to the mood of the day... Eventually after the gig in Pierre's home town of Strasbourg the pro-Pierre faction met with him in the Café de la Gare and Pierre agreed to rejoin... at least until the third LP in the Gong Trilogy was completed..."

In March '74 Gong found a new community base at Middlefield Farm in Witney, not far from The Manor Studio. In quick successions Rob Tait and Di Bond[24] departed and Pierre Moerlen arrived.

You

The band immediately began to work on the next album. In order to expand their musical vision, Gong decided to create the new music in a more collaborative and deliberate way.

Allen: "We had come to the conclusion that, because I was contributing a lot of the material, that it was too much my original creation. It was time we created something completely together."

Howlett: "We rented a cottage in Little Bedwyn to concentrate on writing the *You* album collectively. Maybe there were too many distractions at the farmhouse? It was a fairly isolated place where we jammed and put together ideas."

Of course what may have been 'distractions' to other bands were a central part Gong's creative process. Allen: "We saved up some wonderful acid and we took this acid together as a group. And this was one occasion where there was no paranoia, it was just a wonderful, wonderful trip and we all played and played and played... then at the end of the day, we would listen to the recordings and take the pieces out that we wanted to learn."

Hillage recalls the day he discovered the 'Om Riff' from 'Master Builder': "I woke up really early one morning and I just had this riff come into my head. I went: *wow!* And I thought 'don't forget it, don't forget it!'... I found Mike Howlett and I said listen to this man, listen it's amazing init? And he went 'That's great!' *(laughs)* So we rushed to the rehearsal place, we had to drive about 20 or 30 miles to get there. We plugged in and we started throwing this riff around... and we really thought this was this is the greatest thing ever! *(laughs)* And I still love it!"

Creativity was sparking, and new tracks kept coming: "The next day Mike arrived with a great new bass riff... This tune evolved into 'The Isle of Everywhere'. After more time spent jamming and refining we felt we had another winner... In the meantime Tim had been working on a rich synthesiser tapestry that he called 'A Sprinkling of Clouds'. We proceeded to add some rhythmic parts and Mike and Pierre came up with some more glorious riffs. Daevid came up with a beautiful glissando guitar part, and by now we were feeling that we had the essential material for a great album." [25]

Their first opportunity to play this new music to an audience was at Birmingham City Hall on 24 April. That hadn't originally been the plan, but that changed when Daevid Allen lost his voice and couldn't perform.

Blake: "In the bus we changed the entire set to base it around the new music we'd written. When we got to Birmingham Venux was there, and he said 'right I can see there's going to be some changes here.' *(laughs)*

"We started the gig with me just droning on synthesisers, then Steve came in and joined me, then Mike and Pierre and before we knew where we were, we were playing the 'Om Riff' for the very, very, very first time! Birmingham City Hall was full, but when we finished playing there was total silence. No-one clapped, everyone was saying 'What the fuck was that!' - including us! After about two minutes Mike bursts out laughing, which changed the spell and brought the whole house down. It was certainly the most amazing gig we'd ever played."

The new music was flowing, but Daevid Allen was finding it difficult to incorporate his lyrical concepts: "I still had not written the lyrics that would work with the new music and complete the tale of Zero the Hero's return home to planet Earth. The longer I left it, the more the feeling arose in the band that the music stood strong as it was. That it did not need words. I saw I had nudged myself out of the composing arena and now I felt I was being vibed out of my verbal and mythological tower."

Tim Blake and Pierre Moerlen were most active in pushing the less-is-more-vocals line, but Mike Howlett admits that the rest of the band were sympathetic to the idea: "For me, the trilogy (including *Flying Teapot*) is a profound work, inspired by Daevid, and given power by the musicians involved. It is really a restatement, in modern terms, of the ancient mystery school lesson - a journey of self-discovery which, like all good fairy stories, goes as far as the reader is capable of following. Nevertheless, I'm guilty of conspiring to minimise the amount of vocals on it, if only by not resisting those pressures more. In retrospect I believe *You* got it right in the balance of vocal versus non-vocal sections. But that balance was achievable only in the context of the preceding two albums."

In June '74 Gong moved into The Manor to record the album. Hillage: "Although there was some instability and tension at the recording sessions at The Manor, there were some wonderful moments, especially the recording of the entire second side from 'The Isle of Everywhere' right through to the end of 'You Never Blow Yr Trip Forever (You Are I and I Am You)' which was all one live take, solos included. For me that was an absolute peak moment."

The vocals remained problematic, and for Allen the nadir came while recording 'The Master Builder': "The rhythmic placement of each word was esoteric in the extreme. First Pierre tutored me and when he grew impatient Steve took over. I made maps. I counted. I tried it phrase by phrase. Still it eluded me. Finally after much struggle with my ailing self-esteem I miraculously started doing it right though I wasn't entirely sure how. By trusting my intuition and going with the flow I finally succeeded. But it killed my desire to ever do it again."

The simmering music vs. lyrics debate finally exploded late in the sessions. Howlett: "Tim was a very excitable and energetic character... but I noticed him getting a bit out of control towards the end of recording *You*. He stayed up all night tripping and haranguing Daevid, who was trying to finish the lyrics and artwork for the album. He was telling Daevid that he should never have come back from Majorca and that he wasn't good enough to play with such brilliant musicians as us. I know this hurt Daevid a lot but none of us had discussed it, or agreed with Tim about this."

Just before wrapping up the *You* sessions, Gong played a show at Hyde Park to an audience of 25,000. A recording was made by the Manor Mobile which reveals a band on searing form, that has created the perfect mix of sparkling musicianship, rhythmic drive, and vocal intervention. The performance peaks with 'The Isle of Everywhere' showcasing Gong's fusion of musical complexity and muscular funk with Smyth's cosmic and Allen's derisive vocalisations.[26]

However Allen found the experience of playing to such a huge crowd totally alienating: "When you play to more than 2000 people you don't have eye contact with everybody, and if I can't see into somebody's eyes then I'm not really playing for them... It's a harder vibe, it's a high professional vibe that *squeezes* you and starts to make a machine of you... I mean I *tried* it with Gong. When we went into Hyde Park... it was ludicrous... there was *no* connection... There's a point at which you can't be spontaneous, you can't change, and everyone's saying you have to do the same thing you did last night. Then there's the economic pressure. So I figure the best thing to do is just *jump out* at that time."

With *You* completed Gilli Smyth decided it was the right time to move on from Gong, playing her last concert at the London Olympia on 7 July. Allen remembers it as a disappointing gig, with no soundcheck and terrible on-stage sound: "It was a sad finale and further proof of the fragility of my position in the band. But the next day the shit really hit the fan."

All Change (again)

After the Olympia gig Pierre Moerlen rounded on the band telling them he'd had enough. Allen: "Pierre was furious with everybody. We were terminally untogether... We played too much and didn't listen to each other... He couldn't play with a band like that! Finally, I was guilty of usurping his compositions and covering them with silly vocals. That was it. He was finally leaving... forever!" [27]

A dark gloom descended, flaring into outright conflict when Blake laid the blame for Moerlen's departure squarely on Allen and Smyth. The situation was eventually diffused when Allen suggested that *You* should be mixed without his input, he would let the rest of the band decide on the role his vocals would play.

With the tensions lessened, Allen was free to travel to Spain to help Smyth and the children settle into their new home. In the calm of Deya Allen once again considered leaving Gong. Not only was there another upheaval to face, there was also a potential choice looming between band and family. He and Smyth resolved to try to balance the two, Allen would come to Deya when Gong were off the road, and Smyth and the children would join him whenever it was possible.

Allen arrived back at Middlefield Farm just as the *You* mixes were completed: "We crowded around the best sound system in the house and with my art in my mouth I emptied my mind and surrendered to the spirit of the music. I was powerfully impressed... and thankful to everybody for keeping my needs in mind... it was the best Gong sound yet."

After completing a three-week UK tour Allen returned to Spain, while the remainder of the band reentered The Manor to record Steve Hillage's debut solo album. *Fish Rising* is often seen as a de-facto Gong album, a view given weight by the fact that the complete 'Paragong' line-up, including Pierre Moerlen, play on it.[28] However it has to be acknowledged that Hillage was developing a compositional voice quite distinct from that of Gong. Nevertheless, in the months leading up to its release, much of the album would be integrated into the band's live set.

In September Gong set off on a major tour to support the imminent release of *You*. In three months the band would play more than fifty concerts across the UK and Europe. Moerlen's departure had restarted Gong's drummer-go-round. Chris Cutler had stood in on the August tour, but now Laurie Allen returned as their permanent drummer. That was until he was busted carrying drugs across the French border, and banned from returning to France (not a tenable situation for a member of Gong). Bill Bruford (ex-Yes, ex-King Crimson) was called in at short notice to complete the tour.[29]

This would come to be seen as only a minor bump in the road when a major crisis erupted after the release of *You* on 4 October '74. Virgin had just shipped the album to shops when a resurrected BYG slapped an immediate injunction on the sale of all Gong records. The injunction was lifted on appeal, but this was merely the first salvo in an epic battle over the ownership of Gong's catalogue.[30]

Allen returned to Deya in the new year, and again pondered his future with Gong.[31] The drum stool was empty again, a corporate battle was being waged over their future, and there was still simmering intra-band conflict, with Tim Blake acting as a lightning rod.

Allen: "I intuitively flashed that some of the band were discussing my departure from Gong. A similar seeing a few days before provoked my own questions about being in Gong. Did I like the new music? No. Had I ever liked it? No. Did this matter? No. Did I want to leave the band? Yes... but could I afford to?"

The end of an era

On his return Allen was plunged straight into open conflict with Blake. Allegiances in the band shifted over the course of a few weeks until an impasse was reached. Steve Hillage had been absent for all of this, and when he returned he was asked to break the deadlock.

Hillage: "Unfortunately [Gong] went through some real problems at the end of '74, beginning of '75, when I was away finishing *Fish Rising*... They were having a lot of problems in the house and I wasn't there. I was feeling kind of impotent because I couldn't really resolve this thing. It was all starting to crack up. It was frustrating for me."

Finally in mid-March '75, Tim Blake was asked to leave. Howlett: "We sacked Tim after a particularly insane outburst involved throwing a carving knife while standing on the dinner table and screaming abuse."

Blake: "I have to admit it, when I should have been at my strongest I totally cracked up, and started behaving in a way that rapidly became unacceptable to my colleagues..."

Allen: "It was the beginning of the end for the classic Gong band... Without Moonweed, would Gong ever be the same again? Who could know? Gong was dead. Long live Gong."

Allen's feeling that he had become musically redundant in Gong was compounded when he judged himself unable to do justice to the guitar parts on Hillage's new piece 'Aftaglid'.

His decision was finally made: "It was increasingly clear that Gong as I had helped to create it was dying... Yoni's departure had cut it off from the vital feminine source of its power. Pierre's inability to punch with the floaters & spacers & his constant on:off participation had weakened our male spiritual warrior rhythms & deep roots...

Obviously Gong needed to go in a new direction with Steve at the helm and I was in the way. The truth was that I had lost interest in playing but in my exhaustion was unable to confront the reality that I was only continuing out of habit and fear for the survival of my family."

In April Gong left Middlefield Farm to embark on a major tour: twenty dates in the UK, and a further twenty in France. Allen would only play the first. At the second concert in Cheltenham he didn't join the band on stage.

Malherbe: "It was a surreal evening. We were in the dressing room and Daevid was all dressed up for Gong, with fluoro make-up on his nose and cheeks, dressed in his stage clothes with a big hat and tights - the whole costume *(laughs)*. And I really don't know... Nothing against him, but he flipped out."

Allen: "I couldn't actually get on stage. It was as though there was an invisible curtain of force that was stopping me from going through the door. I threw myself at the open door and bounced back, off nothing. And this blew my mind so thoroughly that I just ran out of the theatre."

Linon: "Life had become complicated. Tim had created too much tension, and Gilli had left, so I wasn't surprised when Daevid arrived at the console to tell me he wouldn't finish the concert. He stayed with me for a bit and then disappeared. I knew he wasn't coming back... I never forgot that moment, it was as strong as our meeting."

Malherbe: "It was raining and he hitchhiked back to [Witney]. I can see the whole thing *(laughs)* in his stage costume, in the rain, hitchhiking! I don't know why he did it. Did he get paranoid because of Steve? I don't know. Pierre Moerlen had some problems with Daevid and the mythology because his mind was very French, very rational. He accepted the Gong scene, but there was maybe a bit of friction with Daevid. I don't know the reason, but Daevid flipped out that night, that was the reality."

The day after Allen's departure *Fish Rising* was released, and the band continued on the tour with Hillage taking on Allen's role.

Howlett: "After Daevid and Gilli left, Steve more or less took over with our consent, although theoretically there was no 'leader'. We also started to incorporate more material from Steve's album *Fish Rising*, which we'd all played on."

"On reflection, Daevid had often expressed a vision of Gong being a sort of ongoing vessel that musicians could come into and do work with then move on. Perhaps like the Sun Ra Arkestra..."

Linon: "I think that everyone's paths took another direction at this exact moment and what came next was going to prove it. He had achieved a goal, the trilogy existed, the group was well supervised and could continue its story without him.

"I went to the end of the tour. It was at a festival in Rome that I made my decision. I told Steve that I wasn't coming back to England and that I would stay in Nice for a while before I got my things back in Witney. It was five years, to the day, from my first concert with Gong."

A Brave New Gong? (*Shamal*)

Virgin contacted Pierre Moerlen in August '75 to ask him to rejoin Gong in a leadership role.[32] Moerlen agreed and over the next few months brought several new members into the band, the first being keyboard player Patrice Lemoine (ex-Catherine Ribeiro + Alpes).

A September performance recorded by the Manor Mobile at The Marquee captured the band in transition.[33] The set is almost evenly split between tracks from the Trilogy albums and material from Hillage's solo record, along with two new tunes (Malherbe's 'Bambooji' and Howlett's 'Wingful of Eyes').

At the end of September Moerlen enlisted Mireille Bauer[34] to add marimba, glockenspiel, and xylophone. Under his influence the music was quickly moving away from the psychedelic flavour of classic Gong towards percussion-led jazz-fusion.

Hillage began to reassess his position: "Miquette and I resolved to sort of keep in there and make a go of it, but there was this kind of pressure to move away from the fantasy and the psychedelia and go more into instrumental prowess. It wasn't very satisfactory for me, really. I mean I loved the fact that Gong had this jazzy element... [but] focusing just on that wasn't enough for me."

In October, while rehearsing for the upcoming recording, Hillage and Giraudy announced they had decided to leave at the end of the year.[35]

In November the new line-up entered Basing Street Studios to record *Shamal*, the last Gong album to feature a cast of players mostly drawn from the classic Trilogy line-up. By writing most of the music Malherbe and Howlett proved to be the most significant contributors, but Moerlen's inimitable drumming cannot be discounted, nor can the stamp that Hillage and Giraudy leave with their guest spots. The music has changed, but the spirit of Gong is still there on *Shamal*.

Malherbe: "I composed more for *Shamal* than for the previous albums. And Mike Howlett composed some things as well. We enjoyed making the album, even though it wasn't really the same kind of music as before. The good thing was that we had a very good producer: [Pink Floyd's] Nick Mason. He was very good technically and also on the human level, because there were, I wouldn't say arguments, but different directions in that group."

Howlett: "*Shamal* was a collaboration in that we all brought our own pieces to the party and arranged them together. I liked the music, I just felt that we should keep some lyrical connection with the previous material. The vocal element on *Shamal* was largely the result of my efforts... I felt a responsibility to those listeners who had stayed with the story so far to leave them with a few clues as to where Zero had disappeared to... I'm a believer in the power of words to communicate concepts and emotions, the more so when coupled well with music."

When is a Gong not a Gong? (*Gazeuse!*)

At some point did the group that carried the name "Gong" actually cease to *be* Gong? A purist might argue that happened on 10 April '75 at the exact moment Daevid Allen left the Cheltenham Town Hall. However *Shamal* showed that while the spirit of Gong may have evolved since his departure, it was still there. What *is* incontestable is that over the next twelve months the band would be transformed beyond recognition, as Pierre Moerlen's vision won the day. By the time the album *Gazeuse!* was recorded in November '76 all traces of psychedelia had been jettisoned in favour of a sleek, percussion-led jazz fusion.

Howlett : "I held the banner for lyrics after Steve fell in the line of duty. Perhaps inevitably, I was next to come under attack from the anti-lyrics camp... The group was split between me and Patrice Lemoine on the lyric side, and Pierre and Mireille Bauer in the instrumental camp, with Didier as ever not really ready to decide either way... Things came to a head and Virgin was given the choice between my version and Pierre's. Simon Draper, the true creative head of Virgin from the beginning... chose Pierre's way."

Mike Howlett left in May '76, quickly followed by Patrice Lemoine. A new line-up was created with high-profile fusion guitarist Allan Holdsworth[36], bassist Francis Moze (late of the *Flying Teapot* line-up) and two additional percussionists (one of them Moerlen's brother Benoît).

It was on 24 October '76 that Didier Malherbe realised this Gong was no longer *his* Gong: "We played a big gig at the Olympia in Paris, a show with proper French Gong aficionados. So I was at the front telling stories about the Pixies, making the link with the *Gazeuse!* Gong which was completely jazz-rock. Everyone else was behind me... very cold, very stiff, not having a good time. There was a big dichotomy, I was the only one to really be a Gong man. So I thought it was time for me to go."

Malherbe participated in the recording of *Gazeuse!* but on the understanding that he was leaving the band afterwards.

Malherbe: "*Gazeuse!* had some really incredible players: Alan Holdsworth, Francis Moze, and the percussionist Mino Cinelu who played with Miles Davis. Instrumentally it was a big advancement, real progress. But it's too different from the Gong atmosphere, it had become cold... not free at all."

With Malherbe's departure Gong's story was definitively over. Pierre Moerlen dissolved the band before *Gazeuse!*[37] was released in January '77.

Epilogue (*Gong est Mort, Vive Gong!*)

Hillage: "One thing about Gong that I really like is the fact that we've got the Gong Family. Unlike a lot of bands from that time, and even though we've had our disagreements, we've managed to keep the whole thing as one family. We see every Gong solo project or spin-off project or sister project as part of the overall Gong thing. And I think that's a really beautiful thing."

The first reunion of the Gong family came only months after the release of *Gazeuse!*. A festival at the Paris Hippodrome on 28 May '77 brought together the *Angel's Egg* line-up, the *Shamal* line-up, and the current projects of each member: Daevid Allen & Euterpe, The Steve Hillage Band, Tim Blake's Crystal Machine, Pierre Moerlen's Gong, and Strontium 90 (an early version of The Police with Mike Howlett on bass).[38]

There was a gap of over a decade before a new line-up of Gong appeared for a one-off TV performance in '90 (later released on video as *Gong Live*). This band was Daevid Allen, Gilli Smyth, Didier Malherbe, and Pip Pyle, with three members of Here & Now[39] (Keith Bailey, Stephan Lewry, and Twink).

During the '90s Gong became a going concern once again, with an album of new material, *Shapeshifter*, released in '92. Another three albums were released with the last, *I See You*, released in the last year of Allen's life. Allen asked the line-up that recorded that album to continue as Gong after his death. Their most recent album, *Unending Ascending*, was released in 2023.

Daevid Allen continued to record as both a solo artist and a member of Gong until his death in 2015, aged 77.

Gilli Smyth formed the band Mother Gong in '79, and continued performing and writing until her death in 2016, aged 83.

Didier Malherbe continues to record and perform, most recently in Hadouk with Loy Ehrlich.

Pierre Moerlen formed Pierre Moerlen's Gong in '77. They recorded eight albums before finally disbanding in '88. Moerlen continued to play live and studio sessions, and had only recently started a new band when he died in 2005, aged 52.

Steve Hillage continues to play live with the Steve Hillage Band and record as System 7 with his partner Miquette Giraudy.

Mike Howlett has had a very successful career as a record producer, and academic.

Tim Blake continued his Crystal Machine synthesiser project after leaving Gong. He continues to record and play live, often as a member of Hawkwind.

Francis Linon ran a successful audio engineering company for almost twenty-five years. He has been Magma's sound engineer since '78.

Notes

1   See *Chapter 20*: 'A Tale of Two Moons' for more on this era.

2   The soundtrack of the play was issued by CBS in '67 and a film (in which Malherbe reprised his role) was released in '68.

3   Barclay Records released the album in early '70. "None of us made any money, and we never actually heard the product" *(Field)*.

4   Allen describes his signing with BYG in *Gong Dreaming 1*: "One evening, I received a telegram from a mysterious person named Jean Karakos who wanted me absolutely to sign with his new label, and was on his way down from Paris by car with a million old francs advance... He was a good gambler and a good psychologist where I was concerned. I was powerfully impressed and, most importantly my integrity was engaged."

5   Tritsch and Houari had previously played together as the rhythm section for *varieté* star Claude François.

6   Field had played with Malherbe in the 'Morning Calm' trio, while Gewissler had played double bass on the *Magick Brother* album.

7   For more on the Amougies Festival see *Chapter 4*. Malherbe points out that the band had played a few shows before the festival: "Amougies wasn't our first gig. We played at a party to open Jean Bouquin's clothes shop in Saint-Germain-des-Prés, along with Martin Circus."

8   During Laloux's time in Gong, this piece would remain an integral part of Gong's repertoire.

9   These recordings were released in 1995 on the *Camembert Eclectique* CD.

10   See the Introduction to this section to read about Allen's UK visa woes.

11   The last documentation of Houari's time in Gong is a performance broadcast on *Pop 2* at the very beginning of January '71. It includes the songs 'Never Fight Another War', 'Perfect Mystery', and 'Big City Energy'.

12   Pyle's recollection differs somewhat: "...we jammed the whole affair to projected images of film in live synchro. EXTREMELY STONED on Thai sticks... none of your split second film sync..."

13   Didier Malherbe points out: "*Camembert Electrique* was still mainly Daevid... There were some very collective things, it's true, but the general vibe was very 'Daevid-Allenian'. We started co-signing things from the next record."

14   This session was broadcast on 9 November '71. Kevin Ayers's song 'Clarence in Wonderland' was one of the three recorded.

15   Christian Vander was Magma's famously charismatic drummer.

16   The factors that truly led Tritsch to leave Gong remain shrouded in mystery. His slow-motion exit (he would remain with Gong until late January '73) raises many questions. Bob Benamou had this to say: "He was a very good musician, and he spent all of his time with the group in Sens. Christian left because he was fed up with everybody, he wanted to go back to normality."

17   Tritsch's move from bass to guitar seems to have been a step towards a potential solo career. At his last gig with Gong he played a three-song set accompanied by Didier Malherbe and Francis Moze. An article published at the time noted his departure, adding: "All the same he thinks he'll soon be back with his own compositions (with or without Gong?)".

18   In an interview with *Maxipop* in late December '72, Moze commented: "I'm only with Gong for a little while, to help them record their disc. I'm not sure what I'll do after that, but I won't be staying with the band."

19   Although Howlett wouldn't join Gong for some months yet, he was well-connected to Virgin and understood the band's plight.

20   In a 1995 interview Moerlen told Aymeric Leroy: "I knew the Lemoine brothers, who are also from Alsace... in January 1973, they told me that Gong were looking for a replacement for Laurie Allan. I was in Paris, looking for work in the classical field, but I didn't really want to do it, so I said yes, and found myself in the middle of a forest near Sens."

21   Mike Howlett has some insight into Virgin's decision: "Branson had just started the label, and they had this band who'd just racked up a bill of several thousand pounds that was never going to be paid. Simon Draper liked *Flying Teapot*, he wasn't thinking it was going to sell a lot, but he thought it was good. So they thought we might as well sign them."

22   This concert was released in 1990 as *Live in Sheffield, 1974*.

23   Gilli Smyth, who was pregnant, remained in France until December. Di Bond took on her role until she returned. For a short period after that Gong featured two female vocalists.

24   Miquette Giraudy took over Di Bond's on-stage role.

25   Tim Blake's recollection of the writing of *You* differs significantly: "We'd gone to a cottage in the country for an intensive writing period. During this time Daevid and Gilli kept themselves locked in the kitchen making tea. And we were working at it! From time-to-time when something actually started to work as a composition, Gilli would come and say 'yes now you've got my poem just right'. And we said 'no dear, this isn't your poem, it's called the Om Riff'. This went on *all* the time... *You* was written

by Moerlen, Howlett, Malherbe, Hillage, Blake, and nobody else..."

26 This concert is included on the *Love from the Planet Gong* boxset.

27 "I left after the recording of *You* because the atmosphere in the band wasn't very good... Daevid wanted to leave. He found the music too complex and virtuosic. Then there were differences on other subjects. I must admit that, at the time, the band indulged in some substances which in part led to its self-destruction." *(Moerlen)*

28 *Fish Rising* also features Miquette Giraudy's first appearance on record, as well as guest spots from Lindsay Cooper and Dave Stewart.

29 Didier Malherbe was stunned by the drummer's abilities: "Bill Bruford was excellent. He'd learned the whole set in a couple of days."

30 The battle would rage on for decades, eating up any royalties due to the Gong musicians.

31 An anecdote from Marc Blanc suggests that Allen may have made his decision before Gong's concert at Salle Wagram in late '74: "I went up to see Daevid after the show and said, 'It's good now. You're going to become a world-famous band like Yes and Genesis'. He replied, 'No, I'm off'."

32 Moerlen had already negotiated a solo project with Virgin, and this offer was made in lieu of that.

33 Included in the *Love From The Planet Gong* box-set.

34 Bauer had been a guest musician on both *Angel's Egg* and *You*.

35 A live recording from late November (released as *Live In Sherwood Forest '75*) reveals just how quickly the music was changing, with even Hillage's compositions given a new jazz-rock undercurrent.

36 "Alan Holdsworth had been playing in Lifetime, with one of the greatest drummers ever. So Tony Williams was calling Alan on the phone asking him to come back. And Alan would say 'No, I'm going to stay here with my friends from Gong'! I couldn't believe it - Gong was fairly well-known, but not like Tony Williams! I didn't understand why he didn't go back to America. That was one of the strangest things in the whole history of Gong." *(Malherbe)*

37 In the US the album was released under the title *Expresso*.

38 The *Gong est Mort, Vive Gong* album was recorded at this event.

39 Allen and Smyth had joined forces with Here & Now in '77 to perform live and record as Planet Gong.

CHEVAL FOU & NYL

> For the three of us, it was our first experience in a group, that's to say the most beautiful experience that can happen in a musician's life. We discovered everything together, in a naive and spontaneous process. We created our universe with the luxury of being able to totally immerse ourselves in it, almost completely apart from the world.
>
> *Michel Peteau*

The story of Cheval Fou is inextricably linked to the underground newspaper *Le Pop*, launched by Max Peteau in March '70. Peteau's sons Michel (guitar, sax) and Jean-Max (guitar) had joined together with Stéphane Rossini (drums) to form Cheval Fou ("a direct reference to Crazy Horse, the Sioux medicine man and warrior") just beforehand.

At the time Michel Peteau was only sixteen years old (as was Rossini). His experience of May '68 and its aftermath had steered him towards music: "The feeling of freedom that floated in the air spurred me on to quit my studies and to head inevitably towards music. During this time, I saw The Who and Pink Floyd in concert. It was decisive. My life choice was made.

"In France, the radio and TV only played *variétés* singers, performing covers of Anglo-Saxon songs translated into French ... Like many other bands, we wanted to take the opposite position to that... We threw ourselves into savage experimentation, something that joined in with the resistance, that expressed a rejection of political institutions, and of French show-business as it was."

Just as Cheval Fou was coming together, the members of Crouille Marteau (a band that included actors Jean-Pierre Kalfon and Pierre Clémenti) were heading off to India for an indefinite stay. They offered the young band the use of their sound system and amplifiers.

"It was incredible! Nothing else stood in the way of us becoming a group. Except that we didn't know how to play, and none of us had any real knowledge of music... But our desire was so strong that we managed to overcome this problem, by trying every day, very hard... quite insanely in fact!"

Another early break came when the Grateful Dead cancelled out of a concert organised by *Le Pop*, and the elder Peteau suggested that his sons' band fill in for them.

"The room was full, Stéphane, Jean and I felt 'out of this world', the crushing stage fright paralysed us totally, we became aware of the significant gap that existed between our teenagers' dreams and the actual reality of the stage. I remember coming onto the stage, adjusting the settings on my amplifier, and playing the entire concert with my back to the audience! We played for about forty minutes, very much free form, and then we received a wave of enthusiastic applause! Cheval Fou was born!"

A community known as "The Tribe" had grown around the production of *Le Pop*, and Cheval Fou was incorporated as their musical arm. "The community was inspired by the American free press movement, and spurred on by titles like *Le Parapluie*, *La Cause du Peuple*, and the first incarnation of *Actuel*. It began in Paris... then the Hog Farm moved into our premises for a while and convinced the collective to go and preach 'the good word' all over the countryside." In June '70 a group of around thirty people packed themselves into four trucks, equipped themselves with a generator, and headed off.

"My father launched us into the trials and tribulations of a traveling tribe of freaks, a community of people with alternative ideas, politically on the left, and very much on the fringe of consumer society. We settled where the wind took us - mostly in the South of France. We'd set off in search of a house or a piece of land to squat on, set up for a while and *Le Pop* would kick in: designers created, authors wrote... The Tribe made a new newspaper around a new world. And we, the musicians, made the soundtrack to this mini revolution in a lysergic atmosphere!

"So the three of us, Stéphane Rossini, my brother Jean, and I were able to create our musical universe in an extremely inspiring and motivating environment. We were spared all the constraints tied to an adult life. In the Tribe, our only role was to play music."

As well as being an integral part of this Tribe, the band felt themselves to be part of the wider '70s psychedelic movement, alongside bands like Hawkwind, Amon Düül II, Gong and Crium

Delirium. However their influences ranged wider, encompassing musicians like Robert Fripp, Art Ensemble of Chicago, Robert Wyatt, and Can.

"We improvised a kind of psychedelic rock, mostly instrumental... a drum-kit, two electric guitars (and later a bass player), big amps, a light show, smoke machine... it was intense, continuous, without a word being spoken between the pieces. Stéphane Rossini, on the drums, was the engine the entire time - he was tireless. On stage our songs were a mix of written themes and improvisations. Our audience came with us into our wildest, longest deliriums, their listening was deep, inquisitive..."

"The times were very lysergic... We drew our inspiration from deep inside our brains when 'under the influence'... we didn't speak of musical notes, or in tonality, we spoke of colours! 'That piece in turquoise, that piece in rusty shades... etc.' And of course, we never did the same thing twice. Every piece was like a saga that we lived very intensely, very profoundly. In 'Hannibal' for example, we truly experienced the crossing of the Alps with the elephants, and when the piece ended, we needed some time to recover from the journey... On stage, some songs could last half an hour, according to how we felt and the general atmosphere of the venue."

In Autumn '71 the community found a more permanent home and set up camp for the next seven months. "We settled in the foothills of the Dentelles de Montmirail, in the heart of nature. The layout of the place allowed us to play very loudly, almost without restriction. Afterwards, the group retained the need to feel that adrenaline in our DNA." Shortly after settling there *Le Pop* ran out of steam, and Cheval Fou became the main focus of The Tribe.

Having taken the time to hone their playing and develop a powerful sound, Cheval Fou set off on their first major tour in August '72. Using Gong's sound system they played a series of free, open-air concerts along the southern coast taking in Sanary, Cavalaire, St Tropez, and Le Lavandou. Their electrifying and aggressive playing began to gain them a reputation, especially amongst holidaying Parisians making their annual pilgrimage to the Côte d'Azur.

At this point the band was still just a trio made up of two guitars and drums. To fully realise the power of their music, they felt the need for the rock-solid foundation a bass guitar would provide. So in autumn '72 they contacted Ame Son's former bass player, Patrick Fontaine.

"Stéphane Rossini and Michel Peteau contacted me. They were looking for a bassist who not only shared their musical style, but could share their ideas and aspirations. We met in a Parisian apartment and had a long discussion. Michel picked up his guitar and I responded to the long, soaring notes emanating from his instrument, in the style of David Gilmour."

Fontaine was convinced, and moved to join the rest of the band in Lyon, where Cheval Fou had set up a small community in the suburbs.

"I joined the group and we quickly put together a repertoire and landed a few bookings in January/February '73. Then in March '73 we settled in an isolated house near Vacqueyras, a small village in the Côtes-du-Rhône famous for its wine.

"Stéphane was a fiery drummer and a bit crazed too. Very exuberant, both powerful and busy, somewhere between Keith Moon and Mitch Mitchell. Improvisations could last for hours. We regularly gave concerts in the surrounding area: Arles, Carpentras, Avignon, Uzès."

In May they played for a week at Le Rainbow in Roanne, and in July travelled to Tunisia to play in support of Miles Davis at the first Tabarka Festival.

However, as at its beginnings, the life of Cheval Fou remained closely tied to The Tribe, and when that community disbanded in Summer '73, so did the band. "The Tribe had come to the end of the adventure. My father went to New York, my brother Jean went to live his life."

Cheval Fou made no studio recordings during their existence, as much a reflection of commercial realities as of the band's philosophy. "At the time when Cheval Fou was active, record companies were interested in [bands] like Martin Circus... we didn't even think about getting a contract. We lived in such a disconnected way from everything (not to mention the drugs that circulated in The Tribe). We travelled, forgot Paris, and lived music as something completely immaterial." Thankfully though, they did occasionally document rehearsals and live shows, and a selection of these was finally released on CD in the '90s.

After the demise of Cheval Fou, Rossini and Peteau were determined to carry on playing together. They moved back to Paris and formed the band Nyl. "The end of The Tribe left us a little shattered, we had to reassess ourselves, return to the big city, face economic constraints, become independent, become adult in a way."

Fontaine: "Stéphane and Michel left the south of France and went to live in a small house owned by Stéphane's mother in Esbly, 40km from Paris. The first thing they did when they got into the house was excavate the basement and make it a rehearsal space... I would join them regularly for a few days at a time. Other musicians also came to visit. I remember meeting Catherine Le Forestier, Steve Potts the American jazz saxophonist, and Elisabeth Wiener the daughter of the great pianist/composer Jean Wiener. The Nyl album was conceived there, on a TEAC 4-track tape recorder. I contacted [ex-Ame Son guitarist] Bernard Lavialle to come and take part."

While Patrick Fontaine was initially part of Nyl, by autumn '73 he was looking for a chance to both play more structured music and earn a living as a musician. When vibraphonist Robert Wood asked him to join his group Woodlands, Fontaine accepted. Nevertheless, he remained in contact with his former bandmates.

Peteau and Rossini continued to work on new material, with their house functioning as a kind of live-in workshop for developing the music. Saxophonist Patrice Quentin lived with them for a while, as did many others. Peteau: "Many friends came to see us and settled for an undetermined amount of time: Jacques Higelin, Pierre Clémenti, Kalfon, Philippe Garrel, Ariel Kalma... Their presence motivated us to play and we spent many nights improvising."

Finally, with their new pieces sketched out as demo recordings, the pair began to look for a label willing to back recording an album. "Both Stéphane and I started looking for a contract. After a series of failures, we went to see Richard Pinhas."

Richard Pinhas of Heldon had set up his own record label to release his band's music. The venture was so successful that he quickly began to release other acts on the label.

"I remember that he received us at his home one morning in his bathrobe, a cigarette in his mouth, and extremely tired eyes. We had our magnetic tapes with us, we put them on one of the three Revoxes he had in his living room. 'Well, I'm warning you ... don't ask me what I think of it' he said... He listened to our music while taking his coffee, completely emotionless, and suddenly, he burst out laughing, and told us: 'get a studio guys, I'm producing this record!' " With the backing of Pinhas the band organised a recording session at Aquarium Studio in Paris with engineer Dominique Blanc-Francard.

"The album was recorded and mixed in 48 hours. Stéphane and I put down the basic tracks together, I have very fond memories of doing that. Then there was a procession of musicians: whoever was there at the time played. We had to go fast, a flute here, a vocal there… no time to ask too many questions. That record is a stream of music!

"We invited our friends to play: Patrick Fontaine on bass, Bernard Lavialle on guitar, Patrice Quentin and Ariel Kalma on sax, Olivier Pamela who sang brilliantly, Loy Ehrlich on piano, Jannick Top as an extraterrestrial, and Elizabeth Wiener as the icing on the cake, gracing us with her charm, her musicality, and her craziness.

"The connection with Jannick Top was due to Stéphane. Both were totally hooked on Egyptology… Jannick came to the studio to listen to us, he sat down, took some notes and asked us – 'Are you OK with the structure? It is always the same?' 'Hmm, yes and no …' At this point, we did not even know the name of the notes, we had learned to play together by developing systems familiar to us, such as the colours, the energies… etc. Jannick plugged his bass to the Ampeg, started counting '1-2-3-4' and bang! We were on! This moment will remain engraved in my mind all my life! We lift off and were carried, lifted, and at the same time held down from the cliff to produce solos over and over again…"

The result of this 48-hour recording marathon was Nyl's self-titled album, released on Urus Records in '76. While Nyl mainly existed as a recording project, there were infrequent live performances after the release of the LP, featuring a fluid line-up of musicians augmenting the core unit of Peteau and Rossini. One such performance was at the Fête de L'Humanité in '76, with Jacques Lennoz on bass, Patrice Quentin on sax & flute, and Elisabeth Wiener on vocals.

An unexpected encounter that day would upend Michel Peteau's musical orientation, and lead to the disbanding of the group. "That day a buzz was being created by a group playing on a neighbouring stage… it was the Stinky Toys, a French punk rock group that exploded on stage with three-minute songs… I was totally won over, and I immediately wanted to work differently."

It should be noted that Peteau was still only in his early 20s at this point - the perfect age to be swept up by the energy of the coming wave of punk rock . "I felt that something quite powerful had come, a 'new wave' that would very soon wipe everything else under the carpet… The wind had changed, it was imperative to move in a new direction, in order to avoid being swept away by this tidal wave. This was the end of Nyl."

After the break-up of Nyl Stéphane Rossini became a writer, specialising in ancient Egypt (Patrick Fontaine points out that Rossini's interest in Egypt inspired the band name Nyl). A number of his books have been translated into English.

Michel Peteau has remained active in music, forming the bands Pierrot le Fou and La Fiancée du Pirate in the '80s and '90s. His most recent projects are Superbravo (their latest album Sentinelle *was released in 2019), and the revival of Cheval Fou (with the release of the album* Couteau Calme *in 2021).*

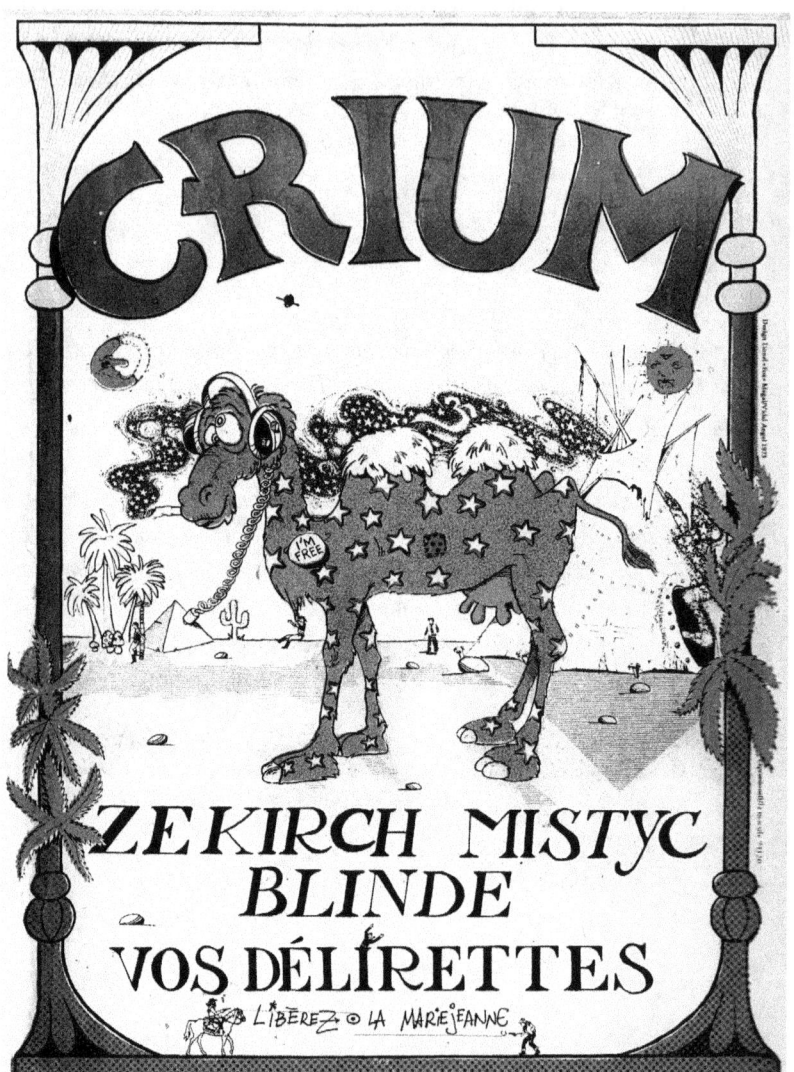

CRIUM DELIRIUM

> "At every concert Fox, the shaman of the stage, initiates the crowd into the ritual of the Cosmic Chillum. The members of Crium Delirium invite the audience to throw pieces of grass and balls of hash onto their flying carpet. As soon as the chillum is lit, Crium Delirium start their song 'Les Road Managers': "We are the road managers, we bring the LSD engine, we bring the pollen to get you high"... The audience sing along as if it's an international hymn!"
>
> *William Belvie*

Crium Delirium has been described as "less of a group, more of a conglomeration, a nebula at the service of the underground". The core of the band were two brothers: guitarist Thierry Magal and drummer Lionel "Fox" Magal. They gathered a loose assemblage of musicians in mid-'68 with the aim of creating happenings rather than playing gigs, and named it Crium Delirium Circus.[1] In 1970, Fox Magal left France for on a road trip to India with the Hog Farm. On his return the Magal brothers created Crium Delirium Circus Theatro & Music Zizanie Association, a group that would be at the heart of the French psychedelic movement for the next three years.

While Crium Delirium may appear to have had multiple lives, Fox Magal insists that it was always a single project: "We played every day between '68 and '75. When I went to India we played as Crium Delirium, and when I came back in '72 it continued. It was all the same thing."

* * *

The Magal brothers were born into an artistic family, with a father who was a jazz musician, filmmaker, and theatre designer. Their introduction to the world of music was at a very early age: "When we were kids my parents took us to the Blue Note, Thierry was eighteen months, and I was five-and-a-half. We were put on seats less than a metre from Kenny Clarke and Art Blakely. I can remember Lester Young, Ella Fitzgerald (who took me in her arms), and Sarah Vaughan. I even nodded off beside Thelonious Monk while he was improvising."

It's not surprising that Magal could be found playing in the Parisian jazz clubs by the mid-'60s: "I worked at Le Chat Qui Pêche opening for the stars who passed through - lots of very good American musicians. I also worked with Jef Gilson, a famous jazz talent scout. Through him I made an album with Jean-Luc Ponty in '68, and another in a big band with Bill Coleman and the organist Eddie Louiss."

While playing at Le Chat Qui Pêche, Magal met a young up-and-coming drummer: "I used to smoke weed with Christian Vander's father, Maurice. Christian came to the club when he was very young - he was just starting out. And he broke my balls, because he wanted to play on my kit all the time, but he played too hard! I had to tell him, 'No, Christian. Stop! Don't break my sticks'."

At the same time he was playing in the clubs, Magal was studying at the School of Applied Arts. There, he tried his hand at silversmithing, tapestry, design, and stop-motion animation. He also met another future member of Magma: Klaus Blasquiz. "We studied together in the same department at art school between '64 and '68. He's been my friend for a long time."

An interest in merging music with the plastic arts drove Magal to dive into the burgeoning avant-garde art scene based around the American Center. In '67 he began to organise happenings, often in collaboration with dancer Graziella Martinez. Around this time he also developed ties to Musica Elettronica Viva, Terry Riley, Didier Malherbe, and Pierre Clémenti.

In May '68 Magal and Blasquiz worked together at the Atelier Populaire making the student movement's iconic posters: "I worked on screen-printing at the Beaux-Arts, but on 13 May, with the barricades up and police confrontations, I was going to Madagascar with Jef Gilson and Gilbert Rever. We were on the last plane to leave Paris. So for the rest of May '68 I was in Madagascar." [2]

Magal spent two months on the island playing in Gilson's trio[3] and immersing himself in the local culture: "I had very good relationships with Malagasy artists. I worked with Odeam Rakoto, a great man of theatre and music, and went on tour with Malagasy dancers."

Out of nowhere he was contacted by the French embassy: "The cultural department wanted to hire me. They asked me to replace the manager of the cultural mission, who was leaving. I'd have the same house, the same maid, the same driver, the same boss, and the same mistress. *(laughs)*"

Magal was ready to accept, but the French army had other plans. He was due for military service, and even with the embassy in Madagascar pleading his case, he was forced to return to France. Happily, he failed the medical: "They discovered I had a kidney condition because I played drums in a bad position. And I smoked too much!"

The army's loss was the counter-culture's gain - in the eighteen months he could have been mouldering in a barracks Magal entered an intense period of creativity. Almost immediately, he created Crium Delirium Circus with his brother Thierry: "My younger brother had been at the conservatory for four years, studying classical guitar under Alexandre Lagoya and Ida Presti. He also studied composition, so it was Thierry who was the composer in Crium Delirium." [4]

They called together a large number of musicians from different backgrounds: "There were eighteen musicians, involved including Jacques Dudon and the musicians from Horde Catalytique Pour La Fin. What was the music? I can't define it; every time it was different: improvisation, jazz, rock, songs... Always a mixture of that.

"We presented everything saying: 'This isn't a show, this is an event'. In my mind it was a non-show, more action theatre."

One of their early performances was a collaboration with actor Pierre Clémenti and musicians from Musica Elettronica Vita. "It was at the Palais de Tokyo with Richard Tettenbaum and Frederic Rzewski. I played a Moog synthesiser with Horde Catalytique and Francky Bourlier & Goa - musicians who made bamboo instruments. I put contact microphones on a naked woman on a water bed and amplified her breathing and movements. So there was a mixture of electronics, bamboo instruments, glass harp, and noises from the girl."

In '69 Magal leased an old furniture factory near the Bastille, where Crium Delirium began living in community. The 'Atelier' sprawled across three floors, providing studio space and accommodation for forty artists, musicians and poets. *Actuel* described it as "a Toureg camp in the centre of Paris".

"I found the Atelier thanks to Bernard Szajner.[5] The owner was an old gentleman who said I could take it *en viagé* - meaning I could rent it until he died, then I would own it. But I told him, 'I don't want to pay for your death', so I bought the commercial lease instead. But when I came back from India he was dead. So I lost the factory." [6]

It became a focal point for the Parisian counter-culture, a place where artists and writers from *Tout!*, *Le Parapluie*, and *Le Pop* could mix with more famous visitors: "Eldridge Cleaver from the Black Panthers, Abbie Hoffman - a lot of crazy people. Salvador Dali even came to take acid." [7] When they arrived in Paris the Hog Farm community also lodged at the Atelier, doubling the building's population overnight.[8]

The Hog Farm left to continue their road trip to India in late '70 with a large group of Parisians (including Magal) joining them. *Actuel* asked him to be their roving correspondent but were disappointed by his output: "The only thing that I sent them while on the road... was a postcard plastered in stars and rainbows." For almost two years, Magal travelled through Turkey, Iran, and Afghanistan before finally reaching India. If he hadn't already been fully psychedelised, this road trip definitely completed the process.

In early '72 he split away from the Hog Farm and returned to France: "I'd had enough; they were too organised and structured for me." With the Magal brothers reunited, they immediately created a trio with bassplayer Daniel Léonard - that they christened Crium Délirium Circus Theatro & Music Zizanie Association.

One of their first projects was a multimedia event sponsored by Electricité de France on the site cleared for the Pompidou Centre. Housed in a futuristic inflatable dome, their show 'The Magik Gazon Vert' (The Magic Green Grass) featured a laser lightshow and robotics, with a soundtrack created by the band featuring a VCS 3 synthesiser donated by the sponsor.

Crium soon doubled in size with the addition of Patrice Quentin (sax & flute), Loy Ehrlich (keys), and Victor Angel (percussion). With Thierry Magal now doubling on guitar and synth the band had a formidable arsenal of sounds at their disposal.

Their appearance at the May Day festival at Place Gambetta was reviewed by *Actuel*: "Crium Delirium use the voice to create cosmic sound effects, make sarcastic interludes, and recite advertising slogans and idiotic proverbs... all floating over great blistering outbursts of energetic and joyous rock music. With long howls of synthesiser and some acoustic moments, Crium make a 'Barbarian Rock' that is both rich and complete."

Pop 2000 was effusive about their performance at the Bagas Cheap Festival in August: "Here is a totally unique group that we'd like to see more of in France. When I say group, I don't particularly think of their music, because this is only one of their aspects... they use other means of expression such as theatre, light shows etc. They are in the ranks of those who look to create new artistic avenues, and have to be thanked for their hard work." [9]

Hard work indeed; a few months earlier Crium Delirium had helped organise the first free festival in France at Bièvres, near Paris. For an anarchic, psychedelic band Crium were proving to be surprisingly resourceful. They would continue working to help set up an alternative musical circuit across the country.

Their level of activity was even more notable given the band led a nomadic existence, setting up camp when they were able to find a temporary home: "We were lent a mill, then a school... Sometimes we had a farm where we made our own bread and grew crops. We were nomadic, but we still had places where we could leave people from the group to develop activities while the band toured."

Crium Delirium finished '72 supporting Kevin Ayers across France.[10] In less than a year they had built an enviable reputation by organising important events and playing powerfully psychedelic live shows. Their performances were unlike anything offered by any other French band.

Magal: "Crium concerts always started with the Magic Carpet. We harvested weed and drugs on the Magic Carpet, then we made the flying teapot[11] and the chillum (a pipe for smoking weed). So the concerts started with the audience sat with the musicians celebrating the Cosmic Chillum. Then my brother started playing the mantra 'om' on the synthesiser, and I made an announcement: 'This isn't a show, this is a moment that encourages sharing'.

"Sometimes we played on the floor with the amplifiers and projectors set up on the stage. We showed films from the road trip with the Hog Farm, and there were dancers or interventions. Crium led the game and set the tone - we guided the audience."

The band's unorthodox approach to performances could create unusual situations, as at a major concert in Paris with Agitation Free and Nico. "At the Opéra Comique concert, we gave the audience acid. And they were so high that they came onto the stage. I had to stop them: 'You're breaking the gear, you're breaking the projectors, you have to get off the stage!'"

Paul Alessandrini chose not to mention the melee in his review for *Rock & Folk*: "[It started] with a call for the audience to participate in celebrating the 'Cosmic Chillum' and it finished with a three-minute song dedicated to the road managers. They have a warm-hearted lunacy, a sense of sonic humour that French groups, apart from Gong, are lacking. Crium Delirium, like the early Grateful Dead and Fugs, are a true band of 'Freaks' on the fringe."

During '73 the band played all over France, often on the MJC circuit: "There were concerts in small venues and sometimes concerts with 3000-3500 people. We played with Gong a lot and with Magma and Lard Free from time to time. We also played with Nico. But the hardcore was with Gong, with Didier Malherbe and Tim Blake."

After the Opéra Comique concert Crium spent several weeks touring with Gong, deepening links between the two bands. Gong's Mike Howlett: "Crium Delirium were good friends of the band. Around the Paragong period we played some gigs with them, and they invited me and Tim Blake to hang out with them while they did a few gigs. I particularly remember one in Dole up in the mountains: this crazy gig where we jammed for two hours, but it felt like thirty minutes. Then we were told it was 3am, and time to shut the venue."

Crium kept up a manic pace - they toured around the country, helped organise the first Fete du PSU,[12] and played at numerous festivals and events in support of striking university students, the anti-nuclear movement, and ecological concerns.

However, as Magal told *Rock & Folk*, their wealth of activity didn't translate into financial stability: "We alternate between spontaneous concerts in the street and concerts with paid entry. But we're still in a bloody huge mess materially: with 5 million (old Francs) debt, no amplifiers (we borrow them when we play), and nothing to pay the guy who fixed our synthesiser."

In July '73 Crium Delirium were invited to perform at the first Tabarka festival in Tunisia, where they were given a slot between Ravi Shankar and Miles Davis. They returned to France in a suitably anarchic manner.

Patrice Quentin: "We came back on foot, hitchhiking via Algeria, Morocco and Spain. In Spain we were playing in the street - Fox Magal was in a djellaba and I was barefoot. We were arrested for vagrancy. This was in Franco's Spain, and we spent three weeks in prison until the Magal brothers' parents got us out. "

As the members dribbled back into France half of them landed in Paris, while the remainder, including the Magal brothers, moved into a dilapidated farmhouse near Alès in the south. The ever-resourceful band used this unusual situation to work to expand the MJC circuit set up by Rock Pas Gaga.[13] Magal: "This split obviously caused a lot of back and forth between the South and Paris. We took the opportunity to start setting up a network for concerts."

They also organised the Clermont-Ferrand Festival in September '73. Magal: "It was set in the middle of nature, surrounded by volcanoes. We had generators for electricity, a stage with a marquee, several tents, and a kitchen. I'd hijacked Guru Maharaji to come with us, he took responsibility for buying and preparing the food. We fed 8000 people over two or three days. We also printed 1000-1500 copies of a special magazine. It was paid for by the insurance from a musician friend who had died, so we had money for the technicians and we could pay a little money to the groups that came."

Over the years Crium Delirium displayed extreme resourcefulness and an impressive work ethic for a self-professed band of freaks. However they gave little thought to the standard goal for a group of musicians: recording their music and releasing an album. When *Rock & Folk* raised this, Magal replied: "The contracts we've been offered are much too demanding in terms of duration and commitments (promotion, festivals...). We'd want our say on price (even if it means reducing our percentage), promotion, the cover design, the content of the ads... We've found no-one ready to agree to that."

Crium Delirium decided to call it a day in '75.

Although they had been so active on the early '70s live scene, they were in danger of being forgotten before Legend Music released a CD in 1994. The band had always shunned recording, but Thierry Magal was an experienced sound engineer and made sure to create an archive of live recordings. These were brought together on the album *Live Concerts 1972-1975*.

Fox Magal emphasises that the disc was programmed to flow in the manner of a typical Crium Delirium live concert: "This CD is really like the unfolding of a performance, reproducing the spirit and the excitement of the concerts. You really have the atmospheres, the moments where we speak with the audience, the showing of the films, etc..."

Fox and Thierry Magal continued to work in music and the audio-visual arts after Crium Delirium parted ways. Alongside Jean-François Bizot, they were both heavily involved in the creation of Radio Nova in '81 - with Thierry on the technical side and Fox as a presenter. Thierry Magal died in India in 1998.

Notes

1 "The name Crium Delirium came from a pen that my father owned - a Criterium. On his pen the "teri" was missing. So the word looked like 'Crium'. So, I said to my brother, that's a great name but maybe we'll add 'Delirium Circus'." *(Magal)*

2 Magal was able to make a contribution to the cause later that year when he played drums on *Descendre dans la rue*, an EP released in support of the May '68 movement.

3 This was Jef Gilson's first trip to Madagascar. He would return to the island three times, before releasing the legendary album *Malagasy* in '72.

4 Thierry Magal had also worked as sound engineer for Jef Gilson, and ran a small recording studio. Etron Fou Leloublan would record their debut album, *Batalages*, in his studio.

5 Bernard Szajner was very active in creating light-shows and visual effects for the underground music scene from the early '70s. In '79 he recorded the album *Visions of Dune* under the name Zed, and went on to become one of the most important French electronic musicians of the early '80s.

6 "While I was in India I rented it to the magazine *Le Pop* but they never paid me - we were always waiting for their money in India." *(Magal)*

7 "When he arrived all these Bentleys and Rolls piled up, pouring out women in long dresses who wanted to hang out with him. The police came along as well, anxious to protect them all." *(Magal)*

8 See the *Introduction* to this section for more on the Hog Farm's arrival.

9 The multifaceted nature of the group was codified in a manifesto written in '73: "CRI OM is not a meeting place, nor a collection of audio-visual specialists; CRI OM is the desire to create encounters... It's not surprising that music gives us the opportunity to have encounters, but it would be catastrophic to leave it at that."

10 It was at one of these concerts that Steve Hillage met Gong.

11 This mysterious "flying teapot" is explained by Magal: "We played at the Milkweg in Amsterdam, and a dealer gave me 3000 trips of liquid acid, It was very important to make the flying teapot, the magic tea."

12 "The extremely resourceful freaks of Crium Delirium... got Michel Rocard's agreement that the Fete PSU would put aside a specifically relaxing space for friends of the rolling paper..." *(Actuel)*

13 Crium Delirium's manager, Jacques Pasquier, was part of the Rock Pas Gaga team.

CLEARLIGHT

> It was a pure game of circumstance that let me hear the music inside myself for the first time. I'd taken a tab of acid (actually a Clearlight, the kind Timothy Leary used to launch his flower-power campaign/crusade) and suddenly I improvised on my piano for the first time. Luckily a friend had lent me a tape recorder, so I was able to save a good amount of that surprise-improvisation.
>
> This was the material that helped me make my first album. In these circumstances I could only call it *Clearlight*, no? Since then, even without acid, I've retained this ability to hear the music from within, thus I've continued to call my group (when I have one...) Clearlight.
>
> *Cyrille Verdeaux*

While Clearlight, a studio-based band signed to an English label, could be considered marginal to the French Underground, its mainstay Cyrille Verdeaux is most definitely a graduate of the scene. Before signing to Virgin Records in '73 he'd spent two years on the Parisian circuit in the band Babylone. This was followed by a brief tenure in Marseille's Barricade II.

The studio-bound nature of Clearlight came about by accident rather than design. Verdeaux made several attempts to build a band, with members of Zao, Gong, Lard Free, and Magma all featuring in the various incarnations of Clearlight. However circumstances dictated that Clearlight would primarily be a recording project showcasing Verdeaux's singular vision of classically-inspired psychedelic rock.

Cyrille Verdeaux had been drawn to the keyboard very early in life. "As in any self-respecting bourgeois house in France at the time, there was a piano in ours that served more as decorative furniture than anything else.

"At around 5 years old I was first drawn to touch the keyboard, and my mother noticed that I didn't chaotically hit the keys like other children, but listened carefully to each note one at a time. This gave her the idea to enroll me in a children's music school. When she realised I had perfect pitch she also saddled me with a home tutor who came 3 times a week to 'torture' me with scales, lessons on music theory, etc..."

These early beginnings set Verdeaux on the path towards a traditional musical education, and at twelve he was enrolled in the prestigious National Conservatory of Music in Paris. "There I developed my taste for classical harmony: something that can be found in the majority of my music."

There was another influence being beamed in on the radio waves, and as the '60s progressed Verdeaux enthusiastically embraced Anglo-American and homegrown rock'n'roll. He expected to graduate from the Conservatory in mid-'68, but the events of May threw a spanner in the works: "As a member of the Revolutionary Inter-faculty Liaison Committee, I landed first prize for megaphone rather than piano that year. As soon as the administration were able to take back control they got rid of the troublemakers. Every member of this nevertheless respectable Revolutionary Committee was struck off the student rolls for life."

Banned from resuming his study in Paris, family connections were able to secure Verdeaux a place at the National Conservatory of Nice. He completed his studies there between '69 and '71.

On graduation Verdeaux returned to Paris and began the second phase of his musical education by immersing himself in the growing underground music scene. He replied to a want-advert for an organist placed by the band Babylone and met guitarist Christian Boulé, who would become an important musical collaborator over the next decade.

Verdeaux still regards his time in Babylone as a formative musical experience. "It was only when I joined them that I discovered a taste for 'psychedelic' music. Christian and his friends[1] were listening to Matching Mole, Caravan, Terry Riley, Pink Floyd, King Crimson, Genesis, Mahavishnu etc. - music I immediately loved. I owe them a huge debt, because without them my fate would have definitely been different and probably less artistic..."

Most of Babylone's music was written by Boulé. "The musical

style encouraged by Christian was oriented towards the English Canterbury scene... At the time, I didn't yet know I was a composer myself, so I created keyboard parts for his compositions, nothing more."

The band performed at festivals alongside Gong, Crium Delirium, and Magma. They also toured through France and made a short foray into the Netherlands, but unfortunately broke up before making any recordings.[2]

Verdeaux's next musical adventure was a short stint in Barricade II. He traveled to Marseille to become their keyboard player in Spring '73, but he was a poor fit for such an infamously anarchic band.

"Their aim was the exact opposite of mine. I wanted and expected serious work and precision. I quickly saw that just wasn't possible with them. It was chaos on stage - with very few people to watch us, fortunately!

"So, after some painful months, I put an end to this useless experience and decided to focus on starting my own band with my own repertoire, making it serious and professional. A few months later, I signed with Virgin, so I guess it was the right move!"

Back in Paris, the events of a single summer night changed the course of Verdeaux's musical career. He took a tab of LSD, sat at his piano, and suddenly began to improvise for the first time... The music flowed and he found his creative voice. "I composed the 'Symphony' during the summer of '73 on a full-moon night with Lucy in the Clearlight Sky. Quite an impressive experience. I obviously received a precious gift from the Universe that night."

Luckily Verdeaux had a Revox tape recorder to hand and was able to record a large part of his acid-fueled improvisation. In the weeks that followed he completed a sketch for the 'Clearlight Symphony' by overdubbing piano and organ parts onto the original recording. When Jean-Pierre Lentin, of Dagon and *Actuel*, heard the tape he suggested a trip to London to present it to a small label he had heard were beginning to make waves there.

"He gave me the addresses of Virgin and the squat where Tim Blake lived. Gong had just signed to Virgin and Tim was a friend of Simon Draper, the No.2 in Virgin after Richard Branson."

The label's success with Mike Oldfield's *Tubular Bells* had laid the groundwork for Verdeaux: "Mike's success probably helped to interest Virgin in my project, which was in the same format as Mike's album - namely long tracks of continuous, instrumental music." In short order he was offered a recording contract.

Tim Blake took on the production role and secured a budget of £10,000. *Clearlight Symphony* was scheduled to be recorded at the end of '73 at Kaleidophon Studios (owned by renowned electronic musician David Vorhaus, of the band White Noise). Gong's Steve Hillage, Didier Malherbe, and Tim Blake along with drummer Pip Pyle were booked to back Verdeaux.

It was decided the first order of business was to record the main piano part on the Steinway grand at The Manor studios. It was a decision that would inadvertently create problems down the line.

"It was the first time I'd set foot in a studio, so I made a lot of beginner's mistakes, including recording the piano first without any metronome in the headphones. I'd taken an express ticket to meet Lucy in the Sky with Diamonds before the recording, so I definitely played in a totally psychedelic way... but with a rather uneven tempo."

When the tapes were brought to Kaleidophon Studios it quickly became obvious that Pip Pyle wasn't going to be able to overdub his drums over the undulating tempo of Verdeaux's piano performance.

"I had the choice to totally give up on drums, or to redo everything from the beginning! Finally Simon Draper and I arrived at a middle ground: to have one side without drums, and another with drums - which would have to be completely rerecorded."

The session at Kaleidophon was used to complete the drumless section of the 'Symphony', with the members of Gong overdubbing their parts on the piano recording from The Manor.

"We played one after the other, no psychedelic madness except for my trip at the first session. The atmosphere was rather hard-working and industrious."

Gong went on tour immediately after this session, so for the re-recording of the other half of the 'Symphony' Verdeaux turned to his musical connections in Paris. His Babylone comrade, Christian Boulé, would be the guitarist on the session, and Lard Free's Gilbert Artman was selected as drummer.

"I set up a meeting with Gilbert Artman and played him the

section reserved for the drums. He liked it and said 'OK'. So we all rehearsed in his practice room to make sure we had a coherent, continuous twenty-minute piece to record. A week later we returned to London."

Virgin gave Verdeaux seven days in The Manor to complete the album. "Christian, Gilbert, and I recorded together in a single session. That way there was no hassle with out-of-sync rhythms."

It had taken longer than anticipated but *Clearlight Symphony* was finally completed and readied for release. Virgin had decided that the piece featuring Gong should be on Side One of the LP, to take advantage of their popularity in the UK. Thus the two parts of *Clearlight Symphony* are actually reversed: 'Part 1' on the album was actually written by Verdeaux as 'Part 2'.

"Finally, finding myself with one side of drums-and-guitar rock and a more romantic and harmonic side, the idea (in vogue at the time) came to designate one side Yin-female and the other side (with the drums) Yang-male. It was a story to give a rational explanation for the rather bizarre concept of having two sides of the same work so dissimilar in form."

Clearlight Symphony was released in early '75 and sold around 45,000 copies, with solid promotion from Virgin. Clearly pleased by its success, Virgin signed Verdeaux for another two albums.

The next, *Forever Blowing Bubbles*, was recorded in June '75. Rather than wanting to treat the album as a solo project using guest musicians, Verdeaux decided to create a permanent band around himself. "For this second experience my project was to create a band. I wanted a stable group that could rise up as a regular team for years to come. The commercial success of the *Clearlight Symphony* really helped gain the interest of good, available French musicians.

"Joel Dugrenot, Zao's bassplayer, had just left the group. We had a couple of work sessions on the new music I had in mind. He agreed to be part of Clearlight as long as he could include some of his own music on the album. Fair enough. We worked on the two songs he wanted to record: 'Chanson' and 'Way'."[3]

The other musicians Verdeaux selected were guitarists Christian Boulé[4] and Jean-Claude d'Agostini (who doubled on flute), drummer Christos Stassinopoulos, and François Jeanneau[5] on synthesiser, sax and flute. This was intended to be Clearlight for the foreseeable future. "We spoke about making a really close band, so I found it natural and logical to give the members every chance to express themselves on the album."

With a cohesive band assembled work began on Clearlight's second album. "The recording itself is a wonderful memory. We were living at The Manor, sleeping in beautiful rooms, eating excellent food and relaxing in beautiful gardens outside. It was June and the weather was very sunny. Our girlfriends were there with us, and four of them were pregnant (Jean-Claude's, Joel's, Christian's, and my own). How could it possibly be better?? We spent fifteen quite unforgettable days there.

"We were recording one song every day from morning to evening, with a night session to mix. That allowed us to finish *Forever Blowing Bubbles* on schedule."

A few English musicians made guest appearances at the recording session, the most notable being ex-King Crimson violinist David Cross (a friend of Joel Dugrenot). The backing vocals were provided by Amanda Parsons and Ann Rosenthal (the "Northettes") of Hatfield and the North.

To promote the release of the album Virgin had arranged for Clearlight to open for Gong on a twenty-five date UK tour. The band that went on the road in November '75 had one additional member and one substitution.

"I crossed paths with an Argentinian violinist, Jorge Pintchevsky, between the recording and the tour. He was living in a squat in Paris with very little money. His playing was very interesting and I offered him hospitality for a few months as well as a place in the band, because I've always loved having violin in my music. Christos had to go back to Greece after the recording, so Coco Roussel[6], a very good drummer, replaced him."

The tour with the Steve Hillage-led Gong went very well for Clearlight. Too well, in fact, for some peoples' tastes: "A magazine article published in the second week said Gong's support group had a better sound and a better repertoire! The outcome: the rest of the tour was sabotaged by Gong's sound engineers, who also provided the sound for my group! An order from above..."

It looked like the future was secure for Clearlight. The tour had been a success and Virgin were willing to support this French band, with only one proviso: "The condition was that I come to live permanently in London to be totally at their disposition for interviews etc. For me it was a dream becoming reality. Where it came unstuck was with my companion, who was six months pregnant. She categorically refused to emigrate!"

Virgin made it clear that the continuation of Verdeaux's contract was contingent on his relocation to the UK. "I had to make a painful choice, and I chose my wife's will. So, after the tour, Richard Branson canceled my contract. End of the dream…

"Double end, because my wife dumped me five years later, and my son died accidentally one week later. So I'll always wonder what would have happened if I'd chosen to stay in London and continue my adventure with Virgin…"

Verdeaux returned to Paris and the band he had so carefully assembled fell apart.

* * *

A welcome diversion thankfully presented itself just a few weeks later. Yvan Coaquette[7], who had been Babylone's sound engineer, approached Verdeaux to work with him on a project: an experimental film being made by Pierre Clémenti.

"Clémenti was quite a famous movie actor, and was looking for a musician able to create a genuine soundtrack for his new 'avant-garde' movie. We became friends very quickly and he gave me the green light to try to make it happen."

The album session has become legendary: a three-day drug-fueled whirlwind of musical activity at the rather staid EMI/Pathé studios.

"Three crazy, crazy, crazy days with more than eighteen musicians… the faces of the sound engineers who'd never seen such an environment in a studio, with all the hash pipes that were constantly burning, plus incense etc…

"It was around Christmas '75…Very cold outside…But very hot in the studio!"

Coaquette and Verdeaux quickly composed the basis of the tracks. They called in Joel Dugrenot on bass, François Jeanneau on

ARP synth and sax, plus a number of drummers (including Gilbert Artman) for the recording. As they got to work they were taken aback by the unexpected arrival of more than a dozen other musicians.

"Little by little the rumour of an open door at EMI's studio spread, and several other friends showed up offering to take part in this moment of total freedom. It wasn't planned at all."

The basis of each track was recorded live by Verdeaux on piano and Coaquette on guitar along with one of the drummers.

"Afterwards everyone was freely improvising over it... almost non-stop. The poor engineers were making a relay team between themselves...

"When a track was free in a song I gave it to whoever I could, until we had forty-five minutes of half-improvised music recorded. Then we had one day left to mix the whole thing! A lot of hash and LSD was circulating during the two days recording session but we never lost our focus! A true miracle, I may say! We were young and strong…"

By the end of the session the contributing musicians included Tim Blake, Christian Boulé, Jean-Claude d'Agostini, Antoine Duvernet, Ariel Kalma, with singers Valérie Lagrange and Olivier Pamela.

The mysterious title of the movie, *Visa de Censure no. X*, is explained by the censor's refusal to grant the film a visa for screening.[8] While it never officially saw the light of day, the soundtrack was released by EMI under the band name Delired Cameleon Family.

* * *

The serious work of writing the third Clearlight album began just a few months after this legendary studio session. Joel Dugrenot from the *Forever Blowing Bubbles* band had stayed on as Verdeaux's musical partner. Together they began to work on *Les Contes du Singe Fou*.

For his first post-Virgin album Verdeaux had decided to break from the symphonic space-rock of his earlier albums to move towards a vocal-led, progressive-rock sound. "Being an ardent admirer of Genesis, the idea was to make a space opera with philosophical-science fiction themes, that were actually of a New Age leaning before its time."

He found a lyrical collaborator in keyboard player Francis Mandin. "I gave Francis a synopsis of the kind of philosophy and message I wanted to communicate on the album, along with a recording of the skeleton of the songs and the melodies."

Although the title is French, the lyrics for *Les Contes du Singe Fou* ('Tales of the Mad Monkey') are in English. Asked why, Verdeaux simply responds, "Oh, it's a lot easier to sing this kind of music in English than in French, and it was easier to find an English singer than a French one… and it didn't bother Francis to write the lyrics in English."

Joel Dugrenot was responsible for sourcing the musicians who appear on the album (this time around there was no thought given to creating a permanent band). Ian Bellamy was chosen as vocalist. Bellamy was an Englishman living in France who had been a member of Zoo. Another important element in the group was violinist Didier Lockwood.

"Joel knew Didier and had heard that he'd quit Magma a few weeks before. I met him for the first time at the session and was immediately seduced by his style and the speed of his musical understanding. We both came from the same school (The French Conservatoire), so no need for words, really…"

The band assembled in November '76 at Studio Léo Clarens in Vincennes. It was a world away from the environment that Verdeaux had become accustomed to.

"Everything was different! The studio was OK, but quite small. And every day, I had to make it through the city's horrible morning traffic jam to get to the studio. At The Manor we were living in the middle of a park and forest… with just a twenty yard walk to the studio!"

The recording session for *Les Contes du Singe Fou* went well, but time ran short during the mixing session. "We recorded all the songs in ten days, then had five days for the mix. Unfortunately, we didn't get it finished in five days. I played the producer a rough mix, and when he heard it, he said 'it's fine like that, I'm not paying for more studio time just to fix a few details.' And he released it as it was!

"Isadora was a very small new label, but I didn't appreciate what he did, and decided that my next album would be just me as producer, composer, player, mixer, etc…"

Immediately after completing this album Verdeaux began composing the music for the next.

"I was happy in this period (1975-1977). I had my young son Jonathan with me, so the music I was channeling was harmonious. I worked on the piano each morning at home, recording my improvisations. When I was satisfied with a melody or a rhythmic pattern I learned it by heart, and built the songs little-by-little so that a story appeared between the first and the last note. I can write music, but prefer to play in the here-and-now - it leads to a less intellectual and more spontaneous style... the Clearlight style, in fact..."

By the Summer of '77 the music for the next Clearlight album was written, and Verdeaux looked around for the best players to bring it to life. "In the two years before the birth of *Clearlight Visions*, my musical notoriety gave me the opportunity to meet and become friends with a lot of French musicians. So when I felt ready, I picked the people that I wanted to record with.

"This time I wanted to be my own producer, and the feeling of artistic freedom was so good that I never worked with a producer again..."

It was the first time in his career that Verdeaux had organised to record an album without the backing of a record label. He paid the musicians with the royalties from his English and French record sales, and was able to work out a deal with the studio owner to help finance the recording costs.

"It was expensive to pay all the costs of an album without a label or a producer to sign the cheques! But I worked out an arrangement where I could pay for the studio three months later - just enough time to find a label to pay an advance that would cover the studio fee. And that's exactly what happened with Eric Brucker, the A&R of Polydor, who appreciated my music and bought my tape."

While his last album had been partially inspired by Genesis, Verdeaux took John McLaughlin as a major musical reference in composing *Visions*.

"I was very seduced by the Mahavishnu Orchestra's fantastic dialogues between violin, moog and guitar... 'Spirale d'amour' is the result of this influence. Instead of violin-guitar-moog, it was violin-sax-moog with Didier Malherbe and Didier Lockwood. 'Full Moon

Raga' is also quite inspired by the East-West fusion sublimated by McLaughlin. I found Lockwood's solo so good that I asked him to dialogue with himself in the second half of the tune. I was very happy with the result... Jean-Luc Plouton, from Didier Lockwood's band, played the solo in the first half."

Visions was recorded at Studios Mannderly in Feucherolles, to the east of Paris. In addition to Didier Lockwood and Didier Malherbe, Verdeaux called on long-time collaborators Christian Boulé and Francis Mandin, session drummer Jacky Bouladoux, and ex-Oedipe bassplayer Philippe Melkonian.

"The recording studio was in the countryside near Paris. We started in the morning and finished late evening: eight days to record, eight days to mix. A lot of different musicians and no musical score, as it was all based on improvisation, so it was a bit risky. But I picked musicians knowing that they were talented improvisers and my trust in them was totally validated.

"It was a wonderful two-week creative journey. I wished I could have done that forty hours a week for my whole life! My favorite times as a professional musician have always been in recording studios, more than playing live on stage."

After the successful completion of *Visions*, a project at the beginning of '78 allowed Verdeaux to close a musical circle by working with Christian Boulé on his first solo album. "After releasing *Clearlight Visions*, Polydor asked me to be artistic director for Christian's first album, *Photo Musik*."

In parallel to his work on Boulé's album, Verdeaux tried one last time to create a group. This involved all the major musicians from the *Visions* sessions: Didier Malherbe, Didier Lockwood, Francis Mandin, Jacky Bouladoux, and Philippe Melkonian. With Christian Boulé focusing on his own solo career, Jean-Michel Kajdan was brought in to play guitar.

This line-up of stellar musicians was unveiled at a major concert at the Olympia on 8 April '78 organised to support the release of *Visions*. However Polydor's inability to promote Clearlight's style of music resulted in disappointment.

"Polydor had no experience working with instrumental prog rock bands, only singers. And the only song on the album was too different from the usual format to help promote my music to radio or set up a tour. Contrary to my most legitimate expectations, considering the rather exceptional potential and musical quality the group displayed, no-one offered us anything after the concert.

"I would have been very happy to continue with these excellent musicians. But they all went back to their own projects and I moved on without a band for the next few years."

An unexpected, tragic event put an end to Cyrille Verdeaux's French musical career. "The accidental death of my son made me leave France for good. In 1980 I went to the US to live in an ashram. This is when my second life began…Yoga, New Age, Californian experience, etc... But that's another story!"

In the '80s Verdeaux's muse took him away from the classical-psychedelic fusion Clearlight had pioneered. He began to create therapeutic and cosmic music that could be loosely be classified under the New Age rubric. By 2016 he had released over 25 albums, some recorded under the Clearlight name. The last of his Clearlight albums was 2014's Impressionist Symphony. *Recorded 40 years after* Clearlight Symphony, *it reunited Verdeaux with Didier Malherbe, Tim Blake, and Steve Hillage to produce a fitting culmination to his impressive body of work.*

Notes

1   The other members of Babylone were Loppo Martinez (vocals, bass), René Soler (drums), and Antoine Duvernet (sax, flute). Duvernet would go on to join Lard Free and Urban Sax, as well as contribute to the Delired Cameleon Family LP.

2   Although Verdeaux points out: "excerpts of the music can be found on Christian's record *Photo Musik*, which I produced."

3   Verdeaux: "Joel was writing his music more precisely than me, so his style can sound a little different to my own compositions, which were mostly unnotated except for the chord chart."

4   Boulé was touring the US with the Steve Hillage Band during the recording of *Forever Blowing Bubbles*, so he doesn't make an appearance on the album. A piece *was* recorded with him, but due to time restrictions couldn't be included on the album. "Christian did play on the piece 'Sweet Labyrinthe' which was real psychedelic musical poetry with an esoteric text (and the participation of Gilbert Artman). But unfortunately it was too long to fit on either of the sides." *(Verdeaux)*
Note: A version of this track (without the recitation of the text) is included as a bonus track on later CD releases of *Forever Blowing Bubbles* under the title 'Sweet Absinthe'.

5   Jeanneau had been a member of Triangle.

6   Roussel had been the drummer in Richard Pinhas's early group Schizo.

7   Guitarist Coaquette had been a member of Musica Elettronica Viva, and would go on to form Spacecraft with John Livengood.

8   *Visa de Censure no. X* is described by Verdeaux as "a one-hour musical clip without any dialogue at all, very *nouvelle vague français*..." A copy of the film is held at the Centre Pompidou in Paris.

part five:
the jazz underground

INTRODUCTION

> As practising proponents of free jazz, we were anathema to the 'serious' jazz musicians. There were extremely rigid distinctions even within the different types of jazz, and for a jazz musician to be associated with rock in any shape or form was seen as a heinous betrayal of 'good music'.
>
> *Robert Wood*

The French underground's embrace of jazz, and particularly free-jazz, was a major force in the development of its musical culture. Dominique Grimaud: "Everyone, not only those in direct contact, was influenced by the strong presence of free-jazz musicians in our country. Some French musicians incorporated free elements into their compositions, others embarked on long, totally free improvisations. It can almost be called a 'contagion'... a good match for libertarian ideas." The rare international rock acts that incorporated elements of jazz (Captain Beefheart, Soft Machine, The Mothers of Invention etc.) were correspondingly popular in France - usually more-so than in their home countries.

Given these factors it's unsurprising that a number of the first bands to emerge from the underground were clearly inspired by the jazz players around them (notably Magma and Moving Gelatine Plates). What *is* surprising is the very one-sided nature of the relationship between rock and jazz at the beginning of the '70s.

Through the '60s and into the '70s, the jazz scene maintained cordial relations with pop acts. They may have viewed *varieté* and *yé-yé* as lesser forms of music, but jazz musicians were happy to accompany these performers on stage and in the studio. It was a symbiotic relationship allowing jazz musicians to pay the bills, and lending cachet to what could be otherwise dismissed as frivolous music. Jazz musicians displayed little fear that exposure to *varieté* or *yé-yé* would dilute their jazz purity, but rock was a different matter entirely.

Robert Wood's experience provides an inside view. The English vibraphonist established a strong reputation in the Parisian jazz world after settling in the city in 1970. This was consolidated in late '71 with the release of his debut album *Tarot* (recorded with members of Steve Lacy's band). Wood was, however, blindsided by the reaction of the jazz community to his brief association with an underground band just a few months later.

"I was asked to perform with my jazz trio at the Festival de Bièvres, a month or so after playing with Lard Free at Évry. Word of my being on stage with a rock band had gotten around amongst the Paris jazz musicians, so when I told my bass player and drummer about the upcoming gig they refused to have anything to do with it. Left with a gig and no band, I asked Gilbert [Artman] if he would play drums. He agreed and found Phil Cassegrain to play bass. At the festival we played my usual numbers, some from the *Tarot* album, but with a 'rock' rhythm section.

"I was still a 'jazz' musician in my head. For my second album, *Sonabular*, I'd composed and arranged a series of numbers for jazz quartet and a guest cellist. A couple of days before the recording session I encountered resistance from the musicians, mainly due to having 'sold myself out' by playing at rock concerts... I began to sense they were worried that a 'rock' musician might appear at the session!"

Wood's response to this incipient mutiny was to scrap his initial plan and simply record the album as a duet with drummer Gilbert Artman. Artman was probably exactly the kind of 'rock' musician the other jazzmen had feared might appear, although ironically he'd cut his teeth in the very same jazz clubs they frequented.

This experience helped convince Wood to leave the strictures of the jazz world behind. He developed a new style featuring amplified (and often distorted) vibraphone and formed Woodlands, a band that would go on to become a fixture on the underground rock circuit.

As jazz-fusion became more accepted, the delineation between jazz and rock musicians appears to have become less rigid, although vestiges of suspicion remained. However, at the same time the direct influence of jazz on the underground was waning.

By late '72 Magma had begun to move far beyond their jazz roots, creating a unique mix of jazz-fusion and symphonic elements - a style that would become known as Zeuhl. The bands that splintered from Magma, like Zao and Weidorje, were inevitably influenced by their time in the band, and their music was often classified as Zeuhl (whether warranted or not). In the mid to late '70s a group of bands began to consciously align themselves with the Zeuhl style. These included Xalph, Univers Zero (from Belgium), and Potemkine.

MOVING GELATINE PLATES

> Jacques Souplet, the Director of CBS, wanted to sign us. But we had reservations about the "system", we were afraid of losing our creative freedom. In a truly underground spirit we didn't want to be "drowned" in a record company more specialised in *variété*. Our style was also difficult to define, being neither rock nor jazz, and the French always want to label things.
>
> *Didier Thibault*

Of all the bands from the French underground, Moving Gelatine Plates is the one that could be referred to as an "overnight sensation". They burst onto the French music scene at the Le Bourget Festival in March '70, just three weeks after playing their debut gig, with a triumphant performance that garnered effusive press coverage and overtures from record companies. Incredibly, at this point half of the band were still high-school students. Inevitably the realities of the French music scene would temper these heady days, but for a brief, sweet moment the Parisian four-piece was touted as the next big thing.

Guitarist Gérard Bertram and bassist Didier Thibault met as schoolboys in Sartrouville, to the west of Paris. Discovering a common interest in British R&B they began to play music together as fourteen-year-olds. An older student, Michel Coulon, was drafted as their drummer in '67, and they christened themselves The Lines. The young trio cut their teeth playing covers of The Beatles and The Rolling Stones.

The school gymnasium would become an important venue for the young band. It hosted their first performances in '67 and in May '68 the band "occupied" it during the weeks of strikes and disruption, allowing them to practise and perform whenever they wished. Over time The Lines' music evolved beyond R&B, taking on influences from Pink Floyd, Soft Machine, and The Mothers of Invention. In early '69 they renamed themselves Moving Gelatine Plates[1] to reflect their new, more experimental musical approach.

At the end of the year there were two significant personnel changes. Michel Coulon vacated the drum stool after becoming a young father. His replacement, Gérard Pons, was chanced upon at the local MJC youth centre where he was auditioning for a hard-rock band. While Pons didn't get that job, Didier Thibault had been listening in and knew that he was the ideal drummer for Moving Gelatine Plates.

The line-up was finalised with the recruitment of experienced multi-instrumentalist Maurice Helmlinger. Thibault: "Gérard had a neighbour who played in a *variété* group that lent us equipment. Maurice was a member of the group." When approached, Helmlinger jumped at the chance to play more contemporary and challenging music. "Maurice became the fourth member and largely completed the line-up all by himself - playing sax (tenor, alto, soprano), flute, trumpet, and organ."

Pons and Helmlinger were both twenty-three when they joined Moving Gelatine Plates, a full six years older than Thibault and Bertram. Asked if there was any issue about the age difference Thibault replies, "Gérard and I were younger but already playing very well! *(laughs)* We found a rapport immediately." Three years of playing together had given the younger pair time to truly hone their musical skills. Now with the addition of Pons and Helmlinger, MGP was ready to make a quantum leap.

The first three months of '70 were spent in intensive rehearsals, with the band bunkering down to write original material and develop their own sound. "We really only started writing when Gérard and Maurice joined. Even today, I can't understand how we wrote more than an hour of music in barely three months!"

The new line-up played their first gig on 7 March '70 at the MJC youth centre where Thibault had met Pons. They performed a full set of new, original material to a capacity crowd of 250 people. "The welcome was more than warm, even if this style of music left the audience a little disconcerted. People weren't very used to rhythm changes, compound bars, and certain 'dissonances'."

Just after this debut the band made an audacious move, approaching the organisers of the Le Bourget Festival for a spot on the bill. Rather than evidence of searing ambition it was the expression of youthful exuberance: "We were very carefree and didn't ask ourselves too many questions. Our main goal was to see Pink Floyd, because we didn't have the money to afford seats! We were given the chance to play on a small annex stage the day before the festival really started."

So, on 27 March, Moving Gelatine Plates played their second ever show to an enthusiastic crowd of around 400. The audience was so impressed that a petition was circulated demanding the band be given the chance to play on the main stage. It was successful, and MGP found themselves scheduled for a second performance just before The Pretty Things. "The next day we played on the main stage in front of 5000 people! We got a really warm reception. We even kicked off the news report at 8pm! Almost all of the newspapers called us the 'revelation of the festival'." [2]

Their performance at Le Bourget created a surge of attention in the national music press, with *Best*, *Actuel*, and *Rock & Folk* all lauding the band.[3]

On the same day that MGP had approached the Le Bourget festival they'd also registered for the *tremplin* battle-of-the-bands at Golf Drouot. Another impressive performance on 3 April '70 won them the competition. However their desire to keep things 'underground' soured relations with the venue: "Henri Leproux offered us the chance to play for a weekend. We told him we weren't making music for 'trendies' to dance to, which was pretty pretentious in hindsight." They were banned from Golf Drouot.

The buzz created by their Le Bourget performance led to record company interest. CBS offered the fledgling band a record deal, but it was turned down. MGP had decided to follow a more independent, "underground" route. In June '70 they entered into a management and recording contract they believed would give them the independence they desired, signed with Claude Rousseau, organiser of the Le Bourget festival ("He'd given us our opportunity and trust, so we owed it to him to give ours in return").

The association with Rousseau led to the band playing at the Valbonne Festival in July '70, allowing MGP to maintain its high profile. However the festival was a financial disaster for Rousseau[4], leaving him in a precarious position. "From an artistic point of view we were in perfect agreement, but he just didn't have the means to produce us."

Under pressure from the band, Rousseau eventually scraped together the cash for a short session at Saravah Studios in November

'70. Moving Gelatine Plates recorded two tracks: early versions of 'London Cab' and 'X-25'. Only a single acetate disc of the recordings was produced, but it made its way into the hands of Patrice Blanc-Francard, host of France Inter's *Pop Club*. He played the record on air the next month.

Once again youthful exuberance paid off for Thibault: "As a faithful listener of *Pop Club*, I was stunned to hear it on the radio! I picked up the phone immediately (because I had *no* idea at all) and an arrangement was made for MGP to play live for 40 minutes the following week! We played again for 20 minutes, then a third time for 10 minutes." [5]

December '70 proved to be a decisive month for MGP. In addition to receiving unexpected exposure on national radio, they opened a high-profile concert for Brigitte Fontaine at the Fac de Droit. The press gave a glowing assessment: "Moving Gelatine Plate *(sic)* makes music that is distinct, relatively straightforward, and has a strong impact achieved without resorting to clichés... Until further notice they are to be considered one of the best groups around. It's high time that they were captured on record."

This last remark proved quite prescient. Claude Delcloo was in the audience that night. He had moved on from BYG/Actuel to set up the specialist AKT label under the auspices of CBS. Impressed with Moving Gelatine Plates' performance he quickly organised a meeting and declared an interest in signing them. "We trusted Claude Delcloo immediately. Firstly he was a musician himself, and secondly he had an independent label within CBS, which guaranteed that we would be a little 'separate' from the company."

By now the band had realised that their favoured 'independent' route simply wasn't feasible. However, to take up Delcloo's offer they had to extricate themselves from their contract with Rousseau. An outstanding debt provided the opportunity: "Claude Rousseau couldn't pay us for a tour that we'd completed in the summer of '70, and that served as the bargaining chip."

MGP signed with AKT on 4 February '71. Delcloo wasted no time at all in organising a recording session. The band entered Davout Studios on 8 March to record their debut album. Thankfully lack of preparation time posed no problem for such a tightly-rehearsed band. The week-long recording sessions saw MGP record entire instrumental takes live to tape, capturing the raw energy of their live performances.

As promised, Delcloo ensured that the band had total artistic freedom in the studio. He also provided them with an experienced recording engineer, François Dentan. Thibault remembers Dentan with real fondness: "He was enthusiastic about innovating, finding new things. For example he was very surprised to record a distorted bass for the first time in his life, and was happy to tamper with the sound of the drums during the solo in 'Last Song'."

The result of the sessions was the album *Moving Gelatine Plates*. Its eclectic style certainly shows some Soft Machine influence, but with more of an anarchic (slightly punky) energy - perhaps Soft Machine's *Third* would have sounded more like this if Robert Wyatt's dadaist spirit had been given free-rein.[6]

Not long after the recording Thibault and Bertram finally passed the Baccalaureate ("I still wonder how..." muses Thibault), and were at last able to devote themselves solely to the band.

*Moving Gelatine Plate*s was released at the beginning of June '71. The band were obviously keen to capitalise on the release, but CBS's distribution was patchy at best, and their promotional effort was practically non-existent. It was left to the band members themselves to send copies to the music press.

Thibault: "The AKT label was a bit separate from straight-up CBS productions. That was good for creative freedom, but not so good for 'promo'."

Thankfully the print journalists who managed to get their hands on a copy gave the album a very good reception. One wrote, "Their rich and dense music seduces the ear immediately. Their recipe for success is remarkable: instrumental virtuosity at the service of an unequalled wealth of ideas, a taste for a joke, and clearly eclectic influences... Hopefully the underground nature of the group, and the incredibly gelatinous look of the disc's cover art won't deter people from buying it. They'd be missing out on something very important: great music."

They received positive reviews, but editorial copy was hard to come by. Thibault puts this down to a music press that directed its attention to politicised groups like Red Noise and Komintern, the resolutely non-political MGP was ignored. They fared little better on television and radio. The band was filmed playing live at ORTF's Studio 105, but it was never broadcast.[7] Lack of exposure coupled with poor distribution resulted in disappointing sales of their debut, with only 2,500 copies sold in France.

Moving Gelatine Plates had been self-managed since parting ways with Claude Rousseau in early '71. Claude Delcloo had helped to find them gigs, but opportunities were drying up as changes in the music scene saw underground-friendly clubs close their doors. However when MGP approached the Gibus Club for a spot, they impressed the venue's booker Francis Clarel. "When Francis heard us he immediately proposed managing us for live work. With Francis, we played more often in provincial nightclubs in exchange for local groups that he programmed at Gibus."

Unfortunately these regional audiences were generally there to dance, and MGP's complex and undanceable music was a poor fit. Nevertheless their performances in Paris and at festivals were enthusiastically received. A review of a Gibus Club gig was typical: "They are a total success everywhere they play... pretty remarkable when you realise the audience hasn't been primed by their discs. Indeed, to this point, Moving Gelatine Plates has recorded only one album whose distribution is rather restricted.

"People want to see Moving Gelatine Plates as the French Soft Machine, but that's an overstatement. However, their music does have something in common with that of Matching Mole: it's intelligent, and that's uncommon."

In spite of the poor performance of their first record, MGP's contract with CBS required them to deliver an album per year, so a session was booked for the band at the 16-track Studio des Dames from 7-15 December '71. Thibault says that the band were more than happy to enter the studio again so quickly, as they had new material ready to go.

On *The World of Genius Hans*[8] Moving Gelatine Plates were keen to exploit the possibilities offered by the studio. While their recording time was constrained, both the studio and the engineer, Roland Guillotel, were a good fit for the band.

Thibault: "The second album was much more 'produced' than the first. From the outset it was developed more for the studio. Some titles were totally composed, leaving little room for improvisation.

Naturally we'd found some rhythmic- and sound-signatures that gave us originality (for example the sax-guitar themes in fifths or thirds). The 'Moving System' was refined, reinforcing the idea that each instrument could move out of its primarily rhythmic or melodic role. Bass and drums weren't limited to a 'supporting' role, but could play entire melodic lines.

"We spent more time in the studio, and added outside musicians (bassoon, vibraphone, trombone, a vocal chorus). There were also some surreptitious discoveries. For example, deciding to use the studio's harpsichord on 'Cauchemar'."

The music brought into the studio was the most sophisticated they had written so far. Thibault describes it as the apotheosis of the 'Moving System', pointing out that over 450 different musical themes are sewn into the fabric of the LP.

"We'd put a lot of themes aside, and others to link them together, which prolonged the 'puzzle' of 'The World of Genius Hans'. Other titles were entirely written by one of us ('Astromonster' by Gérard Bertram, and 'Cauchemar' by myself).

" 'We Were Loving Her' was composed at the last minute to finish off the album. We used a kalimba that we'd been given, and the Hammond organ that was sitting in the studio (you can hear the sound of the Leslie almost giving up the ghost). I discovered the sung theme the same morning while walking, clapping my hands in 7-time. The singing and the sax are in 6-time, hence a little cheating at the end to get back together."

The music on *The World of Genius Hans* is hugely ambitious; much more complex and layered than that on the band's debut. However some of the energy captured on that first LP is lacking. Thibault agrees: "It appears very sophisticated, but less spontaneous, perhaps to the detriment of a certain impact."

1972 should have been the year that Moving Gelatine Plates finally received the success they so richly deserved. While editorial support was still rare, critical acclaim was flowing and a new album was primed for release in February. Instead, as Thibault laments, "1972 was the beginning… and the end of the end!"

It had initially seemed that CBS were making up for past errors by preparing a serious promotional push for *The World of Genius Hans*. A single, 'Funny Doll', was released at the beginning of the year. "They had the idea to release a single before the second album, with the aim of doubling the promotion. But they forgot to send the album to the radio!"

Once again it fell to the band to promote the album themselves. The journalists who managed to obtain a copy wrote positive reviews, and those among the band's audience who were able to track down an LP were impressed. But once again ineffective distribution and zero promotion capped the number of sales at around 2500.

The lack of income from record sales or concerts left the band drowning in a sea of debt. To give themselves a fighting chance as a working band MGP had invested in a sound system, a truck, and decent amplifiers - all purchased on credit. Their record label also proved to be part of the problem rather than the solution: "CBS wasn't giving us any financial support. They simply paid for posters. Any concerts that they found for us were for promotion, so weren't paid. The fees for the extra musicians on the second album were even deducted from our royalties!

"We couldn't afford the repayments on the gear any longer. Gérard Pons and Maurice Helmlinger had burdens that neither Gérard Bertram nor I knew, as we were still living with our parents. It's very sad because we were getting along perfectly."

The first casualty in the battle to reduce the band's debt was Helmlinger's organ. He sold it to make some cash, and moved exclusively onto brass. An advert was placed for a keyboard player with his own equipment, and Philippe Patron (who had played with Paris group Reaction) became MGP's keyboard player.

The war of financial attrition continued into '72 and in May Gérard Pons was forced to sell his drum kit and quit the band. Their manager's son, Alain Clarel, took over. Clarel was an experienced drummer who had played in Michel Polnareff's band.

This new line-up supported the UK's East of Eden at the Paris Olympia on 6 May '72. A contemporary review lauded their performance: "This group, unfairly little-known in France, seduced an audience that received them warmly... With their performance at the Olympia, Moving Gelatine Plates proved that they are among the very best groups in the country."

Another live performance on 26 May was recorded by the ORTF, and released many years later on Monster Melodies Records. This recording reveals a band with a ferocious sound. The title track of their second album is satisfyingly cerebral on record, but in this performance it's crushingly aggressive, with the jazz rolled back and the rock pushed to the fore.

The fact that these two shows in May '72 were obviously played by a band reaching the peak of its power makes the finale to Moving Gelatine Plates' story all the more tragic.

A lifeline finally seemed to have been thrown when the band was booked for a residency in Summer '72. This would have earned enough money to pay off their entire debt, allowing MGP to face the future with some hope.

"We had a booking for the whole of August in a hotel in Honfleur, but due to bad weather and the resulting lack of clients, the contract was cancelled after three nights."

Their lifeline was cruelly yanked away, and the battle was over. Moving Gelatine Plates were forced to sell their truck and sound system to clear their debts. The band called it a day on 5 August '72.

Thibault still regrets the circumstances around their demise. "It's a pity that financial problems brought about the end of MGP, because we'd started to write very promising new songs. Unfortunately they were never recorded, not even as demos."

Didier Thibault's reputation as a bass player saw him asked to join Magma at the beginning of '73, but he declined, wary of their austere reputation. He did, however, join Gong when asked, playing with them for a few months before they left France to relocate to the UK.

He then founded Yasmina, a free jazz group with Eastern overtones. Parallel to this project, Thibault backed the singer Gilles Ulivier and started a career as an arranger and session man.

In '78 he restarted MGP, shortening the name to Moving. A self-titled album was released in '80.

Gerard Bertram played in Zao and Mama Lion after MGP split. He later became a music teacher in Sartrouville and a producer of library and children's music. He released a privately pressed LP, L'Avenir Du Monde, *under the name Gerard Bertram & Le College Romain Rolland de Sartrouville in '86.*

Notes

1   "Moving gelatine plates" was a phrase that Michel Coulon had discovered while reading John Steinbeck's *Travels with Charley*.

2   Footage of the band at Le Bourget is available to view on the INA Madelan website and on YouTube.

3   In his review of the Le Bourget Festival in *Rock & Folk* Paul Alessandrini wrote, "Moving Gelatine Plates are the most interesting of the new bands, with consummate music that is absolutely good to go..."

4   See *Chapter 6*: 'Summer '70 - *L'été Pop*'.

5   The band's first live performance on *Pop Club* was on 29 December '70.

6   The lyrics on *Moving Gelatine Plates* are in English, and with the exception of 'Last Song' are composed of nursery-rhymes and non-sequiturs. The rationale was similar to Robert Wyatt's oft-times wordless vocalisations: "We use the voice as an instrument. We don't want to attract attention to the words, it's the music that counts." (*Actuel*)

7   The broadcast had been scheduled to air on 22 July '71. Magma, Triangle, and Total Issue were also to have been featured.

8   Thibault: "The title and the cover are based on the idea that genius lies in madness."

MAGMA

> What's the point of reproducing a pale imitation of Anglo-American music. British and American musicians made good music but I didn't identify with it. I wanted to leave them to it, and make something different.
>
> *Christian Vander*

From the beginning, French pop and rock was under intense pressure to conform to proven Anglo-Saxon models; however in late '69 a band emerged that refused to genuflect before the British and American idols. In a country struggling to define what French rock could be, Magma's jazz-rock-classical-fusion provided a bold rush of blood to the head. Magma didn't even consider their music to be French. It was from another place entirely. From a different *planet*.

Magma was driven by Christian Vander's vision of a music that could communicate pure feeling. His goal was to evoke a similar epiphany to his on first hearing John Coltrane: "What I looked for in Coltrane's music is what I've looked for with Magma as well... spirituality, a cry... that would in some way awaken this sleepy and somewhat formless world."

In following his muse, Vander was certainly not going to let the boundaries of rock, or any genre, constrain his music. Nor would he allow the limits of French or any other language to circumscribe it - so he invented his own: "Kobaïan isn't a language born from intellectual reflection... People don't understand Kobaïan... But you know, if they listen to an opera in Russian they won't necessarily understand that either."

Klaus Blasquiz, Magma's vocalist, shared in Vander's quest for a new language that would help music to cut straight through to the emotions: "[Kobaïan] is a physiological language, a ritual, a form of universal Esperanto. It's a musical language. It's easy to sing, and at the same time stops people from thinking about the meaning of this lyric, or that line... It has a united content, and that's what's important."

Alongside the Kobaïan language, a new planet with a labyrinthine mythology was created to provide the foundation for Magma's musical explorations. While they distanced themselves from the progressive rock movement, in many ways Magma were the progressive band *par excellence*. Other bands produced self-contained concept albums, while Magma were a concept *band*. Their first two albums told the story of a people leaving the corrupted Earth behind to search for enlightenment on Kobaïa. It was a story of struggle, conflict, and violence, with music to match.

Vander's vision was out-of-step with the prevailing counter-culture: "A lot of groups at the time... dreamed about things... like birds and flowers and peace and love. But that wasn't really what was needed – did we really have time to dream?"

Saxophonist Richard Raux expanded on this in an early interview: "We really believe in the violence of music. We aren't at all in favour of calming or cool music... We want music that spurs people on, that sets something off in their heads, that shatters their consciousness..."

Beginnings

Christian Vander's *entrée* into jazz came at an early age, via a giant of the scene: John Coltrane's drummer of choice, Elvin Jones. "My mother was friends with Bobby Jaspar whose best friend was Elvin. Bobby brought him to the house one day, and my mother told him I was starting to study drums. That's how it started."

After Jones had tutored him, Vander had a stint playing in the jazz clubs around Paris: "At sixteen, when I tried to play at jams, the musicians made sarcastic comments. It was a very tough atmosphere... [and] discouraged me a little from playing jazz, I thought they were slowly dying in their ghetto."

Vander moved on from jazz, searching for a better forum for his own ideas: "I gave everything I had on the drums... But the day I had the opportunity to be completely free, in free-jazz, I realised that the music I heard was too weak. I was at the peak of my physical potential, but I wasn't satisfied with what was happening musically... To be able to hear what I wanted to, I had to have everything in my head played by other musicians."

The seeds of a new direction were sown in summer '69 when

Vander left for the Côte d'Opale in northern France with the Carnaby Street Swingers. The soul-blues band featured Laurent Thibault on bass, Lucian Zabuski (Zabu) on vocals, and Francis Moze on organ.[1]

Vander: "The Carnaby Street Swingers' music was pretty good, with quite bluesy vocals, but I wanted to spice things up by playing tracks from Pharoah Sanders' album *Tauhid*, along with a piece I'd just composed..." This was an early version of the track 'Kobaïa', the centre-piece of Magma's first album: "I hit three chords and began to sing the melody in an unknown language: 'Kobaïa, Kobaïa kobashi bewa, somewa ossü...' The words came by themselves... I wanted to play it in the style of Pharoah Sanders, an incantation... with the singer stirring the crowd, like a political oration. It was definitely incongruous in the places we were playing, with people sipping on their glass of champagne."

This musical incongruity was likely a contributing factor in the sacking of both Vander and Thibault from The Carnaby Street Swingers. Vander: "On the drive back to Paris we constructed a whole story, we created another world: Kobaïa! We ended up inventing this planet, a planet that could be like ours, which actually is ours, [but] as Laurent put it, 'Without the assholes'."

With the musical and conceptual foundations laid Vander set about recruiting the players he needed: "I was well regarded as a drummer, and I knew a lot of musicians, so I got them together to explain our project... There were about twenty of us around a big table... They were 'the cream', the best musicians in Paris... or at least they claimed to be." The meeting was a disappointment, with the assembled musicians more interested in how much it would pay than in the musical adventure Vander proposed.

He decided to look elsewhere, calling in bassist Laurent Thibault and vocalist Zabu from the Carnaby Street Swingers, along with René Garber, a saxophonist he'd bonded with over a common love of John Coltrane. The group was completed by American pianist Eddy Rabin, Claude Engel on guitar, and Guy Marco and René Morizur filling out the brass section. The new band was named Uniweria Zekt Magma Composedra Arguezdra (which was soon shortened to Magma).

Klaus Blasquiz entered the orbit of the band in September '69, when he was invited along to a rehearsal by Claude Engel. Blasquiz was impressed by what he heard: "The *cave* was filled with a shaggy but hard-working clan, communicating with the help of incredible sounds, furtive glances, and ritual gestures. The music was streamlined, futuristic, tropical, precise, symphonic, and limitless."

Blasquiz had been active on the Parisian music scene since '67, building a strong reputation as a blues singer, notably during his time with Blues Convention. Alan Jack (of Alan Jack Civilization) had introduced him to Engel as "the best blues singer there is." Blasquiz continued to come to rehearsals while the band's vocalist was busy elsewhere: "Zabu was the singer, but he was never there. By chance, one day I was singing just beside the grand piano, and they were recording. Not recording me, but the piano..."

Vander describes the moment he listened back to the tape: "I was listening with my friend [René Garber] and suddenly I heard a voice in the background. It was unreal. We were stunned, where did that voice come from? The next day, at rehearsal, I played the tape to the others and asked them who was singing. They told me: 'It's Klaus.'"

Blasquiz: "Christian and Laurent Thibault came to see me, 'We heard your voice... that's the voice we need!' And I said 'Yes, but you have to make a choice between me and Zabu.'" A band meeting was held and Klaus Blasquiz officially become the band's singer.

Of this early line-up only Vander, Engel, and Blasquiz would actually play on Magma's debut album. Rabin simply disappeared (it was assumed that he'd returned to the US), Thibault dropped bass and began to manage the band, while Garber was temporarily left as the sole brass player when the others moved on.

After a long series of disappointing auditions, François 'Faton' Cahen was taken on as pianist, Francis Moze from the Carnaby Street Swingers replaced Thibault on bass, and Jacky Vidal joined on double bass. The brass section was filled out by Alain "Paco' Chalery on trumpet and Richard Raux on sax.

The first performance of this line-up was at the Rock'n'Roll Circus. The American classical pianist, Carl Knutt, was in the audience. Blasquiz: "A lanky American leaps onto the table and literally explodes: 'Are you guys deaf? Do you not realise what you just heard?'" Knutt was an instant convert, renting the band a residential rehearsal space in the countryside outside Paris where they could take the time to refine their music.

Magma stayed in the Chevreuse Valley from October '69 until the end of January '70. Vander: "We could practise night and day. It was a disciplined environment: get up at seven in the morning, jog, have breakfast, and rehearse all day long. In this house we really earned our stripes, and got ourselves ready to record our first album."

During their stay Teddy Lasry (sax and flute) arrived to replace René Garber.[2] Blasquiz was impressed by Lasry's multi-instrumental abilities: "He already played flute, sax, clarinet, and piano, but he picked up new instruments seemingly without effort: oboe, bass, drums... If Francis, Christian, or even Faton were absent he played their instruments with frightening facility."

Rather than slowly build a reputation doing the rounds of the clubs, Magma went directly to the record labels looking for a deal. A series of showcases were organised, for both the press and the labels' artistic directors. Philippe Paringaux from *Rock & Folk* was won over by the showcase he attended: "In Magma's music there is a drama constantly on the verge of hysteria... Magma will be the bomb to demolish every convention of music... Finally, here is music that is deeply disturbing, physically uncomfortable, and attacks the mind."

While the music press were stunned by Magma's musical ambition, the labels were having trouble coming to terms with it. Vander: "The artistic directors weren't getting excited... they were taken aback: 'What is this music? What's it called, how do you classify it?' Then Gérard Davoust, Philips' director of production, arrived. I sensed he was mystified. He was the last to come, and if we didn't convince him we were screwed... When we came to the speech in 'Stoah' I got up from the behind the drums and stood right in front of him, two centimetres away, screaming right into his face, with all the madness I could muster. He was backed against the wall, he couldn't move, terrorised. Afterwards Gérard Davoust would say he signed us out of fear!"

Magma

Magma inked their contract in April '70, and a recording session was quickly booked at Studio Europa Sonar.[3] Vander: "When we arrived in the studio we just played the whole repertoire live in one go... We recorded the tracks one after the other, but Claude Engel's

'Thaud Zaïa' was accidentally erased, so we had to do a second take, not as good as the first, unfortunately."

Vander was responsible for just over half of the compositions, with other contributions made by Engel, Cahen, Lasry, and Thibault. Vander: "The album has great unity even though it's the work of a number of composers... There's a lot of freedom on that record, everyone expressed themselves while keeping to the spirit of the project."

While he was more than satisfied with the performances, Vander was frustrated by the studio staff: "The sound engineer, Roger Roche, didn't know our music and when he saw our wild energy, he turned the levels right down... There was almost nothing on the tape, it didn't ring out. For me, a cymbal should scream when you hit it."

As Roche started mixing the album, the band, underwhelmed by the sound he was achieving, took over. Vander: "The sound engineer was horrified. He was in a corner, watching on in disbelief... I looked after the three or four drum tracks, Francis [Moze] took care of his bass, and everyone did the same for their own instrument. We were all clustered around the mixing desk, everyone adjusting the knobs and the faders, mixing the record even though none of us had ever touched a console! Collective hysteria!... There may be some distortion, but the record has a sound. It's a very dynamic mix, that we probably wouldn't have been able to achieve otherwise."

The thrill of listening to Magma's first album is still considerable, with Lasry's quasi-Afrobeat brass arrangements, Moze's thundering bass, and Vander's astounding drums capped by Engel's almost post-punk guitar. What sounds cataclysmic today must have sounded positively apocalyptic at the time. *Magma* was recorded in the same year as Soft Machines' *Third* - and is arguably just as definitive.

When the album was released in May '70 it received unanimously positive reviews. Philippe Paringaux wrote in *Rock & Folk*: "Neither pop, nor jazz, not the music of yesterday, or the music of tomorrow... this is some of the most impressive music you'll hear today, not only in France, but anywhere... It slaps the listener straight in the face, combining flawless musical technique with fiery expression."

Jazz Hot: "Let's immediately clear up any misunderstanding: Magma is not a jazz band - and doesn't claim to be... We simply want to draw attention to this particularly original group, because, among other things, it includes some of the young jazzmen of the rising generation... The group have undeniably discovered a different sound... jazz lovers, here's an opportunity to leave your ghetto."

While Paringaux had praised the ambition of Magma's music, he also noted "real concern" at hearing vocalisations he felt recalled Hitler's speeches. The suspicion of a fascist undertone in Magma would be a constant thorn in its side[4], one that Vander directly addressed the next month in *Best*:

"Straight away we have to correct those who think that we are fascists and Nazis. It's pretty much the opposite - more or less all of us were members of leftist movements when we were young... As for Nazism... of the eight members in the group, three are Jewish, one is black, and another is married to an Israeli... Every day we live in the midst of horrors worthy of the Third Reich. The Vietnam War is Nazism, Biafra is Nazism, the Siberian camps are Nazism... Nazism is always present. We aren't Nazis. Our hatred isn't directed to this or that race of people. Our war is against bullshit, against people who pass comment on you without knowing you, who grant themselves the right to judge."

These charges of a darkness in Magma's music were amplified when they also took to dressing uniformly in black, with their distinctive symbol prominently displayed. This was yet another misunderstanding according to Vander: "Dressing in black was a way to be sober, in tune with the gravity of our music... What matters in my music is the sound, the image is secondary."

Magma's music certainly has a violence and an anger at its core, foreshadowing the dark turn the European counter-culture would take in the mid-'70s with the rise in support for groups like the Red Army Faction in Germany and Red Brigades in Italy. Militancy mixed with a taste for nihilism doesn't necessarily predicate an adherence to the extreme right.

Magma's first major public concert was held at Gaîté Lyrique on 22 May with Triptique and Moving Gelatine Plates supporting. This was followed a month later by their first TV appearance, on *Discorama*, where an interview preceded a mimed performance of 'Stoah'.[5]

In July '70 the band took on legendary music mogol Giorgio Gomelsky as their manager.[6] He first encountered their music during an interview with a *Rock & Folk* journalist: "They played me a tape of a French band, which somehow seemed puzzling to them and asked for my opinion. I remember it well, even today. The music was original, with influences derived from non-Anglo folk, classical, jazz and experimental music... I said something like 'very ambitious stuff, these guys seem to want to take on a lot, if they are really serious, it could be interesting.' There must have been a conspiracy, because wherever I went in Paris, people were asking me if I had heard *that* tape! It turned out to be Magma!...

"A few days after the interview was published, I got a phone call from Faton, Magma's pianist. They had read it and wished to ask me if I was interested in checking them out. I think they were playing one of their rare gigs a few days hence... the rest is history. I had never heard anything like it."

Blasquiz notes that at this point Gomelsky was just the tonic the band needed: "[He] is the mythical being that everyone hopes for. We were waiting for a Giorgio Gomelsky... The first words he said were: 'Listen guys, Magma's music is fabulous, but you are royal fools... with the music you have, with the musicians you have, you absolutely have to do something to make yourself known.' We were only playing one concert a month at the time. The brass section were using charts, and he made them work to learn everything by heart. Giorgio was the first to really take care of Magma's production."

Magma continued to receive plaudits for their live shows, including their first show at the Olympia on October 17: "Magma's music is indefinable and totally indescribable: free-pop, free-jazz, hard-rock, rock, it's all the labels you'll want to attach to it... Magma has given us a joy that no other current music can give - the joy of having heard the sublime, the joy of having witnessed an unforgettable show, the joy of knowing that we can finally listen to something other than pap."

1970 had been an extraordinary year for Magma, they had signed to a major label, released a universally praised debut LP, and built a fearsome live reputation. However, at the end of the year, in what would become something of a pattern, the original Magma line-up suddenly broke apart. Vander: "Giorgio Gomelsky wanted to make me a leader, a solo artist, his technique was to divide and conquer... It created a bad atmosphere in the group. Add to that the question of money... The fatigue, and the endless touring without any payment... had worn out the musicians. That had a part in making the first line-up implode...

"Claude Engel left while we were getting the second album together. In the middle of a rehearsal he took his amp and left." [7]

According to Vander, Engel was "one of the driving elements of Magma". His departure was a body blow, doubly so as it precipitated the exit of Richard Raux and 'Paco' Chalery from the brass section.[8] While Engel wasn't replaced, Jeff 'Yochk'O' Seffer (sax) and Louis Toesco (trumpet) from Eddy Mitchell's backing band were brought in to join Lasry in the brass section.

Magma 2 & *The Unnameables*

The reconstituted band set about preparing the material for a second album, before entering Château d'Hérouville for seven days in April '71. There they recorded three long tracks - one each from Cahen, Lasry, and Vander.

Vander's side-long composition provided the centrepiece, pointing the way forward for Magma, veering from the jazz foundation of the debut towards something much more individual. Vander: "This album is important because in 'Rïah Sahïltaahk'[9] you can already find the framework of syncopated rhythms that I was going to elaborate in 'Mëkanik Destruktïw Kommandöh'."

Lasry's brass arrangements are a highlight of the LP, although Vander felt they only partially compensated for the loss of Engel: "The brass parts made up for the lack of Claude Engel's guitar, which had given a wonderful colour to the ensemble. [But] Engel's absence left us with a feeling of incompletion."

The critical response to *Magma 2* was every bit as glowing as for the band's debut. *Rock & Folk*: "How can one express how remarkable is Magma's slap to the face of French musical mediocrity... Christian Vander creates music that is more forceful, more beautiful, and more intelligent every day..."

Four months after recording their sophomore album Magma returned to Hérouville to record one of the most atypical records in their catalogue: *The Unnamables*. The album was recorded for Laurent Thibault's Thélème label, and featured the band playing a more accessible style of jazzy blues-soul with English lyrics. For the project they took on the identity of Univeria Zekt.

Blasquiz saw it as a way for the band to blow off some steam: "We let ourselves live a little. This project was a long way from Magma's characteristic musical density and suppressed energy." Francis Moze: "It's the music we would've played if we hadn't played Magma's. For this album, we reunited with Claude Engel and made our own style of pop music..." In addition to Engel's guest turn there are vocal contributions from Zabu and Ergo Sum's Lionel Ledissez. *Best*'s review suggested that "with these pieces, an audience outside France has the opportunity to discover a unique band", but there is no indication that *The Unnamables* was ever released outside of France, and even there the LP quickly faded into obscurity. It remains a curio in Magma's discography.

An important event occurred in the first half of '72 when Magma signed to the US-based A&M Records. Blasquiz: "Giorgio Gomelsky negotiated the change. I don't know if there was a buyout or what. We played at Michel Magne's wedding in Hérouville, and there were lots of guests, including the trumpeter Herb Alpert, the 'A' from A&M. He loved our music, so we signed with him, which was really good for us because it was a real international label." The band remained in the dark about the details of the deal, a pattern that was beginning to tarnish their opinion of Gomelsky. Blasquiz: "Every time, the transactions were carried out in the greatest secrecy, with, I imagine, obvious exchanges of dollars or pounds sterling... 'Don't worry: it's happening', he tells us each time, smiling. Without any more detail. We'll never see a Franc, apart from a few royalty advances, allowing us to buy a sound system, amplifiers and a truck... we only survived thanks to concerts."

After a slow start to the year, Magma toured regularly on the MJC circuit during '72, and that summer embarked on a run of appearances at jazz-oriented festivals in Montreux, Avignon, and Châteauvallon. The last of these performances, at Châteauvallon on 23 August, would see the band spectacularly implode once more.

Best judged their performance to be a musical triumph: "Magma confirmed what we already know, they are the best group in Europe and can equal the Anglo-Saxon giants. The atmosphere and climate they create is reminiscent of James Brown, a hypnotic rhythm crushing everything in its path." However *Rock & Folk* noted an incident that had left a bad taste in the mouth: "Gomelsky, their manager, comes on stage before the group, displaying grotesque puffed-up pride and pretension. To boost Magma, Gomelsky speaks with contempt about the [other] musicians... followed by ridiculous remarks such as 'Art and politics are related.. we're for the politics of good taste'."

More than half of Magma's musicians shared *Rock & Folk*'s distaste, for them Gomelsky's speech was the last straw. Cahen: "[Giorgio and I] had a fabulous connection for a year, then I got tired of his character, nothing he said surprised me anymore. He got on really badly with Francis Moze, and in the end with me too... little by little the tension got worse... Giorgio's speech at Châteauvallon was too much, intolerable, even bordering on fascistic. We couldn't stand it anymore." Cahen, Toesca, Seffer, Moze and Lasry all announced their intention to leave.[10]

Magma had to rebuild from a core of Christian Vander, Klaus Blasquiz, and Jean-Luc Manderlier.[11] René Garber returned on bass clarinet, Jean-Pierre Lambert took over the bass, and Stella Vander joined on vocals.

Stella Zelcer had married Christian Vander after the formation of Magma. As a teenager she had been as a *yé-yé* singer performing under the name 'Stella', with a string of singles released on Vogue and RCA Victor between '63 and '67. She had set herself apart by writing her own lyrics, which often offered a satirical take on the *yé-yé* scene. Stella Vander would be an important presence in Magma for the remainder of the '70s, and beyond.

Mëkanik Destruktïw Kommandöh & Jannick Top

In January '73 this transitional line-up demoed a major piece that was to form the basis of Magma's next LP. This forty-minute suite, 'Mëkanik Destruktïw Kommandöh', had been developed in performances over the past two years.[12] According to Vander an integral part of the band's writing process was giving material the chance to evolve on stage: "For Magma, live performance is essential. Whereas most musicians initially record their albums in the studio then 'reproduce' them on stage, Magma operates differently. In the first phase we refine pieces on stage after shaping and rehearsing them exhaustively. As performances go on, we get to know them, finding ever new depths... Often we improve certain parts and sometimes make radical changes... The second phase involves harvesting all the ideas and information generated at concerts and recording them in the studio."

Between recording the demo and the final version, Magma underwent a major transformation. Firstly three new recruits were added: Marc Fossett (guitar), and Mickey Graillier and Gérard Bikialo (keys). Not long afterwards Jean-Pierre Lambert came to a rehearsal raving about someone he'd seen playing with the band Troc, insisting that he'd found the bass player Magma needed. The next night a delegation went to Le Bulle to see the man who'd inspired their bassist to offer up his own position. Blasquiz: "When Jannick begins to play we understand immediately. Our hair stands on end and shivers run down our spines... The next day at rehearsal everyone agrees: Jannick's what we need! He's the bassist Magma's been waiting for. No doubt about it."

Jannick Top had originally studied cello before moving on to the electric bass. He quickly distinguished himself as a distinctive player, adapting cello tuning to the bass and developing a powerful, driving playing style. He had formed Troc with drummer André Ceccarelli, and recorded an eponymous album in '72.

Top: "Musically I have a very complementary role to that of Christian. My playing is 'earthy', a kind of ground on which you can rest, while his playing is made up of flashes, of surges towards the sky. I build a very solid 'bubble' that he tries to break all the time. It's this tension that gives a good rhythm."

Blasquiz: "The way [Top] plays the bass is very particular and very *in there*. He's a great musician, a freak. He's playing the right things in the right time and in the right place. It was the first time that Christian had nothing to say about [the bass part]."

The new line-up was completed with the arrival of Claude Olmos, who replaced Marc Fossett on guitar. His strong pedigree included stints with Alan Jack Civilization, Cœur Magique, and Alice. Blasquiz: "It turns out that Olmos is from Marseille, as is Jannick, and the two know each other. His tuneful way of playing adds a strong colour to the band when we're still searching for a new form."

Magma had recovered from yet an other implosion, emerging with possibly their strongest line-up to date. Blasquiz told *Best*: "There are now seven of us... There is a new dimension, in that several of the musicians are multi-instrumentalists. One singer plays sax, I play glockenspiel and alto sax, the organist plays alto sax, the pianist plays alto sax, and everyone sings." The influx of singers would become an important element in the evolution of Magma's music.

The new band's first Paris appearance was greeted enthusiastically by *Best*: "The addition of a chorus of between one to three people, depending on the piece, pays dividends... 'Mëkanik Kommandöh' is, without the slightest exaggeration, one of the greatest things we've ever seen, from any international musicians. The chorus is used magnificently, while the instruments, led by the drums, hurry them along superbly in a climactic trajectory."

The group decamped to the UK in April '73, to record *Mëkanik Destruktïw Kommandöh*[13] at The Manor Studio. As Gong had during the recording of *Flying Teapot*, they alternated shifts with Mike Oldfield, who was finishing his *Tubular Bells* album. Teddy Lasry returned to the brass section for the recording, while Gérard Bikialo was absent due to a miscommunication.

The session went smoothly, but an unfortunate mistake during the recording of vocal overdubs drained the power from the drum performance. Vander: "I admit it was my fault. To begin with, we had a fat sound... I heard 'Mekanïk' as a huge piece, with sixty voices ... why not five hundred! And after a while we found ourselves with a few scrawny voices and no more tracks... I thought, 'Hey, I don't use the low tom much on the record. So let's take the mike off the low tom and add vocals on that track'. The problem is the mike also picked up the snare drum and cymbals. I removed two of the five tracks that caught all of the drums, and bass as well (since I recorded live with Jannick). The drums and the bass were easily cut down by half. Afterwards, I tried to get the [same] drum sound, without realising that it was me who had destroyed it. It was with good intentions... to add more voices, to make it even more beautiful."

While it's true that the sound of Vander's usually thunderous drums is surprisingly anaemic on the album, the overwhelming power of the music mostly compensates. Nevertheless Blasquiz opines: "The sound isn't strong enough... It's too small for that piece of music."

As Magma was now signed to A&M, *Mëkanik Destruktïw Kommandöh* was their first LP to be given a full release in the US and UK. Steve Lake gave the album a glowing review in *Sounds*: "Like their major rivals, Gong, Magma have a specific mysticism that the music is almost subservient to... Magma, though, take the whole trip a little bit further by actually purporting to sing in the language of the planet which, not surprisingly, no listener understands. Theoretically, it seems like a good way to condemn your rock and roll band to obscurity, and I'm sure that's exactly what would happen to this lot if their music wasn't so damn fine... the combination of pumping rock electricity, massed neo-operatic voices and Vander's direct percussion is almost overwhelmingly exciting. When something genuinely out of the routine rock rut comes along, you really have to raise a cheer. And Magma is certainly different. I can't understand a word of it, and I think it's bloody great."

Quite apart from the positive critical response, Christian Vander views *Mëkanik Destruktïw Kommandöh* as a defining album for Magma, the vindication of his search for music that could communicate feelings directly: "For me, Magma was born with *Mëkanik Kommandöh*... The previous group had several directions, everyone brought a bit of their own style, because we weren't all in total agreement on the philosophy of the group. We had turned away from the original spirit a bit. We fully returned to it with *Mëkanik Kommandöh*. I had the opportunity to meet musicians who have the same state of mind."

To realise the ambition of his music Vander had employed an equally ambitious musical form. Not only did this single piece take up both sides of an LP, it was merely part of a larger work: "[It's] the last movement of a trilogy... I composed the first two movements ('Theusz Hamtaak' and 'Wurdah Ïtah') in '70 when we released the first double album... When 'Mëkanik Destruktïw Kommandöh' was completed, it was a revelation, so we recorded it immediately... If it had been possible I would have recorded 'Theusz Hamtaak' and 'Wurdah Ïtah' at the same, and the trilogy would have been complete." [14] For the next few years Magma would devote themselves to this expansive musical format.

A&M organised a promotional tour to the US in July '73, including a performance at the Newport Jazz Festival. This was followed by a well-received appearance at the UK's Reading Festival in August. With momentum building for the band outside of France, disaster appeared to strike when Klaus Blasquiz was called up for national service in September. He was stunned to be posted to Germany, where he was forced to stay for almost a month before a medical exemption was finally granted.

With tragedy averted, Magma embarked on their first major UK tour. *Melody Maker* reviewed their performance at the Marquee on 5 December: "Listening to Magma requires a lot of mental adjustment, a rethink about musical values, but it's nonetheless a shattering experience. And the group are so unlike anything else on this earth, that the thrill of discovery when you first see them is just unreal, like stumbling upon the Velvet Underground must have been for questing New Yorkers. That's how important Magma are. The New York Dolls and their ilk are great fun, absolutely, but Magma are important." The band returned to the UK many times over the next twelve months, building a strong reputation with their live shows, and recording an important session for the BBC in March '74.

Wurdah Ïtah/Tristan et Iseult & *Köhntarkösz*

Vander was able to document another movement of his trilogy in April '74 when *Wurdah Ïtah* was recorded at the Studio de Milan. The session had an unusual genesis. Vander: "At the beginning of '72 we had no concerts. Seeing us walking around like caged animals, Giorgio suggested going into a studio to make a demo. On the 2nd and 3rd of January Klaus, Stella, Jean-Pierre Lembert and I found ourselves in the Chappell studio to work on a new composition: 'Wurdah Ïtah'...[15] The [film] director Yvan Lagrange heard this demo in the studio and asked us for permission to use the music in his film *Tristan et Iseult*. After seeing the film I turned [him] down..." Laurent Thibault had engineered the session and without Magma's permission gave the tapes to Lagrange, who went ahead and used the music to soundtrack his film. Blasquiz: "It's a very bad movie, a joke. We were very angry, and decided to force Laurent Thibault to make a good recording of it."

Thus several years later Thibault finally made good his promise, and Vander was able to go into the studio with Top, Blasquiz, and Stella Vander. Blasquiz points out that even with a reduced line-up like this, Magma's music would always shine through: "It actually doesn't matter about the instrumentation, because the concept is keyboards, rhythm and a melody. The rest is only orchestration - it's important, but not the most important thing... Even if we play on stage with only a grand piano and voices, it will be exactly the same music."

According to Vander it was a very quick session: "Jannick came to my place at ten in the morning, and picked up the parts by listening to me at the piano. At two in the afternoon we went into the studio, and [the session] was finished by four. We recorded both sides of the disc in two hours. We played live with me at the piano and Jannick on bass. After that we recorded the voices: Klaus, Stella, and myself. I added the drums last.

"We hadn't even harmonized the piece, it was very fresh. Everyone improvised a bit. The vocal lines often meet, there's unison, things like that. But still, the colour is beautiful. I find it to be a very fresh record."

The album was released by Barclay as a Christian Vander solo recording under the title *Tristan et Iseult*.[16]

Only a matter of weeks after this recording Magma was back in the studio. Rather than taking the opportunity to complete the 'Theusz Hamtaahk' trilogy, the band recorded a new long form work. It was a movement from yet another trilogy[17] that had been obliquely inspired by Mike Oldfield's *Tubular Bells*.

Vander: "While we were recording *Mëkanik Destruktïw Kommandöh* in England, I composed a theme with my grandfather in mind: 'La Dawotsin'. I was constantly playing the introduction to this theme... Later on when I saw *The Exorcist* I found the music fantastic, for good reason, it was my introduction! So I no longer dared play the melody and dreaded releasing it on record, afraid I'd be accused of plagiarising *Tubular Bells*. The world turned on its head! So I worked on something else: 'Köhntarkösz'."

As with 'Mëkanik Destruktïw Kommandöh', Vander decided that this new work should be recorded as soon as the band had been able to fully explore it in live performance. Thus in May '74 the band moved into a villa in the south of France and the Manor Mobile pulled up outside. Claude Olmos had left Magma just before the recording, so English guitarist Brian Godding (ex-Blossom Toes) was brought in to play his parts.

Blasquiz: "We took over a huge house owned by one of Giorgio's friends, Milou de la Tour. It's near Valbonne, and is still surrounded by a wild pine grove... It's magnificent. The Manor Mobile was set up on the south side, beside the long, narrow lounge where the band sets up. We also used the enormous grand entrance, with its marble staircase and paved floor: it has a celestial reverb. To avoid having Jannick's giant Ampeg [amp] 'spilling' onto the other tracks, especially the piano, we had the idea to set it up in a little shelter over a well. The sound was perfect and deep, and the amp could be pushed as loud as we liked..."

While 'Köhntarkösz' was another extended work that ran over two sides of the LP, there was space left for two shorter pieces: 'Ork Alarm' written by Top, and Vander's 'Coltrane Sündia'.

The reviews were again filled with superlatives. *Extra*: "Perhaps for the first time, Magma has successfully put all the life that illuminates their concerts onto record. *Köhntarkösz* is less aggressive than their other albums, [but] it is a full and thoughtfully arranged work. Each instrument occupies a specific place, decisive in the design of the piece. The sound rises majestically in an atmosphere of explosive tension... The intoxicated music breaks out without ever dissipating, exploding to its limits, pushing back every barrier."

Blasquiz sees this album as a pinnacle, marking the point where Top really made his mark on Magma: "For this album, Jannick wasn't coming to play an existing work, the piece was created with him. It was in this moment that the Vander/Top rhythm section came into its fullness... That rhythm section was a steamroller."

After the recording Magma toured extensively through Holland, England, and Scotland, finishing with a catastrophic tour through Franco's Spain.

Jannick Top departs & *Magma Live*

The rigours of touring, financial strain, and his explosive relationship with Vander caused Jannick Top to announce his departure in September '74: "As we worked, little by little, things accumulated that, in themselves, weren't important. But there was a number of misunderstandings that I personally took as something more... Certain things had bothered me quite a lot, so I stopped; we made two records: *Mekanïk Destruktïw Kommandöh* and *Köhntarkösz*, which had 'Ork Alarm' on it, my first composition for Magma. Musically it was going well, we'd had five English tours and things were happening. We could really have done something if we hadn't had a personal problem."

Both Mickey Graillier and Gérard Bikialo left with Top. Although they helped the band to fulfil its commitments, Magma was reduced to Christian Vander on drums and Klaus Blasquiz and Stella Vander on vocals. As a result, the remainder of '74 was taken up with rebuilding the band, followed by relentless rehearsals.

Vander could think of only one person capable of replacing Top. Bernard Paganotti was an old friend who was well-known from playing in the band Cruciferius. Blasquiz was impressed by the power of his playing: "He literally sculpts jumping, purring bass lines that stand out next to the rest of the band, [who're] relatively weak in comparison."

A guitarist, Gabriel Féderow, was poached from a jazz trio that supported Magma at one of their last gigs with Top, and Rene Garber returned on bass clarinet. The other players were all selected from a round of auditions: Benoît Widemann and Jean-Pol Asseline settled behind the keyboards, and Didier Lockwood was taken on as violinist. Both Lockwood and Widemann were only seventeen years old.

This line-up would be captured after only a few months on *Magma Live, a* double-LP recorded at a run of shows at the Olympia in early June '75. The record contains only Vander compositions: a live rendition of 'Köhntarkösz', a truncated version of 'Mekanïk Destruktüw Kommandöh' and three shorter tracks including 'Hhai', an extract from 'Emëhntëht-Rê'. Blasquiz thinks this album functions as the best introduction to Magma: "This disc is the first I recommend for people to discover Magma. In the studio... we didn't always have the right engineers, so we rarely reached the intensity of the concerts... For me it's the album that sounds closest to the *real* Magma sound. When I listen to it I *feel* Magma, very close."

Twenty year-old Patrick Gauthier, who was already known to the band, was brought into Magma just after these shows: "They played three dates at The Olympia, and I went of course. It was incredible. After the concert, I heard Klaus Blasquiz telling some people that Jean-Paul Aseline was leaving the group, and they were looking for a new pianist. I was walking by, and as a joke said: 'Hey, me!" Klaus said, 'Sure', and brings me to Christian saying 'Patrick wants to try out'. I studied the pieces with Benoît and he brought me along to the rehearsals. Christian make me try out, just drums and piano, in front of all the others. I played, and he said, 'OK, you're in the band.' "

The two new keyboard players were the first to introduce synthesiser into Magma, initially with Vander's misgivings. Gauthier: "Benoît bought an ARP Odyssey, and brought it on stage. Christian was looking at it like a snake: 'What's that?' *(growls)* Then I bought a Mini-Moog, so there were two synthesisers on stage."

Blasquiz believes that this was possibly Magma's greatest line-up: "For the first time Magma attained recognition, in terms of record sales, media, and the public. Things were getting better and better. Christian wondered if it's not too good to be true. He just has this feeling, even though... he admitted that musically and humanly, its the best line-up of Magma we've had yet."

Gauthier highlights the enthusiasm of this new, youthful line-up: "There was a fantastic feeling in the group. We were all very young, playing tricks on each other, it was really fun. The concerts were fabulous. Really, I'd never heard anything like that. The bass drops, woah! Powerful, you know. I don't think they were as punchy afterwards as with Bernard and Christian together. Incredible!"

However, Vander just couldn't shake the idea that things would be even better with Jannick Top in the band. Blasquiz: "Christian dreams of going back to the previous line-up. Especially of getting Jannick back, who remains for him the only real bassist for Magma... He's obsessed."

Finally by mid-'76 Vander decided he had to bring Top back. Blasquiz: "Christian broke Magma up... For no reason. He's a little suicidal, he thinks you have to suffer for things to be good... That's why he ended the group with Bernard Paganotti... we had no more problems, we made money, we started selling discs. Christian thought to himself, if it went too well, he wouldn't find his thing."

Gauthier: "We were pushed out! *(laughs)* We were fired! Christian talked to us and said, 'I want to make a band with Jannick again'. He wanted it to be tougher. So he re-made the band with Didier, Jannick Top, Gabriel, and Mickey Graillier."

Üdü Ẁüdü & the return of Jannick Top

In May-June '76, while this upheaval was underway, *Üdü Ẁüdü* was recorded at Studio de Milan. Magma didn't really exist as a band at this point, and apart from the opening pair of tracks it was made by a trio of Christian Vander, Jannick Top, and Klaus Blasquiz. Although Widemann and Gauthier only appear on one track, their legacy can be heard in the amount of synthesiser used on the album.

Blasquiz was unconvinced by the LP: "Jannick Top's 'De Futura' is superb, and 'Weidorje', composed by Bernard Paganotti, is also very good... [but] it's a record made up of odds and ends." On reflection Vander seemed to agree: "*Üdü Wüdü* was made at a time when there was actually no group. So it's a transitional album. I didn't have any of my own pieces prepared, I just took extracts from 'Emëhntëht-Rê', which don't mean a lot in isolation. So... in fact Üdü Wüdü isn't really an album, or [made by] a group."

However, it was received well by the critics. *Atem*'s Gerard Nguyen was particularly enthusiastic: "*Üdü Wüdü* testifies to the incredible complicity that reigns between [Top and Vander] both on the musical and spiritual [level]...Top isn't just an exceptional musician who (finally) finds the path to fulfil his potential, but also an invaluable creative force to complement Christian Vander." He was particularly taken with 'De Futura': "This piece was first performed by the Utopic Sporadic Orchestra at Nancy.[18] Here, it has been fully purified, keeping only the *essential*, the single term that could sum up Magma at present... Everything has been economised, every note, every sound carries within it dozens of notes and sounds, fully concentrated, combining to give the music extraordinary power and beauty."

The new 'VanderTop' line-up of Magma was finally ready to go out in public by October '76. It saw the remaining members (Vander, Blasquiz, Féderow and Lockwood) joined by the returning Jannick Top and Mickey Graillier. Top's return had been eagerly anticipated, and Giorgio Gomelsky had been able to arrange a block of almost six months touring: through France in October/November, into Europe and the UK in January/February '77, and onto the US in March/April.

Jannick Top departs (again) & *Attakh*

In the end the band never made it out of France; Top pulled the plug after less than two months. Top: "I forgot what had happened a little too quickly... It didn't take long to realise that our relationship hadn't changed: namely that when we decided to do something, straight away the opposite had to happen...

"Christian offered to share the responsibility for the group with me. I realise now that it couldn't work. Christian needs complete freedom to create the thing he has been fighting for over the past seven years."

This was the final straw for Giorgio Gomelsky: "Magma did very well in England. We took that country by storm! Unfortunately, the 25-day tour that was to establish the band permanently got cancelled because of internal struggles and the subsequent break-up of the Vander-Jannick Top collaboration... Frankly speaking, I lost interest after the cancellation of the UK tour and the break with Jannick. Unfortunately, most of the times, when a band hits the 'top', and there is real, substantial success, all kinds of conflicts appear." [19]

Patrick Gauthier was surprised to be contacted by Vander in December '76: "Christian called us! He wanted us to come back to Magma, but it was too late, Bernard and I had formed Weidorje." [20]

Benoît Widemann had also put together his own band with drummer Clément Bailly (ex-Triptique), bassist Guy Delacroix (ex-Voyage), and guitarist Jean de Antoni (who had played with Swiss progressive rock band Welcome). However, when he received Vander's call, he agreed to return - and the band he had assembled became Magma's new core. This new line-up had three dedicated vocalists with Klaus Blasquiz joined by a returning Stella Vander and Lisa Bois. The addition of Bailly as second drummer allowed Christian Vander to come from behind his kit on occasion to sing and play piano on stage.

By February '77 this band was on tour and Georges Leton had taken over from Gomelsky as manager. But in the second half of the year Magma was thrown into turmoil once more with the resignation of Bailly and de Antoni. The band ground to a halt.

During the enforced hiatus Vander began to feel a need to reinvent the music and ethos of Magma: "I hadn't yet realised that it was the new Magma cycle that was preparing; the new seven-year cycle... We had to stop this cycle and prepare something new that could create as great a shock as Magma's music did seven years ago." With the encouragement of Laurent Thibault, he entered Hérouville studio (which Thibault now managed) to create the album that would inaugurate this next seven-year cycle. In September '77 the remnants of Magma joined him in the studio, for the last time in the '70s. The pieces Vander chose to record for *Attakh* explored a more commercial style that incorporated elements of funk, jazz-fusion, and gospel.

Blasquiz describes the creation of the album as "laboured": "The pieces weren't ready, we hadn't played them for months, the opposite of what's normal for Magma." In retrospect he is dismissive of both this album and its predecessor: "These albums aren't very representative, they aren't really Magma records. They were made on the spot. Christian brought in the piano parts... He knew the pieces, but we had never rehearsed them. This results in a lot of vocal improvisation, which is not good for Magma."

Vander seemed to see this inversion of the normal writing process to be integral to the new Magma: "The record is all fresh [material], with the songs composed then played in the studio straight away, without having the time to completely mature. On stage, everything will be developed, and arranged... people will hear what they couldn't on the record. The album will leave them a little hungry, because there are very beautiful melodies..." To Blasquiz's consternation, Vander chose to sing these melodies by himself, with his own role consigned to the chorus.

Attahk was released in May '78 in a cover designed by H.R. Geiger on which the band was billed, for the first time, as "Christian Vander's Magma". The album received generally positive reviews, but *Best*'s Michel Lousquet was less impressed: "I would have liked to help Magma start this new era by adding my voice to the chorus of praise welcoming *Attahk*... [But] we know what Christian Vander is capable of, so we're entitled to expect more than... melodically-weak compositions that only occasionally evoke the formidable impulses, and emotional torrents that Magma has accustomed us to... That Christian Vander has abandoned extended sagas in favour of shorter pieces isn't a problem in itself. What is at issue is that these new pieces generally have neither the richness nor the finesse, nor even the violence of the past... But don't forget, even a disappointing Magma record is infinitely superior to a successful record from many other groups."

By the end of '78 Magma had yet another turnover. Blasquiz continued in the band for another twelve months, but by this time he felt that Magma had lost its moorings: "Now I realise that it wasn't really Magma any more. We were trying to find the way, but we had problems, not of quality - the musicians were very good - but of cohesion. For three years, the never-ending quest to find something as strong as what we'd known with Jannick Top or Bernard Paganotti hadn't succeeded. That's one of the reasons why I left the group."

His departure brought the first cycle of Magma to a definitive conclusion. Magma continued to struggle to bring its "second cycle" to fruition. In contrast to the productivity of the first seven years of the band, the years after *Attahk* saw only a brace of retrospective live albums released until their final studio album, *Merci*, was recorded in '84. Shortly after its release in '85, Vander called an end to the band.

Magma remained in abeyance until 1996, when Christian and Stella Vander restarted the band with a totally new line-up. The fire that was lacking in the last years of the original Magma seemed to rekindle, and the new band developed a reputation for fearsome live performances. They returned to recording in the new century, finally completing the "Emëhntëht-Rê" trilogy with the release of K-A *(2004) and* Emëhntëht-Rê *(2009). They continue to perform and record, with an album* Kartehl *released in 2022.*

Notes

1 Thibault, Zabuski, and Moze had played together in Zorgones, who had released the psyche-pop single 'Herr Doktor Reich' in '69.

2 Over the years Garber would often return to Magma, and remained an important adjunct to the band even when not officially part of the line-up.

3 Vidal was let go just before recording, because the power of the band totally overwhelmed his contribution on double bass. Blasquiz: "Even when Jacky gives it his all he's constantly drowned out by the electric bass and Christian's bass drum."

4 Richard Raux: "There was controversy from the start, but it has to be understood that above everything else our goal was to be unlike anyone else... There was a truly special creative atmosphere within the group. [But] of course there was a sectarian side. The speeches could seem a bit partisan, to the extent that sometimes guys from the far-right came to congratulate us at the end of a set, which was downright embarrassing."

5 'Stoah' was the very track that Paringaux had singled out for its provocative vocal declamation. It's interesting to note that Magma nevertheless continued to use it as their calling card. When they appeared on *Pop 2* in November '70, it was again the track they chose to play.

6 Gomelsky first came to prominence as the owner of London's Crawdaddy Club, which took on The Rolling Stones as house band. From there he managed The Yardbirds, and started Marmalade Records. He also organised Soft Machine's first recording session.

7 In '73 Engel told an interviewer that he had left Magma "for non-musical reasons regarding the relationships between musicians."

8 Raux: "There were almost no solos in Magma... I got tired of that after a while, I wanted to play jazz, to swing, to improvise... I didn't have any problems with [Vander] in particular, but rather with some of the musicians who only wanted to play 'Magma'... Francis Moze swore by Magma. He became a fundamentalist and that ended up in clashes."

9 Magma recorded a revised version of 'Rïah Sahïltaahk' in 2014 that according to the liner notes "is more faithful to the spirit of the original composition". It undoubtedly makes the piece's relationship to 'Mëkanïk Destruktïw Kommandöh' more explicit.

10 Lasry began a successful solo career, Moze joined Gong, and Cahen and Seffer started Zao. Seffer: "We'd both decided to set up 'our' formation, Zao... [But] replacing a pianist at short notice is not an easy thing, so Faton stayed on for another three months..."

11 Manderlier's trio, Arkham, had supported Magma in Belgium at the end of '71. The band were impressed enough to invite him to be Magma's second pianist, and bandmate Daniel Denis, to be their second drummer. Denis only stayed with Magma for one concert, but would go on to form Univers Zero.

12 Three recordings made during '71 give an insight into the development of the piece. In January a short version had been recorded for the compilation *Puissance 13+2* (released on Laurent Thibault's Thélème label), and in October another short rendition was made for a Europe 1 radio session. A seventeen-minute live take was later released on *Concert 1971 - Bruxelles - Théâtre 140*.

13 Vander has noted that the title "isn't Kobaïan - it was chosen deliberately to shock." The term 'kommando' references guerrilla warfare - in the early '70s often used in reference to urban guerrilla groups like the German Red Army Faction and Italian Red Brigades.

14 The third part of the trilogy, 'Wurdah Ïtah', was recorded the next year, however 'Theusz Hamtaahk' wouldn't be released until '81's *Rétrospective* live album.

15 The '72 demo of 'Wurdah Ïtah' wasn't released until 2017, when it appeared as a bonus track on a remastered CD of the original album under the title 'Wurdah Ïtah (Prima Materia)'

16 The rights to the album reverted to Magma in the late '80s, and since then it has been reissued under its correct title.

17 Vander explained the concept behind the new trilogy when *Köhntarkösz* was released: "It's the story of a guy who, during an excavation, discovers the temple of Emëhntëht-Rê. The tomb has never been desecrated and for the first time in seven thousand years, a man enters it. As he does, dust from the ground is released spreading through the space for a quarter of a second; and during this short time, he sees the whole life of Emëhntëht-Rê, the creator of Kobaïan... It's the introduction to a piece that I'll record in two years' time, which will be made up of three discs."

18 "Gomelsky suggested that I do something for the Nancy jazz festival. I'd just composed 'De Futura', so it suited me. But in Nancy it was billed as: Giorgio Gomelsky and Christian Vander's Utopic Sporadic Orchestra, even though I'd spent six months working on this thing." *(Top)*

19 Blasquiz dates Gomelsky's loss of interest back to a gig in London twelve months before: "I begin to feel, at this key moment, that Giorgio is no longer really interested in the group. We had toured all over Europe, thanks to him we'd even made a (cobbled together) foray into New York in July '73. Large groups of fans flocked to the concerts and the records

began to sell, but it didn't seem to be going fast enough for him."

20 In addition to Gauthier and Paganotti, Weidorje featured Michel Ettori (guitar), Jean-Philippe Goude (keyboards), and Kirt Rust (drums). At one point Klaus Blasquiz was approached to be the band's vocalist, before Paganotti decided to take on vocal duties himself.

CONTREPOINT

> The business side of things was really a series of failures. Lots of crazy stories! For example, we traveled 1000km to a studio in Menton, and after setting up we played a single note and the Studer [tape machine] broke down! Then we were almost the first French group on Virgin. I don't know exactly why that didn't happen. We had lots of opportunities, but we never really took advantage of them.
>
> *Jean-Pierre Weiller*

On a British holiday in '69, a teenage Jean-Pierre Weiller struck up a friendship with Hugh Hopper after a Soft Machine concert. Hopper introduced him to Kevin Ayers, and days later Weiller was making his recording debut - at Abbey Road studio.

"It was just a bit of fun... I was in London; I'd met Kevin Ayers and was staying at his place for a few days. This was while he was recording *Joy of a Toy*. So I went to the sessions in the big studio at Abbey Road. Robert Wyatt, some of Kevin's friends, and two young girls he'd met on Portobello Road were there, and *voilà*, we all recorded the little piece that gave the album its title."

Weiller had formed his first band a few years earlier: "I was about fourteen, with a group of friends the same age, from the same neighbourhood: the 13th arrondissement of Paris. The only interesting thing to do seemed to be forming a band."

By the time he made his surprise debut at Abbey Road, Weiller had formed his first serious band, a trio named Brave New World.

"I played bass, and Jean Pierre Carolfi, who lived next to me, played piano. We met Mike Freitag, who was a pretty well-known drummer... We were really very young. Mike was fifteen, and I was seventeen."

By the middle of the year the name had been changed to Contrepoint ("I thought it was better to have a French name") and saxophonist René Garber was added to the line-up. At the end of '69

Garber left to join Magma and was replaced by American saxophonist Robert Taylor. Taylor was classically trained but had been playing free jazz in a Philadelphia-based group, The Image, before relocating to Paris.

Contrepoint began to explore an avant-garde musical style sitting between rock and free jazz: "We took inspiration from Soft Machine, the free jazz of Archie Shepp and Art Ensemble of Chicago, as well as from Jean-Pierre Carlolfi's classical training.

"There was an evolution, but we were already writing our own pieces which were, in my view, truly original... It's often said that Contrepoint makes aggressive music, and at other times it's a very calm, very beautiful music. I really feel that it represents Paris... It's a music of the city."

By the end of '70 the band was becoming well known, and Laurent Thibault invited them to record a track for the compilation *Puissance 13+2*. René Garber returned to add soprano saxophone to the track 'Unfathomable of the Seventh Time'. It would be the only recording the band released while together.

In March '71 Contrepoint secured a coveted spot on the *Pop Club* radio programme. "It was our first introduction to the Parisian and French pop scene. We found Blanc Francart, and I asked him, 'Would you be interested in coming to hear us?' He said yes, so we arranged a meeting, but he didn't come. He telephoned to apologise, a little embarrassed. The second time he came, liked it and said: 'Okay, you're coming on to *Pop Club*'."

A few months later they were one of the few bands actually able to complete a performance at the disastrous Auvers-sur-Oise Festival. The rainfall that had started while they played turned into a deluge, and their well-received set turned out to be the last of the festival.

"It was a really exciting time... We played at Auvers, then the next day we played in front of ten people, then in front of 250. It was always different, but always, we really felt that something was happening."

A promising start to the year led to the opportunity to tour through France, but touring in the early '70s was not for the faint of heart.

"It could take drastic turns, which is why a lot of groups break up... Concerts often take place in incredible conditions: you would arrive, and the organiser had forgotten the concert, or there are no posters, no key to the hall, or they'd forgotten to ask for council permission. We could travel 800km and be unable to play, often when an audience had arrived that really wanted to hear us. This created absurd scenes, with the group searching for a venue at the last minute with the audience trailing behind them. Really unbelievable.

"At the Communist Youth festival in Marseille we were thrown out without being paid because they thought that we were making fun of them during our 'free' section. We returned to Paris, penniless..."

The political atmosphere of the times could also lead to other absurdities: "A friend called me one morning to ask if we could come and play at the Faculté de Vincennes that afternoon. In the '70s that was the mecca of intellectuals and leftists in France. When he asked how many people the group could bring along. I said around 2000 (a huge exaggeration, of course!). The university was bugged, and the police Special Branch suddenly appeared at my home... They didn't ask too many questions; they'd already done their research and knew I was just a simple bass player."

At the beginning of '72 the band lost Robert Taylor, who was replaced by another American saxophonist, Hugh Levick.

Contrepoint's performance at the Troyes Festival in March was reviewed by *Pop 2000*: "Contrepoint's music [has] astonishing contrasts between violent and aggressive explosions and calm and restrained passages with great sensuality. The music has a constant 'freedom' but never loses its very individual character. Contrepoint has a unique ability to take possession of their audience and have them live its music until the very last measure, leaving them breathless, wanting more."

The article noted that the band had just made a live recording for Theleme (which may be the source of the album released by Monster Melodies) and was preparing a studio album: "We were supposed to record on Laurent Thibault's label but it went under before we could."

Weiller points out that he had trouble navigating the business side of the music scene: "I admit that it's an environment I find difficult to move in. It has always been very hard to take your tapes to people who are often ignored, or afraid of their superiors. They all say the same thing: 'Well, you know, that's great. You're really great musicians, but

I can't take it to my boss'... So no-one takes the risk to do anything."

Contrepoint closed out '72 with a four-date run at the Paris venue Gibus, and a support for Kevin Ayers in Orléans: "Just before we played, the stage was bombarded by the extreme left from the front and the extreme right from the back: those were the days!"

In June '73 Contrepoint was invited by Pierre Lattès to appear on the *Rock en Stock* TV show. They played alongside the German band Agitation Free, in a programme devoted to the European 'progressive rock'. "Pierre Lattès had been following us for a long time; we had made our first appearance on José Arthur's *Pop Club* with him. The program was broadcast, but to my great regret I can't find any trace of it."

Towards the end of the year Hugh Hopper and Weiller planned a joint tour through France: "I spent a few days at Hugh's place after he left Soft Machine. I said to him, 'Why don't you do a tour in France? You're well-known and the public likes what you do...' He said, 'That would be good, I could bring musicians over with me, and Contrepoint could play too.'"

The plan was altered when the musicians Hopper had in mind became too busy with their own band, Hatfield & The North: "At the time Hatfield were in high demand... so Hugh said: 'Listen, the tour's going ahead, would you like to take second bass, I'll take Jean Pierre Carolfi on piano, and I'll bring Elton Dean, Lol Coxhill and Laurie Allen with me.'... Hugh came to Paris a month beforehand with the scores for Jean Pierre and I to work on."

However, Contrepoint were just about to head off on a three-week tour, so very little time was available for rehearsal. When they arrived back in Paris, in the second week of March '74, Weiller and Carolfi headed off immediately with Hugh Hopper's band.

"We were dead beat when we met up with Hugh, Elton, Lol and Laurie, and set off [to play at] Lyon the same night... I was wondering how it was going to go, then Elton simply took out his instrument and off we go! We started playing and everything flowed smoothly, it happened in such a simple and easy way that was so musical...

"We'd told ourselves, 'Okay, we'll rehearse before the concert.' Then we never arrived on time for a concert, so we never practised, but everything went well, and we played really excellent concerts...

That was a really rewarding experience... Hugh gave us a great deal of freedom, and he taught us a lot."

The final performance in Bordeaux on 20 March '74 was recorded and released as the second side of Hopper's *Monster Band* album.

After beginning the year with a major tour, Contrepoint's existence became very precarious. By the middle of the year the brass section had left (a trombonist had been added late in '73): "We spent some time finding other musicians before putting together the last line-up, which toured in '75 with two saxophonists: Richard Foy and Joel Lallouette."

With things winding down, Weiller left France to travel to the US in mid-'75: "Nobody said: 'Contrepoint no longer exists.' Everyone went their own way, always leaving a door open to the possibility of continuing, to a reformation... We had been doing this for five years, and at one point, you have to move on and do something else."

When he returned in early '76 Weiller made an attempt to relaunch the band. He gave an interview to *Atem* in April, telling them: "I think Contrepoint is going to do something... Firstly we'll make the record we never made; in my opinion, this will be decisive in our development." The record was never made and as Weiller recalls: "The band didn't last long, and I don't think we ever played live."

Jean-Pierre Weiller went on to work in the French record industry. He started as label manager for Island Records and became it's French CEO. Unfortunately he doesn't know what became of Contrepoint's other members ("I've always wondered why we never heard any more from such a good saxophonist as Robert Taylor, and I really regret losing touch with Mike who was a naturally kind person.")

part six:
the avant underground

MUSICA ELECTRONICA VIVA
FILLE QUI MOUSSE KOMINTERN
FLAT 5F
DAGON MAJUN
POP DAUPHINE
5 Février

INTRODUCTION

> When I say that we play 'wholes' instead of 'pieces', it's not just wordplay. On stage we are creating our music directly in front of the people. There are strong sections and parts that [could be] termed 'failures' or 'monotonous', but are sections like that pointless?... It's somewhat related to Erik Satie's 'furniture music'... We aren't the only ones in France doing this, there's also Berrocal, Nu Creative Methods, Mozaïk.
>
> *Dominique Grimaud, Camizole*

The meeting of free-jazz and indeterminate music (as championed by John Cage*) gave rise to a new musical form in the mid-'60s. Groups like the UK's AMM and Scratch Orchestra, and Italy's Gruppo di Improvvisazione Nuova Consonanaza were created by musicians from the contemporary classical and jazz worlds coming together to improvise without any restriction. Every sound was equally valid, even silence.

The French underground became familiar with this new musical style mainly through the presence of the multinational collective Musica Elettronica Viva. It had been formed in Rome in '66, and by the time *The Sound Pool* was recorded in May '69† the collective included two French members: Yvan and Patricia Coaquette. Musica Elettronica Viva played at the Amougies Festival in October, but in early 1970 it splintered into three groups, one based in Rome, one in New York, and one in Paris. The French group, centred on the Coaquettes, was active for several years, playing live and recording *Leave The City* for BYG in June '70.

The first French expression of the "avant underground" emerged

---

* Cage was a guest of the Journées de Musicale Contemporaine in October '70. A series of concerts culminated in a staging of his Musicircus. This event involved the simultaneous performance of multiple bands alongside musical participation by audience members. Red Noise, Komintern, Horde Catalytique pour la Fin, and Dynastie Crisis all took part in the performance.

† *The Sound Pool* was recorded during a live performance in Paris.

in '67. Horde Catalytique pour la Fin came together in Nice, initially as a free-jazz group, but became more and more drawn to "gestural" music. They moved to Paris in 1970, and recorded an album for Futura Records in '71. Futura was a major supporter of the avant-garde end of the early underground, with its SON series featuring releases from Bernard Vitet, Jean Guérin, Semool, and Jac Berrocal.

Camizole, Jac Berrocal, and Birgé Gorgé Shiroc all took aspects of the free improvisational approach to develop their own idiosyncratic musical languages. There was also another group of underground bands epitomised by Etron Fou Leloublan, ZNR, and Art Zoyd who played more structured music while maintaining an affinity to the musical ideals of the avant-garde.

CAMIZOLE

> It seems essential to me that no-one in Camizole should be able to make a living from its music. That allows us total freedom to do what we want. I even believe it would be harmful if that wasn't the case. Working in Camizole would involve playing a huge number of concerts, constantly being on the road, and making compromises in the music. Making it into a job would mean no longer having a choice.
>
> *Dominique Grimaud*

Chartres is a sleepy provincial town famous as the site of an imposing gothic cathedral. While it is less than a hundred kilometres from Paris, when Camizole formed in 1970 it felt more like a thousand.

A lesser-known architectural site in Chartres is the Maison de Picassiette - an *art brut* masterpiece built over thirty years by local cemetery worker, Raymond Isidore. Dominique Grimaud recalls its untutored, dreamlike excesses as one of his early inspirations: "I think everything in artistic creation stems from childhood... Things like making huts or Indian tents from bits of wood and canvas were very important for my education. Everything was thrown together, but the dream behind it was immense..."

While Dominique Grimaud would become the driving force in Camizole, in the early days it was Jacky Dupéty who provided the impetus. Grimaud: "Jacky had been a student at the School of Applied Arts[1] in Paris, where he participated in the turmoil and unrest of May '68. He was forced to leave Paris when he refused to sign a document promising not to disrupt the smooth running of the school.

"Jacky was the instigator and undisputed leader of the group for the first two years. Thanks to the encounters and experiences from his time in Paris, he had a knowledge of avant-garde art and the counter-culture that none of us shared."

Grimaud met Dupéty for the first time in September '69, during a photo-shoot for a local hard-rock band. They met again at the very beginning of 1970 at the Halles Festival in Paris. A few weeks later Grimaud was taking part in his first 'happening' as a member of a loose-knit collective centred around Dupéty: "Jacky conceived an event in the spirit of the Living Theatre. It took place in a small chapel where young Catholics were organising shows and meetings. There were about twenty of us, aged eighteen to twenty. The audience was about the same age, and not much bigger than our group."

They were arranged in a circle, quietly seated in the lotus position. Grimaud: "Jacky had given us no instructions beforehand, it was completely improvised. There was a long silence to begin with. Then breaths, screams, and groans started coming out of our bodies. It all ended in a violent and totally anarchic melee. The audience applauded. Jacky told us: 'We have to start a free jazz group!' "

A few weeks later they were back in the same chapel, in front of the same audience: "There were still about twenty of us, all seated on the ground with an instrument or a sound accessory (I remember there was a brass band bass drum, a box fitted with rubber bands, various flutes, Indian tablas, cans, a guitar, a triangle, sleigh bells). Jacky stood in front of us directing our interventions with arm gestures and hand signals."

The performance was deemed a success, so the group decided to continue its adventure: "We got together in the basement of the youth hostel once a week to refine our improvisations, still under Jacky's direction. Each time, two or three of the hostel's residents came down to listen to us."

In the first half of 1970 the group performed five times: "There was a concert for the Communist Party in a working-class area of town, and another at a Foyer Culturel in a nearby neighbourhood; the city council was meeting in an adjoining hall and the mayor suddenly burst in yelling, 'Stop this racket immediately!' "

When summer arrived, the youth hostel became too busy to host their rehearsals: "The group was reduced to five: Jacky (tenor sax), his brother Jean-Luc (trumpet), myself (violin and flute), Alain Loüet (bongos), and Christian Delatre (acoustic guitar). We organised improvisations in the woods, without any power."

Then, with the end of summer Camizole moved their rehearsals back into the Youth Hostel. They were joined by Daniel Ossig ("He was a well-known local saxophonist, older than us, with a well-developed classical jazz technique, but open enough to be confronted with our libertarian music") and drummer Eric Delaunay. Delaunay's pedigree was impressive - his father had founded *Jazz Hot* magazine, and the Swing record label.[2]

In January '71 the band were invited to support the American jazz organist Lou Bennett. However the organiser was concerned the audience may have difficulty with Camizole's improvised music, and asked them to play after the main act. The eight-piece that performed that night was spontaneously joined on stage by the organiser (who played piano) and a violinist and cellist who lived next to the venue.

Grimaud points out that their performances were surprisingly well received: "Even though we couldn't play more than 50 km from our town, there were always people at our concerts. We were the only band of our kind in the area, and there was an extremely limited amount of rock and pop on offer in small provincial towns."

Grimaud believes that Camizole had much in common with Barricade: "I think our approach and operation was comparable. We both had a large membership, with some permanent foundational members and a shifting and somewhat random group of other people. Our performances were as much a happening as a concert, with a good dose of improvisation and provocation. Like us, Barricade was in the provinces, except they were in Marseille, the second-largest city in France, and we were in a much smaller town."

Camizole seem to have trumped Barricade on at least one measure. While the Marseille band was known for its huge cast of characters (up to thirty musicians passed through the band), Grimaud remarks that over *eighty* were involved with Camizole: "The commitment varied from person to person. Some were devoted, others went with the flow, curious, or just amused by what was going on. Some only played the one gig. Very few had a musical education, and they were never the most active or influential."

In early '71 Camizole trekked to Paris to visit the offices of *Actuel*: "There were about thirty of us in their small premises, which made a strong impression on the editorial team. A few days later, one of their journalists came to interview us in our small town. Unfortunately his account wasn't published until four years later, in *Actuel*'s last issue... a bit late for our liking."

Camizole played only a small number of concerts during '71,

capped by a performance at the Ecole Normale (teachers college) in Chartres. After this they went on a hiatus.

The break would ultimately last almost two years.

Dominique Grimaud undertook solo musical projects: "I constructed a large zither and experimented with the sounds of scraped, rubbed, and struck strings - recording it onto a small cassette recorder.[3] My comrades rented a house and formed a community. They gave a single concert in April '72, under the name Magic Mushroom."

Grimaud attempted to set up other group projects, but they all faltered. First was a duo with drummer Eric Delaunay, then he started working with guitarist José Castilla: "We tried out various [line-ups] with different musicians, including Jacky Dupéty, his brother Jean-Luc, and the drummer Xavier Jouvelet, but it didn't really work."

Finally, at the end of '73, Grimaud revived Camizole as a quartet with Jacky Dupéty, Jean-Luc Dupéty, and Françoise Crublé.[4] "Our first concert was thanks to José Castilla who invited us to play with his group. We improvised to a tape with various recorded sounds and sound effects, and Jean-Luc cooked peas on a portable stove, then distributed them to the audience in a parody of the Eucharist. A local reporter was hard on us, but two days later, the same newspaper published a long article titled "Mr. Jean Brédelou explains Camizole's music to us" written by an art teacher we had never met!"

Early in '74 they began collaborating with the Biberon art collective, and three artists from the group joined the band: Vincent Mery (percussion), Françoise Maury (percussion), and Catherine Lienhardt (violin). The influx of artists steered them towards a more theatrical performance style, incorporating costumes, make-up, and even pyrotechnics.

"Jacky had conceived a piece in three movements devised to be played outdoors with movement, hats, masks and painted tunics. We performed it on a bandstand on 18 May. We seized every opportunity to play: there was a second bandstand performance, and a Mother's Day concert in a park. In June we worked on a tape inspired by Stockhausen (which included 'The Internationale') for a concert organised by the communist CGT union, then played at a party in a detention centre for children."

Early in '74 Grimaud had bought his first synthesiser (a Korg 700), and was becoming more and more interested in electronic music: "I was fascinated by the German bands, especially Neu, *Kraftwerk 2*, *Cluster II*, Tangerine Dream's *Zeit*, Klaus Schulze's *Irrlitch*... But my comrades didn't share my enthusiasm at all." By the end of the year Grimaud decided to leave Camizole, disappointed that their music wasn't developing fast enough; "For the last concert of the year we presented two versions of Camizole. I played solo (synthesiser, flute, violin, lap guitar), and then Jacky, Jean-Luc, Françoise, and Catherine Lienhardt played as a group."

Grimaud continued to perform solo into '75, playing concerts in Paris and Orléans early in the year. At Orléans he was booked to support Ash Ra Temple: "But they were held up at the border and I was the only one to play!"

By March it had become clear that the rest of Camizole didn't intend to continue playing music: "When I left, I thought my comrades would continue without me, in that free and happening style we had practised from the start. But, unfortunately that wasn't the case. They hung up their musical instruments, and started doing street theatre." Grimaud decided to take on the name, reconstituting Camizole as an electronic duo: "I bought a second synthesiser, the famed Synthi AKS (a wonderful instrument, ideal for experimental music). Then I placed an ad in *Actuel*, and Bernard [Filipitti] replied. Our first concert together was on 18 April in Troyes."

The duo sent a cassette to Jean-Pierre Lentin at *Actuel*, who began mentioning Camizole in his monthly music column, raising their profile: "This gave us the opportunity to play at a lot of festivals during summer '75. If our interview from 1970 had appeared on time, maybe the recognition would have come sooner."

The band recorded their set at the Festival de Solémieux in June '75 and sent tapes to several people in the media and music business.[5] They received an enthusiastic response from Klaus Schulze, who asked if he could take the tape to German record labels, hoping to be able to produce an album for Camizole.

However Grimaud found the duo's music too close to the *kosmische* style of Schulze and Tangerine Dream: "I thought we weren't distinguishing ourselves enough from the bands across the Rhine... I appreciated Bernard's skills and energy. But we weren't in full agreement; importantly I wanted more originality, uniqueness and unconventionality... We broke up in autumn... In such a short time we'd played about ten concerts, which was good for the days when big tours only existed for very well-known groups." Grimaud and Filipitti played their last show together on 16 November.

Another concert had already been organised for the end of December, and Grimaud called on his old comrades: "I suggested we do it together, and they were in complete agreement. There were eight of us; it was a very eclectic concert: free, electronic, folk, Native American texts, Tibetan horn, toy instruments, sounds on tape..."

This reformed Camizole continued to benefit from the publicity the electronic duo had generated. Finally they had progressed from a local to a nationally-known group. They were also aided by a relationship with Etron Fou Leloublan, who Grimaud had met at the Montluçon Festival in September '75: "It was the start of a long friendship, and several collaborations. We organised an Etron Fou concert in Chartres at the beginning of '76. Then their saxophonist, Chris Chanet, joined Camizole. In Summer we visited them at their community in Ardèche."

During this visit the two groups discussed setting up a collective, the fancifully named Dupon et ses Fantômes: "We wanted to unite our efforts and share resources; rejecting competition was quite a worthy intention. There were four groups [Camizole, Etron Fou, Mozaïk and Grand Gouia].[6] We sent out a joint newsletter, and there was a Dupon Festival held in Grenoble on 12 and 13 November '77, but every group had different problems, and it didn't go any further. It was exactly the same for other similar initiatives: FLIP, Les Bas-Rock, etc." [7]

Another encounter in May '76 was important to Camizole's progression: "Gilbert Artman came up to us at a festival organised by the newspaper Political Hebdo, and told us he liked our performance. I was very honoured because I'd already seen Lard Free play several times, and I loved their first two albums. Gilbert gave us generous help and support, especially with recording. He'd just started his Urban Sax project, which Chris, Jacky and Françoise all took part in."

Chris Chanet left Camizole at the beginning of '77, the year that would be the band's peak.

In March, the band's growing reputation brought them to the attention of Pierre Lattès: "He was a very open, warm person. We were invited on to *Ecoute*, a radio show he hosted with Paul Alessandrini and Jean-Pierre Lentin on France Musique. As we didn't have any recordings to play, he arranged a session in one of the Maison de la Radio studios a few days before the show.

"It was the first time we'd been into a studio, we were very impressed. We recorded under professional conditions and had complete artistic freedom. We recorded about thirty minutes of the live set we were playing at the time, pieces that were more or less composed (the term 'organised' might be more accurate)."

After the recording session the band decided to return to the total improvisation that had been Camizole's hallmark in the beginning: "We decided to take improvisation as far as possible and give ourselves unlimited freedom. In my opinion it was the best period of the group. In the time we'd been playing together we'd become very close friends. We played together, but also in opposition - one against all, or all against one, etc. We set up a sofa on the stage so we could sit down and quietly wait for an unwelcome moment to intervene in an improvisation already in progress, or to totally butcher a passage.

"One of us would lock ourselves into a chest before the concert, leaving the audience wondering where the sound was coming from. We chopped logs with an axe (Jean-Luc was the most inventive in this area). Everything was possible. There was also the idea of composing, of constructing a piece in the moment. I made this pun: "Camizole does not make pieces, it makes wholes!" (I'm not sure it works in English)."

Their audacity paid off with coverage in the national press - notably two large articles in the newspaper *Liberation*. One of these described the unfolding of a Camizole concert of this era: "In the middle of the drum 'solo', firecrackers go off at our feet, hubcaps are randomly thrown onto the cymbals disturbing and inspiring the drummer. The tenor saxophonist wanders into the hall playing, waits while two concealed speakers spew out synthesiser, then responds with a long free improvisation that breaks off at the point of physical exhaustion... Saxes, violin, synth, guitar and drums are thrown together so violently and intensely that it can't be expressed in words... Their music lies far beyond the commonplace imagination, it's no longer art reserved for and performed by an elite, it becomes an extension of communication where everyone has to participate."

With the beginning of '77 came the emergence of the French

punk scene. Like their comrades in Etron Fou, Camizole felt no fear of the rising movement. In fact, they found themselves somewhat bemused by the performative "anarchy" of the French bands: "I have to say that when punk came along it didn't impress us that much. People said punks don't care about technique and don't even bother to tune their guitars. Well, *no-one* in Camizole learned to play their instrument before going on stage, and my guitar was never properly tuned... As for simplicity of lyrics, I remember Jacky relentlessly shouting into his microphone, 'I want real rock'n'roll, I want real rock'n'roll...' Spontaneity, anarchy, we knew that too. We were punks without knowing it, we'd been practising all these things for years. We just didn't have the outfit."

After seven years of on-again-off-again existence, Camizole was finally offered the chance to make a record by Jean Karakos (ex-BYG) in late '77: "He'd launched his new label Tapioca... He was interested in a Camizole album, provided he didn't have to pay for recording sessions, as was the case for the entire Tapioca catalog. That wasn't a problem for us, as Gilbert Artman had convinced us that it was much more apt for Camizole to capture our music outside of a recording studio.

"So, we had the idea to record at the Théâtre de Chartres in front of an audience. We sent out invitations to record stores and bookstores in the region, and to places in the Parisian underground. It wasn't so much a concert, as a public recording [session]."

The recording was made on 26 November '77: "Our sound engineer set up his two tape recorders and mixer on the stage. We were aware that we shouldn't make the interventions too long, and we focused on the sound without paying attention to the visual or theatrical [aspect]. The audience of around 150 people was very attentive and respected these constraints. These were the ideal conditions for our music, and we enjoyed making the recording.

"If memory serves, we recorded around an hour of music. We selected the best twenty minutes for the A-side of the album. We wanted the B-side to be an excerpt from a stormy concert we'd played a few weeks earlier as opening act for Océan, a pretty well-known French hard-rock band... It was a good expression of how a Camizole concert should unfold."

The band expanded on this experience in *Liberation*: "We were literally thrown off the stage by the audience. There were catcalls, and while we were playing a rumble built up that quickly became very loud, louder than us. So we turned the microphones towards the audience... Jean-Luc played 'L'Hymne à la mort' on tuba which mixed in with the protests from the hostile section of the crowd and the part of the audience that was defending us. It was pretty incredible..."

Camizole entered '78 with an LP recorded and scheduled for release. The promise of the year was scuppered when their label went out of business: "We found out Tapioca had folded while we were still working on sequencing the tapes." As was the case for so many bands, the disappointment of the abandoned record proved fatal. Rather than being the year that Camizole finally received the attention it deserved, '78 became the year they decided to call it a day.

Rather than fizzle out, the last few Camizole concerts saw them join together with Lard Free to form something of a free-improvising supergroup. The collaboration came together by chance: "On 13 May we were both playing at a festival that was running a long way behind schedule. To make up some time, Gilbert Artman suggested the two groups play simultaneously on the one stage. We played together spontaneously and naturally without exchanging a word. Everyone enjoyed the experience, so we decided to do it again as soon as possible."

The larger group size and mix of different musical influences gave the combined band its own unique sound: "Camizole always had a spirit of irony and humour, but it wasn't like that when we played with Lard Free. Their personality brought in darker, oppressive and relentless ambiences, making for much more dense music. We were able to play together four times during summer '78, every time with a different mix of musicians.[8]

"These were the last concerts for both Camizole and Lard Free. Gilbert was about to devote all his time to Urban Sax. For my part, I wanted to turn to music that was more structured and recorded in the studio."

Dominique Grimaud formed Vidéo-Aventures with Monique Alba in 1979; they released several albums during the '80s. Grimaud continues to record and release music.

Jacky Dupéty stopped his musical activity after Camizole, and bought a farm with Françoise Crublé in the south-west of France. He published a successful book on farming practices in 2007.

Françoise Crublé accepted Lindsay Cooper's invitation to join the Feminist Improvising Group in 1978. She continued to play saxophone and developed an interest in the cabrette (bagpipes from south-west France).

Like his brother Jean-Luc Dupéty stopped his musical activity after Camizole.

Catherine Lienhardt worked with Alan Silva, appearing on the album The Shout - Portrait For A Small Woman. *She joined Silva's Paris-based Institute for Art, Culture and Perception in the '80s.*

Chris Chanet joined the street theatre troupes Le Poteaux Rose, and Délices Dada. He also worked on electroacoustic creations, winning a prize from the CNR in Marseille.

Eric Delaunay released a solo album Antagonnisme *in 1980. He then joined the band Tiemko which released several albums in the '80s and '90s.*

Xavier Jouvelet joined Chemin Blanc after leaving Camizole, then created the duo Bex and Jouvelet in the early '80s before recording two solo albums.

Bernard Filipetti created the groups Art & Technique in the '80s, and Prime Time Victim Show in the '90s.

Notes

1 Dupéty attended the School of Applied Arts for fours years, where he had been a student alongside Klaus Blasquiz from Magma and Lionel Magal from Crium Delirium.

2 His grandparents were even more impressive - two of the most famous French painters of the early 20th Century: Robert and Sonia Delaunay.

3 These recordings were remixed and released in 2023 on the album *Erahtic*.

4 An article in *Liberation* explains that it was only at this point that the band took on the name 'Camizole' - derived from that first two letters of each musician's *nom de guerre*: CA (Camille - Jacky Dupéty), MI (Migraine - Françoise Crublé), ZO (Zorba le Grêle - Dominique Grimaud), LE (Leonard - Jean-Luc Dupéty).

5 The recording was released in 2015 as *Camizole 1975*.

6 According to Guigou Chevenier from Etron Fou there were actually *six* bands in the collective. He adds Nouvel Asile Culturel, and Au Fond du Couloir à Gauche to the list.

7 For more information on the FLIP see *Introduction* to *The Political Underground*.

8 The concert in Montagnac on 30 July '78 was recorded and released in 2018 as *Camizole + Lard Free*. The line-up for that concert was Gilbert Artman, Philippe Bolliet, Françoise Crublé, Jacky Dupéty, Jean-Luc Dupéty, and Dominique Grimaud.

JAC BERROCAL

> I think my music can be categorised as improvised music, a term that can appear pompous, but at least has the merit of being expressive. That said, it isn't totally accurate as elements of composition enter into my music... Actually a kinship can be established with many "experiments" from northern Europe and Germany, experiments made by people who, while tending towards jazz, started making music that no longer showed an American influence.
>
> *Jac Berrocal*

Jac Berrocal remains a mainstay of underground French music to this day, having released more than twenty albums under his own name, and appearing on scores more. His music is as indefinable and free-ranging as it ever was, carousing in a liminal space of his own making somewhere between jazz, rock and free improvisation. He may be known as a trumpet player and vocalist, but his musical conception is open to incorporating anything and everything (including bicycles, explosives and livestock!).

Berrocal's musical journey began at ten, when he volunteered to sing at Mass in a bid to avoid maths lessons. "I sang in a choir specialising in Renaissance music. We sang motets in Latin. That four-part polyphony was beautiful. We didn't understand the words, of course, we just learnt it by ear – it might as well have been in Arabic... In 1956 we sang at the funeral of Archbishop Lamy in Sens... We were performing in front of thousands of people, plus all the nuns and priests in costumes, with the incense and the candles. Better than the Olympia, better than Carnegie Hall!"

After leaving school (and the choir) a 16-year old Berrocal had a short stint as a rock'n'roll singer in Les Gitans, a band formed by a group of friends. However, his most formative early musical experience was hearing free jazz while listening to Europe 1 ("I heard Ornette Coleman and Don Cherry on the radio and I went *mad*!").

"I'd always liked jazz because my father was a fan of traditional jazz, Duke Ellington, Count Basie, and a little bit of bebop, and I fell straight into free jazz and also modern jazz – Charlie Parker, Art Blakey, Miles Davis and then Coltrane, Albert Ayler, Ornette Coleman and all those people. So my influences were free jazz and then rock."

In '66 Berrocal was called up for 18 months national service. It was in the army that he picked up the trumpet for the first time. "The trumpet came in a rather bizarre way. I never knew either of my grandfathers – they both died in the First World War… – but at home there was a photo of my grandfather (on my mother's side) when he was young, in his village brass band, playing the cornet. It must have stuck in my mind, because when I discovered jazz later on the radio, that was the instrument that touched me immediately."

Berrocal met two trumpet players with diverging styles and personalities, and took lessons from both: "I couldn't let either of them know that I was seeing the other, because they detested each other. The first was billeted at the gunsmiths and played New Orleans style, the second was in my barracks and played in the style of Georges Jouvin. I took what suited me from each of them."

On returning to civilian life in the late '60s Berrocal began to make connections with the people who would become his main collaborators for most of the next decade.

"I tried a few things out with friends, but it was difficult. It was a bit like what happened in England later with punk: none of us knew how to play anything, but we wanted to play. Our drummer Bruno was mad keen on Art Blakey and Elvin Jones but he was actually losing his eyesight, going blind, and he had no rhythmic sense at all. Sometimes he actually missed the drums altogether! That was how I met [accordionist] Claude Parle, who was into Cecil Taylor and John Cage… I'd already met Michel Potage in 1967. He was involved in theatre, and wrote and painted too."

Berrocal had a third important encounter on a trek through Finland to the Arctic Circle: "One night in August 1970 a broken-down 2CV stopped at the side of a trail where I was camping: it was Roger Ferlet… A couple of hours later, after arriving at the edge of the northern lights, we decided to form the Musiq Ensemble."

Within a few months a group had been assembled in Paris, with

Berrocal and Ferlet joined by Claude Parle, Michel Potage, and Dominique Coster. The Musiq Ensemble developed its own take on free improvisation with a musical language that happily mixed found objects and other non-musical elements together with ethnic percussion and brass.

Soon after the formation of the band Berrocal and Ferlet travelled through the Middle East and on to India. It was during this trip that Berrocal had an experience that consolidated his musical vision: "One day in Pakistan, in a village north of Karachi, I had a sort of revelation (which isn't too strong a word). Around five o'clock in the afternoon I heard a muezzin's call to prayer for the first time in my life, in the midst of a whole sonic landscape composed of crying children, car horns, camels' bells... I think it was there that I really became aware of the richness of the paramusical universe."

Musiq Musik (recorded in late '73) was intended to be something of an aural postcard documenting the experience of this trip, featuring a variety of ethnic instruments he and Ferlet had brought back. By the time of the recording Claude Parle had left the Ensemble to play with Don Cherry, so it was made by a trio of Berrocal, Ferlet, and Coster with Michel Potage manning the tape recorder.

One of the most essential musical elements on *Musiq Musik* is the recording space itself, the crypt of an 11th century church in Berrocal's home town of Sens. "It's one of the oldest churches in the region... back then studio reverb cost a fortune, and I realised that natural reverb was more beautiful, and cost nothing at all! Thanks to the local priest we were allowed to record in this church... For the music itself we started with a kind of basic plan, but that soon fell by the wayside. We just fell in love with the sound of the church, that thousand-year-old reverb."

Musiq Musik plays as an extended piece of music, quite unlike the eclectic stylings of Berrocal's later albums. As the album is recorded in mono the reverberation of the environment becomes an integral component of the music rather than a discernible "effect". The physical environment of the crypt also seems to have influenced the content of the music. The predominance of bells, occasional trumpet peals, fanfares, and short bursts of vocal polyphony (recalling Berrocal's choral past) lend the music a ritualistic feel.

The album was released on Gérard Terronès' Futura Records,

one of the few French labels that could provide a natural home for such uncategorisable music: "It wasn't a jazz record, and it certainly wasn't rock, and it didn't have much to do with contemporary music either... But as a result of that we started to get a bit of work. We tried to recreate the kind of stuff that was on the disc, but by then people had moved on to other things, a kind of music theatre."

Over the next few years Michel Potage's theatrical and artistic connections led to concerts at a variety of festivals and venues like Théâtre Mouffetard and the Musée d'Art Moderne. Before making his next album Berrocal took part in François Tusques' Opération Rhino Creation Collective, an 18-piece improvising ensemble whose performance at the Politique Hebdo festival in Lyon was recorded and released in '76.

In late '76 Berrocal recorded *Parallèles*, which was released on his own label, d'Avantage. Breaking with the cohesive musical flow of *Musiq Musik*, this album ventures through a series of vignettes that continue to explore the extra-musical possibilities of brass and string instruments (most notably on the title track and 'Bric-à-brac').

Once again the choice of recording environment was a major factor in the creation of the album: "I believe that locations are very important for music... I have such an acute awareness of this that I arranged for all the pieces on the record to be recorded in different places. It's essential that the location corresponds to the intention behind the piece, without mentioning that there is a response of the location to the music itself."

The most extreme example of this philosophy in action was the recording of the track 'Post-card' in the middle of a Burgundian piggery.

"We found the text on a postcard in a rubbish bin... We adapted the text - originally it was half French, half English - but left it pretty much intact. We decided that Michel would read it, because he had some experience in theatre. Then we wondered what sound we could have in the background... One day we were talking about animals with [sound engineer Daniel Deshays], and Michel mentioned that a friend of his father's had a pig farm. So we called this guy up and he said yes. So off we went to record with the pigs. Live, with the pigs. Not stick them on top afterwards in a studio. We had to do it quite fast because when we started playing the pigs got quite agitated." [1]

Parallèles also includes Berrocal's most well-known composition: 'Rock'n'Roll Station'. Distinguished from the other tracks on the album by its strong, rhythmic pulse (courtesy of Pierre Bastien on double bass), it's a somewhat nostalgic, abstract meditation on the birth of rock music.[2]

"I wanted to sum up my vision of the '50s in an abstract, jumbled way – the spirit and the energy of the post-war years, things that had made an impact on me, the importance of radio in spreading culture… The upright bass was also a quintessential instrument of the era, so it all made sense… We recorded very quickly, in only two takes."

The track is especially notable because of the involvement of Vince Taylor - the embodiment of early rock'n'roll rebellion in France.

" 'Rock'n'Roll Station' was originally written for me to perform… but as it happened I had some friends who ran an antiques shop, and it was there I met Vince. As soon as I heard him speak, I knew that was the voice I wanted. Maybe in the text I had been thinking of Vince without realising it, in a way."

The final track on *Parallèles*, 'Bric-à-brac', takes up the whole of the second side. It's a deep dive into Berrocal's interest in non- or extra-musical sounds, tellingly dedicated to Luigi Russolo, author of the Futurist manifesto 'The Art of Noises'.

"I think that there's a family relationship between this piece and some of Russolo's creations… To put the noises of life into music is to have already adopted an attitude at odds with soothing and pacifying music. I mean that the intervention of certain noises, like the intervention of themes that evoke a revolutionary or insurrectional history, isn't just a touch of aesthetic 'style'. Every time it's a discourse that I want to hold with the listeners. That said, it's perfectly likely that many of them will be oblivious to that aspect of my work."

Jac Berrocal's story continues far beyond the period covered in this book. In '79 it took a new turn with the formation of the avant-post-punk trio Catalogue with drummer Gilbert Artman (Lard Free, Urban Sax) and guitarist Jean-François Pauvros.[3] In the last 40 years there have been many more twists and turns, and throughout Berrocal has maintained a constant output of essential and uncategorisable music. His most recent activity has been in another trio alongside David Fenech and Vincent Epplay.

Notes

1   In another interview Berrocal commented: "A piggery is maybe the furthest thing from the impersonal, sound-proofed desert of a modern recording studio. By installing our microphones in Jouancy, we posed a question about the external conditions imposed on musical expression in 1976. In a dramatic way we showed that the location can and must contribute to the music." (*Jazz Magazine, 1976*)

2   Berrocal was initially unsure whether this track fitted on *Parallèles*: "It was so different that I felt compelled to ask other musicians if they didn't think it was a problem that it was on the record!" (*Jazz Magazine, 1976*)

3   Berrocal commented on the strong influence of the post-punk milieu on him at the time: "Michel and I listened to a lot of stuff. We'd heard about the Sex Pistols and The Clash, but we came to them a bit late. What really blew us away was PiL – I remember when Michel bought the first PiL record, it was much more powerful than the Pistols, with Jah Wobble's enormous bass sound and Lydon's voice... fantastic." (*interview with Dan Warburton, 2004*)

ETRON FOU LELOUBLAN

> Our first ever concert was supporting Magma at the Théatre Municipal. Back then I was already playing a drum solo ('Sololo Brigada' from *Batelages*). We had to play two shows, and between them Giorgio Gomelsky (Magma's manager) came up and asked me, in a patronising tone of voice, whether I was going to play my solo again that night. I reassured him: "Yes! Of course!"
>
> *Guigou Chenevier*

In '71 a sixteen year-old drummer, Guy 'Guigou' Chenevier, went in search of people to create music with. He had been immersed in underground music for most of his teens: "Between '68 and '72, I saw a lot of important bands playing in Grenoble. One of the most influential was the French band Komintern. I also saw Sun Ra, Gong (on the same bill with Kevin Ayers and Nico!), Can, Amon Düül II, Caravan, etc... After seeing all these groups, the one thing you want to do is make music, the most creative and alternative possible!"

His first co-conspirator was organist Claude Achard: "I was looking for musicians, and met Claude. At the time our music was a mix of The Doors, Soft Machine, and Gong... plus some strong influence from free-jazz (Art Ensemble of Chicago, Ornette Coleman etc...) - meaning we were playing a lot of long improvisations!

"In '72 we were joined by Chris Chanet, who played alto sax. Chris was three years older than me, and we spent hours listening to music together at his flat after my school day..."

Chanet: "I was an actor, stage manager, and self-taught saxophonist practising improvised music. I joined a free-jazz band, Libre Cours, whose double bassist was Ferdinand Richard. Then, to my great regret, the band separated. At this time, Guigou Chenevier came to knock on my door, suggesting I join his organ-drums duet."

Achard came up with a name for the new trio. Chenevier: "We hadn't played a single gig, [but] Claude had found a name for us:

Etron Fou, a derisive take on the name of the band Cheval Fou, who Claude thought took itself too seriously." The irreverence of the name (which roughly translates as "Crazy Turd") was a first indicator of the satirical humour that would inform so much of their music.

For most of '72 the embryonic Etron Fou practised, and then began playing locally. Chanet: "Some gigs in Grenoble, some tries with a bass player (Alain Courbis), then Claude stopped playing music to dedicate himself to teaching. Guigou and I were playing in a duet, Grâce Molle, [when] I asked Ferdinand to join us."

Ferdinand Richard already had some experience in bands: "I'd dabbled in total improvisation (playing double bass, very badly, in Libre Cours...) and rock (Zoo Express) before Etron Fou." He agreed to join the band on a temporary basis, on one condition: "I wasn't that convinced by the band's aesthetic... wasn't at all into saxophone, and wasn't a great fan of the drummer's playing ... [but] on the condition that 'Leloublan' was added to the name (which I found particularly naff) I agreed to be a short-term fill-in. This lasted for thirteen years..."

Chenevier: "Ferdinand had this idea to add 'Leloublan' (which means 'the white wolf'). The French expression 'known as the white wolf' means to be very famous. So the idea was just a stupid 'commercial campaign'. Calling ourselves 'leloublan' would necessarily imply that we will become famous! And as you know, this worked perfectly!"

By the end of '72, Etron Fou Leloublan was established in the form it would remain in for the rest of the decade: a trio with the unusual line-up of drums, bass, and saxophone. Such trios could be found in the jazz world, but were almost unheard of in rock. With no model to work from, the band opted for a 'democratic' style where each instrument (including drums) would alternate between melodic and rhythmic roles.

Chenevier: "Our music was rather unique, almost all of the bass was played in chords, the saxophone was frenzied and theatrical, and I played the drums in a very melodic way, treating my instrument more like a set of tuned percussion than as the usual engine of rhythmic support." The result was a skeletal, nervy music invoking the rhythmic energy of Captain Beefheart, while anticipating the stripped-down sound of post-punk. Chenevier notes the obscure English trio Back Door as an early inspiration: "They were one of the only sax-bass-drums trios we ever met. We loved their music, and most of all, Back

Door confirmed that a strong trio could play with only three nested melodic and rhythmic lines, and no chordal instrument!"

Richard credits Chenevier's unorthodox drumming as a major component in Etron Fou's style: "Guigou is the one who brings something fundamentally new to his instrument... since there are only three of us, he's obliged to give his drums another role, he's not a rock drummer, but tries to create harmonies..."

Chenevier explains that this approach developed naturally: "I started playing drums by myself, and very quickly became interested in developing a more 'melodic' style than just playing the usual constant 4/4 beat used in rock'n'roll. When I discovered Drumbo's drumming in Captain Beefheart it was a real shock, and a confirmation, for me... So I never considered my place in a group to be different from any other musician... I've always been very interested in 'composing', as much as in playing."

Richard's unusual style of bass is another distinctive element in Etron Fou's sound. As the only instrument able to play chords, it was often deployed in that role (although in the early days he would occasionally double on guitar): "I play in chords a lot because there is no harmonic instrument in the group. It's kind of my role... the kick drum often plays the role of the bass and I have to do something else... My bass [also] has a particular sound, because it is tuned with the alto sax (there is a two and a half tone difference)."

Much later, during an '82 US tour, Richard found the perfect solution to his unusual requirements in a New York pawn shop: a Fender VI six-string bass. "A perfect fit for my messing about... It's like a big motor in a little body. If you put a double Marshall [stack] behind, with a Hiwatt head on top, it'll make your pants move, that's always been my only aesthetic aim in music; it's beautiful [when your] pants move!"

Etron Fou Leloublan's first gig was booked for 27 December '73 as support band for Magma. Chenevier: "Magma was already quite famous in France in '73, and Etron Fou was just beginning, but... there were a lot of good concerts in Grenoble, and the organiser of these concerts (that we knew very well) proposed us to open for Magma."

It was the perfect (mis)match for a band dedicated to pricking the bubble of musical pretension. Richard: "EFL was a quite cynical and satirical underground group, and although we could appreciate the technical and aesthetic musical approach of Magma, we found (and still find) Magma's image and message quite ridiculous." A number of the pieces played in their set specifically parodied Magma's bombast.[1]

It would be three years before Etron Fou recorded their first LP, however the majority of the songs on *Batelages* were already written by their live debut. One of these, the eighteen-minute epic 'L'amulette et le petit rabbin', is described by Richard as "the essence of Etron Fou".

Chenevier confirms the song's importance in the band's early career: "[For] at least two or three years, we *always* began concerts with 'L'Amulette et le petit rabbin'. It contributed to a certain 'success' for Etron Fou... We became a kind of 'attraction' at festivals because this song's humorous, musical, and theatrical aspects were so different to what other groups were playing around '74-'76 (mostly inspired by Genesis, Pink Floyd or Magma)."

The writing of this song gives insight into some extra-musical influences on Etron Fou. The lyric was created by Chenevier and Chanet while playing the 'exquisite corpse' game, developed by the Surrealists in the 1920s. In the game a piece of collaborative writing is constructed by passing a sheet from author to author with only the last few words visible - encouraging the creation of a text filled with unexpected twists and juxtaposed imagery. These lyrical ruptures were mirrored in the music by abrupt changes in melody and rhythms, with sly winks along the way to other bands like Magma and Gong.

In live performances Chris Chanet would declaim the lyrics while stalking the stage. Chenevier: "As an actor Chris added a theatrical dimension... we were trying to build each piece as a real 'story', even if the stories were quite surrealistic and crazy." Chanet himself saw this theatrical element as essential: "What's important to the group, and what we've tried to do, is to bring music towards theatre."

In May '74 the band had a fateful musical encounter when Chenevier and Richard travelled to Lyon for a Captain Beefheart concert. Chenevier: "Unfortunately, it was the worst period of Captain Beefheart, when he toured with some quite bad studio musicians. No Drumbo, no Zoot Horn Rollo etc..." Disappointed, the pair left before the performance was over, but earlier in the evening they had been stunned by the support band: Henry Cow. "Their music immediately won us over. Hearing a rock band with such an instrumental depth was brand new for us... Those six musicians had the punch of a full philharmonic orchestra and the wildness of... Sun Ra." This chance musical encounter would have on-going resonance in Etron Fou's career.

In the summer of '74 the group moved from Grenoble to the small hamlet of La Peyre in the Ardeche region to begin an experiment in communal living. Chenevier: "Personally I'd never had any community experience before going to live with Etron Fou in Ardeche. You have to remember that we were living only seven years after '68 - the idea that the new generation will make the revolution and change the world was still in the minds of many young people.

"Ferdinand had a political idea in mind. This 'utopian' idea was to generate enough income with our farm to gain a certain independence from the musical 'business' - to be 'free' to accept (or refuse) this or that concert, or to sign this or that record contract... But in fact we never succeeded in realising this utopia - our agricultural and musical activities became too important to allow us to do both at the same time. And that led to big tensions between the musicians and the non-musicians of the community... We weren't especially in touch with other [communities]. On the contrary, for political reasons, we were mostly trying to create relations with the local farmers. This was our Maoist way of thinking *(laughs)*..."

However Chenevier points out that the locals weren't so interested in proletarian solidarity: "The only neighbours we had were two aggressive, suspicious, and hostile farmers... I imagine that our arrival was the worst thing that could have happened to them."

Richard's memories of life in the community illustrate the hardships of band life in such a remote location: "Rehearsals in the barn or in an unheated room! I suffered a lot from the cold, and played bass with mittens, it's distinctive: maybe that's the origin of the sound that's so recognisable! International management from a phone booth five kilometres away... Sending posters from the Cheylard Post Office, maintaining the Citroën TUB: changing the motor, and the gearbox on the side of the road in the snow... Obviously no fax, no internet, no typewriter, [just] a pen, paper, and stamps..."

Despite their extreme isolation, mentions in the music press led to offers to perform arriving in the mail. Chenevier: "In Ardeche, it was not uncommon to receive several letters a week. They usually came from promoters who had heard of us through *Actuel* or *Libé*, or simply by word of mouth."

In '75 there were invitations to play at a number of festivals, including at Montluçon where Chenevier met Camizole's Dominique Grimaud: "We initiated a regular correspondence, sending one or two letters a week for several years... These exchanges between Etron Fou and Camizole rapidly led us to the idea and the desire to create a collective. Later on, Dominique and I had a great musical collaboration."

Together Camizole and Etron Fou started Dupon et ses Fantômes. Chenevier: "The main groups in the collective were Mosaïc, Au Fond du Couloir a Gauche, Nac, Camizole, Grand Gouïa and Etron Fou. It was a kind of 'Rock in Opposition' before Rock in Opposition... The main differences: there were only French groups, and we didn't take ourselves very seriously! Dupon et ses Fantômes generally had a pataphysical approach to things, always acting with humour and detachment. The collective existed no longer than two years, and we mainly shared contacts. The most interesting point is that it clearly shows how radically opposed we were to the *music business* at the time."

In October '75, Chenevier and Richard boldly made a 1000km round-trip to meet the members of Henry Cow over breakfast at a Paris hotel. Chenevier: "We heard that they were playing in a festival close to Paris. We took our old car, went there to meet them, and gave them a cassette of our music!" It would take more than a year, but the relationship they forged with Henry Cow would eventually allow Etron Fou to become one of the few French underground bands known outside of their own country.

'76 was an important year in Etron Fou's development, with live performances at major festivals like the Fete de Politique Hebdo in Lyon and the Fete du PSU and Fete d'Humainité in Paris. It was also the year the band finally entered a studio to record their debut album. Chenevier: "Etron Fou (more than ever in '76) was only a *stage* band. We started the group to *play live*, and during the first three years of the group we played a lot of concerts in France. In '76, it became important for us to do an album, mostly to help the promotion of the group."

Before the recording there was a strange episode which could have seen Etron Fou become Catherine Ribeiro's backing band. Chenevier: "There were, briefly, talks of us becoming her musicians. I don't remember why, but she was considering getting rid of her Alpes band and she was looking for other musicians... Pierre Lattés was the middle-man. Basically he told us that performing with her could be a launching pad for us... For whatever reason, the idea didn't move forward. I think Ferdinand called Catherine Ribeiro once or twice and things stopped there. It probably turned out to be a good thing in the end. I don't think the sidemen role would have suited us."

When Etron Fou finally recorded *Batelages* in November '76, their goal was to capture the music they had developed with as little studio trickery as possible. Chenevier: "Etron Fou was certainly not a 'conceptual band'... our idea going into the studio was more to play the music we were playing on stage [as well as possible] than to make a conceptual album with a lot of sound treatments and over-dubs."

Chanet believes they succeeded in their goal even though there were important elements of Etron Fou's live performance that couldn't be captured on a recording: "This album is a good representation of what we were playing in concert then, without [the] theatre, the visual aspect..." Richard goes a little further, viewing the record as secondary to their live performances: "Songs were written to be played on stage. The recording was more to be seen as an additional experiment."

Batelages was recorded by Thierry Magal of Crium Delirium in a small four-track studio owned by jazz pianist Jef Gilson. Chenevier: "Thierry Magal was a very cool and calm guy (the opposite of his brother Renard who'd always been very eccentric and extrovert). He liked Etron Fou a lot, and fixed a studio session for us in Paris. The session was really effective and a very pleasant time spent together!"

Batelages was released in late '76 on Gratte-Ciel Records, a label set up by *Rock & Folk* journalist Jean-Marc Bailleux.[2] It was very well-received by the music press.

Rock en Stock: "The music of Etron Fou Leloublan is rich and very diverse. In its own way *Batelages* is a major event just as Gong's *Camembert Electrique* was in its time. That's not the only thing they have in common with that group. One finds... the same refusal to take themselves too seriously or to use gratuitous technical effects. In certain passages you find the same colour and spirit that enlivened Gong's *Camembert*... *Batelages* is a record that has to be listened to with great attention to grasp its full inventiveness."

The album was even reviewed positively in the British music press:

"This is the most interesting new band I've heard from the continent in some years. Their music is complex, but in a Beefheartian sort of way, rather than the assumed complexity of other bands... There's a bit of Can, a bit of Faust... This band is very good."

During the recording of *Batelages*, Etron Fou had played their last gig with Chris Chanet at the Bas-Rock Festival in Paris.[3] Before leaving Chanet had arranged for Francis Grand to take over from him. Chanet: "I met Francis during a visit to my parents. We lived in the same small town... Before definitely leaving EFL, I asked him if he would like to replace me, Guigou and Ferdinand agreed."

Richard: "When Chris left, we wanted another instrument, not just a saxophone. But we didn't want a harmonic instrument: we wanted to have three melodic lines and have people create the harmonies in their heads... Francis [was] much more technical than Chris... We [asked] him to work on riffs, the rhythmic side of the sax."

Chenevier: "When Francis Grand replaced Chris Chanet of course it changed the balance between the three of us. Francis had a completely different personality to Chris - much less extroverted!... Chris added a theatrical dimension. When he left the band, this dimension changed a bit, but didn't disappear completely."

Etron Fou's 1000km round-trip to Paris finally paid off when they were invited to join Henry Cow's UK tour in June '77, with concerts in Brighton, Southend, Guilford, Cambridge, and Leeds. It was during this tour that Etron Fou was exposed to the UK punk/new wave scene.

Chenevier: "In Southend, I noted that some pure punk guys were in the audience, and loved our concert. We spoke with them afterwards, and it was a real pleasure to discover that English punks could appreciate our music. It was a surprise, because in France most bands from the punk scene were only focused on their clothes and appearance. It was mostly a superficial musical fashion... Most of these young musicians in France didn't have a strong political background, and even though we sometimes played on the same stages, we didn't have much in common. The only very interesting French punk group that I remember was Metal Urbain, but unfortunately we never met.

"Later (in '78) we met some crazy and interesting young punk guys in the South France. They were playing as a duo named The Fab Two, and they loved Etron Fou. Two years later one of these guys, Serge

Novi, designed the sleeve for our fourth album: *Les Poumons Gonflés*."

The association with Henry Cow deepened in September when Etron Fou supported the band at three Italian concerts, including one in Rome in front of 3500 people. On their way back to France the band stopped off in Milan where they met Umberto Fiori, the singer of Stormy Six. He was involved with l'Orchestra Co-operative which, among other things, released records and organised tours in Italy for non-mainstream bands. Over the next three years Etron Fou would play more than twenty concerts in Italy thanks to l'Orchestra.

Atem's review of their next Parisian concert noted how well Francis Grand had integrated into the band: "There are lots of new, long pieces where the emphasis is sometimes placed on Henry Cow-style ruptures. Francis, the new saxophonist has managed to overcome Chris's rhythmic/melodic dilemma and the three madmen now seem to be at maximum coherence and unity, without the music losing a single ounce of its madness."

With so many performances under their belt, Etron Fou were well-drilled when they entered the studio in November '77 to record their second album, *Les trois fous perdégagnent (Au pays des...)*. Chenevier: "It was our intention to do a more 'produced' album. We started Etron Fou as a live band, not as a studio band. *Batelages* was mostly a reflection of what we were playing on stage... But we wanted to work more on the production of the second album."

They chose Jean-Pierre Grasset to record the LP. Grasset had already recorded two solo albums under the name Verto, showcasing his ability to use the studio as an instrument.[4] Chenevier: "We were playing in the south-west of France a lot... and Jean-Pierre was living in Toulouse. We liked him and his music, and he'd started working as a sound engineer in different studios."

The album was recorded at Studio Tangara, where Grasset had already produced Art Zoyd 3's *Symphonie pour le jour ou bruleront les cités* and Potemkine's *Foetus*.

Chenevier: "It was a little eight-track studio that wasn't especially well-equipped, if I remember well. We asked Jean-Pierre if he would like to play guitar on some pieces. The idea came pretty naturally as we were recording with him and he was a guitar player! It was also a way to change our usual sound on some pieces...

"We multiplied the sax tracks on a piece inspired by Urban Sax: 'Je veux danser avec toi' [and] we allowed ourselves [flights of fantasy] during the mix by using all sorts of effects."

Les trois fous perdégagnent (Au pays des...) was released on 9h17 Productions, Dupon et ses Fantômes' short-lived label.[5] Chenevier: "It was the logical consequence of our political engagement. And also very much implied by the musical business situation. I am not sure anyway that any major record company would have been interested in releasing our music. For us it was also a step more in the direction of our 'economic independence'."

Atem gave the album a positive review, but noted that the lyrical humour that served Etron Fou so well on stage didn't translate perfectly onto record: "The instrumental humour is much more interesting, particularly the manic sax/drums dialogue (notably on 'Nave de Bilande'). This is the Etron Fou we really like, unencumbered by verbiage or a jumble of imagery. But this is only the airing of very small reservations that shouldn't make you forget that Etron Fou are the kings of syncopation..."

Not long after the release of the album Etron Fou returned to the UK. Chenevier: "In March '78, we toured England with Henry Cow, and played the 'famous' first Rock In Opposition Festival in London.[6] In a sense, we'd been the first band that Henry Cow 'co-opted' as a band that shared some musical and political background even before RIO started."

From '78, Etron Fou and Rock In Opposition would become inseparable in many people's minds. What began as a loose affiliation of bands morphed into a genre label that stuck to the band for the rest of their career. While it was beneficial in many ways, it also became something of a millstone around Etron Fou's neck.

The Rock In Opposition concept had been born from Henry Cow's frustration with the music business. They had seen too many bands ignored because they were from the wrong country, played the wrong style of music, or were signed to the wrong (or no) label. In response they gathered bands from France (Etron Fou), Belgium (Univers Zero), Italy (Stormy Six), and Sweden (Sammla Mammas Manna) to play alongside them in London.

The collective nature of RIO was formalised in December '78 when the bands met together in Switzerland.[7] However, after a second festival in Milan there was a split in the ranks as Stormy Six argued for more political and social activism. The issue was never resolved, and by the end of '79 Rock In Opposition was no more, even though the bands continued to work together informally.

Chenevier: "You have to understand that RIO was Chris Cutler's and Nick Hobbs's project.[8] There were very positive points: we played in festivals and places all over Europe, it brought us important interest from the media, and of course, it was really great for us to meet all these great bands and musicians. The bad aspect was that it put us in a kind of 'musical ghetto' soon after it began... for example, it was very strange for Etron Fou playing in London in '78, to see RIO completely ignore the punk scene that was in full explosion at the time! We weren't very comfortable with that."

Ferdinand Richard finds it problematic that some still view Etron Fou as an "RIO band": "The only thing in common was that we didn't want to be a part of the regular music business, that's all... I have to say that I'm a bit upset by the way the RIO branding has been instrumentalised by people who didn't have anything [to do] with its beginning, aims, objectives, and who made it a fashion, or an aesthetic movement."

In summer '79 Richard traveled to the US with ex-Henry Cow guitarist Fred Frith. While there he was able to organise a series of gigs for Etron Fou that November.

As they prepared for this short US tour the band changed saxophonist again.[9] Bernard Mathieu: "I met Ferdinand just before the US tour... We started to rehearse together three or four weeks before the US tour... The tour was fantastic. We played at Boston, Hartford, NY, Philadelphia and Baltimore."

The next Etron Fou record, *En Public aux Etats-Unis d'Amérique*, was recorded on this first American tour. Chenevier: "Our plan from the beginning was to record all the concerts... Unfortunately, the guy who organised the tour fucked everything up. So, when we arrived in the US nothing was planned. Luckily Fred Frith (who was already living in New York) helped us a lot to plan the recording at the Squat Theater in NY, and it is mostly recordings of the two concerts we did there that you hear on the record."

Richard: "We recorded it on a four-track machine, although one of the tracks was out of duty most of the time, so you can consider it was recorded on three tracks... I think we were the first French group to tour there, at least the first to record a live album, which was unbelievable for the regular French music business. Some of these Parisian guys declared that this was a fake US tour, that we had invented everything and had never been there." *En Public aux Etats-Unis d'Amérique* was released on Jean Karakos's Celluloïd label.[10]

In the following years Etron Fou became a truly international band, with more than two-thirds of their performances taking place outside of France. In September '80 they became a quartet with the addition of keyboardist Jo Thirion. At this point their music moved more definitively in the post-punk direction it had always hinted at. In late '83 Etron Fou became a trio again when saxophonist Bruno Meillier departed. The band broke up in '86 after releasing another three albums (two of them produced by Fred Frith).

Guigou Chenevier remains very active as a musician. Since the mid-'80s he has released over twenty albums both under his own name and in the bands Les Batteries, Buga Up, and Volapük.

Ferdinand Richard was an active recording musician in the '80s and '90s releasing albums as a soloist and in the bands Gestalt et Jive, Bruniferd, and Ferdinand et les Philosophes He has organised the MIMI festival since '85, and advises several institutions, including UNESCO, on cultural policy.

Chris Chanet played on the first Urban Sax LP. He later specialised in electroacoustic music and composition for theatre, and continued to practise street theatre with the company Delices Dada.

Notes

1   Satirical jibes at Magma would become common fare at Etron Fou concerts. Chenevier: "I regularly made jokes against Christian Vander... I remember that I played some concerts with a golden *etron* [turd] on my chest, to poke fun at the golden eagle claw the Magma musicians were always wearing!" Nevertheless he confesses that an "odd feeling of admiration for Christian Vander" eventually led him to buy the same drums as Magma's leader.

2   "Jean-Marc approached us with this very new idea of self-production... Record production and distribution at that time was totally under the control of big national companies or international majors, which were totally dedicated to the mainstream. The music we (and other underground musicians) made was really too weird for these companies." *(Richard)*

3   Urban Sax also made their first appearance at this festival, with Chris Chanet among the sixteen saxophonists on stage.

4   The first Verto album, *Krig/Volubilis* was released on the synth-based Pole Records, with the sleeve proudly boasting: "This record was made without synthesisers".

5   9h17 Productions was run by some of Camizole's members. *Les trois fous perdégagnent (Au pays des...)* was also released in Italy by the l'Orchestra Co-operative label in '79.

6   Etron Fou Leloublan's performance from this evening (12 March '78) was recorded and released in 2015.

7   At this meeting three more bands were added to the group: The Art Bears (created after the break-up of Henry Cow), Art Zoyd, and Aksak Maboul.

8   Chris Cutler was Henry Cow's drummer and Nick Hobbs was the band's manager.

9   Gérard Bole du Chaumont, who had replaced Francis Grand in mid-'78, left Etron Fou in September '79 just before the US tour.

10 Etron Fou had been associated with Karokos since he took over distribution of their second album (after 9h17 Productions shut up shop in Summer '78). Chenevier: "He was a real character! Karakos was a sympathetic crook (!) but he was also a very funny guy, and certainly a real fan of music!"

BIRGÉ GORGÉ SHIROC
& UN DRAME MUSICAL INSTANTANÉ

> There were two records I listened to when I was very young, maybe five or six: a very strange album by Michel Magne called *Musique Tachiste* where he mixed odd sounds with an orchestra, and a single with a girl singing while she played with telephone sounds. I'd forgotten about them, but when I listened back, I thought: 'Wow!' It sounded like the music I've made since. I thought I'd inventing everything, but I was just remembering my childhood!
>
> *Jean-Jacques Birgé*

Jean-Jacques Birgé's childhood was soundtracked as much by sound-effects from science fiction stories as by the few orchestral records his parents owned: "My father was fond of science fiction, and reviewed records for science fiction magazines. So when I was quite young I listened to LPs of science fiction stories mixing music, sounds, and actors' voices."

This immersion in story and sound intensified with his exposure to the world of film. "My parents didn't have much money, and the only thing they could take us to was the cinema. I wasn't taken to concerts or museums when I was a kid, and I think this history with film made an impression on me."

As for most of those who became involved in the underground, '68 was a turning point. It started with the events in May: "I was only fifteen at that time [but] I used to take my motorcycle and join in with the group handling security during the demonstrations, deliver posters printed at the Beaux-Arts school, or sell *Action*, the newspaper run by neighbourhood action committees in Paris." An already significant year was capped when Birgé set off on a road trip across the USA.

The precocious fifteen-year-old travelled through the country in the summer of '68, witnessing the Grateful Dead, Kaleidoscope, and It's a Beautiful Day playing at the Fillmore West, and returning with a motherlode of vinyl: "I brought back a stack of records, Zappa and the Mothers of Invention, Silver Apples, Jefferson Airplane, Iron Butterfly... and the passion for music."

Back in Paris, Birgé began to become seriously involved in making music. He took up saxophone, and developed an interest in the creation of light-shows: "I started scratching ruined slides after attending a workshop at the neighbourhood MJC in '67... [and] discovered that setting fire to hairspray produced interesting effects on undeveloped film."

His fascination with audiovisuals led him to London in summer '70 for an internship with Krishna Lights. During his stay he helped produce light-shows for Kevin Ayers and Steamhammer.

In his final year of school, Birgé made his on-stage debut: "Keen on setting up light-shows for the high school's rock band, I would sit aimlessly through rehearsals, unable to project psychedelic images in daylight. So I just grabbed a tambourine and then began singing lyrics that I had written..."

On 3 February '71 his band, Epimanondas, played at their school, Lycée Claude Bernard, alongside Dagon and Red Noise: "The band brought together Francis Gorgé on guitar, Edgard Vincensini on bass, Pierre Binsard on drums. Francis wrote the music and I wrote the lyrics. I sang (in English!), manipulated magnetic tapes[1], played alto sax and flute, percussion, jew's harp and an electronic instrument made from a telephone amplifier."

On graduating from school Birgé had decided to focus his energies on playing music and creating light-shows. Along with a half-dozen school friends he formed H-Lights, who created visuals for bands like Gong, Red Noise, Crouille Marteau, and Dagon. While he intended to follow a career in music, Birgé's parents encouraged him to pursue further study: "When I told my mother a friend had gotten into the national film school, she said, 'Why don't you do that?' I didn't want to, but just to please her, I sat the test. There were 600 candidates and only eighteen succeeded. It turned out that I was the youngest, and had the best results. I was so proud to be there for maybe three of my best years. I loved it!"

While attending the IDHEC film school, Birgé continued to work with H-Lights and began to deepen his musical relationship with guitarist Francis Gorgé: "Francis was a big fan of The Beatles, The

Who and King Crimson, while I was more into Frank Zappa, Captain Beefheart and Soft Machine. I discovered free-jazz at the Amougies festival in Belgium in '69 but at the time we were already interested in all kinds of music."

Gorgé points out that his influences were actually much more varied: "[My favourite guitarist was] Django Reinhardt... his disabled left hand made me feel close to him because I personally had a handicapped right hand... Later on, I discovered Sonny Sharrock, Derek Bailey and a few others, but the essential was already in place and my subsequent influences weren't guitar players." About his work with Birgé, he drolly states: "The potential guitar hero that I was became an avant-garde musician when I met Jean-Jacques Birgé."

As they began playing together the duo documented the results on the recording set-up Birgé had assembled: "Francis and I started recording our improvisations in my bedroom, playing through headphones. [I had] a powerful sound system with a mixing desk and two Shure microphones. Francis used to plug his Gibson SG guitar directly into the system, and we both had a multitude of effects pedals... we surprised ourselves by the originality of the results."

By the time he and Gorgé were playing together, Birgé had taken on keyboards as his main instrument. He made the change from sax for the most obtuse reason: "At the beginning I rented a soprano saxophone, but I thought it was very heavy to hold while playing. I got an alto saxophone, but it was still hanging around my neck...

"I went to visit some guys who had a lot of instruments in their country house, and I discovered a Farfisa Professional organ, the same one Sun Ra and Pink Floyd had. I loved it because I had a seat! *(laughs)* I just had to play with my hands; I didn't have to carry anything."

While switching to the keyboard had been a step forward, things really fell into place when Birgé discovered the synthesiser: "I didn't like synthesiser music at that time because it was Walter Carlos's *Switched on Bach* and things like that... But there was a guy in a shop who demoed an ARP 2600, and I went, 'Wow! I want this!' I didn't like the Moog; it was too shiny, it sounded too electronic, and I was trying to make my synthesiser sound acoustic. I loved the ARP! My father didn't have much money, but he said, 'I'll pay for half of it.' So I had to work during summer to get the other half. That's how I bought my ARP, and everything began.

"My taste for symphonies found an echo in this unbelievable machine which, alongside Francis's guitar, transformed our duo into an orchestra... The first improvisations for guitar and synthesiser were recorded in '74 in the living room of the community I'd joined."

As a self-taught musician, Birgé had suffered from impostor syndrome, but the synthesiser gave him the confidence to develop a new way of thinking about music and composition: "With absolutely no knowledge of harmony or counterpoint, I found a way of learning as I played, helped by the synthesiser. Instead of thinking in terms of notes and rhythms, I heard all kinds of music through sound waves, filters, envelopes, clock, white noise, etc..."

His experience at film school also gave Birgé access to a different musical language: "My idea has always been to compose evocative pieces where the listener creates their own cinema. If you want to understand my music, you have to look to the rules in cinema rather than in the history of music... I use montage, ellipses, close-ups, perspectives... For me, melody or harmony comes after the narrative structure. It also made it easier for me to write for the cinema, and always in a complementary way, as opposed to illustration, which highlights with a fluorescent marker." [2]

By early '75 the duo believed that they were ready to release a record, and Birgé went in search of a deal: "I had the feeling that our 'work' could easily compete with what I heard on the radio. Back in those days it was still a medium where experimentation was possible! For a whole week, I called record labels that may have been interested, with no results. On a Saturday evening, trying to forget about the failure, I went to a party in Louveciennes [and] started to talk about my depressing week...

"A balding guy sat on a sofa tells me that he is the producer of a label called Sun Records and that he is interested. It was Sébastien Bernard, who was also recording Frank Wright, Bobby Few, Alan Silva... He arranged a meeting two days later at my place at 5 p.m. At 5:05 he was listening to one of the tracks, told me to stop the tape, and asked if fifteen days in the studio would be OK? We recorded the first part of *Défense de* at his father's place."

The *Défense de* sessions took place between 25 March and 2 April '75. with Birgé and Gorgé joined by saxophonist Antoine Duvernet, a former classmate, who would go on to play with Lard Free and

Urban Sax. While Sébastien Bernard had been enthused by the duo's home recordings, he was strangely non-plussed by the results of the session. Birgé: "Sébastien was totally taken aback by what we'd done. He asked the free-jazz musicians he worked with: Alan Silva, Frank Wright, and Noah Howard - but they didn't understand what we were doing any more than he did... [So] he gave me the eight-track tape and advised me to do something other than music!"

It was a few months after this experience that Birgé and Gorgé entered the studio again, this time to contribute to an album by vocalist Hugues Ométaxalia. At the session they met two members of the jazz-fusion band Speed Limit: pianist Jean-Louis Bucchi and percussionist Shiroc. They were particularly impressed by the percussionist: "We asked Shiroc to come over to our place and play together... We were happy to find someone who had the same approach to music as we did: improvised, narrative, colourful, varied, electric!"

The trio clicked, and Birgé and Gorgé decided to replace two of the pieces already recorded for *Défense de* with new recordings made with Shiroc. A session was held on August 13 and 14 at Studio Adam. Jean-Louis Bucchi joined the trio to play electric piano on one track.

Birgé had no desire to resume the search for a deal to release the album and decided they should create their own independent label: "I found the only patron of my entire career to pay for mixing, and I made the first GRRR record... which Sébastien Bernard agreed to distribute. The record was a great success, probably my best seller..."

Birgé and Gorgé had played only a couple of live shows before the release of *Défense de*. To promote the album and launch the new trio, Birgé Gorgé Shiroc embarked on a run of eight Sunday night concerts at the Théâtre de la Gaîté in Montparnasse (with the first held on 9 November '75). They continued to play regularly for the first half of '76: "We played a few concerts with Shiroc, but he wasn't very available, so we played more and more with [percussionist] Gilles Rollet. We did a lot during that period. It was easy to find places to play, but you know, sometimes there were only ten people in the theatre."

Things were progressing well, but everything changed in July '76 when Birgé had a fateful encounter with jazz legend Bernard Vitet: "Looking back it all seems to have been very quick - the duo recordings ('74), the arrival of Shiroc ('75), then Gilles Rollet, and *bam* Bernard!"

The meeting with the trumpeter took place at a festival in support of the La Borde psychiatric clinic: "I was playing alto saxophone and synthesiser in Operation Rhino... There were fifteen of us. I was on one side, and there was a guy on the other side playing percussion on beer bottles, TAK TAK TAK TAK! They were exploding - there was broken glass everywhere around him. I knew it was Bernard Vitet - one of the most experimental guys."

Unlike the rest of Operation Rhino ("everyone else was afraid of my synthesiser, and just wanted me to play saxophone"), Vitet had been fascinated by the sounds coming from Birgé's ARP: "At the end of the concert we went to talk to each other. And for the three days of the festival, we talked about Edgar Varese, Thelonius Monk, things like that. He was an intellectual; he knew everything about everything. I was totally fond of the time I was having with him. So I went to his place, and we recorded a few pieces in his studio."

By the mid-'70s Vitet had already had a long career on the French jazz scene. While he'd been featured on over a dozen records, only one had been recorded under his own name: *La Guêpe*, released by Futura in '72. Birgé: "He was always the second guy in the band, because he had no ambition for money or for being famous. In '64 he made the first French free-jazz with François Tusques. He played with Brigitte Bardot, Barbara, Serge Gainsbourg, all these very famous French singers, but he stopped that in '68, and played only jazz or free-jazz. He played with all the famous American musicians. And in '74, just before we met, he stopped everything. He wanted to do his own thing."

Meeting Vitet made Birgé rethink his approach to music, and he put an end to Birgé Gorgé Shiroc to create a new band with Vitet: "I was already playing with Francis Gorgé, so I got them together. The first trio concert was organized by the Communist Party's cinema unit at the Fête de l'Humanité." It was the beginning of a lifelong friendship and musical partnership.

"From the second performance, we called it Un Drame Musical Instantané... 'Un' signified the uniqueness of each performance: we'd never repeat ourselves, and we invented a new plan every time. 'Drame Musical' refers to musical theatre... drama in the theatrical sense of the term because, even if we have always been more gifted for drama than for comedy, we don't neglect the humorous aspect of some of our shows. 'Instantané' corresponds to the idea we have of improvisation: contrasting instant composition to prior composition. We believed we'd entered an era where music doesn't always have to be written before it's made, that paper would give way to magnetic tape, and that the music world's social hierarchy had to be rethought from top to bottom."

Un Drame Musical Instantané would become one of the longest-running groups produced by the French underground, lasting over thirty years. While it functioned as a democracy, the roles were divided, with Birgé as organiser: "I was the driving force in Un Drame even though creatively we were all equal... Bernard brought his immense experience, but I laid the foundations of Drame, if only because I had gone to find both of them. Francis had incredible energy and Bernard soared with his magnificent trumpet tone. For my part, I was the orchestra, and they were two concert soloists...

"[Bernard] was eighteen years older than us: he was forty-two and we weren't twenty-four yet. He was a father to us, but since he was chaotic, I was his mother! He had the intelligence to [get together with] two young people who wanted to let rip... He taught us silence; he brought melody. He was a researcher, an experimenter, and prevented us from going in circles."

Birgé credits the band's longevity partly to the egalitarian spirit that flowed through their improvised music and into their day-to-day affairs: "I said to both of them, let's share everything three ways - for the rights, for everything. Even if it's a flute solo, we share everything. So we never had any problems with money because each of us got a third. That was a first for Bernard because he'd been used and [cheated] by a lot of musicians before. That's why we had thirty-two years of friendship and music, because when you don't have money arguments, ninety-five percent of the problems are gone."

Not that there was a lack of strong opinion within the band: "We were always arguing, but we loved each other. Bernard had his card as a communist and was a bit of a Stalinist. I was more like an anarchist or a Trotskyist, and Francis was more like a rightist. *(laughs)* But at the end of the day we were always together, because it was the object that counted: the best idea for the project. So we always found a way."

The first Un Drame Musical Instantané album wasn't released until '79, but the pieces on it were recorded during their first year together - an intense period of creation. During this time the trio met up three times a week to record their 'instant compositions'. In addition to the three pieces that would feature on *Trop d'adrenaline nuit*, they stockpiled a plethora of tracks that were never released: "In '77 we recorded the *Poisons* series, which lasted more than 24 hours! Enough to make dozens of albums." [3]

Un Drame Musical Instantané continued as a trio until '92 when Francis Gorgé left to pursue a career in information technology. By that time the band had released fourteen records. Birgé and Vitet continued as a duo, releasing three more records during the '90s. Birgé: "Francis and I continued to play together for seventeen years following our first album and have always remained close friends. I went on with Bernard until I stopped Un Drame Musical Instantané in 2008. The last recording made with Bernard was in 2000, and the last concert we did together was in 2004."

Jean-Jacques Birgé continues to release records, usually in collaboration with other artists.

Francis Gorgé became a computer engineer specialising in QuickTime and multi-media. He still makes music, but not professionally.

Shiroc disappeared from the music scene in the mid-'70s, becoming a music teacher in the south of France.

Bernard Vitet died in 2013, aged 79

Notes

1 The tape recorder had in a sense been Birgé's first musical instrument: "I started making electro-acoustic magnetic tapes at the age of 13, shortly after my parents gave me a tape recorder for an unexpected prize of excellence."

2 Writing scores for cinema became an important component of Birgé's creative life after starting his film studies: "Having composed music for my own films, some friends asked me to take care of theirs. From film to film, I became a composer. Directing was a fantasy. It became a ghost... To preserve my independence, which up to now has allowed me to pursue my hopes, I naturally opt, without realising it, for a less expensive form of artistic expression than cinematography. Music..." Birgé estimates that he composed soundtracks for up to thirty films between '71 and '78.

3 The forty tracks that make up the *Poisons* series have been made available for download from the remarkable archive hosted on Birgé's *drame.org* website.

part seven:
the electronic underground

MINI MOOG	12 485 F
MOOG SATELLITE	4 985 F

Pour tous renseignements
Écrivez vite à **SEIMATONE**
(importateur, vente exclusivement en gros) 17, rue Froment, PARIS-XI - Tél. : 700.89.63

UTILISÉ PAR
JEFFERSON
AIRPLANE
FAMILY STONE
LED ZEPPELIN
WHO
C.T.A.
BLOOD SWEAT
　　AND TEARS
JOHN LENNON
ZAPPA

GAFFAREL MUSIQUE

3, rue Guy-Mocquet
MARSEILLE-1er
Tél. : (16-91) 48.34.24
18bis, r. de Bruxelles
PARIS-9e
Tél. : 874.40.03

L'EXTRAORDINAIRE SYNTHETIZER A.R.P. (USA)
PRIX PUBLIC : 22.000 FRS
MODÈLE ODYSSÉE : 13.300 FRS

INTRODUCTION

> Synthesisers introduced a sonic continuum along with an extraordinarily wide tonal range that wasn't available on the guitar at that time. I was attracted to their ability to create sonic texture, and the potential of running my guitar through their filters and LFOs. When I got my first EMS Synthi A, I took it with me everywhere I went.
>
> *Richard Pinhas, Heldon*

When the synthesiser arrived in the late-'60s it came with a price tag that put the instrument out of reach of any musician not sponsored by a cultural institution or already wealthy.[1] This allowed experimental musicians like Morton Subotnick to explore their possibilities, but left acts from the UK and US psychedelic underground (who could have exploited their wild sonic potential to the full) without access.[2] Within a rock context the synthesiser became the province of already established acts (e.g. The Beatles) and well-connected session players.

At the dawn of the '70s, the instrument found a new home in the British progressive music scene, becoming synonymous with keyboard wizards like Keith Emerson and Rick Wakeman. At around the same time, portable and more affordable synths like the Moog Mini-Moog, EMS VCS3, and ARP 2600 were released, making electronic instruments more accessible.[3] The underground music scene in the US and UK had begun to dissipate by then, but new scenes in France and Germany were emerging just as these cheaper synthesisers became available. Musicians in both countries were searching for new modes of music, and were naturally drawn to experiment with these new instruments.

In Germany this gave rise to the "Berlin school" (based around Tangerine Dream and Klaus Schulze) along with pioneering bands like Cluster, Kraftwerk, and Popol Vuh.[4] The French were also early adopters of the new technology, as Richard Pinhas notes: "At the time I started to play... not so many people were using synthesizers. France was one of the two or three countries... There were four or five bands in Germany, one or two in Japan, and in England, there was mainly Eno.[5] That's all." France witnessed a broad adoption of the synthesiser, far beyond the purely "electronic" musicians featured in this section, with bands like Lard Free, Crium Delirium, Camizole, Gong, Birgé Gorgé Shiroc, and Clearlight all integrating them into their diverse styles.

Pinhas was one of the first musicians from the French underground to explore the synthesiser. In '71 he travelled to London to buy a Synthi A (a more portable VCS3) directly from EMS ("It was impossible to find synths here, you had to go to London to order them... I had to sell all my cameras to pay for one.") Another early pioneer of the French electronic underground had already made the same trip: English musician Tim Blake.

Blake had moved to France in March '71 to settle into Gong's community at Sens. He'd been invited to join as the band's sound engineer, but instead spent his time at Pavillon du Hay learning synthesis: "During my first two months there I sold some sound equipment I had in England, and bought my first synthesizer." He was readying to play on the *Camembert Electrique* LP, when Pip Pyle, Gong's new drummer, issued a "him or me" ultimatum regarding Blake and his synthesiser. He was forced to move on, spending the rest of the year honing his synthesiser skills in a variety of communities outside Paris.

At the end of '71 Blake travelled to the capital: "I met a woman who was quite a few years older than me, who said 'You've got to come with me to Paris. I'll introduce you to some people I know'. I said, 'How do you know these people?' She replied, 'Oh, I used to be a dancer', and this is where I discovered that my friend was Michèle Seigneuret, Maurice Béjart's dancing partner in Pierre Henry's ballets."

He made significant contacts, including Henry himself, and was convinced to settle in Paris: "As soon as I got there I was contacted by someone from the film industry who wanted to sell EMS synthesizers in France. I also set up Crystal Machine Studio, and was getting work by the beginning of '72."

In addition to his studio, Blake founded the band Crystal Machine, the first fully electronic underground act in France. While it would became better known when revived after Blake left Gong, Crystal

Machine was already active in early '72. Blake: "Live shows were pretty rare, although we played at the Bièvres Festival, which went unexpectedly well. We were very much into huge echoes and very calm music, and that went down quite well at the end of a rock show. There was also something in the Musée d'Art Moderne, and I played at a protest at the Renault factory."

By mid-'72 Crystal Machine had recorded a demo tape: "We produced a cassette which went out to a very select number of people.[6] Soon I was getting feedback, including from Open Light, who were really important." This connection introduced Blake to Patrice Warrener and Bernard Szajner, two lighting artists who would become integral to Crystal Machine.

In August '72 Blake had rejoined Gong, and Crystal Machine was on the back-burner ("I think I did a show with Open Light towards the end of the year, despite already being on the road with Gong.") Reflecting on this time Blake states: "What I noticed was the presence of the Germans and myself, and we were probably a leg and an arm in front of other people. Had I not been involved with Gong, I'd probably have been busy with Tangerine Dream and Klaus Schulze... I believe parallel to this, Richard Pinhas would have been making an album."

Blake and Pinhas had been the first to experiment with synthesiser-based music, but by early '73 other acts had incorporated synthesiser into their sound. Gong's *Flying Teapot* featured Blake's VCS3, Crium Delirium introduced their own VCS3 into their live performance, and Lard Free crafted a new minimalist sound catalysed by Hervé Elhyani's ARP 2600.[7] However it was the autumn '74 release of Heldon's *Electronique Guerrilla* that signalled the arrival of a new wave of electronic music in France.

Within months the floodgates opened. During '75 there was a steady stream of releases on Pôle Records (Pôle, Fluence, Besombe-Rizet, Henri Roger), a debut from Birgé Gorgé Shiroc, and the appearance of a synthesiser-based incarnation of Camizole on the festival circuit. From '76 the number of projects continued to multiply. Barclay were even inspired to set up the Egg Records imprint to cater for the new bands, releasing albums from Tim Blake's revitalised Crystal Machine, Patrick Vian (ex-Red Noise), Ose[8], and Heldon.

Notes

1 The only commercially available instruments at this time were massive modular synthesisers from Moog and Buchla, which (depending on specification) were priced anywhere between $25,000 and $65,000 in today's money.

2 There were however a few acts like Lothar and the Hand People, and Silver Apples in the US, and White Noise in the UK that experimented with more primitive electronics.

3 Affordable is, of course, a relative term: in today's money the Minimoog was approximately $10,000, the VCS3 cost $7000, and the ARP 2600 came in at a cool $17,500.

4 Florian Fricke from Popol Vuh was one of the first to invest in a $65,000 Moog 3 in '69. It featured on the albums *Affenstunde* and *In Den Gärten Pharaos*.

5 The UK's own electronic underground (Cabaret Voltaire, Throbbing Gristle, The Human League, etc.) emerged in the mid-'70s. Until then the synthesiser was largely ignored outside of progressive rock, except for rare acts like Hawkwind and Brian Eno.

6 This recording was likely the very first from the French electronic underground. Three tracks from the demo cassette are included on Tim Blake's *Lighthouse* box-set, released in 2018.

7 Elhyani's job at Gaffarel Music had given him early exposure to the synthesiser: "After the '72 summer holidays my boss, Jean-Marie Gaffarel, introduced me to a new import: the ARP, which along with Moog was one of the top synths of the time. I was seduced by the instrument, and quickly discovered its vast, new potential..."

8 Ose was the project of journalist Hervé Picart.

PHILIPPE BESOMBES

> "I was thirsty for electric sounds; distortion, echo, and reverb. Even though I didn't play the guitar well, it didn't matter as long as my body was wrapped in those striking sounds. I remember my first experience in a recording studio when I pushed up the volume of my amp to create a marvelous distortion sound. The engineer ran up to me, explaining that the sound is nice when you put the volume at one or two... I was disappointed!"
>
> *Philippe Besombes*

At thirteen Philippe Besombes was introduced to rock'n'roll by hearing Elvis Presley on a jukebox: "It was exciting, something impalpable and underground... The music was violent, it was so incisive and the rhythm was fast. It was electric!" A trip to England accelerated his musical education: "I was staying in Sheffield and The Beatles' 'She Loves You' was on the radio all the time. I felt like Christopher Columbus discovering America."

Besombes soon took his first steps in making music: "I spent my time staring through the window pane of the music shop, but it would have been impossible to buy a Fender Stratocaster... instead, I built a home-made electric guitar and started with that."

While his early inspirations came from American rock'n'roll and British beat, as the '60s progressed Besombes discovered jazz before finding his musical touchstone in *musique concrète*. It was Pierre Henry's work that particularly inspired him: "When he worked with arranger-composer Michel Colombier it was the first time we'd heard electronic music mixed with drum sounds. After that he was asked by a record company to 'recompose' an electro-rock album with British group Spooky Tooth. The collaboration was amazing, but I felt there was no cohesion between the group and Pierre... Even if I loved the result, I was disappointed. I wanted to try and do the same."

In 1970 Besombes embarked on two new ventures: he enrolled in chemistry at the CNRS (Centre National de la Recherche Scientifique), and began making music with Jean François Dessoliers, a friend who shared his passion for free jazz and *musique concrète*. Chemistry and music would be parallel pursuits for Besombes until he attained his PhD in '75.

By the time he and Dessoliers began composing music together (under the name PJF) the tape recorder had become Besombes's instrument of choice: "As a composer, I've always felt a deep attachment to sounds, atmosphere, tone... The use of the tape recorder led me to unknown sounds... I could change the speed and tone of the sound. I could slow it down with my hand, make it cry, turn back the tape, cut it and create loops... I realised my own world of sounds."

Besombes's musical and academic activities briefly converged when he discovered surplus electronic equipment being sold off at the neighbouring physics labs. Soon oscillators, signal generators and processors were added to PJF's sonic arsenal. 'PJF 137', an early piece presented at the '71 Paris Biennale, showcases the blend of acoustic instrumentation, tape manipulation, and pure electronics they were able to create.

In '72 they got the opportunity to work with Anne Beranger, creating music for contemporary ballet. This would become Besombes's main focus for the next four years: "Choreographers were the only people who needed the kind of music I was doing. These people were not in the French music business, looking for a hit... It was easy to work together."

Also in '72, Besombes was given was an *entrée* into the world of academic electronic music with his appointment as technical director of the Festival de Musique Contemporaine at La Rochelle. A three-year tenure allowed him to work closely with composers such as Iannis Xenakis, Pierre Boulez, and Karlheinz Stockhausen.[1]

In mid-'72 PJF dissolved. Jean Francois Dessoliers left Paris to continue his studies, while Besombes embarked on a journey through Europe to Turkey, Iran, Afghanistan, and Pakistan ("two months that changed my life").

On his return Besombes struck up a new musical partnership with Jean-Michel Jarre: "Jean Michel was one of my best friends' cousins. We got on well as we shared the same desire to renew electro-acoustic music. Compared to Pierre Henry, Pierre Schaeffer and Bernard

Parmegiani, we were the new generation." They organised a series of live events together, and Jarre put Besombes's name forward to compose a soundtrack.

The film-making collective Groupe Pattern (directors Roland Moreau, Georges Perdriaud and Jean Talansier) had attracted attention with a short film, *Eloah*. They were about to begin their next project, *Libra*, an experimental feature film without any dialogue.[2]

"At this time, I wasn't working for a career; I just wanted to make music I liked... The directors were lovely, so I said okay without very much thought...

"When they shot *Libra*, they did it at their own tempo, without worrying about the music. When they reached the post-production stage, they used Pink Floyd's *Ummagumma*, but didn't have the rights..."

Besombes was given the task of composing a totally new soundtrack that reflected the rhythms and feel of the original pieces ("Pink Floyd, but not Pink Floyd, a nightmare!") He took on the challenge, exploring the electronic/rock hybrid that had caught his imagination in Pierre Henry's work with Spooky Tooth.

"I wanted to work with rock musicians... I called guitarist Patrick Verbeck, drummer Jean François Leroi, bassist Alain Legros and... Alan Jack[3], a Hammond organist. Once finished we were far from the music played by Pink Floyd. The filmmakers liked it."

Besombes began work on the soundtrack in '73, but the pace was dictated by Groupe Pattern's finances, so it wouldn't be completed for almost two years.[4] In the meantime Besombes continued to develop contacts in the world of contemporary dance. In '74 he began working with American choreographer Carolyn Carlson, who had just become director of the Groupe de Recherches Théatrales of the Paris Opera (GRTOP): "She was looking for half electronic and acoustic music - exactly what I was doing." Besombes created scores for a number of GRTOP ballets.[5]

Working with the high-profile choreographer brought Besombes much more work in dance, but at a cost: "It was hard working with Carlson. It was good at first, but got less amusing when she took scissors to tape whenever it suited her. Every musician she worked with had a nervous breakdown afterwards."

1975 was a pivotal year for Besombes. He completed his academic studies with the award of a PhD, but he'd already decided to devote himself to a career in music.⁶ Early in the year he worked with Luc Ferrari⁷, and began a collaboration with Brigitte Lefevre, the choreographer of the La Rochelle-based Le Théâtre du Silence.⁸

An eventful year culminated in two fateful encounters. Besombes met sound engineer Jean-Louis Rizet during the staging of a ballet at the Théâtre de la Ville, and they quickly began working together. Then, later in the year, he came across the founder of Pôle Records: "Paul Putti was a bit of a nutcase, a business tycoon with a futuristic vision, but something of a megalomaniac. He'd created a label called Pôle and produced groups that absolutely had to be called 'Pôle'! He didn't check the quality of recordings as long as musicians agreed to put 'Pôle' on the album."

Putti released Besombe's soundtrack for *Libra* on Pôle Records in late-'75, and the next project, a double album recorded with Jean-Louis Rizet (unsurprisingly titled *Pôle*) would be released on Pôle the following year.

In '74 Besombes had set up his own recording studio, Studios du Chesnay, in the west of Paris. In '75 Rizet joined him in running the business, and they pooled their resources to expand the sonic possibilities of the studio. Rizet had a friend who imported instruments into France and they were given the opportunity to experiment with a plethora of synthesisers.

To this point Besombes had created his soundscapes using pure electronics and tape manipulation, and he was ambivalent about the change of technique: "Synths weren't the soul of my music, they were just a help when I needed certain electronic sounds." In spite of these misgivings the new album became something of a showcase for contemporary electronic instruments.⁹

Even with the abundance of electronic sounds the duo made sure to include acoustic instruments: sax (Alain Petit), drums (Jacky Vander Elstraete), and vocals (Françoise Legros). Rizet also contributed flute, trumpet, and guitar while Besombes played accordion and guitar.

"The Besombes-Rizet record attempts to humanise technology, with a constant mix between performed parts and added sonics. We were trying to convey the message that music has to have a soul."

When the album was released in '76 the duo had no commercial expectations: "We were making fringe music and money wasn't our priority."

However Pôle's unorthodox distribution system (an army of students selling albums door-to-door) managed to rack up somewhere between 10,000 and 20,000 sales. Unfortunately Putti's accounting was as improvised as his distribution method: "They sold carloads of records with this technique, and at the end of the day the profits were shared equally between Putti and the students. So, as you can imagine, there wasn't a single franc for the ones who actually wrote the music!"

The partnership between Rizet and Besombes broke down when another, more mainstream, band entered the picture: "Rizet and I divorced after he married Au Bonheur des Dames. The band wanted us to merge studios and relocate to their place. I didn't want to be their resident flunky, spending the rest of my life recording Au Bonheur des Dames. But Rizet was different, and he ended up living right next to their studio."

After years of writing music in collaboration with musicians and choreographers, Besombes decided it was time to concentrate on his own project. He entered into a lengthy period of experimentation: "It wasn't so easy to swap from pure electro-acoustics with no [beat] to a structured music, and still stay faithful to my feelings." In the next year he amassed over 500 hours of musical ideas stored on tape.

The outcome of this process was Hydravion, a band project giving Besombes license to combine sequenced electronics, rock music, and 'sampled' sounds played from tape. He was joined by the gloriously-named guitarist, Cooky Rhinoceros, whose unusual style was the catalyst Besombes needed: "He was one of the best guitarists I ever heard... He was playing a double-neck Gibson SG 6-string and 12-string and was using the resonating of the 12 strings to produce incredible sound.

"He had a very strange style, working in atonal scales that obviously grate in blues or rock, but were wonderful as I very often work at the boundaries of a key."

An eponymous album was recorded between October '76 and November '77 at Besombes's studio with bassplayer Christ Saint Roch, guitarist Patrick Verbeck, and drummers Pierre Bataillet and Dominique Esnault. When it was released by Cobra at the end of '77 *Hydravion* was lauded by reviewers.

Rock en Stock wrote: "The music on offer here is more rich and varied than that coming from Germany, and more lively and original than that of Jean-Michel Jarre."

While the reviews were good, it was the reaction of television programmers that drove its success, with many of the tracks from *Hydravion* featured as theme tunes on popular series.

Unfortunately Hydravion's second album, *Stratos Airlines*, released in '79, wasn't able to repeat the success of the debut: "It was in the middle of disco, electronic music, and Jean-Michel Jarre was signed to the same label. But my music was not as commercial as his, and I wasn't married to a famous actress. This is the music business after all..."

Besombes decided it was time to invest in his studio and production work: "It didn't cost me to finish my career as a musician. At the time we were flying by the seat of our pants a bit, so I continued to have a life in music, but behind the console." He relocated Studios du Chesnay to Versailles and built a successful career as a sound engineer, producer, and studio manager.

Before this, however, Bescombes was able to finally release his early music on the album *Ceci et Cela*: "I was proud to put this ballet music on a record... For me, it was the way to release all the things that were not published at this time. It was the moment to turn a page in my music."

Philippe Besombes made sporadic returns as a recording musician. His library record La guerre des animaux *was released in '82, then after a gap of almost twenty years he re-emerged with a very successful series of instrumental albums for children. He died in 2018, at the age of 72.*

Jean-Louis Rizet made a career as a sound engineer and producer in the '70s and '80s before branching into animation in the '90s. His recording credits include Jean-Philippe Goude's Drones, *Georges Grunblatt's* K-Pris, *and the* Video-Liszt *collaboration between Richard Pinhas and Hervé Picart. He died in 2021, at the age of 72.*

Notes

1 The most important connection he made was with Xenakis: "He appreciated my work both as a sound engineer and as a composer, and he very soon took me under his wing and often called on me." However, others didn't make such a good impression: "Working with Stockhausen was never pleasurable. He made me a lot of money, and I thank him for that, but I didn't admire him as a person. His behaviour reminded me of the Germany of a certain era...."

2 The film depicts the story of four youngsters living in communion with nature, an idyllic life shattered when an American satellite crashes in the area.

3 Alan Jack and Patrick Verbeck had both been members of Alan Jack Civilization.

4 "Afterwards I worked for the same directors, Groupe Pattern, on other short films in a friendly and interesting environment."

5 These included the music for the ballets *Trio, Pawa 1, L'Or des fous,* and *Synthetik*.

6 His priorities are illustrated by the fact that Besombes went straight from a long studio session to face the academic panel judging his PhD thesis: "I pulled an all-nighter and showed up for the exam wearing flares and with a beard."

7 In early '75 Ferrari invited Besombes to join L'atelier de Libération de la Musique. The improvising ensemble performed a series of multimedia concerts at art galleries around Paris. In 2018 Alga Marghen released an album of their rehearsals that were recorded Feb-Mar '75.

8 The scores for *Ceci est Cela, Traversée,* and *Seul* were the outcome of that collaboration.

9 The roll-call of equipment is formidable. It includes an EMS VCS3, ARP 2600, EML Electrocomp 101, Farfisa Synthorchestra, Oberheim Expander, Solina String Ensemble, and a Mellotron M400. Besombes was particularly taken with the Mellotron and would later become their French agent.

HELDON

> I make the music I like - it isn't up to me to go to the people, it's up to them to come to me... The perspective from which I make my music is to shatter people... I deliver a discourse that's not formed from words, but is persuasive, and against which there is no argument.
>
> *Richard Pinhas*

At the beginning of the '70s Richard Pinhas was at the Sorbonne working towards a doctorate in philosophy, in what seemed to be the perfect *entrée* to an academic career.

"I started university in '68 when I was just seventeen. It was mainly a debt I owed to my grandfather, who really wanted one of his grandsons to have a good diploma. I began in history, completed a Masters degree in sociology, then changed to philosophy and did my PhD with Lyotard. It was a great time in France with great professors like Deleuze, Lacan, Foucault, Lyotard.[1]

"While working on my PhD I did some teaching, but I hated it! I'm a very bad teacher, even on guitar... I always have the idea in my mind that people already know whatever I can teach them. *(laughs)*"

Rather than a career in academia, Pinhas had already decided his vocation was in music. In '73, while still studying, he had approached a British record label with demos of tracks that would feature on the first Heldon LP: "I had only one obsession, I absolutely wanted to be on the same label as King Crimson and Brian Eno...

"I went to see Muff Winwood at EG Management in England. He told me, 'Well, we're really interested, but you'll have to wait for a year'. I was twenty-two, I was in a hurry so I didn't wait. But I have a beautiful letter from him. *(laughs)*"

Only a few months after completing his PhD, Pinhas released the first Heldon album, *Electronique Guerrilla*.

While Pinhas definitively chose a career in music over philosophy, he still views the two fields as irrevocably linked. In a 2009 interview he asserted: "These are the two realms in which, and by which, I live... For more than thirty years I've believed that there is no music without philosophy and no philosophy without music. They are equally important in my process of creation." [2]

The title of Pinhas's PhD thesis was "The Unconscious, Science Fiction, and other Machines". Science Fiction, in particular the conceptual worlds of Philip K. Dick and Norman Spinrad, is another major influence on Pinhas, and the music of Heldon[3]: "We are living in Philip K. Dick's world today. He had a prophetic vision of the world, sixty years ago, that has became real today. He's like one of our last prophets.

"I had the chance to meet Norman Spinrad in New York and get to know him. The name Heldon came from his book *The Iron Dream*[4]."

While his extra-musical influences are idiosyncratic, Pinhas's early musical influences were fairly typical for a guitarist of his generation: "Of course Jimi Hendrix was the most important - I saw him play seven times, and met him too.[5] So Hendrix first, Clapton, Peter Green, and the Three Kings [Freddy King, B.B. King, and Albert King]. I was mainly influenced by so-called British blues - what was originally black American blues."

Pinhas's musical tastes went well beyond blues: "I started listening to the minimalists, like Steve Reich, at fifteen or sixteen. Before that I listened to modern classical music, like Stockhausen[6], and The Beatles of course! *(laughs)* My father took me to see them in '64." As the '70s dawned, two bands rose to prominence in Pinhas's musical life: "I was very fond of Soft Machine - they were way ahead of anything at the time, in sound, texture, everything... Then of course King Crimson."

King Crimson and guitarist Robert Fripp were major touchstones for Heldon's early music. Pinhas has always openly acknowledged this, even going so far as to dedicate individual pieces to them.[7] Fripp's work with Brian Eno became even more influential: "I was able to see a lot of King Crimson concerts around '72. Before and after each concert they played a deeply simple, metallic, and repetitive music... which made a lasting impression on me." Some time later he realised this music was from the Fripp & Eno collaboration *No Pussyfooting*, which he considers to be "one of the *chef d'oeuvre* (masterpieces) of the 20th Century... equivalent to Ravel or Debussy."

This eclectic mix of musical and extra-musical influences led

Heldon down a highly individual path forging it into one of the most distinctive bands to emerge from '70s France. Pinhas also became one of France's most prolific artists of that decade, releasing ten albums in just five years.[8]

* * *

Schizo

Richard Pinhas began playing semi-professionally at sixteen, working with singer Klaus Blasquiz: "I met Klaus in '67. We played in a little band in Saint-Tropez for a month, performing every night." The pair then joined Blues Convention, a heavy blues-rock group that became a fixture on the Parisian club circuit. It would record a number of singles in the early '70s, but by then Pinhas and Blasquiz had already left. In '69 they formed a new band, named Stuff, but it came to a premature end when Blasquiz was tempted away by a promising new group: "Klaus went to Magma. I was actually at the recording of the first Magma album at Philips." [9]

Pinhas occupied himself with his studies for the next few years. Then in '71 he formed Schizo with brothers Pierrot and Coco Roussel, the rhythm section from Royal Show. They were joined by singer Olivier Pamela, synth player Georges Grunblatt, and pianist Patrick Gauthier.[10] During its short lifespan the band released two singles. The first, 'Schizo (And The Little Girl)', was a hard-rocking psychedelic track driven by Pinhas's relentless guitar and strong (English) vocals from Olivier Pamela.[11]

Pamela had left by the recording of the next single, so a guest vocalist features on 'Le Voyageur': philosopher Gilles Deleuze. "I didn't know Deleuze very well at the time. We found ourselves in the studio one day without really knowing what we were going to do... I gave Gilles a badly cut-out text and suggested that he read it.[12] He agreed to play along..." The band backed Deleuze's recitation of Nietzsche with a moody, psych-rock groove given a jazzy edge by Gauthier's distorted Rhodes piano.

This single was produced to be given away: "I'd met an actor from Germany, Mathieu Carrière, at Deleuze's courses at Vincennes University and we became friends. I proposed this project to him - if you have money and there's a good project, you give it, no? He paid for pressing 2000 records, and we offered it to the people for free. Not for promotion, just as a militant act of faith. *(laughs)*"

Schizo disbanded in late-'72, just before 'Le Voyageur' was released. For the next two years Pinhas was mainly focused on completing his doctorate, but he also nurtured a growing fascination with synthesisers: "I was listening to a Herbie Hancock album, and there were some very strange sounds that I really loved. I wanted to find out what was making them: it was a synthesiser.

"It was a shock to me… What attracted me to synths was their capacity to create texture in sound."

In addition to their sonic possibilities, Pinhas was attracted by the new paradigm of music creation they inspired. In an early interview he noted: "I try to push the use of synthesisers to the extremes. I'm fascinated by… pure sound. I want to create a kind of music that would be impossible to attach images to, a totally cold music: an immense block of ice. The synthesiser is a mirror, everyone using it sees their own image. For me it doesn't have to convey emotions or feelings."

The Birth of Heldon

Heldon's first album, the outcome of several years of experimentation, was recorded in Pinhas's apartment.[13] *Electronique Guerrilla* is essentially a solo record, featuring Pinhas playing guitar and a VCS3 synthesizer. The only exceptions are a guitar duet with Alain Renaud[14] and a reprise of Schizo's 'Le Voyageur' (remixed and renamed 'Ouais, Marchais, mieux qu'en 68'). Pinhas had originally hoped to make the album with ex-Soft Machine drummer, Robert Wyatt: "He said yes, but we didn't have the money to rent a studio or to pay for him to come over. *(laughs)*" In recognition of his readiness to participate, the LP is dedicated to Wyatt.

The opening tracks ('Zind' and 'Back to Heldon')[15] show how far Pinhas had progressed since Schizo. Synthesiser is to the fore, and when guitar finally appears it snakes through interlocking layers of synth with an unmistakably Frippian tone. 'Circulus Vitiosus', on Side 2, provides the blueprint for Heldon's musical development. Interlocking synth arpeggios are overlaid with languid fuzz guitar, creating a sonic Möbius strip. This creates the impression that the piece is extracted from an eternal music, with no discernible beginning or end.

The raw, unadorned use of synthesiser on *Electronique Guerrilla* is striking. Pinhas makes no attempt to soften the alienating, mechanical impact of the instrument. There is no Kraftwerkian melodicism or Enoesque ambience in Heldon's music; here the synthesiser is unapologetically a machine. This is an aesthetic that wasn't normalised in popular music until Acid House and Techno emerged a decade later.

Rock en Stock noted how distinct the sound of Heldon's debut was: "Despite being created with the same equipment... it was nothing like the music coming from Germany... This led to confusion amongst those who couldn't resist the urge to associate Heldon with German [*kosmische*] music." Pinhas points out that he was in fact unaware of the German scene: "To be honest, I only found out about people like Klaus Schulze, Tangerine Dream etc. four years after the first album. I love the first four Tangerine Dream albums and the first two solo albums, but I wasn't making that kind of music. It was too soft. I wanted something like a guerrilla music, something that really moves you."

The guerrilla aspect of Heldon's music was also reflected in the radical way it was produced and distributed: "I released *Electronique Guerrilla* on a label I set up myself, because I wanted to know every step of the process." By creating both a home recording studio and record label, Pinhas become an early pioneer of DIY music. Disjuncta Records, run by Pinhas and guitarist Alain Renaud[16], pressed 1000 copies of the album and distributed it by mail order and through sympathetic record stores.

"We had an immediate stroke of luck. The album got airplay on the radio... and we very quickly did shows like *Pop Club* on France Inter... But it was the magazines that were particularly important: *Actuel*, *Rock & Folk*, *Best*, and so on."

The unexpected media support resulted in over 10,000 sales, more than enough to fund the release of another album.

Heldon II: Allez-Teia[17] was released less than six months later. Pinhas recorded it in collaboration with his ex-Schizo band-mate Georges Grünblatt. The expanded line-up of synthesisers listed on the cover suggests the electronic quotient would be raised, but nothing could have been further from the truth. Heldon's sophomore outing is something of an anomaly in its catalogue: an almost pastoral record focused firmly on guitar, which is often bathed in swirls of lush Mellotron strings. The music on *Allez-Teia* is contemplative, melancholy, and quite beautiful, but it lacks the hardness and underlying menace that would come to characterise Heldon.

The necessary corrective came with *Heldon Third: It's Always Rock & Roll*, a double album recorded between December '74 and March '75. Here Pinhas was joined by a number of guest musicians including Georges Grunblatt, Alain Renaud, Patrick Gauthier, Ariel Kalma, Jean-My Truong (Zao), and Gilbert Artman (Lard Free).

"We recorded it after having met with Philip K. Dick in California for two days. This was such an event for a twenty-three-year old... We talked about Jung, we talked about a lot of things. Maybe this encounter gave birth to all of *Heldon Third*."

The album introduces several elements that would be integral to the band's evolution. First was Patrick Gauthier's first appearance with Heldon: "Richard phoned and said come and play a Minimoog solo. Why not? It was very interesting to play with Magma and Richard at the same time - it was so different... With Magma, everything was notated, but with Richard it was a more anarchic situation."

While Gauthier doesn't consider himself to have ever truly been a member of Heldon, he is featured on every album from this point onwards. Pinhas: "Patrick is like a brother to me. When he had time he came and played, he's such a gifted guy that he can do anything in two minutes."

The second development was the introduction of live drumming courtesy of Jean-My Truong and Gilbert Artman.[18] This was a major evolutionary step, and became a core feature of Heldon's sound. The claustrophobic atmosphere conjured when Truong's churning drums pile on to Pinhas's cyclic synth riffs at the end of 'Dr. Bloodmoney' is a foretaste of the future.

When *Heldon Third* was released in mid-'75, *Rock & Folk* praised the band's evolution: "[This album] represents a culmination... when Pinhas is concise he absolutely succeeds in creating an atmosphere of violence: in 'Mechamment Rock', 'Cocaine Blues' (it must have been a rough come-down!), and the electric 'Bouille Blues'... This is synthesiser-based music that is completely different to the [tedium] of German *kosmische*."

In its first twelve months Heldon had released three albums, but had not yet played live. Their public debut was finally made on 7 June '75 at the massive Fete du PSU. "We played just before Claude Nougaro. It was only myself and Alain Renaud. We had an ARP, a Mellotron, and were both playing guitar. Luckily I need glasses to see anything in the distance *(laughs)* because there were 80,000 people in the stadium. The sun was going down, and thankfully I couldn't see them because that would have made it impossible for me to play." [19]

Heldon would tour with Lard Free later that year, but live performances remained a rarity.

At the end of '75 Pinhas gave up the reins at Disjuncta. In eighteen months the label had released seven albums (including Alain Renaud's debut and Zao's *Osiris*). "I realised it wasn't my vocation to run a record label... so I sold it to someone who made it Urus Records. I gave up the label on the condition that Alain Renaud had enough to record his next album... and I wanted a modular Moog." [20]

Disjuncta's last action was to release Heldon's 'Baader Meinhof Blues' as a single, distributed free of charge like Schizo's 'Le Voyager'. Thus the life of the label was bookmarked by equivalent acts ('Le Voyager' had actually been the first record to carry the Disjuncta imprint): "[Music] is irredeemably political... To give away a disc is to at least partially break the relations of exchange imposed by Kapital."

The single was also political in a more literal way, as it was recorded in support of the jailed members of the Red Army Faction.[21] "Make no mistake, we weren't at all in the political line of the Red Army Faction. I have never been a Leninist... but there was the story of the trial... Incidentally, I distributed the disc in the army barracks when I was doing my required three days there."

Heldon Finds its Voice

In its first two years Heldon was in effect Richard Pinhas's solo project. The albums featured musical collaborations, but Heldon had no real group identity. In '75 he told Gérard Nguyen: "For the time being I don't think that it's necessary to have a band to make this kind of music. One day that might come. I've tried things with a group - drums, bass etc, and it was a total mess... I don't see the point in doing things in a group that you can do alone." This began to change with Heldon's next album.

Agneta Nilsson was recorded between September '75 and January '76, and is most definitely a transitional album. While mostly recorded in Pinhas's home studio, for the first time he was able to hire a professional recording studio. "[It] marked the end of an era for me. A period in which I mainly played alone, where I had written a kind of chamber music.

"I'd realised that the best idea was to have electronic instruments with a real drummer and real musicians at the same time. But it couldn't be done because everything was recorded at my home. A studio cost $1000 to $2000 a day at the time *(laughs)*, so it was difficult."

Pinhas took Patrick Gauthier, drummer Coco Roussel, and bassist Alain Bellaiche into Studio Davout to record 'Perspective IV', which fills Side 2 of the album. The final section of 'Dr Bloodmoney' on *Heldon Third* had hinted at the future, while 'Perspective IV' created the template for Heldon's evolution.

Only half of the evolution evident on *Agneta Nilsson* was due to access to a professional studio. The acquisition of a new synthesiser might seem to be of little consequence, but Pinhas's Moog modular fundamentally changed his approach to electronic music. "It became an immovable monster covering my living room wall. You had to take time to construct the slightest sound, opening the way to things that had never been done before. I experienced electronics as a kind of neural connection..."

The bulk of the machinery seemed to add a corresponding heft to the music. It had first been evident on 'Baader Meinhof Blues' where the sonic density of the Moog perfectly matched the drive of Pinhas's overdriven guitar.

Pinhas has tended to downplay the albums Heldon made before *Agneta Nilsson*: "I like the first album, it was a really good attempt. I think *Heldon 2* is too smooth. *Heldon 3* was a chance to play with other musicians, and to try something like a disjointed blues, you know. *(laughs)* I started to be happy around *Heldon 4*."

After the session at Studio Davout, Pinhas had a fateful encounter with its owner, Yves Chamberland: "When I went to pay him for the session he said, 'Oh, you're an honest musician!' Then he said, 'Look, what you do is impossible to sell, so take the key and do what you want'. *(laughs)* So we had the keys for the best studio in Paris. He just asked me to do some sessions on synthesiser for other people."

The arrangement allowed Pinhas to permanently move his gear into Studio Davout, and gave him free access to the studio during downtime. "We were playing every night. That allowed us to record all of the other Heldon albums, Patrick Gaultier's first LP, and even half an album for Jannick Top." [22]

The first Heldon album made under this arrangement was *Un rêve sans conséquence spéciale* recorded from March to June '76. Heldon's music had already transcended the early influence of Robert Fripp, and here Pinhas deliberately chose the name (it was the title of a popular King Crimson bootleg) to mark the fact: "... it was a way to say: this is a legacy, and here I've finished with this legacy."

The significance of this album is hard to overstate. It was the first to be recorded entirely at Davout, the first to feature drummer François Auger[23], and the first to fully reflect Pinhas's musical vision.

Auger's contribution would be crucial to every subsequent Heldon record. In '78 Pinhas stated: "[He is] essential to Heldon's creative process. François is as important as I am... I don't envisage making 'new' music without him." Pinhas had found his rhythmic muse in Auger, and together they would form the core of Heldon.

With the exception of Auger's composition 'Elephanta', the pieces on *Un rêve sans conséquence spéciale*) are recorded by different trios - with Patrick Gauthier, Jannick Top, and Didier Batard holding down the bass position (Gauthier using his Minimoog in that role). This set the scenario for Heldon's future development as an electronic power-trio.

After this recording Heldon was established as a group made up of four musicians: Richard Pinhas, François Auger, Didier Batard, and Patrick Gauthier. However it would generally operate as a power-trio in concert, and on most recordings.

Un rêve sans conséquence spéciale was a manifesto of musical intent that finally expressed the symphonic power that Heldon had previously hinted at. Reviewers were stunned by the raw power of the record.

Best: "A dream or a nightmare? More the second, as there is nothing enchanting about this record... Pinhas has combined the lessons of free jazz with the lessons of metallic rock... he hasn't chosen the easy road, but has truly created something out of the ordinary."

Atem: "Abysses. Apocalypses. Tormented sounds, senses, robot brains. This album is impossible to describe, there is no point of reference... I love it, then I don't. It scares me."

Fear. Nightmares. Violence. These reactions corresponded to Pinhas's intentions. The sleeve of the record quoted from the book *Nietzsche and the Vicious Circle:* "... in the experimental domain to create is to do violence to what exists, and thus to the integrity of beings. Every creation of a new type must provoke a state of insecurity..."[24]

Just after the album's release Pinhas commented: "On the first four discs my goal was to attain a certain kind of violence that I couldn't reach... Here I had sufficient time to record and think, and I believe that I reached a first draft of what I wanted, music with a degree of violence it had never really had before."

He discussed this sonic terrorism further in another interview: "We have always experienced our music as a war machine, pure sound, which aims to shatter certain lines of permanence to put in place pure intensities... This production is a violence, the violence of a war machine in the process of creating its own lines of activation."

Pinhas's talk of violence and war machines may seem unusual, but the social context of the time is essential to understand it: "Violence can change society. You know, this was just after '68, and in France there was still a strong [social] movement until '78."

In 1981 Pinhas told *Rock & Folk* that the pursuit of sonic violence was something he'd moved on from: "At that point, my philosophical theories were for a kind of reversal of perspectives at a 'social' level, at least an attempt at that; and that's no longer the case... As the saying goes, 'before changing the world, you have to change the problem'."

Un rêve sans conséquence spéciale has an important place as the most extreme expression of Pinhas's intent to create a music of violent rupture. In the same 1981 interview Pinhas expressed some pride in that achievement: "In the history of electronic music, *Un rêve sans conséquence spéciale* represented a break. It was the first album in the world of hard electronic music - it was seen that way in America, as industrial music. It was also the first experiment to integrate drum-bass-style rock and synthesisers. It was only the beginning..."

It's no accident that at exactly the moment Pinhas realised his vision for Heldon he also began to produce his first solo albums. From this point onwards Heldon would be reserved for the "symphonic" side of Pinhas's musical output, and his "chamber music" would be released under his own name. "The solo records are constructed according to a totally different process... it's another mode of expression, more 'charming', needing neither the same means of recording nor the same time to prepare... It's a pleasant music... another aspect of sonic creation."

The first to be released (in early '77) was *Rhizosphere*, but the first to be recorded, *Chronolyse*, was created in parallel with the sessions for *Un rêve sans conséquence spéciale*. It illustrates the other pole of Pinhas's new musical paradigm - with most tracks creating an almost glacial ambience constructed from pure electronics. "It was initially meant to be an all-Moog album... The majority of the tracks (Side 1 on the original *Chronolyse* LP) were made using only a big Moog 3P... They flowed in a natural way, just like in a dream, and I recorded them in a very simple way, direct to stereo, no re-recording."

The second side of the album featured just one 30-minute track, 'Paul Atreides', for which Pinhas took his home-recorded tape into Davout Studios to add mellotron and guitar, with Didier Batard and François Auger providing bass and drums. It was the first long-form track to feature the Pinhas/Auger/Batard trio.

Both *Chronolyse* and *Rhizosphere* would follow this pattern - a side of stripped-back solo performances, with an extended track with extra instrumentation on the second side. Tellingly both of these extended tracks would find their way into Heldon's live sets.

Best lauded the album: "The two sides of *Chronolyse* are very different. The first, a remarkable experiment in cyclic music, offers seven variations on the same piece. Every time we hear different colours and rhythms, and every time we discover something new... The second is more emotional, based on atmospheres and expanses produced by a guitar-bass-drum foundation, supported by waves of electronics... it displays Pinhas's talent of unleashing sounds so amazing they take you by the throat, and leave you breathless... proving once again that he is one of the cleverest, most daring, creators of European music."

Maturity

The next Heldon album, *Interface*, was the first completely recorded by the new core unit of Pinhas, Gauthier, Batard and Auger. The experience of recording two solo albums seems to have informed Pinhas's new music, because *Interface* leavens the claustrophobic violence of *Un Reve* with some of the melodicism and ambience of his solo work. An almost perfect balance is attained, making *Interface* both an essential Heldon album, and arguably their most approachable and satisfying release. There is even a light-hearted moment when Pinhas nods to his blues heritage in the final grooves: "We were finishing the track, the tape was rolling, and I started to play a normal boogie... I think it was a good idea to keep it."

When *Interface* was released the critical reaction was unanimously positive.

Atem: "Heldon mercilessly crush every false pretense... their approach is essential, exemplary and unequivocal... This record will sweep away any reservation you have about electronics, the pulse of the blues, or the coldness of minimalist music, because it goes beyond every genre..."

Best: "Heldon has not only freed itself from its influences... with *Interface* it has boldly taken the lead. No-one has dared to go this far in electronic music, not Schulze, nor Tangerine Dream... It is *completely new* music... While others shuffle along, Pinhas and his companions have cleared the way to unconquered sonic spaces."

Heldon became a more consistent presence on the live circuit after the album's release: "We started playing a lot more, and it was quite a success. But we never had more than three people on stage. I used the big Moog, the big EMU, and the mellotron. The Moog weighed 350 kilos and needed four or five people to move it!"

Rock en Stock reviewed one of these concerts (at Salle Gaveau): "Enhanced by the Laser de Trapèze[25], the music reached truly astounding moments... The crucial point was 'Marie-Virginie C', a powerful, elephantine piece that closed the concert, with Richard wrestling squealing notes from his guitar, infusing the air with supernatural sparks..."

The logistics and economics of touring meant that over time live performances again became rarities. In '79 Pinhas told *Best*: "With all the technology at our disposal... we have the means for our live performance to be at the same standard as our records. But French organisers are too sloppy.... and most of the time we can't even cover our costs. We aren't even talking about profitability..."

The release of *Interface* coincided with the rise of punk rock, and Pinhas was surprised to find his music embraced by the new wave of

French bands: "That was a strange thing. Two bands, Metal Urbain and Asphalt Jungle, asked me to produce them. I was very interested to see what I could do at the service of their music. For example, when we came into the studio there were eighteen mics on the drum kit. I took them all away until only two were left. The drummer from the band was very pleased. *(laughs)*"

His influence flowed on to the emerging industrial music scene. In '78 *Atem* noted: "It's satisfying to see the most extreme contemporary groups (Throbbing Gristle, Chrome, etc.) following the path already cleared by Heldon, a band that an American magazine called 'the first electronic punk group'."

Before recording the final Heldon album, Pinhas released a single under the name THX - a cover version of The Tornados' hit 'Telstar'. "It was a dream for me to record. It's one of the two pieces that made me want to make music: 'Telstar' and 'The Last Time' by The Rolling Stones. One day Patrick and I had some free studio time. He played the melody, and I did all the work on the Moog system. We finished it in two hours."

Stand By, Heldon's seventh album, was recorded between April and October '78 at Studio Davout. The production credit was shared between Pinhas and Auger, showing just how integral the drummer had become to the band. For the first time Heldon's power-trio conception was jettisoned, and the entire album was recorded by the full four-piece.

Interface had seen Pinhas integrate his entire artistic vision into a thrillingly *new* music, and this next album took that process to its logical conclusion. *Stand By* is Heldon's ultimate record, in both senses. As a final word it stands without any need of addendum or explanation.

Whether it was intended or not, the two tracks penned by Richard Pinhas packed the entire Heldon experience into thirty-five thrilling minutes. The side-long 'Bolero' takes the synthesiser-driven aspect of Heldon to multiple peaks over its eight parts (two of which are credited to Auger). The title track then pushes the energy over the red line. On 'Stand By' Heldon sound as close to a traditional guitar-driven power-trio as they ever would. Pinhas plays only guitar on the track, with the synthesiser played by Patrick Gauthier, mostly in a backing role. Pinhas plays guitar with more power, concision, and suppleness than ever before, effortlessly moving from post-Hendrix pyrotechnics to post-punk riffage. Mid-track he even includes a short section that uncannily prefigures Robert Fripp's '80s guitar work.

Patrick Gauthier's composition 'Une drole de la journée' is an interesting inclusion, as it is very much written in his voice. It could have easily have been included on the Weidorje album, but here it's a welcome diversion .

Klaus Blasquiz guests on the album. On Gauthier's composition he plays a familiar role, providing some subtle Magmaesque vocalisation. However his major contribution is on 'Bolero', where his unmistakable voice is totally masked by a vocoder. The wonderfully absurd conceit of transforming such an overpoweringly *human* voice into a mechanical drone works perfectly.

Stand By was released in April '79 on Egg Records, and once again was met with reviews filled with superlatives.

Atem: "Heldon had achieved a remarkable technical and musical feat, with a power that rivals King Crimson's 'Red'... The musicians are cohesive and have that rare thing: a *sound*. Making no concessions, Heldon's music continues to be among the most original there is... It's fortunate that there are still people who believe that integrity will eventually pay off. *Stand By* is Heldon's superb gift to 1979."

Not long after the album was released the classic Heldon line-up broke up: "François was very important for me, and I loved playing with Didier. But after two or three years they said: 'We have to make money playing sessions, it was a good experience, but we have to stop'. So I stopped using the name Heldon because it was not the same musicians."

Pinhas released three more albums under his own name before his temporary retirement from music in '83. The first, *Iceland*, was a true solo album in the line of *Chronolyse* and *Rhizosphere*. It was released in '79, but had been recorded during the sessions for *Stand By:* "When the guys went for two hours to get some food I stayed in the studio and did things by myself *(laughs)*. And at the end I had a full album."

The other albums were in a similar vein to the Heldon albums, but Pinhas had resolved not to use the name without the presence of Auger and Batard: "*East West* and *L'ethique* could have been Heldon albums. They were made the same way but with other musicians - [Bernard] Paganotti on bass, and people from Magma."

After *L'ethique* was released in '82, Pinhas had made the decision to put his musical career on indefinite hold: "During those years, I was a session musician, working 300 days a year playing synthesiser in the big analog studios. I enjoyed it for four years... But then I stopped making music altogether in '82/'83. I felt I didn't have much to say."

Richard Pinhas returned in '92 with the album, DWW, and has been active since. He has released over thirty records, including collaborations with Pascale Comelade, Masami Akita (Merzbow), Tatsuya Yoshida (Ruins), Wolf Eyes, and Oren Ambarchi. He continues to release records and tour, both in France and internationally.

Notes

1 Pinhas attended Deleuze's lectures at the Université Vincennes from '71 until '87 when the philosopher retired: "I went to university (for Deleuze, not for a diploma) for seventeen years. We were very close, very friendly. I took my car to pick him up from home, and we talked during the trip. He asked me what to do next year. And I said, 'Oh, please do Spinoza for me, or Leibniz'. And he said, 'OK, we'll do that.' *(laughs)*"

2 In an interview for this book Pinhas noted: "Music and philosophy are actually the same thing! The same concept, you know: event, repetition, process. Then you work on the *métier*. And of course, duration is the principle in the process of it all."

3 Pinhas playfully credited the production on Heldon records to characters from their books. Joe Chip and Glenn Runciter, both from Philip K. Dick's *Ubik*, are credited on *Third* and *Agneta Nilsson* respectively.

4 In *The Iron Dream* Spinrad explores an alternate timeline where Adolf Hitler quits Germany for the USA after World War 1. There he becomes a second-rate science fiction author who subsumes his fascist ideology into a book, *Lord of the Swastika*, set in the racially-pure High Republic of Heldon.

5 Pinhas was fourteen when he met Jimi Hendrix in Paris: "The promoter knew that I used the same guitar strings... he calls me: 'Richard, Hendrix would like English strings... could you come to Olympia?' I arrived at the dressing room to give him his strings, and Hendrix says to me: 'Groovy man'."

6 Surprisingly the *musique concrète* of Pierre Schaeffer and Pierre Henry was never important in Pinhas's circle: "No, I don't know anyone who liked that. The minimalists were ten times, twenty times more important!"

7 The first was a less than oblique reference on *Allez-Teia* with a track titled: 'In the Wake of King Fripp'.

8 Between '74 and '79 seven LPs were released by Heldon, and three by Pinhas as a solo artist.

9 The relationship between Pinhas and Magma would continue into the '80s. There was even a family connection: Stella Vander is his cousin.

10 Gauthier would become an important member of the Heldon family: "Richard was my neighbour. When he asked me to play in Schizo I was very pleased. But I was at university studying philosophy. I wasn't thinking about playing professionally, so it was only for fun.

11 Pamela would later provide vocals on the *Delired Camelon Family* LP and on Nyl's eponymous album.

12 The text was cut from Nietzsche's book *Human, All Too Human: A Book For Free Spirits*.

13 This home set-up is christened Schizo Studio on the album sleeve.

14 Alain Renaud (who had been Triangle's original guitarist) recorded a number of solo records in the '70s. The first of these was co-produced by Pinhas, and released on Disjuncta.

15 The titles of both tracks refer to Norman Spinrad's *The Iron Dream*.

16 The label would release seven albums, including Renaud's debut.

17 The title is a play on "aletheia," an ancient Greek word for truth that was revived by philosopher Martin Heidegger.

18 Artman's appearance on 'Mechamment Rock' is notable, as the track is actually a reworking of 'Pâle Violence Under A Réverbère' from Lard Free's second album. Pinhas: "I recorded it first for Lard Free, but I had the idea to take the guitar and some other parts for Heldon. I asked [Gilbert] and he said, 'Yes, you can do what you want'."

19 This early duo incarnation of Heldon is captured on the album *Live in Paris 1975*.

20 Disjuncta's sale funded Alain Renaud's *Out of Time* LP, and the purchase of a Moog modular with significant provenance: "It cost £4000 at the time. Ten years later when I saw it in a photo with George Martin, I couldn't believe it! It was exactly the one we had - the *real* Beatles Moog."

21 Pinhas had already dedicated several tracks to revolutionaries who had been assassinated or died under suspicious circumstances, including Salvador Puig Antich and Omar Diop Blondin.

22 The recording of an entire Jannick Top album was scuppered when he became suspicious of Pinhas's motivations. Before this happened a first studio version of 'De Futura' was completed. The recording was released twenty-five years later on the album *Soleil d'Ork*.

23 "When we met François was purely a studio musician. I played him some of my music and he said, 'Woah! That's great let's try it!' *(laughs)* I think he was the first to play live with a synthesiser, without a beat, and he was incredible! He played like Mitch Mitchell." *(Pinhas)*

24 The book's author was Pierre Klossowski, this quotation is from Daniel W. Smith's translation (University of Chicago Press, 1998).

25 Laser de Trapèze are credited with creating the artwork for the *Iceland* LP.

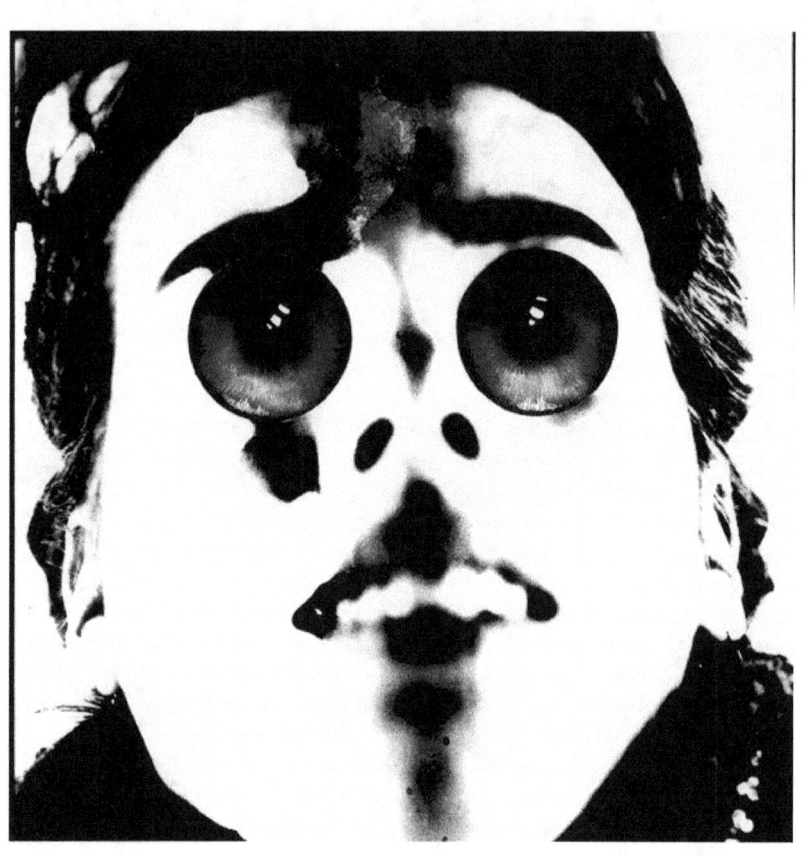

ILITCH

> "I start with a story, an image, a concept, then I improvise with overdubs, *à la* [Brian Eno's] Oblique Strategies. So at the beginning there's an idea of the material, the colour, the intention... I'd say that about eighty percent is improvised, with some albums even completely improvised."
>
> *Thierry Müller*

Thierry Müller's background didn't appear to predispose him to becoming a musician: "There wasn't really a musical atmosphere at home. My father listened to some classical music [and] my older sister listened to French *yé-yé* (Johnny Hallyday, Jacques Dutronc, Françoise Hardy) and English hits (The Beatles, The Rolling Stones, etc.) on her record player... I discovered 'pop music' at the end of the sixties when I was around eleven years old... through radio and TV shows (*Campus, Pop 2*) and magazines (*Rock & Folk, Best*, etc.)."

There was no indication that Müller would develop an interest in making music until a relative came to stay with his family in '69: "My cousin worked for Electricité de France. He was passionate about electroacoustic music, and ran introductory courses to promote this kind of music as part of the EdF Works Council... When he came to Paris with his tape recorders, my brother and I had the opportunity to 'experiment' with tape machines and work with tape. It was one of the triggers in my desire to make music."

Not long afterwards Müller acquired an acoustic guitar, then a small electric organ. He taught himself to play, and began to make music with some high-school friends. His attraction to music was only rivalled by his love of the graphic arts ("As far back as I can remember, I have always drawn") which led him to enter the National School of Applied Arts: "I was there from '74 to '77. At that time, when you entered Applied Arts, you studied a large number of practices: painting, sculpture, typography, design, colors, art history, etc. before turning to a specialisation... These studies allowed me to refine and expand my graphic practice and, of course, make it my work.

"The relationship between music and graphics already existed for me and was interactive. One was inseparable from the other."

The art students he mixed with introduced Müller to new sounds: "My musical tastes at the time went from quality *varieté* to contemporary music, to rock bands like Pink Floyd. My friends from Applied Arts brought their influences, which ranged from jazz to tinkering with electronics, etc."

Quite quickly this musical and artistic mixing led to Müller's first band experience: "The story of Arcane couldn't be more straightforward. It came together at Arts Appliqués in '74. Pascal Potain was in the same class and we liked the same kind of music. He had a friend, Marc Barety, who was also interested in making music. That's how it started. We improvised at Pascal's house; then Frédéric Riches joined us. It was my first group, and lasted a little over a year. We never played live, in fact the idea never crossed our minds.

"I don't think a specific music or style influenced us... [Arcane] was really based on research and experimentation with the means at hand and our capabilities. It was electronic tinkering with what we had access to (recorders, tapes, feedback...), and hitting and blowing into anything that could produce an interesting sound. Only Fred and I had [regular] instruments: he had his flute, I had my guitar and a little Farfisa."

While the group improvised they recorded each session on tape. Müller was able to recover and release three tracks on *Rare and Unreleased 1974-1984*, but most were lost ("I'm sorry we didn't find other recordings, because I remember epic afternoons!")

Müller began to work on his Ilitch project just after beginning his experiments with Arcane, producing the first recordings ('A.B.ss' and 'Micik für brokenpedalboard') in the second half of '74. In hindsight it may seem that Ilitch was designed as a solo endeavour, but this wasn't the original intention: "Ilitch has always been me, my stories, my ravings... I always dreamed that it would become a long-term group, but it didn't.

"To produce under the name Ilitch I need a concept, a strong (generally personal) story... [While] the concepts are personal, I very often called on other musicians, asking them to intervene on my pieces with specific instructions, but without restricting their creativity because, after all, that's why I chose them. On some Ilitch titles that can lead to a joint composition."

The project was studio-based, with Müller recording his ideas directly onto four-track tape. His discomfort with live performance meant that there were only very infrequent forays into the live arena: "I never 'ran' after concerts. The stress before and the almost sickening anxiety during them meant that it really wasn't pleasurable." Nevertheless a rare Ilitch live performance from Spring '75 was recorded, and released in 2011 as the album *Un Jour Comme Tant D'Autres*.

In October and November '75 Müller recorded the material for what he intended to be the first Ilitch LP, made up of the side-long 'Periodikmindtrouble' and three 'Balades Urbaines'.

"I wanted to launch my own project with this album that I saw as a kind of film music. I've always liked the relationship between music and images, whether real or imaginary. Anyway, I never knew how to make music just for the sake of music; it came out of my states of mind as the title of the album indicates...

"I was very tuned in to guitars with long held notes, so at the time that brought me back to [Fripp & Eno and Heldon]... but there was also early Philip Glass and Cecil Taylor. The inspiration for this album was a mixture of all of that."

It would be three years before the album was finally released (in a revised form). In the meantime Müller created the PTM project with his brother Patrick[1], and recorded and released the ultimate limited-edition LP, *Portraits*: "This is my first 'official' album under the Ilitch name, released in '77. They are 'portraits' of girls/women, some of whom were my teenage sweethearts... I had one copy made, a 'collector's edition', which I gave to my girlfriend at the time..."[2]

Müller's main focus in this period was the production of another album, an interlinked sequence of tracks that ran for well over an hour: "*Innerfilmsequences* is a conceptual piece in its own right. Its basis is the composition of scenarios for an imaginary film. The pieces follow one another like the scenes of this 'film'. As for the vast majority of my albums and pieces, they are written from 'visual' stories, whether in still or scenographic images. I had hoped to release them as an album without really knowing how or when."

Müller entered '78 with the music for two albums recorded, but no prospect to release it, until he had a chance encounter: "At the time I was running my own printing company, and Norbert, the creator of Oxygène, contacted us to print his catalog. After some discussions he offered to co-finance and distribute an album."

Müller decided to combine the best tracks from the two recordings for his first release: " 'Periodikmindtrouble' was a no-brainer. On the [other side] I wanted there to be a trace of 'Innerfilmsequences'. It was difficult to make a selection that worked from beginning to end, [but] luckily there were very long pieces, that made it easier for me."

Ilitch's commercial debut was released in the second half of '78, with one review lauding it for picking up the gauntlet laid down by Heldon's first two LPs: "Today there are musicians who appear to take up the legacy where [Pinhas] abandoned it... We noted Verto last month, and this month we must talk of Ilitch's very beautiful album, *Periodikmindtrouble* - without doubt the most successful in the genre since *Allez-Teia*... On Side 1 there are six sequences (from an internal film) where we rediscover the legacy of the undisputed masters, Robert Fripp ('Sequence 4') and Brian Eno... ('Sequence 1', 'Matin d'un Blues'), as well as the delicate ardour of the acoustic pieces from the first Heldon album ('River Scene Theme Variation', 'Derriere la Fenêtre')... [Side 2] opens explosively with broken and strident organ that would please both Cecil Taylor and XTC. Then, almost imperceptibly, chaos becomes organised and leads into a long track reminiscent of Riley's *Persian Surgery Dervishes*; although Riley's music swirls continuously while 'Periodikmindtrouble' has the immobility of Philip Glass..."

When the album was released it credited the recording and mixing to Ruth Ellyeri. Müller: "Ha! The Ruth Ellyeri Mystery! Ruth M. Ellyeri is an anagram of Thierry Müller, a female double... It was a game to express another part of me, more extroverted, more pop, and more feminine. I had created several anagrams at the time, but I only used the one that represented the side of my personality that I wanted to express. Maybe one day I'll have the opportunity to use the others."

In what had been a pivotal year, Müller also worked on the soundtrack to the film *Ceux qui résistent c'est les bons* with Alain Gaillot (under the name Breaking Point), and recorded 'Mescalito', his first track as Ruth[3], which was released on the Oxygène compilation *125 grammes de 33⅓ tours*. Another important event in '78 was the beginning of his musical relationship with Philippe Doray.

"I met Philippe at the launch party for the Oxygène label. We each had the same reaction: we'd fallen in love with each other's albums... We talked, one thing led to another, and we found a lot of common points (music, literature). We decided to work together on each other's projects. I moved onto the farm he shared with other musicians near Rouen, and [that's] where we created the duo Crash."

Müller's story continued into the '80s. He released the second Ilitch album, *10 Suicides*, at the beginning of the decade, then the LP *Polaroid/Romans/Photos* (credited to Ruth) in '85.

"I wasn't following the contemporary sound at all when I made my records. [You can compare] *Periodikmindtrouble* or *10 Suicides* to the minimalism of Fripp & Eno or the electronics of Throbbing Gristle (and frankly, I accept the comparison!) but I was trying to do something a bit different. Perhaps that's why these records are still appreciated today."

In the mid-'80s Müller stopped making records to devote himself to a career in the graphic arts, becoming the artistic director for publishers, magazines, and cultural organisations. He returned to recording music in 2004, and has since released more than a dozen albums (both under his own name, and as Ilitch).

Notes

1 Tracks recorded by Thierry and Patrick Müller under the name PTM were released on the 1980 cassette *PTM Works*, and *The Coma Programma Sessions* download-only release.

2 This 'collectors edition' was in the form of a one-off, lathe-cut vinyl record. Only a single track from *Portraits* was ever released commercially: 'Helena Rodriguez', which was included on the CD *Un Jour Comme Tant D'Autres*.

3 Müller would bring the Ruth project to fruition later in his career, with the release of the album *Polaroid/Romans/Photos* in '85: "I wanted to differentiate this concept from that of Ilitch... Ruth's musical concept is almost the opposite of Ilitch, if not [entirely] different, more 'popular'... When *Polaroid/Romans/Photos* was reissued, a lot of people really believed she was real!"

DISCOGRAPHY

This discography lists all albums and non-album singles released between 1968 and 1978 by groups related to the French musical underground. Other recordings made in this period (live recordings, demos, etc), but that were released posthumously, are also listed. For each record details are provided for the original release and the most current reissues on both CD and LP (current as at June 2025).

There is also an on-line version of this discography hosted at *french-underground.com/discog*. This provides links to those albums that are currently available on streaming services.

ALAN JACK CIVILIZATION

1969   *Se Tu Ragazzo Mio* (7") (Fonit *SPF 31242*)
Shame on You (7") (BYG *129 013*)

1970   **Bluesy Mind** (BYG *529 011*)
(CD) 1997, Spalax *SPALAXCD14824*
(LP) 2018, Music for Special Experiences *MFSE LP 1-0017*
N'y change rien (7") (BYG *129 022*)

ALICE

1970   *De l'autre côté du miroir* (7") (BYG *129 019*)
(CD) *included* on *Alice* (Charly)
Le nouveau monde (7") (BYG *129 024*)
(CD) *included* on *Alice* (Charly)
Alice (BYG *529 016*)
(CD) 2022, BYG/Charly *BYG 529.016 CD*
(LP) 2022, BYG/Charly *BYG 529.016*

1971   *Je voudrais habiter le soleil* (7") (BYG *129 029*)
(CD) *included* on *Alice* (Charly)

1972   **Arrêtez le monde** (Polydor *2393 043*)
(CD) 2007, Second Harvest *423*
(LP) 2014, O-Music *OM 71063-1*
Note: An English Language version titled "All Ice" was released in Germany with the same catalogue number.

AME SON

1970   *Je veux juste dire (7")* (BYG *129 023*)
    (CD) *included* on *Catalyse* (BYG/Charly)
    (LP) *included* on *Primitive Expression* (Wah Wah)

1971   **Catalyse** (BYG *529 324*)
    (CD) 2025, BYG/Charly *BYG 529 324 CD*
    (LP) 2025, BYG/Charly *BYG 529 324*

1998   **Primitive Expression** (Spalax *SPALAXCD14543*)
    Note: demos and live tracks 1969-71.
    (LP) 2011, Wah Wah *LPS103*

ART ZOYD

1971   *Sangria (7")* (Opaline *45 T 1105*)
    (CD) *included* on *Symphonie pour le jour où brûleront les cités* (Belle Antique)

1976   **Symphonie pour le jour où brûleront les cités**
    (AZ Production Michel Besset *001*)
    (CD) 2008, Belle Antique *BELLE 081362*
    Note: This album was totally rerecorded in 1981 and released on Atem (reissued by Sub Rosa in 2011).

Note : Art Zoyd continued to release albums until the 2010s.

L'ASSEMBLÉE

1970   *Le chien (7")* (Odéon *2 C 006-10241 M*)
    (CD) *included* on *Beginner's Guide to French Pop*
    (2012, Nascente *NSBOX092*)
    (LP) *included* on *Psyché France 60-70*
    (2014, Parlophone *0825646320820*)

BANANAMOON

1992   **Je ne fum' pas des bananes** (CD)
    (Legend Music *KZLM 1505 1*)
    (CD) 2014, Gonzo *HST188CD*
    Note: Includes demos from 1968.

2014   **Bananamoon Band**
    (Monster Melodies *MMLP02*)
    Note: Demos from 1968.

BARRICADE

- 2005 **Le rire des camisoles** (CD) (Futura *RED 07*)
  Note: Live recordings and demos 1969-74.

JAC BERROCAL

- 1973 **Musiq Musiq** (Futura *SON 06*)
  (CD) 2001, Fractal *017*
  (LP) 2019, Rotorelief *ROTOR0071*
- 1978 **Parallèles** (d'Avantage *dav 01*)
  (CD) 2001, Alga Marghen *B 5TES.037*
  (LP) 2019, Rotorelief *ROTOR0072*

Note : Jacques (Jac) Berrocal continues to release albums.

PHILIPPE BESOMBES

- 1975 **Libra** (Pôle Records *Pôle 0004*)
  (CD) 2004, Mio *MIO-008*
  (LP) 2017, Purple Pyramid *CLO 0467*
- 1976 **Besombes-Rizet** (Pôle Records *Pôle 0006/7*)
  (CD) 2004, Mio *MIO-009*
  (LP) 2015, Gonzaï Records *FBK003*
- 1977 **Hydravion** (Cobra *COB 37012*)
- 1979 **Ceci Est Celà** (Divox *A3305*)
  (CD) 2004, Mio *MIO-010*
- 2016 **Anthology 1975-1979** (Cleopatra *CLO 0377*)
  Note: This 4xCD boxset contains Libra, Ceci Est Celà, Hydravion, Stratos Airlines, plus bonus tracks.

BIRGÉ GORGÉ SHIROC

- 1975 **Défense de** (GRRR *GR 1001*)
  (CD) 2003, Mio *MIO-026/027*
  (LP) 2013, Fauni Gena *FAUNI 030*
  Note: Reissues include DVD of demos from 1975-76.
- 2016 **Avant Toute** (SouffleContinu *FFL014*)
  Note: Unreleased demos from 1974-75.

CHRISTIAN BOULÉ

1978 **Photo Musik** (Polydor *2473 086*)
(CD) 1999, Musea *FGBG 4296.AR*

1979 **"Non-Fiction"** (Polydor *2393 227*)
(CD) 2002, Musea *FGBG 4350.AR*

CAMIZOLE

1999 **Camizole** (CD) (Spalax *SPALAXCD14549*)
Note: Album originally recorded for Tapioca in 1977.
(LP) 2018, SouffleContinu *FFL029*

2015 **Camizole 1975** (cass) (Ar(t)chiv' *no cat. no*)
Note: live performance 1975
(LP) 2017, Replica *RPC029*

2018 **Camizole + Lard Free**
(SouffleContinu *FFL030*)
Note: live performance 1978

2023 **Erahtic**
(Rotorelief *ROTOR0081*)
Note: Dominique Grimaud solo recording 1972

CATHARSIS

1971 **Masq** (Saravah *SH 10025*)
(CD) 1994, Spalax *CD 14201*

1972 **Les Chevrons** (Saravah *SH 10035*)
(CD) 1994, Spalax *CD 14202*

32 Mars (Galloway *GB 600507*)
(CD) 1994, Spalax *CD 14873*

Illuminations (Explosive *558.004*)
(CD) 1994, Spalax *CD 14281*

1974 **Le bolero du veau des dames**
(Sonopresse ST 69.612)
(CD) 1994, Spalax *CD 14203*

1975 *Cachemire (7")* (Sonopresse *46.610*)

1976 **Et s'aimer et mourir** (Sonopresse *36.613*)
(CD) 1994, Spalax *CD 14280*

Note: A non-album track, 'Charles', appears on **Puissance 13+2** *(Thélème)*

CHEVAL FOU

1994   **Cheval Fou** (CD) (Legend Music *LM 9004*)
Note: Live performances 1970-75
(CD) 2011, Psych Up Melodies *PUM 002/01*
(LP) 2024, PQR Disques *PQR28*

CHICO MAGNETIC BAND

1971   **Chico Magnetic Band** (Vogue *LOXV. 17001*)
(CD) 2008, Free Records *FR 2020*
(LP) 2020, Survival Research *SVVRCH030*

Pop or Not (7") (CBS *5136*)
(CD) *included on Chico Magnetic Band* CD.

1972   *Girls of Ocean (7")* (Tuba *RU 8007*)
(CD) *included on Chico Magnetic Band* CD.

CLEARLIGHT

1975   **Clearlight Symphony** (Virgin *V 2029*)
(CD) 2017, Belle Antique *BELLE 172818*
(LP) 2020, LMLR *783 190*

Forever Blowing Bubbles (Virgin *V 2039*)
(CD) 2017, Belle Antique *BELLE 172819*

1976   **Les contes du singe fou** (Isadora *ISA 9009*)
(CD) 2017, Belle Antique *BELLE 172820*

1978   **Visions** (Polydor *2393 185*)
(CD) 2014, Gonzo *HST211CD*

Note : Clearlight (Cyrille Verdeaux) continued to release albums until the 2010s.

JEAN COHEN-SOLAL

1972   **Flûtes Libres** (Daphy/Sonopresse *69 504*)
(LP) 2018, SouffleContinu *FFL044*

1973   **Captain Tarthopom**
(Connection/Sonopresse *CTN 69.569*)
(LP) 2018, SouffleContinu *FFL045*

2003   **Flutes Libres & Captain Tarthopom** (CD)
(MIO Records *MIO-025*)

CONTREPOINT

1971 'Unfathomable Of The Seventh Time' on **Puissance 13+2** (Thélème *6499 073*)
(CD) 1993, Musea *FGBG 4087.AR*
(LP) 2016, Lion *LP-165*

2017 **Contrepoint** (Monster Melodies *MMLP11*)
Note: live performance 1971

Note: 'Paris la Nuit' (live recording from 1971) appears on **30 Ans d'Agitation Musicale en France** *(Spalax, SPALAXBOX14711)*

CRIUM DELIRIUM

1994 Live Concerts 1972-1975 (CD)
(Legend Music *LM 9005*)
(CD) 2012, Crium Amicorum *no cat.*

DAGON

'Suite Pour Orgue' (live recording from 1971) appears on **30 Ans d'Agitation Musicale en France** *(Spalax, SPALAXBOX14711)*

DELIRED CAMELEON FAMILY

1975 **Visa de censure n° X** (EMI *2C 066 13087*)
(CD) 2014, Gonzo *HST208CD*
(LP) 2010, Wah Wah Records *LPS091*

JACQUES DUDON

1969 *Anita (7")* (Odeon *MEO 174*)
Note: Released under the pseudonym Claude Guilain.

2016 **Erosion Distillée** (Monster Melodies *MMLP09*)
Note: Unreleased recordings from 1969.

Note: Jacques Dudon was also a member of L'Assemblée (see separate entry).

ECLOSION

2015 Eclosion (Monster Melodies *MMLP05)*
Note: Unreleased recordings from 1972

ETRON FOU LELOUBLAN

1976 Batelages (Gratte-Ciel *CIEL 2001)*
(CD) 2015, Belle Antique *BELLE 152455*
(LP) 2013, Replica Records *RPC02*

1978 Les trois fou's perdégagnent (au pays des...)
(9H 17 Productions *7001)*
(CD) 2015, Belle Antique *BELLE 152456*
(LP) 2014, Replica Records *RPC004*

1980 En Public Aux États-Unis D'Amérique
(Celluloid *CEL 6572)*
(CD) 2015, Belle Antique *BELLE 152457*
(LP) 2014, Replica Records *RPC008*

2015 Live At The Rock In Opposition Festival, **1978** (Replica Records *RPC012)*
(CD) 2016, Replica Records *RPC012*

Note : Etron Fou Leloublan released another 3 albums before breaking up in 1985.

FILLE QUI MOUSSE

1971 Trixie Stapleton 291 - Se taire pour une femme trop belle (Futura *not released)*
Note: Only a small run of test pressings was made.
(CD) 1998, Spalax *SPALAXCD14919*
(LP) 2013, Monster Melodies *MMLP001*

FLUENCE

1975 Fluence (Pôle *0008)*
(LP) 2020, États-Unis *etat14*

Note: Pascal Comelade continues to release albums.

BRIGITTE FONTAINE

1968 **Brigitte Fontaine est... folle** (Saravah *SH 10 001*)
    (CD) 2013, Superior Viaduct *SV041*
    (LP) 2013, Superior Viaduct *SV041*

1969 *Le goudron (7")* (Saravah *SH 40 008*)
    (CD) *included* on *Comme à la Radio* reissues

et... (7") (Saravah *SH 40 007*)
    (CD) *included* on *Comme à la Radio* reissues

Comme à la radio (Saravah *SH 10 006*)
    (CD) 2021, Saravah *SHL 1018*
    (LP) 2018, Craftman *CMRS-0017*

1972 **Brigitte Fontaine** (Saravah *SH 10 034*)
    (CD) 2015, Saravah *SHL 1034*
    (LP) 2014, Superior Viaduct *SV043*

Jamai-ai-ai-ai-ai-ais (7") (Saravah *SH 40 024*)

1974 **L'incendie** (BYG *529 026*)
    (CD) 2022, BYG *529.026 CD*
    (LP) 2022, BYG *529.026*

Ça va faire un hit (7") (BYG *129 052*)
    (CD) *included* on *L'incendie* CD (BYG)

Je ne connais cet homme (Saravah *SH 10041*)
    (CD) 2009, Omagatoki *OMCX-1231*
    (LP) 2015, Superior Viaduct *SV044*

1975 **Le bonheur** (Saravah *SH 10059*)
    (CD) 2009, Omagatoki *OMCX-1232*

1977 **Vous et nous** (RCA/Saravah *RSL 1070*)
    (CD) 2009, Omagatoki *OMCX-1233*
    (LP) 2018, Kythibong *KTB67*

2020 **Théâtre musical** (Monster Melodies *MMLP17*)
    Note: Live performance from 1973.

Théâtre musical 2 (Monster Melodies *MMLP18*)
    Note: Live performance from 1973.

Note : Brigitte Fontaine continues to release albums.

GONG

- **1969** **Magick Brother** (BYG *529 305*)
  - (CD) 2022, BYG/Charly *529.305 CD*
  - (LP) 2022, BYG/Charly *529.305*
- **1970** *Garçon ou fille (7")* (BYG *129 021*)
  - (7") 2009, Finders Keepers *FKSP001*
  - (CD) included on *Magick Brother* CD
- **1971** **Continental Circus** (Philips *6332 033*)
  - (CD) 1994, Mantra *089*
  - (LP) 2010, Mercury *6332 033*

  Camembert Electrique (BYG *529 353*)
  - (CD) 2024, BYG/Charly *BYG 529 353CD*
  - (LP) 2024, BYG/Charly *BYG 529 3535*
- **1972** **Glastonbury Fayre** (Revelation *REV 1-3*)
  - Note: Includes Gong set from Glastonbury 1971
  - (CD) 2007, Arkama *AK 390/3*
  - (LP) 2021, Arkama *AK 367/3*
- **1973** **Flying Teapot** (Virgin *V 2002*)
  - (CD) 2019, Virgin/UMC *7714150*
  - (LP) 2019, Charly *L 178*

  Angel's Egg (Virgin *V 2007*)
  - (CD) 2019, Virgin/UMC *7714151*
  - (LP) 2023, Virgin *ARHSLP025*

  Greasy Truckers Live At Dingwalls
  (Greasy Truckers *GT 4997*)
  Note: Side-long Gong live performance
- **1974** **You** (Virgin *V 2019*)
  - (CD) 2019, Virgin/UMC *7714152*
  - (LP) 2025, Replica *RPC064*
- **1975** **Shamal** (Virgin *V 2046*)
  - (CD) 2019, Virgin/UMC *7714153*
- **1989** **Live au Bataclan, 1973** (CD) (Mantra *025*)
  - (CD) 2009, Mantra *MAN 0903206*
  - (LP) 2019, Culture Factory *782 945*
- **1990** **Live Sheffield, 1974** (CD) (Mantra *042*)
  - (CD) 2009, Mantra *MAN 0903207*
  - (LP) 2020, Culture Factory *783177*
- **1995** **Camembert Eclectique** (CD) (GAS *CD 001*)
  - Note: Demos from 1970
  - (CD) 2013, GAS *A GAS CD 001*

Pre-Modernist Wireless: Peel Sessions (CD)
(Strange Fruit *SFR CD 137*)
Note: Peel sessions from 1971-74.
    (CD) 2000, Celebration *CELCD 059 PM*
    (LP) 1999, Turning Point *TPM-99202v*
Paragong Live '73 (CD) (GAS *CD 002*)

2002 **Glastonbury Fayre 1971** (CD)
(GAS *ARC CD 001*)
Note: Includes set from Glastonbury Festival 1971 as released on "Glastonbury Fayre" (Revelation, 1972)

2005 **Live In Sherwood Forest '75** (CD)
(Major League Productions *MLP09CD*)

2006 **Gong in the 70s** (CD) (Voiceprint *VP406CD*)
    (LP) 2022, Culture Factory *CFL1LP*

2019 **Love From The Planet Gong (The Virgin Years 1973-75)** (CDBox)
(Virgin/UMC *675 890-1*)

2021 **Live à Longlaville 27/10/1974** (CD)
(Madfish *SMACD1206*)
    (LP) 2021, Madfish *SMALP1206*

2023 **Live In Lyon, December 14, 1972**
(LMLR *783 564*)

JEAN GUERIN

1971 **Tacet** (Futura *SON 04*)
    (CD) 2001, Elica/Futura *MPO-3560*
    (LP) 2015, SouffleContinu *FFL009*

DASHIELL HEDAYAT

1971 **Obsolete** (Shandar *SR 10 009*)
    (CD) 2016, Replica *RPC023CD*
    (LP) 2020, Replica *RPC023*

Note: Dashiell Hedayat is a pseudonym for Daniel Theron, who also recorded under the name Melmoth (see separate entry).

HELDON

- **1974** **Electronic Guerilla** (Disjuncta *12/13*)
  (CD) 2018, Bureau B *BB 280*
  (LP) 2018, Bureau B *BB 280*
- **1975** **Allez Teia** (Disjuncta *000002*)
  (CD) 2018, Bureau B *BB 281*
  (LP) 2018, Bureau B *BB 281*

  It's Always Rock & Roll (Disjuncta *000006/7*)
  (CD) 2018, Bureau B *BB 282*
  (LP) 2018, Bureau B *BB 282*

  Soutien à la RAF (7") (Disjuncta *101*)
  (7") 2014, SouffleContinu *FFL002*
- **1976** **Agneta Nilsson** (Urus *000.001*)
  (CD) 2018, Bureau B *BB 283*
  (LP) 2018, Bureau B *BB 283*

  Perspective 1 bis complement (7") (Urus *102*)
  (7") 2014, SouffleContinu *FFL002*

  Un rêve sans conséquence spéciale
  (Cobra *COB 37002*)
  (CD) 2020, Bureau B *BB 329*
  (LP) 2020, Bureau B *BB 329*
- **1978** **Interface** (Cobra *COB 37013*)
  (CD) 2020, Bureau B *BB 330*
  (LP) 2020, Bureau B *BB 330*
- **1979** **Stand By** (Egg *900 578*)
  (CD) 2020, Bureau B *BB 331*
  (LP) 2020, Bureau B *BB 331*
- **1983** **Perspective: Compilation 1976-1982**
  (WEA *24 0303-1*)
  Note: Contains 5 tracks recorded live in 1978, these are also included as bonus tracks on the Cuneiform CD reissues of Un rêve sans conséquence spéciale, Interface, and L'Ethique.
- **2006** **Live Electronic Guerilla** (CD)
  (Captain Trip *CTCD-550*)
  Note: 2 live performances from 1975 & 1976

  Well And Alive In France: Live In Nancy 1979
  (Captain Trip *CTCD-551/552*)
- **2015** **Live in Paris 1975** (SouffleContinu *FFL007*)
  Note: live performance from 1975 included on Live Electronic Guerilla (Captain Trip)

        Live in Paris 1976 (SouffleContinu *FFL008*)
        Note: live performance from 1975 included on Live Electronic Guerilla (Captain Trip)
2018 **Live in Metz 1977** (Bam Balam *BBLP055*)

HORDE CATALYTIQUE POUR LA FIN
1971 **Gestation sonore** (Futura *SON 03*)
        (CD) 2001, Mellow Records *MMP 404*
        (LP) 2015, SouffleContinu *FFL013*

ILITCH
1978 **Periodikmindtrouble** (Oxygène *Oxy 09*)
        (CD) 2000, Fractal Records *012*
        (LP) 2015, Superior Viaduct *SV074*

1980 **10 Suicides** (SCOPA *HRH/10007*)
        (CD) 2001, Fractal Records *013*
        (LP) 2015, Superior Viaduct *SV075*

        P.T.M. Works (cass) (Eurock *EDC04*)

2011 **Un Jour Comme Tant D'Autres** (CD)
        (Beta-lactam Ring *mt272*)
        Note: Live recording from 1975.

ARIEL KALMA
1975 **Ariel/Le temps des moissons**
        (Astral Muse *9999*)
        (CD) 2008, Beta-lactam Ring *mt189*
        (LP) 2015, Wah Wah *LPS142*

1978 **Osmose** (SFP *3.5021-5022*)
        (CD) 2006, Blur *blur01*
        (LP) 2013, Black Sweat *BS 007*

2014 **An Evolutionary Music - Original Recordings: 1972-1979** (Rvng. Intl. *RERVNG05*)

2017 **French Archives: 1977-1980** (4LP Box)
        (Black Sweat *BS042*)

2019 **Nuits blanches au studio 116**
(Transversales *TRS12*)
Note: Tracks recorded at GRM 1974-79.

2021 **French Archives Vol 2: 1974-1985** (4LP Box)
(Black Sweat *BS063*)

2023 **French Archives Vol 3: 1964-1989** (4LP Box)
(Black Sweat *BS078*)

KOMINTERN

1971 **La bal du rat mort** (Harvest *2C 062-11 774*)
(CD) 2014, Great Barrier *GBR 52 0 97*
(LP) 2018, Replica *RPC035*

LARD FREE

1973 **Gilbert Artman's Lard Free** (Vamp *VP 59 500*)
(CD) 2008, Captain Trip *CTCD-610*
(LP) 2022, Replica *RPC046*

1975 **I'm About Midnight** (Vamp *VP 59 502*)
(CD) 2008, Captain Trip *CTCD-611*
(LP) 2022, Replica *RPC048*

1978 **Spirale malax** (Cobra *COB 3700*)
(CD) 2008, Captain Trip *CTCD-612*
(LP) 2022, Replica *RPC050*

1997 **Unnamed** (CD) (Spalax *SPALAXCD14915*)
Note: includes unreleased recordings from 1971-72.
(CD) 2008, Captain Trip *CTCD-613*
(LP) 2022, Replica *RPC051*

2018 **Camizole + Lard Free** (SouffleContinu *FFL030*)
Note: live performance 1978

MAAJUN

1971 **Vivre la mort du vieux monde**
(Vogue *SLVLX 545*)
(CD) 2022, SouffleContinu *FFL077*
(LP) 2022, SouffleContinu *FFLCD077*

MAHJUN

1973 **Mahjun** (Saravah *SH 10040*)
(LP) 2016, SouffleContinu *FFL022*
Nous ouvrirons les casernes (7") (CAM)

1974 **Fils à Colin-Maillard** (Saravah *SH 10047*)
(LP) 2016, SouffleContinu *FFL023*

1977 **Happy French Band** (Gratte Ciel *ZL 37049*)
(CD) 1998, Spalax *SPALAXCD14903*

1999 **Maajun** (CD) (Mantra *037*)
Note: Compiles first 2 albums onto 1 CD

MAGMA

1970 **Magma** (Philips *6395 001/002*)
(CD) 2017, 7th Records *REX IV-V*
(LP) 2016, Mercury *6 621 032*

1971 **1001° Centigrade** (Philips *6397 031*)
(CD) 2012, 7th Records *REX VI*
(LP) 2015, Jazz Village *JV33570071*

1973 **Mekanïk Destruktïw Kommandöh**
(Vertigo *6499 729*)
(CD) 2017, 7th Records *REX VII*
(LP) 2022, Music on Vinyl *MOVLP2975*

1974 **Köhntarkösz** (Vertigo *6325 750*)
(CD) 2012, 7th Records *REX VIII*
(LP) 2022, Music on Vinyl *MOVLP3044*

1974 **Tristan & Iseult/Wurdah Ïtah** (Barclay *80.528*)
(CD) 2017, 7th Records *REX IX*
(LP) 2022, Music on Vinyl *MOVLP3045*

1975 **Magma Live/Hhaï** (Utopia *CYL2 1245*)
(CD) 2017, 7th Records *REX X-XI*
(LP) 2015, Jazz Village *JV 33570091.92*

1976 **Üdü Wüdü** (Utopia *FPL1-7332*)
(CD) 2020, 7th Records *REX XII-V2*
(LP) 2015, Jazz Village *JV33570068*

1977 **Inédits** (Tapioca *TP 10001*)
(CD) 1996, 7th Records *REX XIX*

1978 **Atthak** (Eurodisc *913 213, 25376*)
(CD) 2017, 7th Records *REX XIII*
(LP) 2015, Jazz Village *JV33570067*

1989	**Mekanïk Kommandöh** (CD) (7th Records REX *VI*) (CD) 2017, 7th Records *AKT X*
1994	**Théâtre du Taur - Concert 1975 - Toulouse** (CD) (AKT *IV*) Note: Live in Toulouse (24/9/75)
1996	**Concert 1971 - Bruxelles - Théâtre 140** (CD) (AKT *VIII*) Note: Live in Brussels (12/11/71)
	Concert 1976 - Opéra de Reims (CD) (AKT *IX*) Note: Live in Reims (2/3/76)
1998	**Simples** (CD) (7th Records *REX II*) Note: Compilation of non-album singles 1971-74. (10") 2021, Music on Vinyl *MOV10036*
1999	**BBC 1974 Londres** (CD) (AKT *XIII*) Note: Live at the BBC (14/3/74) (CD) 2020, AKT *AKT XIII-V2* (LP) 2021, Music on Vinyl *MOVLP2976*
2014	**Zühn Wöhl Ünsaï - Live 1974** (CD) (MIG *01102 2CD*) Note: Live at Radio Bremen Sendesaal (6/2/74) (LP) 2017, MIG *01101 2LP*
2018	**Magma Marquee Londres 1974** (CD) (AKT *XVIII*) Note: Live at The Marquee (17/3/74)

Note 1: A non-album track, 'Mekanik Kommando', appears on
Puissance 13+2 *(Thélème, 1971)*
[reissued (CD) Musea, 1993; (LP) Lion, 2016]
Note 2: Magma continues to release albums.

MAHOGANY BRAIN

1971	**With (Junk-Saucepan) When (Spoon-Trigger)** (Futura *RED 02*) (CD) 2001, Mellow *MMP 402* (LP) 2014 SouffleContinu *FFL005*
1976	**Smooth Sick Lights** (Pôle *0013*) (CD) 1997, Spalax *SPALAXCD14266* (LP) 2022, Zaius Tapes *ZT-07*

ALBERT MARCOEUR
- **1974** **Albert Marcoeur** (Atlantic *40 546*)
  (CD) 2015, Belle Antique *BELLE 152468*
- **1976** **Album à colorier** (Atlantic *50 215*)
  (CD) 2015, Belle Antique *BELLE 152469*
- **1979** **Armes & Cycles** (Philips *9101 210*)
  (CD) 2015, Belle Antique *BELLE 152470*

Note : Albert Marcoeur continues to release albums.

MELMOTH
- **1969** **La devanture des ivresses** (Arion *30 T 079*)
  (CD) 1992, Mantra *MANTA 076*

Note: Melmoth is a pseudonym for Daniel Theron, who also recorded under the name Dashiell Hedayat (see separate entry).

MOSAIC
- **1978** **Ultimatum** (Production Ekimoz *441.52.78*)
  (CD) 2003, MIO *029*

MOVING GELATINE PLATES
- **1971** **Moving Gelatine Plates** (CBS *S 64399*)
  (CD) 1992, Musea *FGBG 4062.AR*
  (LP) 2015, Replica Records *RPC011*
- **1972** **The World of Genius Hans** (CBS *64146*)
  (CD) 1994, Musea *FGBG 4101.AR*
  (LP) 2016, Replica Records *RPC017*
- **2014** **Moving Gelatine Plates**
  (Monster Melodies *MMLP03*)
  Note: Includes 1970 demos, Live 1972 & 1978.

NYL
- **1976** **Nyl** (Urus *000.013*)
  (CD) 2011, Psych Up Melodies *PUM 001*
  (LP) 2018, Golden Pavilion *GPMUSIC05LP*

PATAPHONIE
- **1975** Pataphonie (Pôle Records *0003*)
- **1978** Le Matin Blanc (Féeri Music *feeri 178*)
  (CD) 1999, Gazul /Musea *GA 8629 AR*

RICHARD PINHAS
- **1977** Rhizosphère (Cobra *COB 37005*)
  (CD) 2018, Bureau B *BB 279*
  (LP) 2018, Bureau B *BB 279*
- **1978** Chronolyse (Cobra *COB 37015*)
  (CD) 2018, Bureau B *BB 291*
  (LP) 2018, Bureau B *BB 291*
- **1979** Iceland (Polydor *2393 254*)
  (CD) 2022, Bureau B *BB 393*
  (LP) 2022, Bureau B *BB 393*

Note: Richard Pinhas continues to release albums.

PLAT DU JOUR
- **1977** Plat du jour (Speedball *1002*)
  (CD) 2016, Paisley Press *PP 117*
  (LP) 2016, Mellotron Records *mlp 015*

PÔLE
- **1975** Kotrill (Pôle Records *Pôle 0001*)
  Inside the Dream (Pôle Records *Pôle 0002*)

POTEMKINE
- **1974** *Mystère (7")* (Disques Polymnie *V 1016*)
  (CD) *included* on *Triton* (Soleil Zeuhl)
- **1976** Foetus (Pôle Records *Pôle 0010*)
  (CD) 2021, Musea *FGBG 5042*
  (LP) 2019, Replica *RPC036*

1977   Triton (Voxigrave *V 30/ST 7162*)
       (CD) 2001, Soleil Zeuhl *SZ 04*
       (LP) 2022, Replica *RPC052*

1978   Nicolas II (Phaeton Records *7801*)
       (CD) 2001, Soleil Zeuhl *SZ 05*

RED NOISE

1971   Sarcelles - Lochères (Futura *RED 01*)
       (CD) 2009, Futura *RED 01*
       (LP) 2014, SouffleContinu *FFL004*

CATHERINE RIBEIRO

1969   Catherine Ribeiro + 2 bis (Festival *FLDX 487*)

1970   no. 2 (Festival *FLDX 531*)
       (LP) 2018, Anthology *ARC 053*

1972   Ame debout (Philips *6332 017*)
       (CD) 1995, Mantra *MANTRA 091*
       (LP) 2018, Anthology *ARC 054*

1973   Paix (Philips *6325 019*)
       (CD) 1993, Mantra *MANTRA 078*
       (LP) 2018, Anthology *ARC 055*

1974   Le rat débile et l'homme des champs (Philips *9101 003*)
       (CD) 1994, Mantra *MANTRA 084*
       (LP) 2012, Mercury *279 506-6*

1975   Libertés (Fontana *9101 501*)
       (CD) 1994, Mantra *MANTRA 083*

1977   Le temps de l'autre (Philips *9101 155*)
       Le blues de Piaf (Philips *9101 156*)
       (CD) 2001, Philips *548 401-2*

1978   Jacqueries (Philips *9101 201*)
       (CD) 2002, Philips *586 642-2*

1979   Passions (Philips *9101 270*)

Note: Catherine Ribeiro continued to release albums into the 1990s.

HENRI ROGER
1975   **Images** (Pôle Records *Pôle 0005*)
Note: Henri Roger continues to release albums.

SEMOOL
1971   **Essais** (Futura *SON 02*)
       (CD) 2000, Mellow Records *MMP 403*
       (LP) 2015, SouffleContinu *FFL006*

SPACECRAFT
1978   **Paradoxe** (no label *SC 7802*)
       (CD) 1995, Spalax *SPALAXCD14928*
       (LP) 2012, Wah Wah *LPS114*

TRAVELLING
1973   **Voici la nuit tombée** (Futura *RED 06*)
       (CD) 2000, Mellow *MMP 390*
       (LP) 2015, SouffleContinu *FFL012*

TRIODE
1971   **On n'a pas fini d'avoir tout vu**
       (Futura *RED 03*)
       (CD) 2000, Mellow *MMP 389*
       (LP) 2015, SouffleContinu *FFL011*

UNIVERIA ZEKT
1972   **The Unnamables** (Thélème *6332 501*)
       (CD) 2008, Arcàngelo *ARC-7313*
       (LP) 2024, Thélème *THE2401*

URBAN SAX

1977   **Urban Sax** (Cobra *COB 37004*)
         (LP) 2016, Wah Wah *LPS152*

1978   **Urban Sax 2** (Cobra *COB 37017*)
         (LP) 2016, Wah Wah *LPS153*

1990   **Urban Sax** (CD) (EPM Musique *FDC 1124*)
         Note: Compilation of Urban Sax + Urban Sax 2.

Note : Urban Sax continues to release albums.

VERTO

1976   **Krig/Volubilis** (Pôle Records *0009*)

1978   **Réel 19.36** (Fléau *FL. 7004*)
         (LP) 2019, Replica *RPC040*

Note: 'Alice' (unreleased track) incl. on **Musiques Electroniques En France 1974-1984** *(CD) Gazul, 2007; (LP) Replica, 2015*

PATRICK VIAN

1977   **Bruits et temps analogues** (Egg *900.541*)
         (CD) 2013, Staubgold *staubgold 126*
         (LP) 2013, Staubgold *staubgold 126*

Note: 'Sarcelles 2' (unreleased track) incl. on **Musiques Electroniques En France 1974-1984** *(CD) Gazul, 2007; (LP) Replica, 2015*

WEIDORJE

1978   **Weidorje** (Cobra *COB 37014*)
         (CD) 2008, Arcàngelo *ARC 7314*
         (LP) 2015, Replica *RPC010*

2023   **Live at Toulon 1978** (CD) (Noizu! *NORCD-001*)

ROBERT WOOD

1972   **Tarot** (Edici *ED 00 61020*)
         (CD) 1996, Spalax *SPALAXCD14507*

         Sonabular (Edici *ED 0061030*)
         (CD) 1996, Spalax *SPALAXCD14508*

1976   **Tombac Vibe** (Polydor *2393 150*)
            Vibrarock (Polydor *2393 137*)
2015   **Live at Lons le Saulnier 1974**
            (Monster Melodies *MMLP06*)

XALPH

2018   **Xalph** (Monster Melodies *MMLP13*)
Note: unreleased demos from 1975

ZAO

1973   **Z=7L** (Vertigo *6499 738*)
            (CD) 2012, Belle Antique *BELLE 121922*
            (LP) 2014, Replica *RPC007*
1975   **Osiris** (Disjuncta *000004*)
            (CD) 2007, Belle Antique *BELLE 071338*
            Shekina (RCA *FPL 1 0097*)
            (CD) 2007, Belle Antique *BELLE 071339*
1977   **Kawana** (RCA *FPL1 0178*)
            (CD) 2012, Belle Antique *BELLE 121923*
            Typhareth (RCA *PL 37121*)
            (CD) 1998, Musea *FGBG 4146.AR*
2003   **Live!** (CD) (Musea *FGBG 4492.AR*)
Note: recorded live in 1976

ZNR

1976   **Barricade III** (Isadora *ISA 900*)
            (CD) 2016, Belle Antique *BELLE 162547*
            (LP) 2015, Superior Viaduct *SV071*
1978   **Traité de mécanique populaire**
            (Invisible Records *SCOPA 10002*)
            (CD) 2018, Belle Antique *BELLE 182872*
2018   **ZNRchive Box** (CDBox)
            (ReR Megacorp *ZNRBox*)
Note: incl. CD 'Demos & Lost Tracks'

BIBLIOGRAPHY

BOOKS

Daevid Allen
    Gong Dreaming 1: From Soft Machine to the birth of Gong
    (GAS,1994)
    Gong Dreaming 2: The histories & mysteries of Gong from 1969-1975
    (SAF, 2009)

Marc Alvarado
    La Chienlit, Le Rock Français et Mai 68: histoire d'un rendez-vous raté
    (Éditions du Layeur, 2018)

Benjamin Barouh
    Saravah: C'est où l'horizon? 1967-1977
    (Le mot et le reste, 2013)

Jean-François Bizot
    Underground: l'histoire
    (Actuel/Denoël, 2001)

Klaus Blasquiz
    Au coeur du Magma
    (Le mot et le reste, 2018)

Jonathyne Briggs
    Sounds French: Globalization, Cultural Communities and Pop Music
    (Oxford University Press, 2015)

Michel Carvallo
    Panique à l'Impérial Palace: Chroniques de l'agitation culurelle 1968-1975 (Asile éditions, 2007)

Antoine de Caunes
    Magma
    (Rock & Folk/Albin Michel, 1978)

Guigou Chenevier
    Une histoire d'Etron Fou Leloublan
    (Lenka lente, 2017)

Maxime Delcourt
    Il y a des années où l'on a envie de ne rien faire:
    (Le mot et le reste, 2015)

Éric Deshayes & Dominique Grimaud
L'underground musical en France
(Le mot et le reste, 2008)

Eric Drott
Music and the Elusive Revolution: Cultural Politics and Political Culture in France, 1968-1981 (California University Press, 2011)

Christian-Louis Eclimont
Rock'O'Rico, 25 ans de Culture Rock en France
(Gründ, 2012)

Steve & Allan Freeman
Twilight of the Alchemists
(Audion Publications, 2024)

Dominique Grimaud
Un certain rock(?) français Vol 1 & 2
(9h17 Production, *1977*)

Philippe Gonin
Magma: Décryptage d'un mythe et d'une musique
(Le mot et le reste, 2010)

Francis Grosse & Bernard Gueffier
La Discographie du rock français
(Musea, 1985)

Warren Hatter
Concrete Science Fiction Riot: The Stories of France's answer to Krautrock
(Strange Attractor, *to be published*)

Hervé Hamon & Patrick Rotman
Génération Vol 1 & 2
(Seuil, 1998)

Steven Jezo-Vannier
Presse Parallèle: la contre-culture en france dans les années soixante-dix
(Le mot et le reste, 2011)

Gareth Jones
French Pop from Music Hall to Yé-Yé
(Music Mentor Books, 2022)

François Jouffa
La Culture Pop des années 70: Le pop-notes de François Jouffra
(Spengler, 1994)

Aymeric Leroy
> *L'École de Canterbury*
> (Le mot et le reste, 2016)

David L. Looseley
> *Popular Music in Contemporary France: Authenticity, Politics, Debate*
> (Berg, 2003)

Serge Loupien
> *La France Underground: Free Jazz et Pop Rock 1965/1979*
> (Rivages Rouge, 2018)

Lionel 'Fox' Magal
> *Crium Delerium: the Psykedeklik Road Book*
> (Crium Amicorum, 2012)

Michel Muzac
> *Le Pop Sauvage*
> (self published, 2024)

Philippe Manoeuvre (ed.)
> *Rock Français: de Johnny à BB Brunes - 123 albums essentiels*
> (Hoëbeke, 2010)

Gérard Nguyen
> *Atem 1975-1979: une sélection d'articles et d'interviews*
> (Camion Blanc, 2010)

Archie Patterson
> *Eurock: Music & Culture Post Millennium*
> (Eurock Publications, 2013)
> *Eurock: The Music of Gilbert Artman & Urban Sax*
> (Eurock Publications, 2016)

Philippe Robert
> *Agitation Frite: Témoignages de l'Underground Français*
> (Lenka lente, 2017)
> *Agitation Frite 2: Témoignages de l'Underground Français*
> (Lenka lente, 2018)
> *Agitation Frite 3: Témoignages de l'Underground Français*
> (Lenka lente, 2018)

François Robinet
> *Rock Progressif Français: Une histoire discographique*
> (Camion Blanc, 2020)

Robert Rossi
    Histoire du rock à marseille 1960-1980
    (Le mot et le reste, 2017)

Christian Vander
    À vie, à mort, et après… Entretien avec Chrisophe Rossi
    (naïve, 2013)

Christian Victor & Julien Regoli
    20 ans de rock français
    (Rock & Folk/Albin Michel, 1978)

Grégory Vieau
    Une histoire de la presse rock en france
    (Le mot et le reste, 2021)

JOURNALS

Published 1968-78

    Rock & Folk
    Best
    Le Parapluie
    Actuel
    *Pop Music**
    Maxipop
    Atem
    Pop 2000
    Le Pop

Published since 1978

    The Wire
    Audion

---

* *Pop Music* changed names multiple times - it was known as *Pop Music-Super Hebdo* from March 1971-April 1972, and as *Pop Music-Maxipop* for a few editions in March/April 1973

WEBSITES

Online Magazines

Fuzzine:
fuzzine.over-blog.com

Gonzai:
gonzai.com

It's Psychedelic Baby Magazine: *(in English)*
psychedelicbabymag.com

The Quietus: *(in English)*
thequietus.com

Resources/Archives

Archive of Pop 2 episodes at INA:
madelen.ina.fr/collection/pop-2

Archives of the French Rock Press:
web2000.bluesfr.net/PRESSE/presse.htm

Magma Web Press Book:
robert.guillerault.free.fr/magma

Paris 70s (Bernard Bacos):
paris70.free.fr

Planet Gong: *(in English)*
www.planetgong.co.uk

Musicians

Art Zoyd:
artzoydstudios.com

Jean-Jacques Birgé blog:
drame.org/blog

Dominique Grimaud:
dominique-grimaud.fr

Ilitch:
ilitchmusic.com

Ariel Kalma:
ariel-kalma.com

Magma:
magmamusic.org

Richard Pinhas:
richard-pinhas.com

Henri Roger:
henriroger.com

Writers

Neospheres (Éric Deshayes):
neospheres.free.fr

ILLUSTRATIONS

Cover Patrick Vian arrested at a street concert celebrating the centenary of the Paris Commune, March '71 *(photographer: Claude Palmer).*
xxiv Jean-Jacques Birgé in the Grand Canyon, USA, August '68 *(courtesy of Jean-Jacques Birgé).*
xxx Poster for Magma at Roundhouse, February '75.
p.2 Vince Taylor et ses Playboys, '63 *(photographer: Hugo van Gelderen).*
p.11 Poster from May '68 *(design: Jacques Carelman/Atelier Populaire).*
p.20 Cover of *Actuel* no. 2, Nov '68.
p.24 Poster for The First Paris Music Festival (before relocation to Amougies, Belgium).
p.28 Title frame of *Pop 2 (ORTF).*
p.34 Poster for Riviera Festival, Biot, July '70.
p.42 Cover of *Rock & Folk* no. 48, Jan '71.
p.50 Cover of *Atem* no. 2, Jan '76.
p.54 Label of Heldon, *Electronique Guerilla (courtesy of Richard Pinhas).*
p.62 Lard Free, publicity photo Vamp Records '73 *(photographer: Francis Goldstein, courtesy of Gilbert Artman)* L to R: Gilbert Artman, Herve Elhyani, Philippe Bolliet, François Mativet.
p.88 Illustration from "Agit-pop", *Actuel* no.6, Mar '71.
p.96 Red Noise, detail of inner sleeve of *Sarcelles - Lochères (collage: Patrick Vian).*
p.105 Barricade II, '74 *(photographer unknown).*
p.126 Maajun, Vogue publicity photo, '71 *(photographer unknown).* Top to Bottom, L to R: Cyril Lefebvre, Roger Scaglia, Jean-Pierre Arnoux, Alain Roux, Jean-Louis Lefebvre.
p.138 Komintern, outside employment office at Citroen factory, '71 *(photographer: Philippe Gras, courtesy of Michel Muzac).* L to R: Serge Cattalano, Richard Aubert, Olivier Zdrzalik, Francis Lemonnier, Michel Muzac, Pascal Chassin.
p.152 Fille Qui Mousse, '71 *(layout: Denis Gheerbrànt, courtesy of Henri-Jean Enu).* L to R: Henri-Jean Enu, Benjamin Legrand, Denis Gheerbrànt, Barbara Lowengreen.
p.164 Dagon playing onboard the USS Mitchell, Aug '71 *(photographer unknown, courtesy Dominique Lentin).* L to R: Fabien Poutignat, Denis Martignon, Dominique Lentin, Daniel Hoffmann, (missing) Jean-Pierre Lentin.
p.178 Poster for La Fenetre Rose, Nov '67.
p.184 Bananamoon in Deya, '68 *(photographer unknown).* L to R: Daevid Allen, Patrick Fontaine, Gilli Smyth, Marc Blanc.
p.194 Ame Son *(photographer unknown, courtesy of Marc Blanc).* L to R: Bernard Lavialle, Patrick Fontaine, Marc Blanc, François Garrel.

p.206 Publicity poster for Gong, '71. Clockwise from top left: Christian Tritsch, Gilli Smyth, Pip Pyle, Venux Delux (Francis Linon), Daevid Allen, Didier Malherbe.

p.244 Poster for Cheval Fou *(Original design: Le Pop collective, courtesy of Michel Peteau)* © Marellemusic (Marellemusic.label@gmail.com).

p.252 Poster for Crium Delirium, '73 *(Original design: Angel Vidal, courtesy of Lionel 'Fox' Magal).*

p.262 Cyrille Verdeaux at the family piano, '75 *(photographer: Georges Litvine, courtesy of Cyrille Verdeaux).*

p.278 Robert Wood and vibraphone *(photographer unknown).*

p.282 Moving Gelatine Plates, '71 *(photographer unknown, courtesy Didier Thibault).* L to R: Didier Thibault, Maurice Helmlinger, Gérard Bertram, Gérard Pons.

p.294 Magma, '70 *(photographer unknown).* L to R: Richard Raux, Paco Charley, Teddy Lasry, Christian Vander, François Cahen, Claude Engel, Francis Moze, Klaus Blasquiz.

p.322 Contrepoint *(photographer unknown).* L to R: Robert Taylor, Jean-Pierre Weiller, Jean-Pierre Carolfi, Mike Freitag.

p.330 Poster for Free Fuck, Dauphine, Feb '70.

p.334 Camizole at Barjouville, '76 *(photographer: Quentin Lemaire, courtesy of Dominique Grimaud).* L to R: Françoise Crublé, Catherine Lienhardt, Jacky Dupéty, Dominique Grimaud, Jean-Luc Dupéty.

p.346 Jac Berrocal *(photographer: Roger Ferlet).*

p.354 Etron Fou Leloublan *(photographer unknown, courtesy of Guigou Chenevier).* L to R: Chris Chanet, Guigou Chenevier, Ferdinand Richard.

p.368 Birgé Gorgé, during the recording of *Défense de*, March/April '75 *(photo © Thierry Dehesdin, courtesy of Jean-Jacques Birgé).*

p.380 Synthesiser ads from *Rock & Folk.*

p.386 Philippe Besombes at Studios du Chesnay *(photographer unknown).*

p.394 Richard Pinhas with the 'Big Moog', '78 *(photographer unknown, courtesy of Richard Pinhas).*

p.414 Photo/collage by Thierry Muller *(courtesy of Thierry Muller).*

SOURCES

Unless otherwise noted all sources were originally published in French, and were translated by the author. For complete details for any book cited as source material see the Bibliography.

INTRODUCTION

Except for those noted below all quotations are from interviews with Jean-Hervé Peron, Patrick Fontaine, Karel Beer, François Billard, and Dominique Grimaud conducted by the author in 2020/21.

Philippe Paringaux in *Rock & Folk* n° 50 (Mar '72)
"Two very clear and distinct, almost antagonistic, currents can be distinguished..."
"It's clear that it's more possible to find originality by playing a style..."
Pop 2000 n° 11 (Nov '72)
"Their musical tastes inclined them towards Soft Machine, Pink Floyd..."
Robert Wyatt quoted in *Wrong Movements: A Robert Wyatt History*
"There is just a great tradition in France of listening to music..."
Gilbert Artman
"For me Captain Beefheart was the synthesis of a kind of free-rock..."
Nick Mason quoted in *Musiq* n° 6 (Nov 2016)
"Pink Floyd may never have survived without the French audiences..."
Daevid Allen interviewed by Lars Fahlin, 2002
"At the time, England was much narrower in its stylistic preferences..."

PART 1 - A SHORT HISTORY OF THE FRENCH MUSICAL UNDERGROUND

1. CHANSON, *YÉ-YÉ* & TEEN IDOLS:
French Pop Before 1968

Marc Blanc interviewed by Alain Hertay (2015)
"At the end of '67, there was a very small underground..."

2. MAY '68:
The Explosion

Except for those noted below all quotations are from interviews with Roger Scaglia, Alain Roux, Michel Peteau, Didier Malherbe, Dominique Lentin, Patrick Fontaine, Guigou Chenevier, and Dominique Grimaud conducted by the author in 2020/21.

Roy Prior in *Anarchy* n° 89 (July '68) *(in English)*
"The great courtyard of the Sorbonne is crowded..."
JD Beauvalet, *Les Inrockuptibes* website (13/4/2018)
"No-one really amplified the hubbub like the Stones and The Beatles..."
Christian Tritsch quoted in *Rock & Folk* n° 57 (Oct '71)
"For me, at the beginning, being a musician was a job line any other..."
Klaus Blasquiz in *Volume* 9:2 (2012)
"In May I worked at the Beaux Arts..."
Cyrille Verdeaux interviewed by Aymeric Leroy
"I was in hospital for weeks recovering from the 'migraine'..."
Olivier Zdrzalik interviewed by Manuel Rabasse (2018)
"There was an incredible atmosphere! The barricades..."

3. A BRIEF HISTORY
Part 1: 1968-69

Philippe Thieyre, transcript of talk on Magma (2009)
"...in the fallout of '68, plenty of groups spring up..."
Didier Malherbe quoted in *La France Underground* (p. 147)
"The era after May '68 was like a bottle of champagne..."

4. OCTOBER '69:
The Amougies Festival

Jean-Noël Coghe in *Best* n° 17 (Dec '69)
"The festival was a huge survey of the different musical trends of today..."
JJ Birgé from his blog (www.drame.org)
"The shock for me was discovering free jazz..."

Sources

5. A BRIEF HISTORY
Part 2: 1970

Daevid Allen, *Gong Dreaming 2* (p. 46) *(in English)*
   "*It was the start of a unique French rock movement..*"
Marc Blanc interviewed by the author (2020)
   "*Paul Alessandrini organised the Halles Festival...*"
Patrice Blanc-Francard quoted in *La Chienlit* (p. 307)
   "*French rock has always had a serious problem leaving behind its ersatz role...*"

6. SUMMER '70:
L'été pop

Hamon & Rotman, *Generation 2: Les années de poudre* (p. 261)
   "*On the road, a growing cloud of dust...*"
Serge Loupien, *La France Underground* (pp. 167-8)
   "*With Gong's set barely finished...*"

7. A BRIEF HISTORY
Part 3: 1971-73

Hamon & Rotman, *Generation 2: Les années de poudre* (p. 261)
   "*On the road, a growing cloud of dust...*"

8. THE MJC CIRCUIT

Hamon & Rotman, *Generation 2: Les années de poudre* (p. 261)
   "*On the road, a growing cloud of dust...*"

9. A BRIEF HISTORY
Part 4: 1974-78

Jac Berrocal interviewed by Dan Warburton (2004) *(in English)*
   "*What really blew us away was PiL...*"

10. INDEPENDENT LABELS

Richard Pinhas interviewed by Philippe Robert in *Agitation Frite*
   "*No-one had started an independent label before Disjuncta...*" (p. 98)
Gérard Terronès interviewed by Philippe Robert in *Agitation Frite*
   "*My priority was (and indeed still is) the world of jazz...*"
Richard Pinhas interviewed by Chloé Cotteur, BnF (2013)
   "*People had the goal to release what they wanted...*"
Richard Pinhas interviewed by the author, 2024
   "*What was important about the label is that we produced...*"
Richard Pinhas quoted in *Un Certain Rock(?) Français Vol. 2*, pp. 3-5

"Alain and I had been run off our feet..."
Ariel Kalma interviewed by the author, 2021
"I'd told Richard I thought it was great..."
Jean-Jacques Birgé interviewed by Philippe Robert in *Agitation Frite*
"We were waiting for producers who couldn't make up their minds..."
Paul Putti interviewed in *Rock en Stock* n° 2 (May '77)
"We sold 3,500 copies of Kotrill *in three months..."*

PART 2 - THE EXCEPTION THAT PROVES THE RULE

11. LARD FREE
Except for those noted below all quotations are from interviews with the author conducted from 2020-23.

Rock & Roll Musique n° 2 (Feb '77)
    "Like the mythical sea serpent, Lard Free surfaces, dives, then resurfaces..."
Gilbert Artman interviewed by Franco Onweb (2021)
    "It allowed you to break all the codes, all the shackles..."
Gilbert Artman interviewed by Philippe Robert in *Agitation Frite*
    "François Mativet was definitely the most iconoclastic..." (pp. 108-9)
    "The music on the first recording is a good reflection of this era..." (p. 109)
Jacques Chabiron, *Rock & Folk* n°55 (Aug '71)
    "Lard Free is a band absolutely without equal in France..."
Actuel n° 17 (Feb '72)
    "Our name already shows several influences..."
Gilbert Artman interviewed by Jean-Rodolphe Zanzotto *BnF* (Nov 2015)
    "So we set up the piano frame, the rest of the band, and we start..."
    "When we knew we weren't going any further we wanted to record..."
    "There was a rift in the group..."
    "We set up and got the sound we wanted. There were no pre-conceptions..."
Actuel n° ? ('73)
    "the use of the synthesiser to the most unsettling effect..."
Gilbert Artman interviewed by Gérard N'Guyen *Atem* n°10 (June '77)
    "The second disc is calmer... the aggressiveness is no longer wilful..."
    "It is quite similar music, if you listen to both albums they border on.."
    "The previous two discs were a little held back by lack of time..."
Actuel n° ? ('75)
    "Lard Free resurface with a new incarnation..."
Hervé Muller in *Rock & Folk* ('75)
    "The first album... dated from a time when Lard Free was still trying..."
    "Lard Free is Gilbert Artman..."
Guigou Chenevier, *Une histoire d'Etron Fou Leloublan*
    "Sixteen saxophonists lined up on the stage..."
Gilbert Artman interviewed by Bobbi Bruno & Paul Putti, *Rock en Stock* ('77)
    "[Urban Sax is] the unitary sound par excellence..."
    "I have never believed in the notion of a group..."
    "All of the current musicians play keyboards..."
    "We created spiral motifs and time-shifted everything..."
Eurock x (p. 92) (in English)
    "There were people from the Cobra label..."
Xavier Beal in *Atem* n°11 (Jan '78)
    "This third disc has lost the sonic coherence..."
Rock en Stock n°14 ('78)
    "Lard Free produces something very similar and very different..."

PART 3 - THE POLITICAL UNDERGROUND

12. INTRODUCTION

Actuel n° 6 (Mar '71)
    "In France, Pop equals helmets, truncheons, cops, iron bars.."
Christian Victor and Julien Regoli, *Vingt ans de Rock Français* (p. 99)
    "These bands were concerned with the ideas of May '68..."
Alain Roux, *Music et vie quotidienne* (p. 143)
    "dreams and contemplates itself... the originality of the French youth..."
Richard Pinhas interviewed by Philippe Robert in *Agitation Frite* (p. 97)
    "We were in the fallout from May '68 and Vietnam War..."
Richard Pinhas quoted in *La Chienlit* (p. 73)
    "To be realistic, the politically committed groups reached four to five thousand..."
Paul Alessandrini, *Rock & Folk* n° 44 (Sept '70)
    "Rushing through the breach opened by Red Noise..."
Michel Muzac interviewed by the author (2020)
    "The idea to create the FLIP was mainly at the initiative of..."
François Joffra, *Pop Music* (13 May '71)
    "Recently the FLIP brought musicians to the Marché au Puces..."
Dominique Grimaud interviewed by the author (2020)
    "It was a rather brief era, beginning in '68..."

13. RED NOISE

Quotations from Marc Blanc are from interviews with the author conducted in 2020/21.

Patrick Vian quoted in *Actuel* n° 17 (Feb '72)
    "I wanted our music to be a kind of rubbish bin..."
    "In the beginning, a good Red Noise concert only ended when..."
    "Revolutionary songs have been sung for a thousand years..."
    "Today our music is built on sonic experimentation..."
Thierry Lewin, *Pop Music* n° 83 (18 Nov '71)
    "May 1968. The students occupy the Sorbonne..."
Jean-Pierre Lentin, *Actuel* n° 17 (Feb '72)
    "the first underground group... a symbol, the unrivalled reference..."
Patrick Vian interviewed by Baptiste Manzinali, *Gonzai* website (2013)
    "I wanted to show that to make music it was enough to take an instrument..."
    "I lacked that Napoleonic side needed to lead a band..."
Patrick Vian quoted in *Rock & Folk* n° 40 (May '70)
    "[music] that doesn't try to make people forget their little day-to-day problems..."

"Instinctively you want to be appealing on stage, or rather cause a reaction..."
Rock & Folk article (*Un Certain Rock(?) Français Vol. 1*)
"There's no respite. Red Noise set off a blinding explosion..." (p. 8)
"Its structure, its form, its approach... is unique in France..." (p.9)
Dominique Grimaud quoted in *La Chienlit* (p. 94)
"A scream. Slogans. Almost continuous electric guitar feedback..."
Olivier Kowalski interviewed by Manuel Rabasse (2018)
"Patrick Vian... considered that with its shattering of structures music itself..."
Actuel record review (*Un Certain Rock(?) Français* p. 9)
"a completely free improvisation where the sound intensifies to a scream..."
Deshayes & Grimaud, *L'underground musical en France* (p. 110)
"a half-success or a half-failure, whichever you prefer..."
Rock & Folk n° 50 (Mar '71)
"You immediately sense their real desire and pleasure in smashing music open..."

14. BARRICADE

Except for those noted below all quotations are from interviews with François Billard, Jean-Louis Tixier, Joseph Racaille, and Cyrille Verdeaux conducted by the author in 2020/21.

Best n° 26 (Sept '70)
"This time it's just too much, there are some groups being political on stage!"
"I want to tell you about a band that left quite a few people speechless..."
François Billard interviewed by Philippe Robert in *Agitation Frite*
"We were pretty clear-eyed about our limitations..." (p. 34)
"The result was predictable, the group never signed the contact..." (p. 29)
François Billard interviewed by Lou, *Fuzzine* website (2010)
"was originally built on a number of very simple ideas..."
Joseph Racaille interviewed by Lou, *Fuzzine* website (2010)
"Actuel was very interested. They asked us to write an article..."
"Barricade was really a live band..."
Rock & Folk n° 44 (Sept '70)
"I had a laugh at some clowns called Red Noise..."
Rock & Folk n° 46 (Nov '70)
"For the first time I witnessed the audience's desire..."
Rock & Folk n° 45 (Oct '70)
"Barricade creates an atmosphere of apocalypse..."
Superhebdo Pop Music (8 Apr '71)
"Barricade are the anti-spectacle, an outrageous provocation..."
Hector Zazou, article from *Actuel* (*Un Certain Rock(?) Français Vol. 1* p. 28)
"Barricade followed the path of 'political music' up to its split..."
"The two survivors of this sad tale..."
Actuel n° 29 (Mar '73)
"From Barricade have come two groups..."
Actuel n° 40 (Mar '74)
"Barricade II is practically the only survivor of a generation..."

15. MAAJUN

Except for those noted below all quotations are from interviews with Roger Scaglia, Alain Roux, and Jean-Louis Lefèbvre conducted by the author in 2021.

Jean-Louis Mahjun quoted in *La Chienlit*
  "The label told us, 'You can record whatever you want to'..." (p. 351)
  "There was tension between a side that was situationist..." (p. 73)
Alain Roux, *Music et vie quotidienne*
  "The conception and creation of the disc..." (pp.133-4)
  "We organised a small festival at Gagny..." (p. 134)
Maajun quoted in article 'Maajun nouveau groupe français' (early '71?)
  "Maajun is a hashish confectionary that can be found in Morocco..."
  "We recorded this record above all else to be able to express what we feel..."
Jean-Pierre Lentin, *Actuel* n° 6 (Mar '71)
  "But when the company's management heard the tape a new problem arose..."
  "There were those who screamed "Go back to Peking, Maoists"..."
Rock & Folk n° 48 (Jan '71)
  "We recorded a disc at Vogue that is still in their vaults..."
Rock & Folk n° 50 (Mar '71)
  "Maajun didn't play, as some line-up problems were still unresolved."

16. KOMINTERN

Except for those noted below all quotations are from interviews with Michel Muzac conducted by the author in 2020/21.

Komintern, *Le Parapluie* n° 6 (Mar '72)
  "We wanted to interrupt the ball, to stop it dead..."
Olivier Zdrzalik interviewed by Manuel Rabasse (2018)
  "We knew the name [Red Noise], we'd even seen them in concert..."
  "We weren't really politicised at the time..."
Paul Alessandrini, *Rock & Folk* n° 44 (Sept '70)
  "The subversive aspect, the reading of political tracts..."
Jacques Vassal, *Rock & Folk* n° 44 (Sept '70)
  "Is this group in the process of making the first 'Leftist co-option of pop'?..."
Yves Adrien, *Rock & Folk* n° 50 (Mar '71)
  "The music of Komintern, can at first appear to be austere and cold..."
Olivier Zdrzalik, in 'Komintern', *Ugly Things* n° 56 (2018) *(in English)*
  "The recording process was quite extraordinary for us..."
Komintern interview in *Actuel* n° 17 (Feb '72)
  "The text on the sleeve is completely unrepresentative..."
  "On the record, we wanted to put entirely spoken passages..."
  "We're basically doing it to secure the survival of the group..."
Thierry Lewin, *Pop Music-Superhebdo* (18 Nov '71)

"Without ever falling into the musical jumble..."
Best n° 42 (Jan '72)
"Above all else this politically motivated band plays..."
John Peel, *Disc* (4 Nov '72) *(in English)*
"One of the LPs I bought was by a band called Komintern...."
Actuel n° 29 (Mar '73)
"Komintern has changed since its 'leftist' period..."

17. FILLE QUI MOUSSE

Except for those noted below all quotations are from interviews with Jean-Henri Enu Benjamin Legrand, Stéphane Korb, Dominique Lentin, and Alain Roux conducted by the author in 2020-22.

Henri Jean Enu, sleevenotes for Spalax Music CD (1998)
  "From it's birth Fille Qui Mousse..."
Henri Jean Enu, sleevenotes for Monster Melodies LP (2013)
  "Fille Qui Mousse was mobilised in this atmosphere of rupture..."
Jean-Pierre Lentin, *Actuel* n° 17 (Feb '72)
  "Fille Qui Mousse embodies the ego-trip of Henri-Jean Enu..."
Benjamin Legrand quoted in *La France Underground* (p. 222)
  "On stage, we didn't really know what we were doing..."
Henri Jean Enu, interviewed by Alan & Steve Freeman, *Audion* n° 32 (1995) *(in English)*
  "Mixing two, or more, antagonising structures..."
  "I was trapped by my visual conception..."
Henri Jean Enu, quoted in *Actuel* n° 17 (Feb '72)
  "When the Spanish invaders arrived in Latin America..."
  "Trixie Stapleton, is a friend of ours..."
Henri Jean Enu interviewed by Philippe Robert in *Agitation Frite 2* (p. 35)
  "I paid no attention to these affairs..."
  "One day Gilles Yéprémain called me..."

18. DAGON

Except for those noted below all quotations are from interviews with Dominique Lentin and Daniel Hoffman conducted by the author in 2021-24.

Jean-Pierre Lentin, sleevenotes for *30 Years of Musical Agitation.* (199x)
  "Dagon mesmerised a generation of French pot-heads..."
Jean-Pierre Lentin interviewed by Aymeric Leroy
  "None of them knew how to play, and they were looking for a bass player..."
  "We started listening to English psychedelic groups like Soft Machine..."
  "We'd smoke joints, everyone would take their instruments..."

Pop 2000 n° 11 (Nov '72)
: *"They had a highly individual vision expressed..."*
: *"Their music lost the surrealism and imagery their singer brought..."*

Yves Adrien in *Rock & Folk* n° 50 (Mar '71)
: *"Their grimy sound creates a noxious atmosphere..."*

Dominique Lentin interviewed by Philippe Robert in *Agitation Frite* (p. 183)
: *"We mixed a happening in with a concert..."*

Gilles Yéprémian interviewed by Philippe Robert in *Agitation Frite 2* (p. 17)
: *"There is a live cassette of a Dagon concert at Nantes..."*

Gerald Moenner, *La Nouvelle République* 24/9/72
: *"Dagon was able to captivate the audience from the very beginning..."*

Gerald Moenner, *La Nouvelle République* 25/5/73
: *"Dagon's music is a continual search for original sounds..."*

Sources

PART 4 - THE LYSERGIC UNDERGROUND

19. INTRODUCTION

Quotations from Bob Benamou and Jacques Dudon are from interviews with the author conducted in 2020/21.

Robert Wyatt quoted in *Wrong Movements: A Robert Wyatt History* by Michael King (SAF, 1994) *(in English)*
"There is just a great tradition in France of listening to music..."

Daevid Allen quoted in *Wrong Movements: A Robert Wyatt History* by Michael King (SAF, 1994) *(in English)*
"People like Bridget Bardot were there and lots of film producers and directors..."
"We only played there about five times..."

Lionel Magal quoted in *La France Underground* (p. 313)
"I was holding a billhook in one hand and a chicken in the other..."

Jean-Jacques Lebel interviewed by Aymeric Leroy (2003)
"Daevid and Kevin [Ayers] said to me several times afterwards..."

20. BANANAMOON

Except for those noted below all quotations from Daevid Allen are from his book "Gong Dreaming 1" (GAS, 1994), and those from Marc Blanc and Patrick Fontaine are from interviews with the author conducted in 2020/21.

Marc Blanc interviewed by Alain Hertay (2015)
"Daevid Allen was playing in the cellar of La Vieille Grille..."

Daevid Allen interviewed by Udi Koomran (1995) *(in English)*
"No one had heard music like that.."
"[it] didn't come from any outside influence that I know of..."

Daevid Allen interviewed by Steve Ward (2001) *(in English)*
"I saw Syd playing a curious sort of slide guitar..."

Marc Blanc sleevenotes for *Je ne fume pas des bananes* (Legend Music 1992)
"We had just enough time to rehearse two tracks..."
"a horror film, shot in Normandy..."

Daevid Allen, interviewed by Mike Barnes, *The Wire* n° 23 (July 2003) *(in English)*
"A friend of ours was arrested..."

Marc Blanc quoted in *La France Underground* (p. 139)
"We had invitations to this concert at the Bataclan..."

21. AME SON

Except for those noted below all quotations from Marc Blanc and Patrick Fontaine are from interviews with the author conducted in 2020/21.

Marc Blanc interviewed by Bester, *Gonzai* website (March 2020)
　　"a girl on the underground told me that the Marquee was finished..."
Marc Blanc quoted in *La France Underground*
　　"I think we are one of the only French groups to have played..." (p. 153)
　　"We could have easily carried on like Magma and Gong..." (p. 170)
Marc Blanc interviewed by Alain Hertay (2015)
　　"We had two days in the studio to do all of the backing tracks for Catalyse..."
Paul Alessandrini, *Rock & Folk* n° 35 (Dec '69)
　　"If everything doesn't yet seem to be perfect..."
Jean-Noël Coghe, *Best* n° 17 (Dec '69)
　　"Ame Son are French and full of promise..."
Philippe Paringaux, *Rock & Folk* n° 46 (Nov '70)
　　"Ame Son express a few snatches of plastic beauty in the style of Pink Floyd..."

22. GONG

Except for those noted below all quotations from Daevid Allen are from his book "Gong Dreaming 2" (SAF, 2009), and those from the other members of the band are from interviews with the author conducted in 2020/21.

Daevid Allen interviewed by Lars Fahlin *(in English)*
　　"At various times in France, Gong was a revolutionary band..."
Didier Malherbe interviewed by Aymeric Leroy (1999) *(in English)*
　　"I was fascinated, they were playing a good fusion..."
　　"That first [album] was a mix of Daevid's songs and free jazz..."
　　"Camembert Electrique was still mainly Daevid..."
　　"We did a first tour of some pretty big places, like Newcastle City Hall..."
Didier Malherbe interviewed by Max Ritter, *It's Psychedelic Baby* (2023) *(in English)*
　　"I met... Leo Gillespie [and] Gerry Field..."
Pierre Lattès, *Best* n° 17 (Dec '69)
　　"You could sense the real freshness..."
Daevid Allen quoted in *Rock & Folk* n° 57 (Oct '71)
　　"It doesn't represent the current group. It was a kind of masturbation..."
　　"He brings a new energy to Gong... he plays so hard..."
　　"This record bears witness to the development of the group..."
Paul Alessandrini *Rock & Folk* n° 57 (Oct '71)
　　"sonic madness, a kind of violence, with so many original components..."
Pip Pyle quoted in *Gong Dreaming 2* (p. 425) *(in English)*
　　"like a flock of deranged psychedelic chaffinches."

Sources

"...*we jammed the whole affair to projected images of film in live synchro.*"
Didier Malherbe quoted in *La France Underground* (p. 145)
"*Every time their styles alternated. A jazzy drummer would be followed...*"
Daevid Allen interviewed by Clive Williamson (1975) *(in English)*
"*I wanted to split about two years ago...*"
Steve Hillage interviewed by Julian Marszalek, *Prog Magazine* (2023) *(in English)*
"*Kevin invited Didier Malherbe to jam...*"
"*One thing about Gong that I really like is...*"
Steve Hillage, *Love From the Planet Gong* booklet *(in English)*
"*Since all the songs on* Flying Teapot *were all pretty much formed...*" (p. 11)
"*Personally I was happy with the way they reintegrated...*" (p. 22)
"*These songs were almost entirely created in Spring 1973...*" (p. 22)
"*Although there was some instability and tension at the recording..*" (p. 36)
"*The next day Mike arrived with a great new bass riff...*" (p. 39)
Didier Malherbe interviewed by Fred Dellar, *NME* (13/7/74) *(in English)*
"*It began as an imaginative game to explain the rapport...*"
Steve Hillage interviewed by Klemen Breznikar, *It's Psychedelic Baby* (2016) *(in English)*
"*Daevid had the fully developed Gong cosmology...*"
Daevid Allen interviewed by Fred Dellar (2002) *(in English)*
"*We arrived at the Manor on New Years Day '73...*"
"*Simon Heyworth was practically driven to a nervous breakdown...*"
"*I had time and space to meditate on a new direction for Gong...*"
"*We could wire up and record from our own rooms...*"
Bob Benamou interviewed by Aymeric Leroy in *L'École de Canterbury*
"*One day, we had an argument over some futile pretext...*"
Steve Hillage interviewed by Anil Prasad *(in English)*
"*He's a key element of the Gong sound in the '70s...*"
Tim Blake, *Love From the Planet Gong* booklet (p. 16) *(in English)*
"*Didier Thibault was finding it difficult to blend in...*"
"*In a couple of months, we had moved on from a repertoire...*"
Mike Howlett, *Love From the Planet Gong* booklet *(in English)*
"*I insisted they must at least hear me play...*" (p. 10)
"*After touring around the UK and Europe to promote* Shamal...*" (p. 52)
Mike Howlett interviewed by Aymeric Leroy (1997) *(in English)*
"*My first jam with Pierre was frustrating..*"
"*Pierre... left after* Angel's Egg, *grumbling about 'silly lyrics'...*"
"*For me the trilogy (including* Flying Teapot*) is a profound work...*"
"*Shamal was a collaboration...*"
"*The group which toured* Shamal *was always fairly tense in my memory...*"
"*Things came to a head and Virgin was given the choice ...*"
Pierre Moerlen interviewed by Aymeric Leroy (1995) *(in English)*
"*I knew the Lemoine brothers, who are also from the Alsace region...*"
"*There were indeed some problems between me and Daevid...*"
"*I left after the recording of* You *because the atmosphere in the band...*"
"*The problem was, I didn't get on very well with the bass player..*"
Gilli Allen quoted in *Gong Dreaming 2* (pp. 338-9) *(in English)*
"*I finished up in the Milkweg in Amsterdam..*"

Daevid Allen, *Gong History (in English)*
   "We had come to the conclusion that, because I was contributing..."
   "I couldn't actually get on stage. It was as though there was..."
Steve Hillage interviewed by Jerry Ewing (2016) *(in English)*
   "I woke up really early one morning and I just had this riff come in my head..."
   "Unfortunately [Gong] went through some real problems at the end of '74..."
   "Miquette and I resolved to sort of keep in there and make a go of it..."
Daevid Allen interviewed by Aymeric Leroy (2007) *(in English)*
   "When you play to more than 2000 people you don't have eye contact..."
Marc Blanc sleevenotes for *Je ne fume pas des bananes* (Legend Music 1992)
   "I went up to see Daevid after the show..."

23. CHEVAL FOU/NYL

Except for those noted below all quotations from Michel Peteau and Patrick Fontaine are from interviews with the author conducted in 2020/21.

Michel Peteau interviewed by Klemen Breznikar, *It's Psychedelic Baby* (2018)
   (in English, translated from French by Antonio Barreiros)
   "It was incredible! Nothing else stood in the way of us becoming a group..."
   "The room was full, Stéphane, Jean and I felt 'out of this world'..."
   "The times were very lysergic..."
   "At the time when Cheval Fou was active, record companies..."
   "Many friends came to see us and settled..."
   "I remember that he received us at his home one morning..."
   "The connection with Jannick Top was due to Stéphane..."
   "I felt that something quite powerful had come, a 'new wave'..."

24. CRIUM DELIRIUM

Except for those noted below all quotations are from interviews with Lionel 'Fox' Magal conducted by the author in 2024.

William Belvie in *The Psykedeklik Road Book* (p.?)
   "At every concert Renard, the shaman of the stage..."
Christian-Louis Eclimont in *Rock'o'Rico* (p.?)
   "less of a group, more of a conglomeration..."
Lionel Magal quoted in *La France Underground*
   "When we were kids my parents took us to the Blue Note..." (p. 308)
   "When he came, Bentleys and Rolls piled up in the neighborhood..." (p. 3?)
   "The only thing that I sent them while on the road..." (p. 314)
   "I'd had enough, they were too organised and structured for me." (p. 313)
   "This split obviously caused a lot of back and forth..." (p. 3?)
Patrice Quentin interviewed by Aymeric Leroy (2014)
   "We came back on foot, hitchhiking via Algeria..."
Jean-Pierre Lentin in *Actuel* (*Un Certain Rock(?) Français* p. 22)
   "Crium Delirium only use the voice for cosmic sound effects..."
Pop 2000 n° 10 (Oct '72)

Sources

"*Here is a totally unique band that we'd like to see more of in France...*"
Lionel Magal quoted in *Rock & Folk* (*Un Certain Rock(?) Français* p. 23)
"*We alternate between spontaneous concerts in the street...*"
"*The contracts we've been offered are much too demanding..*"
Manifeste 1973 quoted in *The Psykedeklik Road Book* (p. 60)
"*CRI OM is not a meeting place, nor a collection of audio-visual specialists...*"
J-F Bizot, *Actuel* n° 29 (Mar '73)
"*The extremely resourceful freaks of Crium Délirium...*"
Paul Alessandrini, *Rock & Folk* (1973)
"*[It started] with a call for the audience to participate...*"
Mike Howlett interview with the author (2021)
"*There was a band called Crium Delirium who were good friends...*"

25. CLEARLIGHT

Except for those noted below all quotations are from interviews with Cyrille Verdeaux conducted by the author 2020-23.

Cyrille Verdeaux interviewed by Laurent Metayer
"*It was a pure game of circumstance that let me hear the music inside...*"
"*Mike's success probably helped to interest Virgin...*"
"*We spoke about making a really close band...*"
"*The condition was that I permanently come to live in London...*"

Cyrille Verdeaux interviewed by Aymeric Leroy
"*There I developed my taste for classical harmony...*"
"*It was only on joining them that I discovered a taste...*"
"*He gave me Virgin's address...*"
"*With the guys from Gong, we played one after the other...*"
"*Finally, finding myself with a side of drums-and-guitar rock...*"
"*A magazine article published in the second week...*"

Cyrille Verdeaux, sleevenotes to Clearlight Music CD (2000) *(in English)*
"*Afterwards everyone was freely improvising over it...*"
"*a one-hour musical clip without any dialogue at all...*"

PART 5 - THE JAZZ UNDERGROUND

26. INTRODUCTION
Quotations from Robert Wood are from interviews with the author conducted in 2020/21.

27. MOVING GELATINE PLATES
Except for those noted below all quotations from Didier Thibault are from interviews with the author conducted in 2021.

Didier Thibault interviewed by Klemen Breznikar, *It's Psychedelic Baby* (2020) *(in English)*
"The welcome was more than warm..."
"As a faithful listener of Pop Club, I was stunned..."
"he was enthusiastic about innovating.."
"it appears very sophisticated..."

unknown "Brigitte Fontaine et Gelatine Plate a la Fac de Doit" - reproduced in *Moving Gelatine Plates* (Monster Melodies, 2014)
"Moving Gelatine Plate (sic) makes music that is distinctive..."

unknown "Moving Gelatine Plates ouvre la voie de la pop français" reproduced in *Moving Gelatine Plates* (Monster Melodies, 2014)
"Their rich and dense music seduces the ear immediately..."

unknown "Gibus Club"
reproduced in *Moving Gelatine Plates* (Monster Melodies, 2014)
"They are a total success everywhere they play..."

unknown review
reproduced in *Moving Gelatine Plates* (Monster Melodies, 2014)
"...this group. unfairly little-known in France, seduced the audience..."

Paul Alessandrini, *Rock & Folk* n° 43 (Aug '70)
"Moving Gelatine Plates are the most interesting of the new bands..."

Didier Thibault quoted in *Actuel* n° 17 (Feb '72)
"We use the voice as an instrument..."

28. MAGMA
Except for those noted below all quotations from Christian Vander are from his book "À vie, à mort, et après..." (naïve, 2013) and all quotations from Klaus Blasquiz are from his "Au Coeur du Magma" (Le mot et le reste, 2013).

Christian Vander interviewed by David McKenna & Ludovic Merle, *Rockfort* (2009) *(translated by David McKenna)*
"What I looked for in Coltrane's music..."
"A lot of groups at the time... dreamed about things..."

Sources

Laurent Thibault Facebook post (5 March 2022)
"Christian wanted a universal musical language..."
"Kobaïan had its origin in the scat that Leon Thomas sang..."
Klaus Blasquiz interviewed by Poul Erik Sørensen, *MM* (Aug/Sept '77)
(translated by Michael Bohn)
"[Kobaïan] is a physiological language, a ritual..."
Richard Raux interviewed on *Discorama* (19 June '70)
"We really believe in the violence of music..."
Christian Vander interviewed by Stanislas Witold, *Extra* n° 1 (Dec '70)
"My mother was friends with Bobby Jaspar..."
"I gave everything I had on the drums..."
Christian Vander interviewed by François-René Cristiani,
Rock & Folk n° 85 (Feb '74)
"At sixteen, I tried playing at jams. I got sarcastic comments..."
Klaus Blasquiz interviewed by Alan Freeman (1981)
"Zabu was the singer, but he was never there..."
"Christian and Laurent Thibault came to see me..."
"The way he plays the bass is very particular and very in there..."
"It actually doesn't matter about the instrumentation..."
"The sound isn't strong enough..."
"For me it's the album that sounds closest to the real Magma..."
"It was a step backwards, it was more improvised..."
Philippe Paringaux, *Rock & Folk* n° 40 (May '70)
"In Magma's music there is a drama constantly on the verge of hysteria..."
Philippe Paringaux, *Rock & Folk* n° 41 (June '70)
"Neither pop, nor jazz, nor the music of yesterday..."
Emmanuel Gray, *Jazz Hot* n° 264 (Sept '70)
"Let's immediately clear up any misunderstanding..."
Richard Raux quoted in *La France Underground*
"There was controversy from the start..." (p. 290)
Christian Vander interviewed by Jean-M. Mareska, *Best* n° 24 (July '70)
"Straight away we have to correct those who think that we are fascists..."
Giorgio Gomelsky interviewed by Archie Patterson, *Eurock* (in English)
"They played me a tape of a French band..."
"Magma did very well in England. We took that country by storm!..."
Klaus Blasquiz quoted in *Best* n° 56 (Mar '73)
"Giorgio Gomelsky is the mythical being that everyone hopes for..."
Jean-Noël Ogouz, *Best* n° 29 (Dec '70)
"Magma's music is indefinable and totally indescribable..."
Eddy Mitchell quoted in *Pop Music* (6 April '72)
"I really love Magma's music..."
Yves Adrien, *Rock & Folk* n° 54 (July '71)
"How can one express how remarkable is Magma's slap to the face..."
Jean-Paul Commin, *Best* n° 36 (July '71)
"This time choosing record of the month didn't come to blows..."
Francis Moze quoted in "Magma la pop a part", *Salut les Copains* ('71)
"It's the music we would've played if we hadn't played Magma's..."
***Best* n° x (?)**
"with these pieces, an audience outside France has the opportunity..."

Klaus Blasquiz, article from 2000?
 "Giorgio Gomelsky negotiated the change..."
Sacha Reins, *Best* n° 51 (Oct '72)
 "Magma confirmed what we already know..."
Rock & Folk n° 69 (Oct '72)
 "Gomelsky, their manager, comes on stage before the group..."
François Cahen interviewed by Michel Bourre, *Rock & Folk* n° 126 (July '77)
 "[Giorgio and I] had a fabulous connection for a year..."
Yochk'O Seffer interviewed by Klemen Breznikar, *It's Psychedelic Baby* (2022) (in English)
 "We'd both decided to set up 'our' formation, Zao..."
Christian Vander sleevenotes for *Kohnzert Zünd* (2015)
 "For Magma, live performance is essential..."
Jannick Top quoted in Antoine de Caunes, *Magma* (Albin Michel, '78)
 "Musically I have a very complementary role to that of Christian..."
 "Christian offered to share the responsibility for the group with me..."
Klaus Blasquiz, *Best* n° 56 (Mar '73)
 "There are now seven of us... There is a new dimension..."
Christian Lebrun, *Best* n° 58 (May '73)
 "The addition of a chorus of between one to three people..."
Christian Vander interviewed by *Big Bang*
 "I admit that it was my fault..."
 "We hadn't even harmonized the piece, it was very fresh..."
Steve Lake, *Sounds* (19 Jan '74) (in English)
 "Like their major rivals, Gong, Magma have a specific mysticism..."
Christian Vander interviewed by François-René Cristiani
 Rock & Folk n° 85 (Feb '74)
 "For me, Magma was born with Mëkanik Kommandöh..."
Steve Lake, *Melody Maker* (15 Dec '73) (in English)
 "Listening to Magma requires a lot of mental adjustment..."
Alain Wais, *Extra* n° 46 (Sept '74)
 "Perhaps for the first time, Magma has successfully..."
Jannick Top interviewed by Michel Bourre, *Rock & Folk* n° 124 (May '77)
 "As we worked, little by little things accumulated..."
 "I forgot what had happened a little too quickly..."
Klaus Blasquiz interviewed by Christian Victor, *Jukebox Magazine* n° 171 (Nov 2001)
 "For this album, Jannick Top wasn't coming to play an existing work..."
 "This disc is the first one I recommend for people to discover Magma."
 "Christian broke Magma up... For no reason..."
 "Jannick Top's 'De Futura' is superb..."
 "These albums aren't very representative, they aren't really Magma records..."
 "Now I realise that it wasn't really Magma any more..."
Christian Vander interviewed by Laurent Buvry & Jean-François Papin,
 Rock en Stock (Aug '78)
 "Üdü Wüdü was made at a time when there was actually no group..."
 "I hadn't yet realised that it was the new Magma cycle that was preparing..."

"The record is all fresh, the songs were composed and played in the studio..."
Gerard Nguyen, *Atem* n° 7 (Oct '76)
"Üdü Wüdü testifies to the incredible complicity that reigns..."
"This piece was first performed by the Utopic Sporadic Orchestra..."
Michel Lousquet, *Best* n° 120 (July '78)
"I would have liked to help Magma start this new period..."

29. CONTREPOINT

Except for those noted below all quotations from Jean-Pierre Weiller are from interviews with the author conducted in 2023.

Jean-Pierre Weiller interviewed by Pascal Bussey, *Atem* n° 6 (Sept '76)
"There was an evolution, but we were already writing our own pieces..."
"It was our first introduction to the Parisian and French pop scene..."
"It was a really exciting time... We played at Auvers..."
"It could take drastic turns, which is why a lot of groups break up..."
"I admit that it's an environment I find difficult to move in..."
"I spent a few days at Hugh's place after he left Soft Machine..."
"We were dead beat when we met up with Hugh..."
"Nobody said: 'Contrepoint no longer exists'..."
"I think Countrepoint is going to do something..."
Pop 2000 n° 4 (Apr '72)
"Contrepoint's music [has] astonishing contrasts..."

PART 6 - THE AVANT UNDERGROUND

30. INTRODUCTION
Quotations from Bob Benamou and Jacques Dudon are from interviews with the author conducted in 2020/21.

31. CAMIZOLE
Except for those noted below all quotations from Dominique Grimaud are from interviews with the author conducted in 2021.

Dominique Grimaud in *WOASCHES*, 12 June 2019
    "I think that in artistic creation everything stems from childhood."
Dominique Grimaud quoted in *Liberation*
    "When I speak of 'wholes' instead of 'pieces', it's not just wordplay…"
Liberation article (*Un Certain Rock(?) Français Vol. 1*)
    "In the middle of the drum 'solo', firecrackers go off at our feet…"
    "We were literally thrown off the stage by the audience…"

32. JAC BERROCAL
Except for those noted below all quotations from Jac Berrocal are from interviews with the author conducted in 2021.

Jac Berrocal interview in *Jazz Magazine* (*Un Certain Rock(?) Français 2* p. 33)
    "I think that my music can be categorised as improvised music…"
    "One day in Pakistan, in a village north of Karachi, I had a sort of revelation…"
    "I believe that for music, locations are very important…"
    "I think that there's a family relationship between this piece and some of Russolo's creations…"
Jac Berrocal interviewed by Dan Warburton (2004) *(in English)*
    "I sang in a choir specialising in Renaissance music…"
    "The trumpet came in a rather bizarre way…"
    "I tried a few things out with friends, but it was difficult…"
    "It's one of the oldest churches in the region…"
    "It wasn't a jazz record, and it certainly wasn't rock…"
    "We found the text on a postcard in a rubbish bin…"
    " 'Rock'n'Roll Station' was originally written for me to perform…"
Jac Berrocal interviewed by David McKenna, *The Quietus* (2015) *(in English)*
    "I'd always liked jazz because my father was a fan of traditional jazz…"
Jac Berrocal quoted in *La France Underground* (p. 346)
    "I couldn't let either of them know that I was seeing the other, because they detested each other…"

Jac Berrocal interviewed by Philippe Robert in *Agitation Frite* (p. 54)
"One night in August 1970 a broken-down 2CV stopped at the side of a trail..."
Jac Berrocal interviewed by Pilooski (2020)
"I wanted to sum up my vision of the '50s in an abstract, jumbled way..."

33. ETRON FOU LELOUBLAN

Except for those noted below all quotations from Guigou Chenevier are from interviews with the author conducted in 2021.

Guigou Chenevier interviewed by Philippe Robert in *Agitation Frite*
"Our first ever concert was supporting Magma..." (p. 131)
"Our music was rather unique..." (p. 132)
Chris Chanet interviewed by Klemen Breznikar, *It's Psychedelic Baby* (2014) (in English)
"In 1970, I lived in the city of Grenoble where I was an actor..."
"Some gigs in Grenoble, some tries with a bass player..."
"This album is a good representation of what we were playing.."
"I met Francis during a visit to my parents..."
Guigou Chenevier, *Une histoire d'Etron Fou Leloublan* (in English)
"We hadn't played a single gig.." (p. 209)
"The only neighbours we had were two aggressive..." (p. 214)
"Their music immediately won us over..." (p. 218)
"We initiated a regular correspondence..." (p. 222)
"In Ardeche, it was not uncommon to receive several letters a week..." (p.301)
"There were, briefly, talks of us becoming her musicians..." (p.235)
Ferdinand Richard interviewed by Philippe Robert in *Agitation Frite II*
"I wasn't that convinced by the band's aesthetic..." (p. 46)
"For a long time... I [switched] between bass and guitar..." (p. 46)
"Rehearsals in the barn or in an unheated room!..." (p. 46)
Guigou Chenevier interviewed by Klemen Breznikar, *It's Psychedelic Baby* (2014) (in English)
"Ferdinand had this idea to add 'Leloublan'..."
"As an actor Chris added a theatrical dimension..."
"Magma was already quite famous in France in '73..."
"At the time Jean Marc Bailleux was also a journalist..."
"Etron Fou (more than ever in '76) was only a stage band..."
"Etron Fou was certainly not a 'conceptual band'..."
"I composed it already as a real 'song'..."
Ferdinand Richard interviewed by Klemen Breznikar, *It's Psychedelic Baby* (2014) (in English)
"Almost none of EFL production was improvised..."
"Jean-Marc approached us with this very new idea of self-production..."
"Since the beginning of RIO there were tensions between members..."
"In the summer of '79 Fred Frith..."
"We recorded it on a four-track machines..."

Ferdinand Richard interviewed in *Atem* n° **x** ('7?)
    "the essence of Etron Fou..."
    "When Chris left, we wanted another instrument..."
    "My bass has a particular sound, because it is tuned with the alto sax..."
Chris Chanet interviewed in *Atem* n° 5 ('76)
    "What's important to the group and what we've tried to do..."
Rock en Stock
    "The music of Etron Fou Leloublan is rich and very diverse..."
Review quoted in *Un Certain Rock(?) Français 2* p. ?
    "This is the most interesting new band I've heard from the continent..."
Atem n° 11 (Jan '78)
    "Lots of new and long pieces where the emphasis is sometimes..."
Atem n° 12 (April '78)
    "The instrumental humour is much more interesting..."
Rock en Stock
    "The music doesn't change, it simply evolves..."
Bernard Mathieu interviewed by Klemen Breznikar, *It's Psychedelic Baby* (2014) *(in English)*
    "I met Ferdinand just before the US tour..."

34. BIRGE GORGE SHIROC

Except for those noted below all quotations from Jean-Jacques Birgé are from interviews with the author conducted in 2021.

Jean-Jacques Birgé, liner notes for *Defence de (in English)*
    "I was only fifteen at that time [but] I used to take my motorcycle..."
    "We asked Shiroc to come over to our place and play together..."
Jean-Jacques Birgé, blog at drame.org
    "I brought back a load of records..." (posted 23/2/2007)
    "I started scratching ruined slides..." (posted 15/6/2022)
    "We were very excited about this first concert..." (posted 23/2/2007)
    "We called it Un Drame Musical Instantané..." (posted 11/11/2019)
Jean-Jacques Birgé, liner notes for *Avant Toute (in English)*
    "Keen on setting up light shows for the high school's rock band..."
    "Francis was a big fan of the Beatles, the Who and King Crimson..."
    "Francis and I started recording our improvisations in my bedroom..."
    "My taste for symphonies found an echo in this unbelievable machine..."
    "I had the feeling that our 'work' could easily compete..."
Jean-Jacques Birgé, *Le son sur l'image,* unpublished book
    "I started making electro-acoustic magnetic tapes..."
    "Having composed music for my own films..."
Francis Gorgé, liner notes for *Avant Toute (in English)*
    "[My favourite guitarist was] Django Reinhardt..."
    "The potential guitar hero that I was became an avant-garde musician..."

Sources

Jean-Jacques Birgé interviewed by Philippe Robert in *Agitation Frite*
"*With absolutely no knowledge of harmony or counterpoint...*"
"*My idea has always been to compose evocative pieces where the listener...*"
"*Six months after recording the first version of* Défense de..."
"*I was already playing with Francis Gorgé, so I got them together...*"
"*I was the driving force in Un Drame even though creatively...*"
"*[Bernard] was eighteen years older than us...*"
"*In '77 we recorded enough to make dozens of albums...*"

PART 7 -
THE ELECTRONIC UNDERGROUND

35. INTRODUCTION

Quotations from Tim Blake are from interviews with the author conducted in 2023/24.

Richard Pinhas interviewed by ???
"*Synthesisers introduced a sonic continuum...*"
Richard Pinhas interviewed by Bester, *Gonzaï* website (20/5/2015)
"*It was impossible to find synths here, you had to go to London...*"

36. PHILIPPE BESOMBES

Philippe Besombes interviewed by Kris Needs, *Electronic Sound* n° 27 (2017) *(in English)*
"*I was thirsty for electric sounds; distortion, echo, and reverb...*"
"*It was exciting, something impalpable and underground...*"
"*I was staying in Sheffield and The Beatles' 'She Loves You'...*"
"*When he worked with arranger-composer Michel Colombier...*"
"*As a composer, I've always felt a deep attachment to sounds...*"
"*He appreciated my work both as a sound engineer and as a composer...*"
"*Jean Michel was one of my best friends' cousins...*"
"*When they shot* Libra, *they did it at their own tempo...*"
"*I wanted to work with rock musicians...*"

Philippe Besombes quoted by Dave Thompson in *Anthology 1975-1979* (Cleopatra, 2016) *(in English)*
"*I spent my time staring through the window pane of the music shop...*"
"*Choreographers were the only people who needed the kind of music...*"
"*At this time, I wasn't working for a career...*"
"*Pink Floyd, but not Pink Floyd, a nightmare!*"
"*She was looking for half electronic and acoustic music...*"
"*Synths weren't the soul of my music...*"
"*It wasn't so easy to swap from pure electro-acoustic...*"
"*It was in the middle of disco, electronic music...*"

Philippe Besombes quoted in liner-notes for *Ceci et Cela* (Mio Records, 2004) *(in English)*
"*He was playing a double-neck Gibson SG...*"
"*I was proud to put this ballet music on a record...*"

Philippe Besombes interviewed by Caroline Lamark, *Rock en Stock* n° 5 (Aug '77)
"*Working with Stockhausen was never pleasurable...*"
"*It was hard working with Carlson...*"
"*I really liked working with Brigitte Lefèvre...*"
"*He had a very strange style...*"

Philippe Besombes interviewed by Bester, *Gonzai* website (2014)
"*I pulled an all-nighter and showed up for the exam wearing flares...*"
"*Paul Putti was a bit of a nutcase...*"
"*The Besombes-Rizet record attempts to humanise technology...*"
"*We were making fringe music and money wasn't our priority...*"
"*They sold carloads of records with this technique...*"
"*Rizet and I divorced after he married Au Bonheur des Dames...*"
"*It didn't cost me to finish my career as a musician...*"

JC LaForest, *Rock en Stock* n° 11 (Feb '78)
"*The music on offer here is more rich and varied...*"

37. HELDON

Except for those noted below all quotations from Richard Pinhas and Patrick Gauthier are from interviews with the author conducted in 2023.

Richard Pinhas interviewed by Xavier Beal, *Atem* n° 7 (Oct '76)
"*I make the music I like - it isn't up to me to go to the people...*"
"*[It] marked the end of an era for me...*"
"*... it was a way to say: this is a legacy, and here I've finished...*"
"*On the first four discs my goal was to attain a certain kind of violence...*"
"*It was made during the fourth album, it's a piece that started...*"

Richard Pinhas interviewed by Chloé Cotteur, BnF (2013)
"*I only had one obsession, I absolutely wanted to be on the same label...*"
"*We had an immediate stroke of luck. The album got airplay on the radio...* "
"*I realised it wasn't my vocation to run a record label...*"
"*Make no mistake, we weren't at all in the political line...*"
"*After the last Heldon album,* Stand By, *I made other records...*"

Richard Pinhas interviewed by Julien, *Goute mes Disques*, 27/08/2009
"*These are the two realms in which and by which I live....*"

Richard Pinhas interviewed by Philippe Robert in *Agitation Frite*
"*I was able to see a lot of King Crimson concerts around '72...*" (p. 103)
"*It was a real innovation, a step forward...*" (p. 98)

Richard Pinhas Facebook post 13/4/2020 *(in English)*
"*one of the* chef d'oeuvre *(masterpieces) of the 20th Century...*"

Richard Pinhas interviewed by Bester, *Gonzaï* website (20/5/2015)
"*I didn't know Deleuze very well at the time...*"

Richard Pinhas interviewed by Bruno Heuzé, 2006
"*It was a shock to me. Electronics introduced a sonic continuum...*"
"*[The Moog] became an immovable monster covering my living room wall...*"

Richard Pinhas quoted in *Un Certain Rock(?) Français Vol. 2*, pp. 3-5
"*I try to push the use of synthesisers to the extremes...*"
"*[Music] is irredeemably political... To give away a disc...*"
"*The solo records are constructed according to a totally different process...*"
"*[He is] essential to Heldon's creative process.*"

Richard Pinhas interviewed by Gérard Nguyen, *Atem* n° 1 (Dec '75)
"*For the time being I don't think that it's necessary to have a group...*"

Rock en Stock, 1977
    "*Despite being created with the same equipment....*"
    "*Enhanced by the Laser de Trapèze, the music reached truly...*"
Richard Pinhas quoted in liner notes for *It's Always Rock & Roll*
    (Bureau B, 2018) *(in English)*
    "*We recorded it after having met with Philip K. Dick in California...*"
Rock & Folk review of *It's Always Rock & Roll*
    "*[This album] represents a culmination...*"
Gérard Nguyen in *Atem* n° 16 (April '79)
    "*The long interrogation period ends and the combat...*"
    "*The dream is in fact a long nightmare...*"
    "*It's satisfying to see the most extreme contemporary groups...*"
Atem n° 7 (Oct '76)
    "*Abysses. Apocalypses. The torment of sounds, senses, robot brains...*"
Hervé Picart review of *Un rêve sans conséquence spéciale* in *Best*
    "*A dream or a nightmare? More like the second...*"
Richard Pinhas interviewed by Jean-Marc Bailleux, *Rock & Folk* n° 170
    (Mar '81)
    "*In the history of electronic music* Un rêve sans conséquence spéciale...*"
    "*At that point, my philosophical theories were for a kind of reversal...*"
Richard Pinhas interview, *Best* (1979)
    "*We have always experienced our music as a war machine...*"
    "*The group actually gives few concerts in France....*"
    "*Heldon has an absolutely stable core...*"
    "*I've just finished my third solo album,* Iceland...*"
Richard Pinhas quoted in press release for *Chronolyse* (Cuneiform, 2015)
    (in English)
    "*It was initially meant to be an all-Moog album...*"
Richard Pinhas quoted in liner notes for *Interface* (Bureau B, 2020)
    (in English)
    "*We were finishing the track, the tape was rolling...*"
Hervé Muller in *Rock & Folk* (May 78)
    "*Heldon has become a complex entity...*"
Atem n° 12 (April 78) review of *Interface*
    "*Here Heldon mercilessly crush all false pretenses...*"
Richard Pinhas interviewed by Aug Stone, 2015 *(in English)*
    "*During those years, I was a session musician, working 300 days a year...*"

38. ILITCH

Except for those noted below all quotations from Thierry Müller are from interviews with the author conducted in 2024.

Thierry Müller interviewed by Philippe Robert in *Agitation Frite 2* (p. x)
    "*I start with a story, an image, a concept, then I improvise...*"
    "*I don't think a specific music or style influenced us...*"
    "*Ilitch has always been me, my stories, my ravings...*"

Sources

    "I met Philippe at the launch party for the Oxygène label..."
Thierry Müller interviewed by Klemen Breznikar, *It's Psychedelic Baby* (2022) *(in English)*
    "There wasn't really a musical atmosphere at home...."
    "As far back as I can remember, I have always drawn"
    "This is my first 'official' album under the Ilitch name..."
    " 'Periodikmindtrouble' was a no-brainer..."
    "Ha! The Ruth Ellyeri Mystery..."
    "I wanted to differentiate this concept from that of Ilitch..."
Thierry Müller interviewed by Cyril Lacaud, *Popnews* website (2009)
    "My musical tastes at the time ranged from quality varieté*..."*
    "I wanted to launch my own project with this album..."
    "I wasn't following the contemporary sound at all when I made my records..."
Rock en Stock (Mar '79) review of *Periodikmindtrouble*
    "Today there are musicians who appear to take up the legacy..."

INDEX

Les 5 Apôtres 128
9h17 Productions *(label)* 364, 367*n*

A&M Records *(label)* 304, 307, 308
Abbey Road Studios 142, 323
Achard, Claude 355-6
Actuel xxvii, 23, 30, 31-2, 51, 123*n*, 166, 246, 256, 337, 359, 399
Adrien, Yves 142
Agitation Free 258, 326
Air Studio 226
Aix Festival
    see Progressive Music Festival
AKT *(label)* 286, 287
Alan Jack Civilization 23, 27, 30, 393*n*
Alba, Monique 78, 344
Alessandrini, Paul 23, 37, 95*n*, 98, 103*n*, 141, 199, 200, 210, 211, 258, 293*n*, 341
Alice 31, 32, 205*n*, 306
Allen, Daevid xxi, 9, 21, 29, 49, 179-80, 192, 193, 197
    see **Bananamoon**, **Gong**
Allen, Laurie 216-7, 219-20, 221-2, 234, 242*n*, 326
Allwright, Graeme 204
Alpert, Herb 304
Ambarchi, Oren 409
American Center *(venue)* xxvi, 134, 137, 181, 254
Ame Son xx, xxvi, 22, 23, 25, 27, 29, 32, 33, 37, 39, 40, 43, 44, 55, 107, 137*n*, 182, 188, 191, **195-205**,
    Catalyse 198-9, 203-4
AMM xxiii*n*, 69, 331
Amon Düül II 30, 37, 246, 355

Amougies Festival xix, xxv, xxvii, **25-27**, 29, 35, 36, 39, 191, 199-200, 201, 202, 209-10, 242, 331, 371
Ange xi
Angel Face 52
Angel, Victor 256
Annecy Jazz Action 49
Anthony, Richard 4, 6
Antoine 7, 128
Arcane 416
Arkham 320*n*
Arnoux, Jean-Pierre 150
    see **Maajun**
Arrabal, Fenando 146
Art Ensemble of Chicago xix, xxvi, 23, 27, 39, 66, 195, 247, 324, 355
Artman, Gilbert xx, xxvi, xxix, 52, 95*n*, 147-8, 150, 266-7, 270, 275*n*, 280, 340, 342, 343, 345*n*, 352, 400, 412*n*
    see **Lard Free**
Art & Technique 344
Artur, José xxix, 22, 146
Art Zoyd xxviii, 22, 45, 52, 332, 363, 367*n*
Ash Ra Tempel xxxi, 339
Asphalt Jungle 52*n*, 407
Asseline, Jean-Pol 312
L'Assemblée 180-1
Atelier de Libération de la Musique 393*n*
Atem 51
Atoll xi, 150
Aubert, Jean-Louis 204
Aubert, Richard 163*n*, 167, 175*n*
    see **Komintern**
Au Bonheur des Dames 391

Index

Audat, Alain 70, 75-7, 83n
Au Fond du Couloir à Gauche 345n, 360
Auger, François 403, 405-8,
Auvers-sur-Oise Festival 31, 40, 44, 158, 169, 324
Ayers, Kevin 30, 39, 151n, 183n, 187, 216, 219, 244n, 257, 323, 326, 355, 370
Ayler, Albert 139, 348
Aznavour, Charles 3

Babylone 263-4, 267, 269, 275n
Bachdenkel xviii
Back Door 356
Baez, Joan 38, 39, 40, 41
Bagas Cheap Festival 44, 257
Bailey, Derek 371
Bailey, Keith 240
Bailleux, Jean-Marc 361
Bailly, Clément 315
Ballon Noir *(label)* 150
Bananamoon 9, 21, 180, 185, **187-193**, 208, 195, 197, 209
Barbara 374
Barbetti, Daniel 115
Barclay Records *(label)* 5-6, 55, 179, 190, 241n, 310, 383
Bardot, Brigitte 180, 374
Baum, Ziska 185-6
Barety, Marc 416
Barouh, Pierre 55
Barrett, Syd xx, xxiii, xxvii, 196
Barricade ix, xi, xvi, xxvii, 21, 22, 32, 37, 40, 44, 45, 51, 59, 70, 93, 95n, **105-124**, 337
Barricade I 93, **110-11**
Barricade II 93, **110-18**, 263, 265
Barry, Phil
  see **Red Noise**
Barthélémy, Hector 70
Bashful Beats 137
Bashung, Alain 122
Basing Street Studios 237

Bas Rock 51-2, 340
Bas-Rock Festival 52, 78, 362
Bastien, Pierre xxviii, 78, 351
Bataclan *(venue)* xx, 191
Bataillet, Pierre 391
Batard, Didier 403-408
Les Batteries 366
Battiato, Franco xxxi
Bauer, Mireille 237-8, 243n
Baulleret, Xavier 78
BBC 216, 309
The Beatles 6, 7, 15, 63, 127, 283, 370, 387, 415
Beaupoil, Philippe 137
Beck, Jeff 63
Beer, Karel xviii
Béjart, Maurice 382
Bel, Marcel 149
Bella Ciao (play) 146-8
Bellaiche, Alain 402
Bellamy, Ian 271
Benamou, Bob 47, 48, 179
  see **Gong**
Bennett, Lou 337
Beranger, Anne 388
Bergerat, Hervé 68-9, 83
Berrocal, Jac xxviii, xxix, xxxiii, 6, 44, 45, 52, 55, 81, 136, 331, 332, **347-353**
  Musiq Musiq 349-50; *Parallèles* 350-1
Berté, Michel 141
Bertram, Gérard
  see **Moving Gelatine Plates**
Besombes, Philippe 51, 57, **387–393**
  Libra 389-90; *Besombe-Rizet* 390-1; *Hydravion* 391-2
Best xxix, 22, 32, 201, 203, 399, 415
Bex and Jouvelet 344
Bidineux, Charly 124
Biennale of Bologna 148, 151n
Bièvres Festival 40, 44, 70, 83n, 111, 171, 257, 280, 383
Bikialo, Gérard 306, 307, 312

481

Billard, François xix
see *Barricade*
Binsard, Pierre 370
Biot Festival
see Popanalia Festival
Birgé Gorgé Shiroc xxviii, 51, 56, 332, **369-374**, 382, 383
Défense de 372-3
Birgé, Jean-Jacques xii, xxv-xxix, 56-7, 77, 168, 175*n*
see *Birgé Gorgé Shiroc*
Bizot, Jean-François xxvii, 31, 32, 39, 260
Black Panthers xxix, 256
Black Sabbath 65, 107
Blake, Tim 258, 265-6, 270, 274, 382-3, 385*n*
see *Gong*
Blakely, Art 254
Blanc, Marc xxix, 9, 29, 101, 103*n*, 207, 243*n*
see *Bananamoon*, *Ame Son*
Blanc-Francard, Patrice xxix, 22, 30-1, 250, 286
Blanc-Franquart, Dominique 250
Blasquiz, Klaus 17, 47, 48, 254, 397, 408
see *Magma*
Blodwyn Pig 64
blousons noirs 5-6
Blues Bag 180, 183*n*
Blues Convention 8, 25, 27, 298, 397
The Blues Unit 128
Bois de Vincennes 26
Bois, Lisa 315
Bole du Chaumont, Gérard 367*n*
Bolliet, Philippe 345*n*
see *Lard Free*
Bond, Di 229-30, 242*n*
Bornet, Daniel 47
Bouladoux, Jacky 273
Boulé, Christian 52, 77, 78, 264, 266, 267, 270, 273, 275*n*
Boulez, Pierre 388

Bouquin, Jean 40, 241*n*
Bourzeix, Michel 148
Bouton rouge (TV) xxix, 8-9, 22, 183*n*, 188, 193*n*
Bowie, David 117
Bowie, Lester 108
Branlo, Mario
see *Barricade*
Branson, Richard 119, 120, 220, 226, 227, 242, 265, 269
Brassens, Georges 3
Brave New World 323
Breaking Point 418
Brel, Jacques 3
Breton, François 180-1, 183*n*
Brown, James 304
Bruford, Bill 234, 243*n*
Bruniferd 366
Bucchi, Jean-Louis 373
Buchla 385
Buga Up 366
Bulldog 116-7
Le Bulle *(venue)* 306
Bus Palladium *(venue)* xxvi, 169
BYG *(label)* 23, 25, 43, 55, 56, 191, 198, 199, 200, 201, 202, 203, 204, 205*n*, 209, 213, 221, 226, 234, 241*n*, 286, 331

Cabaret Voltaire 385*n*
Cage, John xvi, 109, 331, 348
Cahen, François 'Faton'
see *Magma*
Camizole xi*n*, 32, 45, 51, 52, 81, 332, **335-345**, 360, 367, 382, 383
Campus (radio) 22, 84*n*, 415
Can 30, 49, 166, 169, 247, 355, 362
Captain Beefheart xv, xvi, xvii, xx, xxvi, xxvii, 9, 22, 26, 65, 106, 107, 109, 119, 140, 156, 166, 169, 279, 356, 357, 358, 370

La Coupole *(venue)* 185, 208
Caravan xxv, 199, 264, 355
Carlos, Wendy (Walter) 371
Carlson, Carolyn 389
Carnaby Street Swingers 297, 298
Carolfi, Jean Pierre
   see **Contrepoint**
Carrière, Mathieu 397
Carvallo, Michel 49
Cassegrain, Phil 280
Castilla, José 338
Catalogue xxix, 52, 81, 136, 352
Catharsis 44, 68
Cattalano, Serge
   see **Red Noise, Komintern**
CBE Studio 190
CBS *(label)* 43, 55, 283, 285, 286, 287, 288, 289, 290, 341n
Celensu, Taner 186
Celluloïd *(label)* 366
Cenci, Jean-Claude
   see **Red Noise**
Chabiron, Jacques 66
Chalery, Alain "Paco"
   see **Magma**
Chamberland, Yves 402
Chanet, Chris 80, 340, 344
   see **Etron Fou Leloublan**
chanson xi, xvi, 3-4, 7, 15, 43, 151n, 155, 185
Chantrier, Jacques
   see **Lard Free**
Chappell Studio 66, 309
Charles, Ray 64
Les Charlots 128
Chassin, Pascal
   see **Komintern**
Chat Qui Pêche *(venue)* xvii, 208, 254
Châteauvallon 304-5
Les Chats Sauvages 5, 7
Les Chaussettes Noires 5, 7
Chemin Blanc 344
Chene Noir xxxii
Chenevier, Guigou xxviii, 18, 78

   see **Etron Fou Leloublan**
Cherry, Don xix, 23, 65, 347, 349
Cheval Fou xvi, 32, 45, 182, 204, **245-251**, 356
Chico Magnetic Band 32, 33, 37, 43, 182
Chrome 407
Cinelu, Mino 239
Clapton, Eric xxvii, 39, 63, 180, 396
Clarel, Alain 290
Clarel, Francis 288
Clarke, Kenny 155, 254
Clearlight 45, 51, 116, **263-275**, 382
   Clearlight Symphony 266-7;
   Forever Blowing Bubbles 267-8;
   Les Contes du Singe Fou 270-1;
   Visions 272-4
Cleaver, Eldridge 256
Clément, Claude 38, 40
Clémenti, Pierre xxv, xxviii, 208, 245, 249, 255, 269
Clermont-Ferrand Festival 259
Cluster 339, 381
Coaquette, Yvan xxxii, 269-70, 275n, 331
Cobra *(label)* 80, 391
Cochran, Eddie 149
Cœur Magique 306
Coghe, Jean-Noel 27, 199
Cohen, Leonard 37
Cohen-Solal, Jean xxxii
Coleman, Bill 254
Coleman, Ornette xix, 185, 347, 348, 355
Colombier, Michel 387
Colosseum xxvi, 37
Coltrane, John 66, 139, 207, 295, 297, 348
Comelade, Pascale 51, 52, 57
Constantin Philippe 140, 142, 144, 145, 147, 149, 151n
Continental Circus (film) 207, 214, 217
Contrepoint 45, 52, 171, **323-327**
Cooper, Lindsay 243n, 344

Corbeau, Jo 122
Coryell, Larry 64
Cosey, Pete 73
Coster, Dominique 349
Coulon, Michel 283-4, 293n
Country Joe McDonald 37, 40, 41n, 133
Courbis, Alain 356
Coxhill, Lol 326
Coyne, Kevin 52
Cream 9
Crium Delirium xvi, xxvii, xxxii, 40, 44, 45, 49, 51, 137n, 175n, 182, 246, **253-261**, 265, 382, 383
Cross, David 268
Crossroad Blues 165–6
Crouille Marteau xvi, xxv, 43, 245, 370
CRS 12, 17, 188
Crublé, Françoise
    see **Camizole**
Cruciferius xxvi, 27, 29, 312
Crumb, Robert 144
Crystal Machine 240, 382-3
Cutler, Chris 234, 365, 367n

Dada xviii, xxiii$n$, 179, 287
Dagon xxv, xxix, 32, 43, 44, 45, 51, 90, 91, 97, 102, 158, 163n, **165-175**, 370
d'Agostini, Jean-Claude 270
Dahan, Simon 107
Dalida 3
Dali, Salvador 256
Dantalion's Chariot 180
d'Avantage *(label)* 350
Davis, Miles 66, 73, 131, 239, 248, 259, 348
Davoust, Gérard 299
Dean, Elton 326
de Antoni, Jean 318
Dédé la Frite
    see **Barricade**
Deep Purple 30, 38

Delacroix, Guy 315
Delatre, Christian 336
Delaunay, Eric 337, 338, 344
Delaunay, Robert 345n
Delaunay, Sonia 345n
Delcloo, Claude 23, 25-6, 31, 286-7, 288, 290, 291
Deleuze, Gilles 395, 397, 411n
Delices Dada 344, 366
Delired Cameleon Family 269-70, 275n, 411n
Denis, Daniel 320
Dentan 287
Deshays, Daniel 78, 350
Dessoliers, Jean François 388
detournement 144, 149
Deya 189, 193n, 207, 208, 218, 223, 224, 225, 234
Dick, Philip K. 396, 400, 411n
Discorama (TV) 301
Disjuncta Records *(label)* 51, 55, 56-7, 399, 401, 412n
Disques Motors *(label)* 71
Doctor John 106
Dolphy, Eric 139
Doray, Philippe 419
Dorothée Bis *(shop)* 197
Draper, Simon 239, 242n, 265-6
Dreyfus *(publisher)* 71, 74
Drumbo 357, 358
Dudon, Jacques 30, 37, 44, 151n, 180-1, 182, 183n, 202, 204, 255
Dugrenot, Joel 267-71
Dupéty, Jacky
    see **Camizole**
Dupety, Jean-Luc
    see **Camizole**
Dupon et ses Fantômes 340, 360, 364
Dutronc, Jacques 128, 415
Duvernet, Antoine 75-6, 80, 270, 275n, 372
Dynastie Crisis 38, 43, 331n

East of Eden 30, 107, 139, 140, 199, 290
Eclosion 204
L'Ecole des Caillols 109, 123n
Ecoute (radio) 341
Edgar Broughton Band xviii, 30
Egg Records *(label)* 173, 383, 408
Ehrlich, Loy 240, 256
   see **Crium Delirium**
Einstein 173
Elhyani, Hervé 383, 385n
   see **Lard Free**
Ellyeri, Ruth 418
Elvis Presley 387
Emerson, Keith 381
EMI *(label)* 142, 145
EMI Studios 269-70
Empire des Soins 173
Engel, Claude
   see **Magma**
Eno, Brian 382, 385n, 395, 396, 415, 417, 418, 419
Enu, Henri-Jean xxvii, 32, 169
   see **Fille Qui Mousse**
Epimanondas xxv, 373
Epone Festival 44
Ergo Sum 45, 304
Escot-Bocanegra, Gérard 129
Esnault, Dominique 391
L'été Chaud 42, 45
L'été Pop xii, **35-41**, 141, 202
Etron Fou Leloublan xi$n$, 45, 51, 52, 59, 261n, 332, 340, 342, **355-367**
   Batelages 360-2; *Les trois fous perdéganent* 363-4, *En public aux Etats-Unis* 365-6
Europe 1 *(radio)* 6, 22, 320n, 347
Euterpe 240
Evariste 15
Évry Festival 83, 280
Exmagma 56
The Exploding Galaxy 160, 163n, 183n
Expression 187, 191, 196-7
Extra 31

Faculté de Vincennes 325, 397, 411n
Fall of Saigon 52
Family 38
Fanfan Belles-Cuisse
   see **Barricade**
Faust xv, 73, 159, 163n, 226, 227, 362
Fechner, Christian 128
Féderow, Gabriel
   see **Magma**
La Fenêtre Rose 180, 183n, 208
Ferdinand et les Philosophes 173, 366
Ferlet, Roger 348-50
Ferrari, Luc 390, 393n
Ferré, Léo xxvi, 3
Festival de Musique Evolution 30, 37, 202, 283, 284-5, 293n
Festival de Solémieux 339
Festival de St Gratien 44, 108, 171
Festival Rock des Biscuits Belin 108, 123n
Fête de L'Humanité 250, 374
Fete du PSU 258, 261, 360, 401
Few, Bobby 372
Field, Gerry 208-10, 213, 241n
Filipitti, Bernard 339-40
Fille Qui Mousse ix, xvi, xxvii, xxxii, 32, 37, 44, 55, 90, 91, 92, 95n, 134, **153-163**, 169, 175n
   Trixie Stapelton 291 158-162
Fillmore West *(venue)* 369
Fillon, Michel
   see **Les Primitiv's**
Finders Keepers *(label)* xii
Fiori, Umberto 363
Fitzgerald, Ella 254
Flat 163
FLIP 90-3, 133, 142, 151n, 158, 167, 340,
Fluence 51, 57, 383
Fontaine, Brigitte xi, xxvi, xxviii, 9, 44, 49, 52, 55, 185, 195, 201, 286

Fontaine, Patrick xvi, xix, xxvi, xxviii, 17
*see **Bananamoon**, **Ame Son**, **Cheval Fou** & **Nyl***
Fossett, Marc 306
Foy, Richard 327
France Inter *(radio)* 22, 188, 286, 399
Francky Bourlier & Goa 255
François, Claude 16, 241
Fred le vicomte electrique
*see **Barricade II***
free jazz x, xvi, xix-xx, xxi, xxvi, xxxi, 25, 27, 43, 59, 103, 106, 107, 110, 123, 128, 129, 130, 143, 148, 185, 208, 209, 324, 336, 347-8, 388, 403
Freeman, Earl 209
free pop/free rock xx, 66, 139, 140, 196-7
Freitag, Mike 171
*see **Contrepoint***
Fripp & Eno 396, 417, 419
Fripp, Robert 247, 396, 403, 408, 411n, 418
Frith, Fred 365, 366
The Fugs 258
Fukushima, Takum 173
Futura *(label)* xxxii, 43-4, 55-6, 99, 103n, 158, 160, 161, 162, 163n, 332, 349, 374

Gaffarel Music *(shop)* 72, 385n
Gaillot, Alain 418
Gainsbourg, Serge 8, 374
Gaîté Lyrique *(venue)* 301
Gall, France 8, 16
Gallagher, Rory 199
Gambus, Gilbert
*see **Barricade***
Garber, René 323-4
*see **Magma***
Garrel, François
*see **Ame Son***
Garrel, Philippe 200, 249
Gauche Prolétarienne 36
Gaumont, Dominique 111
Gauthier, Patrick
*see **Magma**, **Heldon***
Gazeux, Thierry "Kühl le Clown"-
*see **Barricade***
Genesis 30, 243n, 264, 270, 272, 358
Geoffroy, Daniel
*see **Red Noise***
Gérard, Danyel 4, 6
GERM xxvi
Gestalt et Jive 366
Gewissler, Dieter 209-11, 241n
Gheerbrandt, Denis 159
Ghozland, André 148
Gibus *(venue)* xxvi, 72, 288, 326
Gillespie, Leo 208
Gilson, Bernard 158, 163n
Gilson, Jef xix, 254, 261n, 361
Giraudy, Miquette
*see **Gong***
Gisele Today (play) 134-5
Les Gitans 347
Glass, Philip 80, 417, 418
Glastonbury Festival 215
Godard, Jean-Luc 183n
Godding, Brian 310
Golf Drouot *(venue)* 48, 66, 169, 285
Gomelsky, Giorgio xxvii, 48-49, 217, 218, 221, 226, 355
*see **Magma***
Gong (1967-68) 185
Gong (1969-75) xi, xix, xx, xxi, xxv, xxvi, 22, 23, 25, 27, 29, 30, 31, 32, 33, 37, 39, 40,, 44, 45, 49, 51, 55, 111, 129-30, 133, 142, 185, 190, 193, 195, 197, 198, 200, 203, 200, 201, 202, 203, **207-243**, 246, 247, 258, 261n, 263, 265, 266, 267, 268, 292, 307, 319n, 355, 358, 361, 370, 382, 383

Magick Brother 209; *Continetal Circus* 214; *Camembert Electrique* 215-6; *Flying Teapot* 220-2; *Angel's Egg* 227-8; *You* 230-3; *Shamal* 237-8
Gorgé, Francis xxvii, xxviii,
    see **Birgé Gorgé Shiroc**
Goude, Jean-Philippe 392
Grâce Molle 356
Graillier, Mickey
    see **Magma**
Grand, Francis
    see **Etron Fou Leloublan**
Grand Gouia 340, 360
Grange, Dominique 17
Grappelli, Stéphane 3
Grasset, Jean-Pierre (Verto) 363
Grateful Dead 30, 246, 258, 369
Gratte-Ciel (label) 361
Graves, Robert 208
Greene, Burton 209
Green, Peter 396
Griffin, Johnny 207
Grimaud, Dominique ix, x, xiii, xxxii, 18, 52, 78, 81, 93, 99, 101, 279, 331, 360
    see **Camizole**
Groupe Pattern 389, 393*n*
GRRR Records *(label)* xxviii, 56-7, 373
Grunblatt, Georges 392, 397, 399-400
Gruppo di Improvvisazione Nuova Consonanaza 331
Guérin, Beb xxvi
Guérin, Jean xxxii, 44, 55, 332
Guilain
    see Jacques Dudon
Guildon, François 158-9
Guitare au poing/A cause du pop (film) 41*n*
Guru Maharaji 259

Hadouk 240
Halles Festival 29-30, 199, 201, 202, 336
Hallyday, Johnny 4-6, 7, 8, 22, 63, 415
Hancock, Herbie 66, 398
Hardy, Françoise 6, 128, 131, 415
Harvest *(label)* xxxii, 145
Hatfield and the North 268, 326
Hawkwind xxxi, 30, 240, 246, 385*n*
Hayward, Charles 217
Hedayat, Dashiell xxv, 195, 200, 214
    see Melmoth
Heldon ix, xxvi, 45, 51, 52, 56, 73, 77, 80, 195, 383, 384, **395–412**, 417, 418
    Electronique Guerrilla 398-9; *Allez-Teia* 399-400; *It's Always Rock & Roll* 400; *Agneta Nilsson* 402; *Un rêve sans conséquence spéciale* 403-4; *Interface* 405-6; *Stand By* 407-8
Heller, Luc
    see **Barricade II**
Helmlinger, Maurice
    see **Moving Gelatine Plates**
Hendrix, Jimi 9, 63, 65, 111, 128, 396, 411*n*
Henri Salvador 4
Henry Cow 358, 360, 362, 363, 364, 365, 367*n*
Henry, Pierre 81, 84*n*, 382, 387, 388, 389, 411*n*
Herbe Rouge 44, 45, 93
Here & Now 240, 243*n*
Hérouville *(studio)* 214-5, 220, 303, 304, 315
Heyworth, Simon 220-1, 227
Higelin, Jacques 122, 185, 249
Hillage, Steve 52, 261*n*, 268, 274, 275*n*
    Fish Rising 234, 236, 243*n*
    see **Gong**
H-Lights 370
Hoffman, Daniel 158
    see **Dagon**

Hoffman, Abbie 256
Hog Farm 181-2, 246, 253, 256, 258
Holdsworth, Allan 239, 243n
Hopper, Hugh 323, 326-7
Horde Catalytique Pour la Fin xxxii, 44, 55, 255, 331, 332
Houari, Rachid 16
   see **Gong**
Hourbette, Gérard xxviii
Howard, Noah 373
Howlett, Mike 258
   see **Gong**
Hugo, Victor 210
Human League 385n
Hyde Park *(venue)* 233
Hydravion 391-2

Les i 52
Les Idoles *(play)* 208
Ilitch 52, **415-421**
   Periodickmindtrouble 417-8
Iron Butterfly 37, 171, 370
Isadora Records *(label)* 271
Isidore, Raymond 335
Island Records *(label)* 327
Island Studios 71-2
It's a Beautiful Day 369

Jack, Alan 298, 389, 393n
Jarre, Jean Michel 388-9, 392
Jaspar, Bobby 296
Jeanneau, François xxxii, 16, 267, 269, 275n
Jefferson Airplane 370
Job, Pierre
   see **Barricade**
Joffra, François 92
Jones, Elvin 140, 296, 348
Jouvelet, Xavier 338, 344

Kajdan, Jean-Michel 273
Kaleidophon Studios 266
Kaleidoscope 369
Kalfon, Jean-Pierre xxv, 9, 208, 245, 249
Kalma, Ariel 51, 56, 249, 250, 270, 400
Karakos, Jean 25-7, 39, 41n, 209, 241n, 342, 366, 367n
   see **Amougies Festival, BYG, Celluloid**
Karam, Dialy 77
Keef Hartley Band 65
King, Albert 396
King, B.B. 396
King Crimson 39, 128, 234, 264, 268, 370, 395, 396, 403, 408
King, Freddy 396
Kirk, Roland 65
Klassik 150
Knutt, Carl 298
Kobaïa/ Kobaïan xxxi, 295-6, 297, 320n
Komintern xvi, xxvii, xxxii, 30, 31, 32, 37, 38, 40, 43, 44, 45, 55, 90, 91, 92, 93, 99, 102, 133, 134, 136, **139-151**, 157, 163n, 167, 175, 287, 331n, 355
   Le Bal du Rat Mort 142-6
Korb, Stéphane
   see **Fille Qui Mousse**
kosmische music 186, 339, 399, 403
Kovacic, Manfed
   see **Barricade**
Kraftwerk 339, 381
krautrock x, xv-xvi ,xxvii
Krishna Lights 370
Kühl le Clown
   see **Barricade**

La Ciotat 111, 122
Lacy, Steve 65, 280
Lagoya, Alexandre 255
Lagrange, Valérie 31, 208, 270

Index

Lagrange, Yvan 309
Lallouette, Joel 327
Laloux, Daniel xxvi, 209-11, 241*n*
Lambert, Jean-Pierre 305-6
Lanes, Yves 78
Laperrousaz, Jérome 27, 187-90, 196-8, 205*n*, 210, 214
Lapeyre, Gérard 107
Les Lapins Bleus des Îles 136, 150
Lard Free ix, xx, xxvi, 31, 32, 44, 45, 52, 59, **63-84**, 93, 95*n*, 147, 150, 258, 263, 275*n*, 280, 340, 343, 352, 372, 382, 383, 401, 412*n*
  Unnamed 68-70; *Gilbert Artman's Lard Free* 72-4; *I'm Around About Midnight* 75-7; *Lard Free* 79-80
Lard Free II 59, 70, 71, 75, 77, 83*n*, 93, 95
Laser de Trapèze 406, 412*n*
Lasry, Teddy
  see **Magma**
Lattès, Pierre xxix, 8, 188, 198, 209, 210, 326, 340, 361
Lautreamont 129
Lavialle, Bernard 191, 249, 250
  see **Ame Son**
Lebel, Jean-Jacques 179-80, 183*n*, 185
Le Bourget Festival
  see Festival de Musique Evolution
Ledissez, Lionel 304
Lefèbvre, Cyril
  see **Maajun**
Lefèbvre, Jean-Louis
  see **Maajun**
Lefevre, Brigitte 390
Legend Music *(label)* 260
Leggett, Archie 213
Le Glou, Jacques 149, 150*n*
Legrand, Benjamin
  see **Fille Qui Mousse**
Legrand, Michel 4, 155
Legrand, Olivier
  see **Fille Qui Mousse**

Legrand, Raymond 155-6
Legros, Alain 389
Legros, Françoise 390
Lelouch, Claude 183*n*
Lemaitre, Maurice 71
Lemarque, Francis 155-6
Lemoine, Patrice 237-9, 242*n*
Lemonnier, Francis
  see **Red Noise**, **Komintern**
Lennoz, Jacques 250
Léonard, Daniel 256
Lentin, Albert-Paul 165-6
Lentin, Dominique xxv, 17, 52, 154, 158-9, 163*n*
  see **Dagon**
Lentin, Jean-Pierre xxv, 43, 97, 158, 265, 339, 341
  see **Dagon**
Le Pieux, Phil 77
Leproux, Henri 285
Leroi, Jean François 389
Leroy, Aymeric xiii, 183*n*, 229, 242*n*
Les Halles ix, 25-6, 29-30, 211
Leton, Georges 315
Lettrisme 32, 71, 153
Leurion, Jean-Jacques 77
Levick, Hugh 325
Lewry, Stephan 240
Libération 51, 52, 165, 341, 343, 345*n*, 359
Libra (film) 389
Libre Cours 355
Lienhardt, Catherine
  see **Camizole**
Ligue Communiste 92, 140-1, 147
The Lines 283
Linon, Francis ("Venux De Luxe")
  see **Gong**
Livengood, John xxxii, 100, 275
The Living Theatre 30, 208, 336
Lockwood, Didier 271, 272-3, 312, 314
Lorquin, Olivier 149
Loüet, Alain 336

Louiss, Eddie 254
Loussier, Jacques 122
Lovecraft, HP 166
Lowengreen, Barabara
    see **Fille Qui Mousse**
Lyotard, Jean-François 395

Maajun xvi, xxxii, 32, 37, 43, 44, 90, 91, **127-137**, 141, 150, 151*n*
    Vivre la mort du vieux monde 130-3
Macadam Cowboy 150
Madagascar 254-5, 261*n*
Magal, Lionel "Fox" 181-2, 345*n*
    see **Crium Delirium**
Magal, Thierry 361
    see **Crium Delirium**
Magic Band xx, 113
Magic Mushroom 338
Magma xxvii, xxxi, 22, 30, 31, 32, 38, 43, 44, 45, 48-9, 52, 55, 108, 118, 124*n*, 148, 195, 203, 218, 240, 242*n*, 254, 258, 263, 265, 271, 279-80, 292, 293*n*, **295-321**, 324, 355, 357-8, 367, 397, 400, 409, 411*n*
    Magma 299-301; *Magma 2* 303; *MDK* 307-8; *Wurdah Ïtah* 309-10; *Köhntarkösz* 310-11; *Magma Live* 312; *Üdü Wüdü* 313-4; *Attakk* 315-6
Magny, Collette xxvi, 185
Magne, Michel 82, 304, 369
Mahavishnu Orchestra 264, 272
Mahjun xxvii, 45, 77, 79, 134, 136, 204
Mahjun, Jean-Louis
    see Lefèbvre, Jean-Louis
Mahogany Brain xxxii, 43, 55, 57
Maison de Picassiette 335
Maisons de Jeunes Culture (MJC) 48-9, 120, 284, 304, 370
Maisons de la Culture *(venue)* 106

Malherbe, Didier 17, 21, 254, 258, 266, 272, 273, 274
    see **Gong**
Malicorne 136, 150, 175*n*
Mama Bea 122
Mama Lion 292
Man xxxi
Manderlier, Jean-Luc 305, 320*n*
Mandin, Francis 271, 273
The Manor *(studio)* 119, 218, 220-1, 226, 228, 230, 232, 234, 266-7, 268, 271, 307
Manor Mobile *(studio)* 227, 233, 237
Manvu, Gérard 113
Marco, Guy 297
Marcœur, Albert xxviii, 51
Marquee *(venue)* 196, 198, 237, 309
Marquee Studios 213
'The Marseillaise' 132
Marseille 22, 49, 107-9, 114, 166, 263, 265, 306, 325, 337
Martignon, Denis
    see **Dagon**
Martin Circus xi, xxvi, 22, 25, 27, 29, 241*n*, 248
Martinez, Graziella 254
Martinez, Loppo 275*n*
Mason, Nick xx, 238
Mason, Roger 151*n*
Matching Mole 44, 216, 264, 288
Mathieu, Bernard 365
Mativet, François
    see **Lard Free**
Maury, Françoise 338
May '68 x, xv, xvi, xix, xxix, **11-18**, 21-2, 25, 35, 38, 89-90, 97, 100, 103*n*, 117, 128, 129, 137*n*, 140, 153, 165, 181, 188-9, 193*n*, 208, 245, 254, 261, 264, 283, 335, 369
The MC5 30, 65
McLaughlin, John 65, 73, 272-3
Meillier, Bruno 366
Melkonian, Philippe 273
Melmoth xxv, 200

Mery, Vincent 338
Merzbow 409
Metal Urbain 52*n*, 362, 407
Middlefield Farm 230, 234, 236
Midi Magazine (TV) 202
Miette, Jean-Jacques
    see **Lard Free**
Milkweg *(venue)* 229, 261*n*
MIMI festival 366
Mitchell, Eddy 6, 15, 303
Moerlen, Benoît 239
Moerlen, Pierre
    see **Gong**
Monk, Thelonious xxviii, 254, 374
Monster Melodies *(label)* xii, 163*n*, 193*n*, 204, 291, 325
Montauban, Gato 115
Montaulieu 190, 205, 212, 215
Montesinos, Francis
    see **Barricade**
Montgomery, Wes 64
Montluçon Festival 340, 360
Montreux Festival 304
Moody Blues 39
Morabito, Marcel 115
Morizur, René 297
Morlier, Jean 143, 151*n*
Morning Calm 208-9, 241*n*
Mosaïc 360
Mother Gong 240
The Mothers of Invention xviii-xix, xxv, 26, 128, 140, 196, 279, 283, 370
Moullet, Patrice xxvi
Mouna, Aguigui 39, 41*n*
Mouyeaux, Dominique 47
Moving Gelatine Plates ix, xxvii, 22, 30, 32, 33, 37, 43, 44, 45, 55, 279, **283-293**, 301
    Moving Gelatine Plates 286-7;
    The World of Genius Hans 288-90
Mozaïk 331
Moze, Francis 218- 22, 239, 242*n*
    see **Magma**
Muller, Hervé 76, 79

Muller, Patrick 417, 421
Müller, Thierry 415-21
Mungo Jerry 37
Murray, Sunny xix, 23
Musée d'Art Moderne xxix, 166, 350, 383
Musica Elettronica Viva xvi, xxxii, 27, 91, 163*n*, 254, 255, 275*n*, 331
Le Musical College 128-9
Musicircus 331*n*
Music Power (film) 27, 205*n*
Musiq Ensemble 348-9
musique concréte xviii, 387-8, 411*n*
Muzac, Michel xiii, 15, 90, 93, 136
    see **Komintern**

Nac 360
Nanterre 11-2, 137*n*
Nektar xxxi
Néneux, Harvey 122
Neu! 73, 339
Neveu, Angeline 77
Newport Jazz Festival 308
New York Dolls 309
Nguyen, Gérard 56, 314, 401
Nico 75, 200, 258, 355
Night of the Barricades 12-13, 188
Nougaro, Claude 401
Nouvel Asile Culturel 345*n*
Nu Creative Methods xxviii, 331
La Nuit de la Nation 6
Nurse With Wound 160
Nurse With Wound List xii, xxviii, xxxiii, 154
Nyl 45, 52, 56, 204, **249-51**, 411*n*,
    Nyl 250

Oblique Strategies 415
Océan 342
Oedipe 273
Oldfield, Mike 220, 226, 265, 307, 310

Olivier Pamela 250, 270, 397, 411n
Olmos, Claude
    see **Magma**
Olympia *(venue)* 73, 239, 273, 290, 302, 312, 347, 411n
Ométaxalia, Hugues 373
Open Circus 30, 211
Open Light 383
Opération Rhino xxviii, 78, 350, 374
l'Orchestra Co-operative 363, 367n
Orff, Carl xxxi
ORTF *(TV)* 8-9, 12, 71, 188, 189, 193n, 288, 291
Ose 384, 385n
Ossig, Daniel 336
Owen, Frank 72
Oxygène *(label)* 418, 419

Paganotti, Bernard 312, 313, 314, 320, 409
Palais de Chaillot *(venue)* 147
Palais des Sports *(venue)* 151
Palladium xxvi
Pamela, Olivier 397, 414
Paragong 223, 225, 234
Parallèles *(shop)* ix, xxvii, 350, 351, 353, 425
Le Parapluie xxvii, 32, 68, 153, 155, 156
Parc Saint-Cloud 30
Paringaux, Philippe xv, xvi, xvii, xviii, xxi, 205, 23, 23 299, 300, 301, 322
Paris Biennale 66, 146, 388
Paris Commune 15, 92, 142, 143, 144, 154, , 158
Paris Hippodrome *(venue)* 239
Parle, Claude 348, 349
Parmegiani, Bernard 389
The Partners 116
Pasquier, Jacques 49, 261
Pataphonie 51, 57

pataphysics 216, 360
Pathé-Marconi *(label)* 25, 43, 55, 142, 143, 144, 145, 146, 147, 149, 183, 181, 183, 190, 193
Pathé-Marconi Studios 142, 147, 190
Patrice Moullet xxvi
Patron, Philippe 293
Pauvros, Jean-François xxix, 136, 153
Pavillon du Hay 212, 213, 215, 216, 218, 219, 223, 224, 225, 226, 227, 228, 382
Peel, John 145, 216
Pépée Minegue
    see **Barricade**
Les Percussions de Strasbourg 222
Peron, Jean-Hervé xv, xvi, 166
Peteau, Jean-Max 160n
    see **Cheval Fou**
Peteau, Max 35, 39n, 160n
Peteau, Michel 3, 16, 31, 204, 245, 246, 251, 248, 249, 253, 250, 251
    see **Cheval Fou & Nyl**
Peterman, Guy 149
Petit, Alain 390
Le Petit Dimanche Illustré (TV) 186
Pharoah Sanders xix
Philips *(label)* 43, 55, 299, 397
Philips, Barre 209
Piaf, Édith 3
Picart, Hervé 385, 392
Picasso, Pablo 179
Pierre Moerlen's Gong 240
Pierrot Le Fou 52
PiL 52
Pillot, Jean-Paul 165–167, 175
Pinhas, Richard xxvi, 51, 52, 55, 56, 57, 73, 75, 76, 77, 90, 95, 249, 250, 381, 382, 383 392, 398–416
    Rhizosphere 405; *Chronolyse* 405; *Iceland* 408;
    see **Heldon**

Pink Fairies xviii, xxxi
Pink Floyd ix, xvi, xvii, xix, xx, xxi, xxv, xxvi, xxvii, 9, 26, 27, 30, 39, 59, 66, 69, 128, 171, 188, 186, 196, 199, 201, 205, 203, 245, 264, 286, 287, 358, 371, 389, 416, 454, 465
Pintchevsky, Jorge 268
PJF 388
Planétarium 43, 103
Planet Gong 246,
Plastic Ono Band 39
Plat du Jour 52
Plouton, Jean-Luc 273
Le Poing 45
Point Chaud (TV) 44
Pôle 51, 57, 383
Pôle Records *(label)* 390
Politique Hebdo 340, 360
Polnareff, Michel 7, 293
Polydor *(label)* 275, 276
Pons, Gérard
    see **Moving Gelatine Plates**
Ponty, Jean-Luc 254
Poole, Mac 217
Le Pop 31, 139, 182, 245-7, 256, 261*n*
Pop 2 (TV) xxix, 30, 41, 66, 103, 142, 144, 151, 244, 322, 415
Pop 2000 44
Popanalia Festival xxvii, 31, 39-40, 41*n*, 44, 90, 108, 133, 141, 202
Pop Club (radio) xxix, 22, 30, 67, 74, 136, 146, 188, 289, 293*n*, 324, 326, 399, 469
Popol Vuh 381, 385*n*
Portal, Michel xxviii
Port Leucate Festival 107
post-punk 52, 300, 352, 353*n*, 356, 366, 408
Potage, Michel 348-50
Potain, Pascal 416
Potemkine 52, 57, 281, 363
Potier, Alain 80

Poutignat, Fabien
    see **Dagon**
Presti, Ida 255
The Pretty Things xviii, xix, 27, 29, 44, 195, 285
Prime Time Victim Show 344
Les Primitiv's 8, 195-6, 204
Procol Harum 30
Progressive Music Festival 35, 37-38, 39, 40, 141
PTM 417, 421*n*
Pulsar xi
punk rock xi, 52, 56, 89, 98, 105, 169, 173, 211, 250-1, 342, 362, 365, 407
Putti, Paul 57, 390, 391
Pyle, Pip 213-16, 240, 241*n*, 266, 382

Quad Sax 81
Quentin, Patrice "Free" 80, 249, 250
    see **Crium Delirium**

Rabin, Eddy 297-8
Racaille, Joseph 106
    see **Barricade**
Radio Nova *(radio)* 260
Rakoto, Odeam 254
Rançon, Jean-Louis 149
Raux, Richard
    see **Magma**
RCA *(label)* 55, 305
Reading Festival 308
Red Army Faction 301, 320*n*, 401
Red Noise ix, xvi, xx, xxv, xxvi, xxxii, 15, 18, 21, 22, 29, 30, 32, 37, 43, 44, 55, 90, 92, 95*n*, **97-103**, 107, 117-8, 127, 139, 140, 142, 145, 151*n*, 158, 204, 287, 331*n*, 370
    Sarcelles-Lochères 99-101
Reich, Steve 396

Reinhardt, Django 3, 63, 371
Renaud 15
Renaud, Alain 56, 398-400, 401, 412n
Replica Records *(label)* xii
Rever, Gilbert 254
Rhinoceros, Cooky 391
Ribeiro, Catherine xi, xvi, xxvi, 31, 33, 38, 44, 52, 55, 113, 360–361
Richard, Cliff 4
Richard, Ferdinand
  see **Etron Fou Leloublan**
Riches, Frédéric 416
Rigaux, Pierre 134
Riley, Terry xxvi, 254, 264, 418
Rimbaud xxv, 129, 143, 145, 151n, 163
Rivera, Diego 144
Riviera Festival 37, 38, 90, 132-3, 141, 285
Rizet, Jean-Louis 390-1, 392
Robert, Philippe xiii
Roche, Roger 300
Rock en Stock (mag) 51
Rock en stock (TV) 44, 326
Rock & Folk xxix, 8-9, 22-23, 29
Rock in Opposition 360, 364-5
Rockin 'Rebels 150
Rock-Music Liberation Front 59, 70, 92-3
Rock'n'Roll Circus *(venue)* 298
Rock'n'Roll Musique 51
Rock Pas Gaga 49, 259, 261n
Roda-Gil, Etienne 103n, 142, 143, 149
Roger, Henri 51, 57, 383
Rollet, Gilles 373
The Rolling Stones xxvii, 7, 15, 63, 107, 283, 319n, 407, 415
  'Street Fighting Man' 15
Rollins, Sonny 207
Les Rollsticks 208
Roquet-Belles-Oreilles
  see **Barricade**

Rossini, Stéphane
  see **Cheval Fou & Nyl**
Rougier, Richard 83n
The Roundhouse *(venue)* xxxi, 216
Rousseau, Claude 37, 285-6, 288
  see Festival de Musique Evolution *and* Riviera Festival
Roussel, Coco 268, 275n, 397, 402
Roussel, Pierrot 397
Roux, Alain-Noel 16, 90, 92, 150, 154
  see **Maajun**
Royal Show 397
Ruins 409
Russolo, Luigi 351
Ruth 419, 421
Rzewski, Frederic 255

Sab, Léo 158-9
Saint Roch, Christ 391
Salle Wagram *(venue)* 243n
Salut les copains (radio) 6, 8, 22
Sammla Mammas Manna 364
Sanders, Pharoah xix, 297
Sapho 122
Saravah Records *(label)* 55, 59, 68, 69, 70
Saravah Studios 149, 285
Satie, Erik xxi, 110, 119, 123n, 331
Scaglia, Roger 11
  see **Maajun**
Schaeffer, Pierre 109, 388, 411n
Schizo 45, 275n, 397-8, 401, 411n
Schulze, Klaus 339, 381, 383, 399
science fiction 290, 369, 396
Scratch Orchestra 331
Seffer, Jeff 'Yochk'O' 303-5, 319n
Seigneuret, Michèle 382
Seloncourt 44
Semool xxxii, 44, 55, 332
Sex Pistols 105, 353
Shankar, Ravi 114, 259
Sharrock, Sonny 64, 371

Sheila 6, 16
Shepp, Archie xix, xxvi, 23, 27, 39, 185, 324
Shiroc
   see **Birgé Gorgé Shiroc**
Sienkiewicz, Roman 171
Silva, Alan xix, xxvii, 344, 372, 373
Silver Apples 370, 385n
Situationist International x, 89, 90, 105, 106, 110, 115, 129, 147, 149, 150
Smith, Patti 208
Smyth, Gilli xi
   see **Gong, Bananamoon**
Soft Machine xvii, xxi, xxiii$n$, xxvi, xxxi, 9, 26, 30, 39, 40, 59, 65, 66, 69, 140, 166, 169, 170, 171, 179-80, 183n, 187, 191, 196, 198, 205n, 208, 213, 216, 279, 283, 287, 288, 300, 319n, 323, 324, 326, 355, 371, 396
Sorbonne 12-15, 16, 97, 129, 185, 395
Souffle Continu xii
Spacecraft xxxii, 52, 275n
Speed Limit 373
Spencer Davis Group 180
Spinrad, Norman 396, 411n, 412n
Spooky Tooth 198, 387, 389
Standlee, Loren 185
Stapleton, Steven xii, xiii, xxxi-iii, 160-1
Stassinopoulos, Christos 267
Steamhammer 370
Stevens, Cat 180
Stewart, Dave 243n
Stinky Toys 52, 250
Stisi, Bernard 204
   see Les Primitiv's
Stockhausen, Karlheinz 228, 338, 388, 393n, 396
Stormy Six 363, 364
Strontium 90 240
Studio Davout 150, 200, 286, 402-3, 405, 407

Studio de Milan 309, 313
Studio des Dames 288
Studio ETA 209
Studio Europa Sonor 198, 209, 299
Studio Ferber 76-7
Studio Hautefeuille 79
Studio Léo Clarens 271
Studio Patay 202
Studios du Chesnay 390, 392
Studio Tangara 363
Studio Vogue 131
Studio Wagram 158, 169
Stuff 397
Subotnick, Morton 381
Sun Ra xxvii, 66, 237, 355, 359, 371
Superior Viaduct *(label)* xii
Surrealism xvi, xviii, xxiii$n$, 171, 358
System 7 240
Szajner, Bernard 256, 261n, 383

Tabarka Festival 248, 259
Tait, Rob 218-9, 229-30
Tangerine Dream 49, 186, 339, 381, 383, 399, 406
Tangerine Studios 198, 199
Tapioca *(label)* 342-3
Taylor, Cecil 348, 417, 418
Taylor, Robert 324-5, 327
Taylor, Vince xxxiii, 5-6, 116, 207, 351
Ten Years After xix, 9, 27
Terronès, Gérard 43, 55, 103n, 120, 158, 161, 162, 349
Tettenbaum, Richard 255
Théâtre de la Gaîté *(venue)* 373
The Doors 157, 355
Thélème *(label)* 303, 320n, 325
The Tornados 407
The Troggs 149
Thibault, Didier 219, 224
   see **Moving Gelatine Plates**

Thibault, Laurent 297-300, 303, 309, 315, 319n, 320n, 324, 325
Thirault, Jean-Pierre 77, 79
Third World War xviii
Thirion, Jo 366
Thollot, Jacques xix, xxvi, 9, 16, 197
Throbbing Gristle 385, 407, 419
Tiemko 344
Tixier, Jean-Louis
  see **Barricade**
Toesco, Louis 303
Tomorrow 180
Top, Jannick xxxi, 250, 403, 412n
  see **Magma**
Total Issue 31, 37, 293n
Tous en Scene (TV) 22
Traffic 39
Travelling 44, 45, 55, 163n
tremplin competitions 48, 66, 166, 285
Triangle xi, xxvii, 25, 27, 29, 32, 37, 43, 275n, 293n, 412n
Triloff, Dominique
  see **Lard Free**
Triode 44, 55, 163n
Triptique 301, 315
Tritsch, Christian 16
  see **Gong**
Troc 306
Troyes Festival 325
Truong, Jean-My 400
Tuder, Roland 180-1
Tunisia 166-7, 248, 259
Tusques, François xix, xxvi, 78, 350, 374
Twink 240

Un certain rock(?) français xxxii
Un Drame Musical Instantané xxviii, 57, **374–377**
Univeria Zekt 44, 303-4
Univers Zero 281, 320n, 364

Urban Sax xxvi, 51, 52, 68, 74-5, 77, 78, 79, 80-1, 84n, 150, 275n, 340, 343, 363, 366, 367n, 372
  Urban Sax 80; *Urban Sax 2* 80
Urbi Flat 81
Urus Records *(label)* 56, 250, 401
Utopic Sporadic Orchestra 314, 320n
Uzeste Festival xxviii

Valbonne Festival
  see Riviera Festival
Vamp Records *(label)* 71, 72, 74, 75
Van der Graaf Generator 65
Vander, Christian xxxi, 217, 242n, 254, 367n
  see **Magma**
Vander Elstraete, Jacky 390
Vander, Stella xi$n$, 411n
  see **Magma**
VanderTop 314-5
Vanilla Fudge 128
Vanille Free Press 74
Varady, Peter 77
Varèse, Edgard xviii, xxviii, 374
Les Variations xi, xvii, 8, 22, 29, 32, 43
variétés 3-6, 22, 47, 48, 241n, 245, 279, 283, 284, 416
Vartan, Sylvie 6
Vassal, Jacques 38, 141
Vaughan, Sarah 254
Velvet Underground xv, 168, 175n, 200, 309
Verbeck, Patrick 389, 391, 393n
Verdeaux, Cyrille 17, 78, 106, 116, 123n, 124n
  see **Clearlight**
Vergne, Marie-Blanche 99, 103n
Vertigo *(label)* xxxii
Verto 52, 57, 363, 367n, 418
Vian, Boris 4, 97, 103n, 173

Vian, Patrick xvi, xxvii, 15, 21, 52, 95, 139-40, 151n, 171–172, 173, 204, 384
see **Red Noise**
Vibrarock 52
Vidal, Jacky 298, 319n
Vidéo-Aventures 52, 78, 344
Video-Liszt 392
Vidon, George 211-2
La Vieille Grille *(venue)* 9, 141, 186, 190, 207
Vietnam xxvi, 11, 21, 90, 170, 301
Vincennes University 325, 397, 411n
Vincensini, Edgard 370
Virgin Records *(label)* 105, 116, 119, 150, 218, 221, 226-8, 234, 237, 239, 242n, 243n, 263, 265-6, 267, 268-9, 323
Visa de Censure no. X (film) 269-70, 275n
Vitet, Bernard xix, xxvi, xxviii, 55, 332, 373–6
Vive le Révolution (VLR) 90, 92
Vogue *(label)* 25, 43, 55, 127, 128, 132-3, 134, 137n, 305
Volapük 366
Vorhaus, David 266
Vuitton, Yves-Louis 383

Wakeman, Rick 381
Warhol, Andy xxix, 156, 168, 175n
Warner, Austin Blue 100, 101
Warrener, Patrice 383
Wavy Gravy 181
We Three/We Free xxvi, 27, 29, 30, 32
Weidorje 52, 280, 315, 321n, 408
Weiller, Jean-Pierre 3
see **Contrepoint**
White Noise 266, 385n
The Who 245, 370
Widemann, Benoît
see **Magma**
Wilen, Barney xix, 9, 16, 142

Wiley, Chris 119
Williams, Tony 243n
Winter, Johnny 37
Winwood, Muff 395
Wolf Eyes 409
Woodlands 204, 249, 280
Wood, Robert 47–48, 52, 67-71, 82, 83n, 93, 151n, 204, 249, 279-80
Woodstock 35, 181
Wright, Frank xxviii, 372, 373
Wyatt, Robert xvii, 179, 187, 213, 216, 247, 287, 293n, 323, 398

Xalph 281
Xenakis, Iannis 388, 393n
XTC 418

Yacoub, Gabriel 175n
The Yardbirds xxvii, 9, 48, 195, 319n
Yéprémian, Gilles xiii, xxxii, 32, 47, 68, 71, 147, 161, 175n
Yes 22, 27, 234, 243n
yé-yé 5, xvi, xvii, xxiiin, 3-9, 15, 21, 22, 43, 47, 132, 279, 305, 415
Young, Lester 254
Yugoslavia 123n

Zaboitzeff, Thierry xxviii
Zabu (Lucian Zabuski) 29-8, 304, 319n
Zao xxxii, 31, 45, 49, 56, 263, 267, 280, 292, 319n, 400, 401
Zappa, Frank xv-xix, xx, xxi, xxv, xxvii, xxxi, 26, 37, 40, 100, 166, 169, 180, 370
Zazou, Hector
see **Barricade**
Zdrzalik, Olivier 18, 99, 136
see **Komintern**

497

Zeuhl 280-1
ZNR 51, 52, 106, 119, 122, 124*n*, 332
Zoo xi, xvii, xxvi, 27, 29, 32, 45, 271
Zoo Express 356
Zoot Horn Rollo 358
Zorgones 319*n*
Zov 173

www.ingramcontent.com/pod-product-compliance
Lightning Source LLC
Chambersburg PA
CBHW071951290426
44109CB00018B/1984